CALIFORNIA **grade K** TEACHER'S EDITION

ELD

Carina Dasilva

PEARSON

LANGUAGE CENTRAL

Consulting Authors

Jim Cummins, Ph.D.

Lily Wong Fillmore, Ph.D.

Georgia Garcia, Ph.D.

Jill Kerper Mora, Ed.D.

PEARSON

Glenview, Illinois • Boston, Massachusetts • Chandler, Arizona
Shoreview, Minnesota • Upper Saddle River, New Jersey

English-Language Arts, English Language Development, Science, and History-Social Science Content Standards for California Public Schools reproduced by permission, California Department of Education, CDE Press, 1430 N Street, Suite 3207, Sacramento, CA 95814.

ISBN-13: 978-0-328-37814-2
ISBN-10:   0-328-37814-3

1 2 3 4 5 6 7 8 9 10 V003 17 16 15 14 13 12 11 10 09 08

 Glenview, Illinois • Boston, Massachusetts • Chandler, Arizona
Shoreview, Minnesota • Upper Saddle River, New Jersey

CALIFORNIA

Contents

Unit 1   Cooperation—All Together Now   **6**

Unit 4   **Adventures—Let's Go Exploring**   **120**

PEARSON

LANGUAGE CENTRAL

The hour of instruction in *Language Central:*

o Focuses on the common unit and weekly concepts presented in *Reading Street* and *Calle de la Lectura*.

o Is consistent with the scope and sequence of *Reading Street* and *Calle de la Lectura*.

o Offers instructional support for English learners of various proficiency levels.

o Follows a systematic and logical sequence of daily lesson plans.

Preteach LS Leveled Support Reteach

Scaffold, Support, and Reteach

- Flexible instruction with daily Leveled Support
- Language transfer and misconceptions
- Weekly Practice Stations
- Corrective Feedback

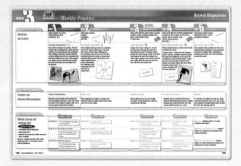

Teacher's Edition, Weekly Practice

FORM & FUNCTION

Connect Function, Form, and Fluency

- Weekly Language Workshops
- Gain access to weekly comprehension skills
- Oral reading fluency practice

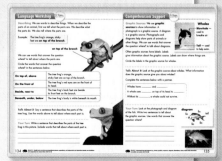

Student Edition, Day 3

Develop and Reinforce Concepts

- Weekly questions and concept goals
- Emphasis on science and social studies concepts
- Overarching unit Big Idea questions

Teacher's Edition, Theme Launch

Poster

Produce Language

- Explicit concept and language goals
- Daily Table Talk activities
- Mixed proficiencies support
- Language acquisition
- Daily writing events

Student Edition, Day 5

Practice Book, Day 5

Develop and Enrich Vocabulary

- Weekly vocabulary includes concept-related and academic vocabulary
- Vocabulary routines
- Word Cards and Song Books reinforce vocabulary
- Challenge Words

 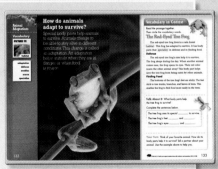

Student Edition, Day 1

Song Book

Word Card

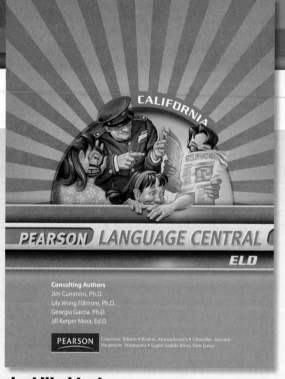

The components of *Language Central* provide students with the concept understanding, academic vocabulary, and written and oral language practice to help them succeed in *Reading Street* and *Calle de la Lectura*.

Language Central offers a variety of opportunities for English learners to produce language and to understand the functions and forms of English.

Guidance in the Teacher's Edition and other components provides a clear roadmap for instruction.

Student and Teacher's Editions provide California ELA and ELD content standards at point-of-use.

Primary grade components emphasize category and high frequency words to expand children's oral and written academic vocabulary.

Student Worktext

- Organized by weekly concepts and academic vocabulary
- Systematic instruction and practice in English language conventions, comprehension, and writing
- Language form and function
- Numerous opportunities for speaking, writing, and fluency practice
- Vibrant color images support active learning

Teacher's Edition

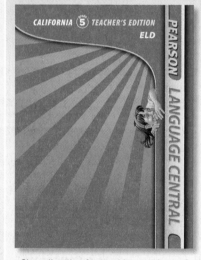

- Clear direction for teaching one hour of explicit ELD instruction
- Leveled Support and Corrective Feedback
- Teacher scripts for direct teaching and modeling
- Language transfer and misconceptions

Practice Book

- Guided or independent practice of skills
- Monitor progress of weekly skills and concept mastery
- Use as homework or as part of in-class reteaching and review

Newcomer Program

- Needs of students with little to no English-language skills addressed in Student Worktext, Teacher's Edition, and Practice Book
- Focus on survival vocabulary and language
- Age-appropriate visuals and content

Leveled Word Cards

- Reinforce, reteach, and review weekly vocabulary
- Synonyms, antonyms, definitions, related words, word families, and example sentences support meaning
- Photos support picturable vocabulary

Progress Monitoring Assessment

- Measure progress in listening, speaking, reading, and writing
- Teacher's Manual includes administration information, evaluation charts, interpretation guidelines, and support and accomodation notes

Song Books

- Engaging songs and images reinforce concept and vocabulary
- Daily warm-ups to build and maintain interest in weekly concepts
- Review and reteach weekly concepts

Posters

- Oral language production activities for speaking and listening
- Preteach, reteach, and extend weekly concepts and vocabulary
- Check for student understanding of weekly concepts

Technology Resources

- Audio Text CD
- Song Book CD
- Student and teacher resources for digital display

Digital Path

- Concept Talk Video
- Background Building Audio Slideshow
- Picture It! Animations
- Grammar Jammer
- Online Journal

Transparencies

- Idea Map Transparencies provide graphic support for vocabulary and weekly concepts
- Genre Transparencies list major genre characteristics with model passages

How to Use Language Central

Language Central provides 180 days of instruction for English language learners. Instruction is organized by week and is consistent with and connected to Reading Street and Calle de la Lectura.

The Teacher's Edition and the Student Worktext provide the core skill instruction for each day. The Practice Book offers daily practice with concepts and skills.

The Posters, Word Cards, Big Books (K–2), and Song Books can be used as needed for additional instruction, reteaching, or practice for oral language, comprehension, vocabulary, and weekly concepts.

180 days of instruction
Organized by Unit, Week, and Day.

Day 1 introduces the weekly concept and academic vocabulary.

Day 2 focuses on Word Analysis and includes lessons on Phonics, Fluency, and Genre.

Day 3 presents the functions and forms of language and how they relate to comprehension.

Day 4 covers grammar and language conventions.

Day 5 revisits the weekly concept and vocabulary by focusing on writing about the concept.

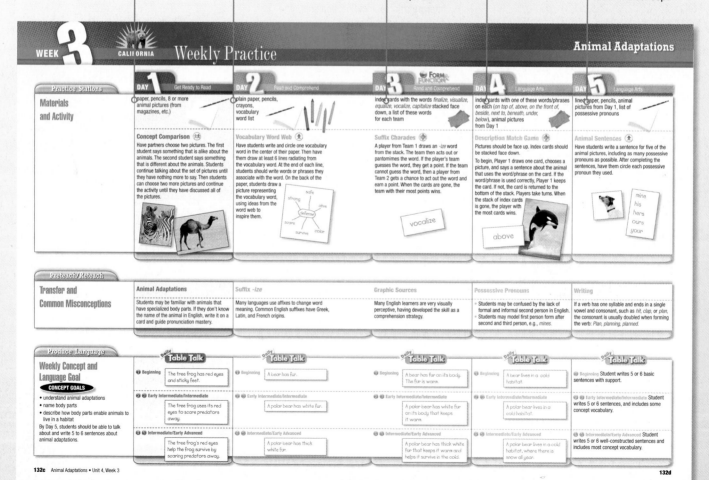

WEEK 3 • CALIFORNIA • Weekly Practice — Animal Adaptations

	DAY 1 Get Ready to Read	DAY 2 Read and Comprehend	DAY 3 Read and Comprehend	DAY 4 Language Arts	DAY 5 Language Arts
Practice Stations — Materials and Activity	paper, pencils, 8 or more animal pictures (from magazines, etc.)	plain paper, pencils, crayons, vocabulary word list	index cards with the words finalize, visualize, equalize, vocalize, capitalize stacked face down, a list of these words for each team	index cards with one of these words/phrases on each (on top of, above, on the front of, beside, next to, beneath, under, below), animal pictures from Day 1	lined paper, pencils, animal pictures from Day 1, list of possessive pronouns
	Concept Comparison — Have partners choose two pictures. The first student says something that is alike about the animals. The second student says something that is different about the animals. Students continue talking about the set of pictures until they have nothing more to say. Then students can choose two more pictures and continue the activity until they have discussed all of the pictures.	**Vocabulary Word Web** — Have students write and circle one vocabulary word in the center of their paper. Then have them draw at least 6 lines radiating from the vocabulary word. At the end of each line, students should write words or phrases they associate with the word. On the back of the paper, students draw a picture representing the vocabulary word, using ideas from the word web to inspire them.	**Suffix Charades** — A player from Team 1 draws an -ize word from the stack. The team then acts out or pantomimes the word. If the player's team guesses the word, they get a point. If the team cannot guess the word, then a player from Team 2 gets a chance to act out the word and earn a point. When the cards are gone, the team with their most points wins.	**Description Match Game** — Pictures should be face up. Index cards should be stacked face down. To begin, Player 1 draws one card, chooses a picture, and says a sentence about the animal that uses the word/phrase on the card. If the word/phrase is used correctly, Player 1 keeps the card. If not, the card is returned to the bottom of the stack. Players take turns. When the stack of index cards is gone, the player with the most cards wins.	**Animal Sentences** — Have students write a sentence for five of the animal pictures, using as many possessive pronouns as possible. After completing the sentences, have them circle each possessive pronoun they used.
Preteach/Reteach — Transfer and Common Misconceptions	**Animal Adaptations** — Students may be familiar with animals that have specialized body parts. If they don't know the name of the animal in English, write it on a card and guide pronunciation mastery.	**Suffix -ize** — Many languages use affixes to change word meaning. Common English suffixes have Greek, Latin, and French origins.	**Graphic Sources** — Many English learners are very visually perceptive, having developed the skill as a comprehension strategy.	**Possessive Pronouns** — • Students may be confused by the lack of formal and informal second person in English. • Students may model first person form after second and third person, e.g., mines.	**Writing** — If a verb has one syllable and ends in a single vowel and consonant, such as hit, clap, or plan, the consonant is usually doubled when forming the verb: Plan, planning, planned.
Produce Language — Weekly Concept and Language Goal **CONCEPT GOALS** • understand animal adaptations • name body parts • describe how body parts enable animals to live in a habitat By Day 5, students should be able to talk about and write 5 to 6 sentences about animal adaptations.	**Daily Table Talk** Beginning: The tree frog has red eyes and sticky feet. Early Intermediate/Intermediate: The tree frog uses its red eyes to scare predators away. Intermediate/Early Advanced: The tree frog's red eyes help the frog survive by scaring predators away.	**Daily Table Talk** Beginning: A bear has fur. Early Intermediate/Intermediate: A polar bear has white fur. Intermediate/Early Advanced: A polar bear has thick white fur.	**Daily Table Talk** Beginning: A bear has fur on its body. The fur is warm. Early Intermediate/Intermediate: A polar bear has white fur on its body that keeps it warm. Intermediate/Early Advanced: A polar bear has thick white fur that keeps it warm and helps it survive in the cold.	**Daily Table Talk** Beginning: A bear lives in a cold habitat. Early Intermediate/Intermediate: A polar bear lives in a cold habitat. Intermediate/Early Advanced: A polar bear lives in a cold habitat, where there is snow all year.	**Daily Table Talk** Beginning: Student writes 5 or 6 basic sentences with support. Early Intermediate/Intermediate: Student writes 5 or 6 sentences, and includes some concept vocabulary. Intermediate/Early Advanced: Student writes 5 or 6 well-constructed sentences and includes most concept vocabulary.

132c Animal Adaptations • Unit 4, Week 3

132d

DAY 1

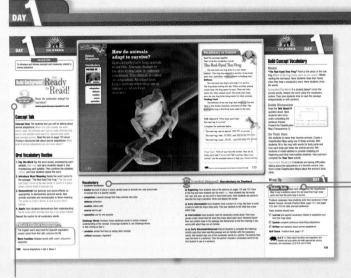

Concept Development

The weekly concept and question are introduced in the Student Worktext with a passage and visual image.

On Day 1, teachers read the introduction and passage with students. Then students discuss the concept using target vocabulary and Idea Maps.

Teachers can also use the Posters and Song Books to introduce, review, and reteach the weekly concept.

Vocabulary

The first day of instruction builds English learners' understanding of the weekly question and concept. A vocabulary routine is used to introduce each vocabulary word.

Several types of vocabulary words are introduced to build English learners' vocabulary:

- academic vocabulary related to the weekly concept
- essential vocabulary from the context passage
- word analysis words covered on Day 2
- relevant vocabulary from *Reading Street*

Wrap Up

This feature brings the day's lesson to a close.

- Daily Table Talk helps students participate in a structured discussion about the concept.
- Produce Language gets students writing about the concept in preparation for Day 5.
- Skill Checks provide practice and monitor progress.

DAY 2

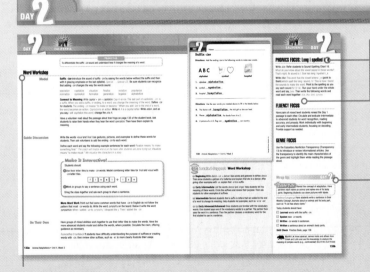

Word Analysis

Language Central instruction on Day 2 covers word analysis using Letter Tiles and the Practice Book. This is the same word work/phonics skill addressed in *Reading Street*.

Teachers present the word analysis skill to students, emphasizing the pronunciation of the example words first and then connecting the sound to spelling and meaning.

Focus Sessions: Phonics, Fluency, Genre

Day 2 offers opportunities for focus sessions on phonics, fluency, and genre.

- The Phonics Focus addresses a sound-spelling related to a word analysis or vocabulary word.
- The Fluency Focus allows teachers to check for decoding, word recognition, reading accuracy, and prosody.
- The Genre Focus allows teachers to use the Genre Transparencies for focused sessions on genre characteristics and models for writing.

Vocabulary and Concept Development on Days 2–4

The weekly question and concept are revisited in the Daily Table Talk, where students produce language about the weekly concept and question in both oral and written activities.

All skill work in the Student Worktext supports the weekly question, concept, and vocabulary.

DAY 3

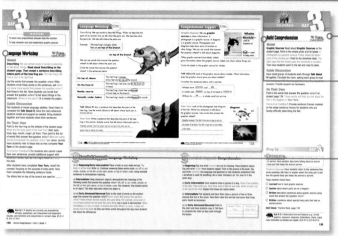

Form and Function

Day 3 addresses the functions and forms of English. The functions of language relate to its purpose. The forms are the grammar, structure, and vocabulary needed for a specific language function.

Comprehension Support

The comprehension skills taught on Day 3 mirror those in *Reading Street* and *Calle de la Lectura*. Students use the language forms introduced in the Language Workshop to discuss the comprehension skills.

Language Workshop

The Language Workshop provides English learners with explicit instruction about functions and forms of language. This provides students with the language needed for academic achievement.

DAY 4

Grammar and Language Conventions

Day 4 introduces the grammar and language conventions addressed in *Reading Street*. Examples and visuals scaffold understanding of the structures and conventions of English. Oral and written activities offer targeted practice.

DAY 5

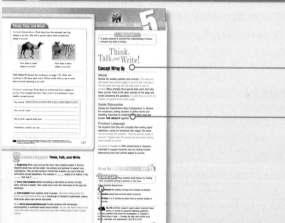

Concept Development

Day 5 represents the culmination of the development of the weekly concept. Students are asked to apply their knowledge and understanding by discussing images and responding to questions. Then they prepare for writing about the concept by reviewing vocabulary and outlining.

Produce Language/Writing

Students use what they wrote during Daily Table Talk/Produce Language as starting points for a writing assignment.

Students outline their writing in their Student Worktext and write their sentences in the Weekly Concept Journal section of the Practice Book.

The Posters and Song Book can be used to revisit and wrap up the weekly concept.

Vocabulary

On Day 5 students demonstrate vocabulary mastery by using academic vocabulary words in their writing.

Preteaching, Reteaching, and Review

Language Central offers ample opportunities for preteaching, reteaching, and review for all levels.

The core instruction targets English learners at the following proficiency levels: Grades K–2: Beginning/Early Intermediate; Grade 3: Early Intermediate/ Intermediate; Grade 4–5: Intermediate/Early Advanced.

 **Leveled Support**

Leveled Support offers daily instruction for each level of English learners. During this small group instruction time, other groups of students can be engaged at the Practice Stations.

Build English Language

Build English Language features transfer and non-transfer information at point-of-use. A linguistic contrastive analysis is also provided.

Practice Stations

The Practice Station for each day is described in detail on the Weekly Practice pages of the Teacher's Edition. The station for Day 1 offers practice with the weekly concept or vocabulary and the stations for Days 2–5 provide review of the previous day's skills.

Corrective Feedback

Corrective Feedback aids teachers in offering feedback and strategies to address common student errors or misconceptions.

Unit-Level Content

A Unit Opener and Wrap-Up suggest a unit project that ties the big question to the weekly questions and concepts.

Teachers also administer the Progress Monitoring Assessment at the end of each unit.

Skills Check and Assessment

Daily Skills Checks and Fluency Checks

The Practice Book provides written exercises for each day's concept, vocabulary, or skills. These checks help teachers evaluate daily progress. Fluency checks on Day 3 offer teachers a way to track fluency progress.

Progress Monitoring Assessments

The Progress Monitoring Assessments formally assess the skills and vocabulary covered in each unit. Oral reading fluency passages are provided in the Teaching Guide.

Poster

The Posters offer an additional way to evaluate listening and speaking skills. Activities on each day help teachers monitor oral language proficiency, vocabulary, and comprehension.

PEARSON LANGUAGE CENTRAL ELD

Consulting Authors

Jim Cummins, Ph.D.
Professor
Department of Curriculum, Teaching and Learning
University of Toronto
Toronto, Ontario, Canada

Georgia Garcia, Ph.D.
Professor
Language and Literacy Division
University of Illinois at Urbana-Champaign

Jill Kerper Mora, Ed.D.
Associate Professor Emerita
San Diego State University

Lily Wong Fillmore, Ph.D.
Professor Emerita
Graduate School of Education
University of California, Berkeley

Consultants

J. Arnoldo Cuevas-Antillón
Language Arts Project Specialist
Escondido Union School District
Escondido, CA

Silvia C. Dorta-Duque de Reyes
Spanish Language Arts/ELD Coordinator
English Language Learners Services Unit
San Diego County Office of Education

Julie Maravilla
Los Angeles, California

English Learner Profiles

English Learners—ELs—are a quickly growing population in U.S. schools. While some are children of recent immigrants, many more were born in the U.S. but have spoken other languages in their homes. ELs may come to classrooms with knowledge of other places as well as diverse cultures and customs. As you work with ELs, you will want to consider how proficient your students are and how you can make the academic content accessible. You will be integrating language and content instruction, most likely within the context of a classroom of students with many abilities and proficiencies. As you consider how to best meet the needs of ELs in your classroom, think about their characteristics, patterns of development, and literacy challenges.

General Characteristics of English Learners

- ELs have a first language—also called a home language, primary language, or native language—other than English and are in the process of acquiring English.

- Some ELs are newly arrived in the United States, while others were born in the U.S. but have lived for many years in households where family members do not speak English.

- Some ELs have already acquired and developed literacy skills in their native languages, while others have not learned the academic vocabulary and background knowledge necessary for continued success in school.

- ELs vary in that some have primary languages that resemble English in word order, sound system, and in the patterns of forming words. Spanish, French, and Portuguese, for example, are languages that share alphabets and left-to-right directionality with English. Some words in English and Spanish share cognates. Some languages, such as Swahili or Vietnamese, do not have as much in common with English. For children who speak these languages, initial learning of English is more difficult.

Types of English Learners

- **Newly Arrived ELs** may come with adequate or limited schooling. Those with adequate schooling will make steady academic progress, although they may have difficulty on standardized tests in English. Those with limited formal schooling may lack a sense of school culture and routines. Their limited literacy development may lead to poor academic achievement until both their background knowledge and English proficiency grow.

- **Long Term English Learners** have been in the U.S. for some time, but they have had limited exposure to English in their communities and little reason to learn or know English. As they begin to acquire English, they may lose proficiency in their native languages and have difficulty grasping new content.

- **Older English Learners** may be more capable of quickly learning academic concepts even though they have not developed the language proficiency of other students their age. Curriculum challenges will help these students bridge their academic gaps while they gain English proficiency. Provide scaffolds for instruction and organize collaborative activities to help these students gain success.

Literacy Challenges for ELs

1. **Phonemic Awareness** ELs may find it difficult to differentiate between certain phonemes in English. Some children may find it difficult to separate groups of phonemes into words.

2. **Phonics** ELs need to be able to match sounds to letters and letters to sounds in order to read and write English successfully. They need to develop both oral vocabularies of frequently used words and written vocabularies of sight words.

3. **Vocabulary Development** Some ELs are able to repeat, pronounce, decode, and produce words in English without really knowing what these words mean. ELs need opportunities to link vocabulary words to meaning through routines, concrete objects, pictures and gestures, physical movement, and experiences. These students need multiple exposures to words through explanation, discussion, and repeated readings.

4. **Fluency** Fluent reading involves reading quickly, accurately, and expressively. This can be challenging for ELs, who need many opportunities to listen and speak English before they can feel comfortable and successful with fluent reading. In large groups, ELs may be reluctant to read orally. They need opportunities to listen and follow along with read-alouds.

5. **Comprehension** Help ELs gain comprehension in reading by choosing reading materials with familiar topics, settings, and concepts. Use nonfiction materials, such as photographs and science experiments. Use anticipation guides and graphic organizers to prepare ELs for reading and allow them to comprehend more of what they read.

Best Practices

Scaffolding instruction for ELs allows them to access content while gaining proficiency in English. Most strategies that help ELs access content and language are appropriate for struggling readers in your classroom whose native language is English, so these strategies can be used with the whole class. Some best practices for teaching ELs include:

- using questioning techniques to elicit experiences that relate to students' native cultures,

- using visual aids, including photographs, graphic organizers, and so on,

- linking learning to a physical response, such as raising hands, doing a "thumbs up," nodding, and moving to a different part of the room,

- actively engaging students in the lesson by including less teacher talk and down time and keeping students involved,

- using scaffolding techniques such as think-alouds, paraphrasing, partnering, and reciprocal teaching, and

- building background with such activities as cloze sentences, creating word walls, and working with students to make personal dictionaries.

English learners are generally divided into five levels. **Language Central** provides systematic leveled support to meet the needs of all students. This chart provides some general characteristics of each level along with teaching strategies for your classroom.

STAGE OF LANGUAGE ACQUISITION	BEHAVIORS	TEACHING STRATEGIES
Beginning	• may be unfamiliar with sounds, rhythms, or patterns in English • respond by pointing, gesturing, or drawing • can use simple yes-no responses or one to two-word answers • read simple language that they have already heard • write labels, patterned sentences, or short cloze sentences	• provide opportunities for active listening and visuals • model language with songs and chants • pair students with more proficient speakers • ask yes/no questions; require responses of one or two words • use manipulatives and pictures • provide writing frames
Early Intermediate	• may understand more details in spoken English • use longer phrases and sentences with better grammar • write for a variety of purposes using models • can read independently after oral previews	• allow students to make personal connections with the material • structure group discussion time • ask open-ended questions and then model, expand, restate, and enrich student language • allow students opportunities to create language for a variety of purposes and audiences
Intermediate	• participate in discussions about academic content • can use higher-order language to describe or persuade • write narratives and expository text • use vocabulary with more accuracy and correctness	• use graphic organizers to prepare students for reading and to discuss selections • promote academic concepts and vocabulary with nonfictional texts, magazines, newspapers, and so on • conference with students about writing to point out areas of progress and areas for improvement
Early Advanced	• have a deeper understanding of everyday language, including idioms • use more extensive vocabulary and produce language with fewer grammatical errors • use standard forms when writing • produce writing about varied topics	• structure discussion for the group • provide reference materials for students and guide them with the research • introduce more variety of literary forms • provide opportunities for more variation in writing assignments
Advanced	• use more complex and varied grammatical structures and vocabulary • read texts appropriate for grade level • write about a variety of topics on grade level • begin to self-monitor and correct as they read and write	• provide opportunities for students to publish their writing for others to read • increase students' production of language through drama and music • continue to make strong links between content-area materials and literacy activities

How People Speak

All languages have both consonants and vowels. Consonants are made with some obstruction of the vocal tract, either a complete stoppage of air or enough constriction to create friction. Vowels are produced with the vocal tract more open; they have no constriction that might cause friction.

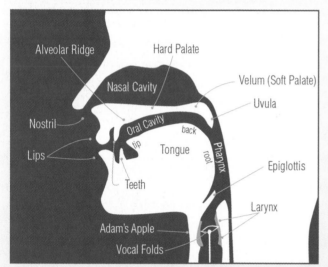

Figure 1: The human vocal tract makes the sounds of speech.

Consonants

Every consonant can be described by noting three characteristics: voicing, place of articulation, and manner of articulation.

Voicing

Many sounds of language, including all vowels, employ vibration of the vocal folds in the larynx. This creates more resonance and energy for the sound. All speech sounds are characterized as either voiced (with vocal fold vibration) or voiceless (with no vocal fold vibration). Feeling the vibration around the Adam's apple can help you understand this difference. If you say "sssss" and then "zzzzz," you can feel the distinction: /s/ is voiceless and /z/ is voiced.

Place of Articulation

This is the location in the vocal tract where the air stream may be constricted. The /s/ sound, for example, is made with the tongue tip close to the alveolar ridge (see Figure 1).

Place of Articulation Terms

Alveolar: tongue tip and ridge behind teeth

Bilabial: using both lips

Glottal: produced at the larynx

Interdental: tongue tip between upper and lower teeth

Labio-dental: upper teeth and lower lip

Labio-velar: rounding of lips; tongue body raised toward velum

Palatal: body of tongue and high part of palate

Palato-alveolar: tongue tip and palate behind alveolar ridge

Velar: body of tongue and velum (soft palate)

Manner of Articulation

This is the type or degree of constriction that occurs in an articulation. For example, the /t/ sound completely stops the airflow with the tongue tip at the alveolar ridge, but /s/ allows air to pass noisily through a small opening.

Manner of Articulation Terms

Affricate: complete constriction followed by slow separation of the articulators resulting in friction

Approximant: close constriction, but not enough for friction

Fricative: narrow constriction; turbulent airflow causing friction

Glottal: produced at the larynx

Lateral: air passes over sides of tongue

Nasal: lowered velum to let air escape through the nose

Stop: complete constriction, closure so that air cannot escape through the oral cavity

Tap: brief contact between tongue tip and alveolar ridge

Vowels

Vowels are open, sonorous sounds. Each vowel can be uniquely described by noting the position of the tongue, the tension of the vocal tract, and the position of the lips. Vowels are described by *height,* where the tongue is relative to the roof of the mouth. They can be high, mid, or low. Tongue backness tells if the tongue articulation is in the front or back of the mouth.

Tense vowels are more common around the world. In English, they are longer and include an expansion of the throat at the pharynx. Lax vowels are shorter with a more neutral pharynx. An example is the tense long *e* as in *meet* versus the lax short *i* as in *mitt*. The lips either can be in a spread or neutral position, or they can be rounded and protrude slightly.

Speaking English

English is the third most widely spoken native language in the world, after Mandarin and Spanish. There are about 330 million native speakers of English and 600 million who speak it as a foreign language.

English Consonant Sounds

The following chart gives the International Phonetic Alphabet (IPA) symbol for each English consonant along with its voicing, place, and manner of articulation. This information can be used to understand and help identify problems that non-native speakers may encounter when learning to speak English.

CONSONANTS OF ENGLISH		
IPA	**Articulation**	**Example**
p	voiceless bilabial stop	**p**it
b	voiced bilabial stop	**b**it
m	voiced bilabial nasal stop	**m**an
w	voiced labio-velar approximant	**w**in
f	voiceless labio-dental fricative	**f**un
v	voiced labio-dental fricative	**v**ery
θ	voiceless interdental fricative	**th**ing
ð	voiced interdental fricative	**th**ere
t	voiceless alveolar stop	**t**ime
d	voiced alveolar stop	**d**ime
n	voiced alveolar nasal stop	**n**ame
s	voiceless alveolar fricative	**s**oy
z	voiced alveolar fricative	**z**eal
ɾ	voiced alveolar tap	bu**tt**er
l	voiced alveolar central approximant	**l**oop
ɹ	voiced palato-alveolar affricate	**r**ed
ʃ	voiceless palato-alveolar fricative	**sh**allow
ʒ	voiced palato-alveolar affricate	vi**si**on
tʃ	voiceless palato-alveolar affricate	**ch**irp
dʒ	voiced palato-alveolar affricate	**j**oy
j	voiced palatal approximant	**y**ou
k	voiceless velar stop	**k**ite
g	voiced velar stop	**g**oat
ŋ	voiced velar nasal stop	ki**ng**
h	voiceless glottal fricative	**h**ope

English Vowel Sounds

Most languages in the world have around five vowel sounds. English has 13 common vowel sounds, which means that many students of English must learn more vowel distinctions than there are in their native language. The lax vowels are most difficult. Some vowels are diphthongs, meaning the tongue is in one position at the beginning of the sound, and it moves to another position by the end of it.

VOWELS OF ENGLISH		
IPA	**Sound**	**Example**
i	ē	b**ea**t
ɪ	ĭ	b**i**t
e	ā	b**ai**t
ɛ	ĕ	b**e**t
æ	ă	b**a**t
u	o͞o	b**oo**t
ʊ	o͝o	c**ou**ld
o	ō	b**oa**t
ɔ	aw	l**aw**
ɑ	ŏ	h**o**t
ə	ə	**a**bout
ʌ	ŭ	c**u**t
ɝ	er	b**ir**d
ɑ ʊ	ow	h**ou**se
ɔ ɪ	oy	b**oy**
ɑ ɪ	ī	b**i**te

Figure 2 is a schematic of the mouth. The left is the front of the mouth; the right is the back. The top is the roof of the mouth and the bottom is the floor. Placement of the vowel shows where the tongue reaches its maximum in the English articulation.

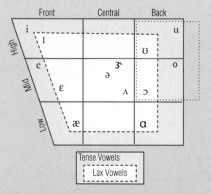

Figure 2: English vowel sounds

Transference

Pronunciation

All languages build on the same fundamentals. All languages contrast voiced and voiceless sound, and have stops and fricatives. Many languages use the same places of articulation for consonants as well. The majority of sounds will easily transfer from another language to English.

However, there will always be some sounds that are not found in a person's native language that can pose a challenge to the English language learner. English has a few relatively rare sounds, such as the interdental sounds spelled with *th*, /ɵ/ and /ð/. The /r/ sound in English is also a very rare type of sound. Most other languages use a tap or trill articulation for an /r/ sound.

In some languages, the /l/ and /r/ sounds belong to one psychological category. This means that they count as the same sound in that language. In this case, it is not the articulation that is difficult, but the perception of the difference and consistent use of one versus the other in any word context. This type of psychological category is called a *phoneme*, and multiple speech sounds all can be categorized as the same phoneme in that language.

This is true for English as well, where, for example, the alveolar lateral /l/ as in *lob* and the velarized lateral /ɫ/ as in *ball* are both counted as the same sound—an *l*—to native speakers of English. It is important to keep in mind that both the phonetic articulation of a sound and its psychological, phonemic category factor into the learning of a new language.

Grammar

Pronouncing English is not the only stumbling block for English learners. The grammar and usage, or syntax, of English may present distinctions that are unique to the language. For example, English syntax requires adjectives to precede the nouns they modify, as in *the tall girl*. In other languages, such as Spanish, Hmong, and Vietnamese, adjectives follow nouns, as in *la chica alta* (literally *the girl tall* in Spanish). This may cause word-order problems, particularly for less advanced English learners.

Other syntactic differences are less obvious and may cause problems even for advanced learners. For example, many East Asian languages (such as Mandarin, Cantonese, and Korean) do not mark agreement between subject and verb. Speakers of these languages may therefore leave out agreement markers such as the *-s* in *The girl like cats.*

The use of articles varies across languages. For instance, Spanish uses the definite article more often than English, while Mandarin and Cantonese do not have articles. A Spanish-speaking English learner might say *The girl likes the cats* instead of *The girl likes cats,* and a Mandarin or Cantonese speaker might say *Girl like cat.*

Plural marking is another potential trouble spot: Vietnamese, Filipino, Cantonese, and Mandarin do not add plural markers to nouns. Learners speaking these languages may have difficulty with English plurals, saying *cat* instead of *cats.*

Grammar Hot Spots

Look for Grammar Hot Spots on the following pages for tips on the most common syntax errors by speakers of languages other than English.

Common First Languages

In the Common First Languages section, you will find details of some common non-English languages spoken in the United States. They are:

- Spanish
- Vietnamese
- Cantonese
- Hmong
- Filipino
- Korean
- Mandarin

You can use the fundamentals of speech articulation already covered to help you understand where the languages differ from English. Differences in the spoken language and in the writing systems are explored as well. These sections pinpoint common trouble spots specific to learners of English.

Culture Clues

Look to Culture Clues for insights into the cultural differences of each language learner as well as ideas for ways to embrace students' diversity.

African American Vernacular English

While not a non-English language, African American Vernacular English (AAVE) is spoken commonly in many student populations and can present barriers to success in reading and writing similar to those facing English language learners. This section provides details on this unique English dialect and suggestions for addressing potential learning problems you may encounter with speakers of AAVE.

Linguistic Contrastive Analysis

The Linguistic Contrastive Analysis Charts provide a quick reference for comparing English sounds with those of other languages. The charts allow you to check at a glance which sounds have equivalents in other languages. For those sounds that don't have equivalents, you can find the closest sound used as a substitute and suggestions for helping someone gain a native English articulation.

In these charts, the sounds are notated using the International Phonetic Alphabet (IPA). This is the most widely recognized and used standard for representing speech sounds in any language. A guiding principle of the IPA across all languages is that each sound is uniquely represented by one symbol, and each symbol represents only one sound.

The chart has columns for each native language with rows corresponding to each English phoneme. Each cell in the chart gives an example word using that sound in the native language, a definition in parenthesis, and transference tips below. If there is no sound equivalent to English, a common substitution used by speakers of that language may be provided.

Transference Tips

Transference tips give you ideas of how the sound will be produced by the learner. Cells highlighted in yellow note where the English learner will have particular difficulty with the English sound.

Spanish

Background

Spanish is the second most widely spoken language in the world. There are more than 400 million native Spanish speakers in 20-plus countries on three continents. Spanish vocabulary and pronunciation differ from country to country. While most dialect differences in English are in vowel sounds, Spanish dialects differ in their consonants.

Spoken

Spanish sounds are similar to those found in English, so there is a strong foundation for the native Spanish speaker learning English. However, there are three key differences between English and Spanish consonants:

1. Most of the alveolar sounds in English, such as /t/, /d/, and /n/ are produced farther forward in the mouth in Spanish. Instead of the tongue touching the alveolar ridge as in English, in Spanish it touches the back of the teeth.

2. Another difference is that the /r/ sound in English is not found in Spanish. There are two /r/ sounds in Spanish. One is the tap /ɾ/, which occurs in English as the quick sound in the middle of the name *Betty*. Psychologically, this tap sound is a kind of /t/ or /d/ sound in English, while in Spanish it is perceived as an /r/. The other /r/ sound in Spanish is a trill, or series of tongue taps on the alveolar ridge. This does not occur in English.

3. The third key difference between English and Spanish can be found in the English production of the voiceless stops /p/, /t/, and /k/. In English these sounds are aspirated, with an extra puff of air at the end, when the sound occurs at the beginning of a word or stressed syllable. So, /p/ is aspirated in *pit*. Learners can add a puff of air to such sounds to sound more like native English speakers.

There are five vowels in Spanish, which are a subset of the English vowels. Spanish vowels include tense vowel sounds /a/ /e/ /i/ /o/ /u/. Lax vowel sounds in English are the problematic ones for native Spanish speakers.

Written

Like English, written Spanish uses the Roman alphabet, so both writing systems are similar. There are a few orthographic differences to note, however:

- The letter *h* in Spanish is silent, but the sound /h/ is written as *j* or *g*.
- A single letter *r* in Spanish represents a tap, while the double *rr* represents a trill.
- Accents are used to show the stress on a syllable when the stress is different from the usual rules. In some cases, words change meaning according to the accents. For example, *el* means *the* while *él* means *he*.

Written Spanish vowels are pronounced like the symbols in the IPA. So, the Spanish "i" is pronounced with the long ē as in the word *beat*. The IPA and Spanish symbol for this letter is the same: /i/.

Grammar Hot Spots

- Double negatives are part of standard grammar in Spanish. Stress the single negative construction in English.
- English prepositions are a common stumbling point for Spanish speakers.

Culture Clues

The Spanish language covers many countries, dialects, and cultures. Always encourage students to share special things about their culture, such as foods, festivals, or social customs.

Vietnamese

Background

Approximately 80 million people in Vietnam speak Vietnamese. The northern dialect is the standard, though central and southern dialects also exist. Most Vietnamese speakers in the United States are from southern Vietnam and speak the southern dialect.

Spoken

Vietnamese is a tonal language, so each syllable is pronounced with a distinctive tone that affects meaning. Vietnamese has a complex vowel system of 12 vowels and 26 diphthongs. Its consonants are simpler, but Vietnamese syllable structure allows few possibilities for final consonants.

Students may need help noticing and learning to reproduce final consonant sounds in English words and syllables. Vietnamese syllable structure allows for limited combinations of initial consonants. Students also may need help with the more complex initial consonant clusters of English words and syllables.

Culture Clues

In traditional Vietnamese education, there is a strict division between the roles of student and teacher. Students may be confused if asked to direct a part of their own study, so encourage group work.

Written

Since the 1600s, Vietnamese has used a Romanized alphabet. Many characters written in Vietnamese have sounds different from their English counterparts, such as *d, x, ch, nh, kh, g, tr, r,* and *e.*

Grammar Hot Spots

- Like English, Vietnamese uses Subject-Verb-Object (SVO) syntax, or word order.

- Vietnamese does not use affixes; instead, syntax expresses number, case, and tense.

Cantonese

Background

Cantonese is one of the seven major Chinese languages, not all of which are mutually intelligible. Cantonese is mostly spoken in China's southern provinces, Hong Kong, and Macau by about 66 million people. It is a tonal language, and the same sequence of letters can have different meanings depending on their pitch.

Spoken

Cantonese has six stops, aspirated and non-aspirated /p/, /t/, /k/; three fricatives /f/, /s/, /h/, and two affricates /ts/, /ts^h/. Some sounds which do not exist in Cantonese can be difficult for the English language learner. The /v/ often gets pronounced as /f/ or /w/; the /z/ is often said as /s/, the sounds spelled with *th* are often said as /t/, /d/, or /f/. Cantonese speakers have difficulty distinguishing between /l/ and /r/, since /r/ is not present in their language. They tend to produce an /l/-like sound for both English sounds in words such as *ride* and *lied.*

Cantonese has 11 vowels and 10 diphthongs. One of the major problems for Cantonese speakers is distinguishing between English tense and lax vowels, because the distribution of Cantonese short and long vowels is determined by the sound context.

Syllables in Cantonese don't have consonant clusters. English consonant clusters are often deleted or broken up by vowel insertion (e.g., *list* becomes *lis*). This may be especially problematic when producing English past tense (e.g., *baked*).

Culture Clues

"Chinese" isn't a language of its own. There are many regional languages spoken in this large country, including Cantonese. For each language spoken, there may be different cultural traditions and beliefs. Talk about where in China students are from and the celebrations and norms that make them unique.

Written

Cantonese is written with standard Chinese characters known as *Hànzi* where each character represents a syllable and has a meaning. Additional Cantonese-specific characters were also added. Cantonese speakers may have difficulty with sound-letter correspondences in English.

Grammar Hot Spots

- English articles and prepositions are difficult for Cantonese speakers. *In, on,* and *at*, for instance, can be translated as the same preposition in Cantonese.

- Plurals, tenses, and gerund endings are difficult for Cantonese speakers to transfer to English.

Common First Languages

CALIFORNIA

Hmong

Background
Hmong is a group of approximately 18 languages within the Hmong-Mien family. There are roughly four million speakers of Hmong, including 200,000 in the United States. They are mainly from two groups with mutually intelligible dialects—Hmong Daw and Mong Leng.

Spoken
Hmong vowels are few and simple, but its consonants are complex and differ from those of English. Notable features of Hmong phonology absent from English include consonantal pre-nasalization (the /m/n/ŋ/ sound before a consonant) and the contrast between nasalized and non-nasalized vowels. Hmong is tonal. Each syllable is pronounced with a distinctive pitch.

Culture Clues
In traditional Hmong culture, learning takes place through hands-on experience. Students may find it difficult to adjust to the use of graphics or print media. Competition, personal achievement, and self-directed instruction may be unfamiliar concepts, so students may prefer group work.

Written
The Romanized Popular Alphabet (RPA), developed in the 1950s, is the usual way of transcribing Hmong. Syllable-final consonants are absent in pronunciation but are used to represent orthographically the tonal value of a given syllable. Students may need particular help in identifying and learning to reproduce the final consonant sounds of English words and syllables.

Grammar Hot Spots
- Like English, Hmong is an SVO language. Personal pronouns are marked for number, including inflection for singular, dual, and plural, though they are not marked for case.
- Because Hmong and English prepositions often have different semantic qualities, students may need help mastering uses of English prepositions. For example, it is correct to say "think <u>about</u> [something]" rather than "think <u>on</u> [something]."

Filipino

Background
Filipino and English are the official languages of the Philippines, where 175 languages are spoken. There are about 24 million native speakers of Filipino, and more than 50 million people speak Filipino as a second language. You may hear the terms Filipino and Tagalog being used interchangeably.

Spoken
Filipino has many similar speech sounds to English. The notable exceptions are the lack of the consonant sounds /f/, /v/, and those spelled with *th*. Of these, the English /f/ and /v/ cause the most difficulty for learners. The distinction between long *e* (as in *beat*) and short *i* (as in *bit*) is also a trouble spot. Filipino does not allow consonant clusters at the end of syllables, so *detect* may be simplified to just one consonant (*detec*).

Culture Clues
Most people from the Philippines can speak Filipino, but for many it is not their first language. Ask Filipino students about other languages they speak. Because English is used alongside Filipino as the language of instruction in the Philippines, most Filipinos are familiar with English.

Written
The Filipino alphabet has 28 letters and is based on the Spanish alphabet, so the English writing system poses little problem.

Grammar Hot Spots
- Filipino word order is Verb-Subject-Object (VSO), which does not transfer well to English.
- Inflectional verb endings, such *as -s, -en, -ed,* and *-ing* do not exist in Filipino, so it is common to leave out the third person singular verb marker (*"He walk,"* not *"He walks"*).

Korean

Background
Korean is spoken by 71 million people in North and South Korea. Standard Korean is based on the speech in and around Seoul.

Spoken
Korean does not have corresponding sounds for English /f/, /v/, /ɵ/, /ð/, and /dʒ/. In word-initial position, all Korean stops are voiceless. Voiced stops /b/, /d/, and /g/ are only produced between two vowels. Korean speakers may have difficulty producing /s/, /ʃ/, and /z/ in some contexts, in addition to English /r/ and /l/ sounds (e.g., *rock* and *lock*). They may have problems in producing English consonant clusters (e.g., *str-, sk-*). These problems can often be eliminated by vowel insertion or consonant deletion. In addition, the distinction between English tense and lax vowels (e.g., /i/ as in *beat* vs. /ɪ/ as in *bit*) may be problematic for Korean speakers.

Culture Clues
Korean uses a complex system of honorifics, so it is unusual for Korean students to use the pronoun *you* or call their teachers by their first name.

Written
Modern Korean uses the Korean alphabet (*Hangul*) or a mixed script of *Hangul* and Chinese. *Hangul* is an alphabetic script organized into syllabic blocks.

Grammar Hot Spots
- In contrast to English, Korean word order is Subject-Object-Verb (SOV). The verb always comes at the end of a sentence.
- Korean syllable stress is different, so learners may have difficulties with the rhythm of English.

Mandarin

Background
Chinese encompasses a wide range of dialects and is the native language of two-thirds of China. There are approximately 870 million Mandarin speakers worldwide. North Mandarin, as found in Beijing, is the basis of the modern standard language.

Spoken
Mandarin Chinese and English differ substantially in their sound structure. Mandarin lacks voiced obstruent consonants (/b/, /d/, /g/, /dʒ/), causing difficulty for speakers in perceiving and producing English voiced consonants (e.g., *buy* may be pronounced and perceived as *pie*). The sounds spelled with *th* are not present in Mandarin, so they are often substituted with /s/ or /t/ causing, for example, *fourth* to be pronounced as *fours*. Mandarin Chinese has five vowels. Due to the relatively small vowel inventory and contextual effects on vowels in Mandarin, many English vowels and tense/lax distinctions present problems for speakers of Mandarin Chinese. Mandarin allows only a very simple syllable structure, causing problems in producing consonant clusters in English. Speakers may drop consonants or insert vowels between them (e.g., *film* may become /filəm/). The use of tones in Mandarin may result in the rising and falling of pitch when speaking English.

Culture Clues
The use of formal and informal forms of English is hard to master for Mandarin speakers. Chinese speakers will often play down complements they receive.

Written
Chinese is written with characters known as *Hànzi.* Each character represents a syllable and also has a meaning. A Romanized alphabet called *Pinyin* marks pronunciation of characters. Chinese speakers may have problems mastering letter-sound correspondences in written English, especially for sounds that are not present in Mandarin.

Grammar Hot Spots
- The non-inflected nature of Chinese causes Mandarin speakers to have problems with plurals, past tense markers, and gerund forms (*-s, -ed, -ing*).
- Mastering English tenses and passive is difficult. Students should be familiarized with correct lexical and syntactic features as well as appropriate situations for the use of various tenses and passives.

African American Vernacular English in the Classroom

To effectively address AAVE in the classroom, the first and most important step for the teacher is to acknowledge the student's use of home language or AAVE as "language different, not language deficit." To accomplish this, a teacher replaces deficit terminology and phrases such as *correct, fix, make better, proper,* or *say it right* with affirming language such as *translate, code-switch, put it in another way,* or *say it for an academic audience.* The second step involves modifying the instruction, focusing on an established technique for second-language instruction called contrastive analysis. With this methodology, teachers have students focus on the rules of the target language through the lens of their home language. The process for doing so is outlined below:

1. **Pre-assessment:** Determine the students' needs for instruction regarding a particular linguistic feature. Use both formal and informal assessments. Listen to students talk; read their writing. In addition, assess the degree to which a student uses a particular linguistic feature. Not all Standard English Learners (SELs) use all Home Language features.

2. **Introduce the AAVE linguistic rule:** For example, explain that multiple negation is the use of multiple negative words in a sentence. The more negative intensifiers in a sentence, the greater the negative sentiment being expressed.

3. **Identify the use of the rule with authentic samples:** For example, explain that the statement *"We don't never have no homework on Friday"* is an example of multiple negation because it contains more than one negative word.

4. **Distinguish between AAVE and the target language:** Give as the SE equivalent *We don't normally have any homework on Friday.* Point out that in Standard English, usage requires one negative word and use of intensifiers (adjectives and adverbs).

5. **Explicitly teach the code switch:** Explain that *We don't never have no homework on Friday. = We don't normally have any homework on Friday.* Point out that Standard English intensifiers *normally* and *any* accurately translate the use of the three negatives in the Home Language sentence.

6. **Address the issue of situational appropriateness:** Emphasize that Standard English is required in many contexts, such as schoolwork, job interviews, and so on.

7. **Assessment:** Assess students to determine their ability to 1) accurately identify the use of AAVE rules, 2) differentiate between home and school language, and 3) code-switch between the two.

AAVE Linguistic Contrastive Analysis Chart

PHONICS	MARKERS	GRAMMAR	VOCABULARY
Digraph /th/ There is no /th/, similar to French as well as other languages. Examples AAVE: *dat*　SE: *that* AAVE: *mouf*　SE: *mouth*	**Past Tense Marker** /ed/ Markers, such as verb tense, are sometimes indicated by tonality versus a use of a morpheme in Standard English. Examples AAVE: *cook yesterday* SE: *cooked* AAVE: *move last night* SE: *moved*	**Regularization** "Hypercorrection" or over-generalizing of the rule linked to the irregular patterns of Standard English with number agreement and subject/objective pronouns Subject verb agreement Examples AAVE: *She walk home sometimes* SE: *She walks home sometimes* Reflexive pronoun AAVE: *hisself (subject pronoun is regularized object pronoun as well)* SE: *himself*	**Culturally Specific Static Vocabulary** Vocabulary specific to the community that is passed down generation to generation Terms like: *kitchen* (back of the hair) or *tripping* (being bothersome)
Same Voicing Consonant Clusters Voiced Clusters *ld, nd, ng* Unvoiced Clusters *sk, st, ft, kt* Examples AAVE: *col*　SE: *cold* AAVE: *des*　SE: *desk*	**Possessive Marker** Possession marked by location of possessor and intonation of word when verbalized Examples AAVE: *Bobby toy* SE: *Bobby's toy*	**Use of *Be*** Habitual *Be* The *be* form is durative, referring to an ongoing state. Examples AAVE: *I be talking with them.* SE: *I often talk with them.*	**Dynamic Uses of Slang** Vocabulary of the youth that changes frequently and can be tied to one specific generation Note: terms for money based on the decade 70s—bread 80s—mula 90s—benjimans 2000—cheddar
Vowel Pairs /ĭ/ /ī/ Mixing of short and long vowels Examples AAVE: *Ah*　SE: *I* AAVE: *Thank*　SE: *Think*	**Plural Marker** Unnecessary when numerically defined Examples AAVE: *fifty cent* SE: *fifty cents*	**Topicalization** Subject announced or "topicalized." Examples AAVE: *That teacher she mean.* SE: *That teacher is mean.*	
Reflexive *R* and *L* *R* and *L* before controlled vowels that do not appear; same occurrence in Asian languages Examples: AAVE: *Sista', Motha'* SE: *Sister, mother* AAVE: *mi'ion, ye'ow* SE: *million, yellow*	**Negation** Uses of multiple negatives to intensify negative in sentences; not equivalent to double negative in Standard English Examples AAVE: *Don't never do that more.* SE: *Don't do that anymore.*	***Is/Are* Form** *Is/Are* linking verbs and helping verbs not always necessary Examples AAVE: *She going to the game with us.* SE: *She is going to the game with us.*	
Two Syllable Stress Patterns Examples: **Po**-lice **Ho**-tel			

Linguistic Contrastive Analysis Chart

The Consonants of English

IPA	ENGLISH	SPANISH	VIETNAMESE	CANTONESE
p	**p**it Aspirated at the start of a word or stressed syllable	**p**ato (duck) Never aspirated	**p**in (battery)	**p**ʰa (to lie prone) Always aspirated
b	**b**it	**b**arco (boat) Substitute voiced bilabial fricative/ɑ/ in between vowels	**b**a (three) Implosive (air moves into the mouth during articulation)	**NO EQUIVALENT** Substitute /p/
m	**m**an	**m**undo (world)	**m**ot (one)	**m**a (mother)
w	**w**in	a**gu**a (water)	**NO EQUIVALENT** Substitute word-initial /u/	**w**a (frog)
f	**f**un	**f**lor (flower)	**ph**u'o'ng (phoenix) Substitute sound made with both lips, rather than with the upper lip and the teeth like English /f/	**f**a (flower) Only occurs at the beginning of syllables
v	**v**ery	**NO EQUIVALENT** Learners can use correct sound	**V**iệt Nam (Vietnam)	**NO EQUIVALENT** Substitute /f/
θ	**th**ing Rare in other languages. When done correctly, the tongue will stick out between the teeth.	**NO EQUIVALENT** Learners can use correct sound	**NO EQUIVALENT** Substitute /tʰ/ or /f/	**NO EQUIVALENT** Substitute /tʰ/ or /f/
ð	**th**ere Rare in other languages. When done correctly, the tongue will stick out between the teeth.	ca**d**a (every) Sound exists in Spanish only between vowels; sometimes substitute voiceless /θ/.	**NO EQUIVALENT** Substitute /d/	**NO EQUIVALENT** Substitute /t/ or /f/
t	**t**ime Aspirated at the start of a word or stressed syllable English tongue-touch. Is a little farther back in the mouth than the other languages.	**t**ocar (touch) Never aspirated	**t**ám (eight) Distinguishes aspirated and non-aspirated	**t**ʰa (he/she) Distinguishes aspirated and non-aspirated
d	**d**ime English tongue-touch is a little farther back in the mouth than the other languages.	**d**os (two)	**Đ**ōng (Dong = unit of currency) Vietnamese /d/ is implosive (air moves into the mouth during articulation)	**NO EQUIVALENT** Substitute /t/
n	**n**ame English tongue-touch is a little farther back in the mouth than the other languages.	**n**ube (cloud)	**n**am (south)	**n**a (take)
s	**s**oy	**s**eco (dry)	**x**em (to see)	**s**a (sand) Substitute sh– sound before /u/ Difficult at ends of syllables and words
z	**z**eal	**NO EQUIVALENT** Learners can use correct sound	**r**òi (already) In northern dialect only Southern dialect, substitute /y/	**NO EQUIVALENT** Substitute /s/
ɾ	but**t**er Written 't' and 'd' are pronounced with a quick tongue-tip tap.	**r**ana (toad) Written as single *r* and thought of as an /r/ sound.	**NO EQUIVALENT** Substitute /t/	**NO EQUIVALENT** Substitute /t/
l	**l**oop English tongue-touch is a little farther back in the mouth than the other languages. At the ends of syllables, the /l/ bunches up the back of the tongue, becoming velarized /ɫ/ or dark-l as in the word *ball*.	**l**ibro (book)	cú **l**ao (island) /l/ does not occur at the ends of syllables	**l**au (angry) /l/ does not occur at the ends of syllables

HMONG	FILIPINO	KOREAN	MANDARIN
peb (we/us/our) Distinguishes aspirated and non-aspirated	*paalam* (goodbye) Never aspirated	*pal* (sucking)	*pʰei* (cape) Always aspirated
NO EQUIVALENT Substitute /p/	*baka* (beef)	**NO EQUIVALENT** /b/ said between vowels Substitute /p/ elsewhere	**NO EQUIVALENT**
mus (to go)	*mabuti* (good)	*mal* (horse)	*mei* (rose)
NO EQUIVALENT Substitute word-initial /*u*/	*walo* (eight)	*gwe* (box)	*wen* (mosquito)
faib (to divide)	**NO EQUIVALENT** Substitute /p/	**NO EQUIVALENT** Substitute /p/	*fa* (issue)
Vaj ('Vang' clan name)	**NO EQUIVALENT** Substitute /b/	**NO EQUIVALENT** Substitute /b/	**NO EQUIVALENT** Substitute /w/ or /f/
NO EQUIVALENT Substitute /tʰ/ or /f/	**NO EQUIVALENT** Learners can use correct sound, but sometimes mispronounce voiced /ð/.	**NO EQUIVALENT** Substitute /t/	**NO EQUIVALENT** Substitute /t/ or /s/
NO EQUIVALENT Substitute /d/	**NO EQUIVALENT** Learners can use correct sound	**NO EQUIVALENT** Substitute /d/	**NO EQUIVALENT** Substitute /t/ or /s/
them (to pay) Distinguishes aspirated and non-aspirated	*takbo* (run) Never aspirated	*tal* (daughter)	*ta* (wet) Distinguishes aspirated and non-aspirated
dev (dog)	*deretso* (straight)	**NO EQUIVALENT** Substitute /d/ when said between vowels and /t/ elsewhere.	**NO EQUIVALENT** Substitute /t/
noj (to eat)	*naman* (too)	*nal* (day)	*ni* (you) May be confused with /l/
xa (to send)	*sila* (they)	*sal* (rice) Substitute *shi*– sound before /i/ and /z/ after a nasal consonant	*san* (three)
NO EQUIVALENT Learners can use correct sound	**NO EQUIVALENT** Learners can use correct sound	**NO EQUIVALENT** Learners can use correct sound	**NO EQUIVALENT** Substitute /ts/ or /tsʰ/
NO EQUIVALENT Substitute /t/	*rin*/*din* (too) Variant of the /d/ sound	Only occurs only between two vowels Considered an /l/ sound	**NO EQUIVALENT**
los (to come) /l/ does not occur at the ends of syllables	*salamat* (thank you)	*balam* (wind)	*lan* (blue) Can be confused and substituted with /r/

Linguistic Contrastive Analysis Chart

The Consonants of English (continued)

IPA	ENGLISH	SPANISH	VIETNAMESE	CANTONESE
ɹ	*red* Rare sound in the world Includes lip-rounding	**NO EQUIVALENT** Substitute /r/ sound such as the tap /ɾ/ or the trilled /r/	**NO EQUIVALENT** Substitute /l/	**NO EQUIVALENT** Substitute /l/
ʃ	*sh*allow Often said with lip-rounding	**NO EQUIVALENT** Substitute /s/ or /tʃ/	*sieu thị* (supermarket) southern dialect only	**NO EQUIVALENT** Substitute /s/
ʒ	*vi*sion rare sound in English	**NO EQUIVALENT** Substitute /z/ or /dʒ/	**NO EQUIVALENT** Substitute /s/	**NO EQUIVALENT** Substitute /s/
tʃ	*ch*irp	*ch*ico (boy)	*ch*ính *ph*ủ (government) Pronounced harder than English *ch*	**NO EQUIVALENT** Substitute /ts/
dʒ	*j*oy	**NO EQUIVALENT** Sometimes substituted with /ʃ/ sound Some dialects have this sound for the *ll* spelling as in *llamar*	**NO EQUIVALENT** Substitute /c/, the equivalent sound, but voiceless	**NO EQUIVALENT** Substitute /ts/ Only occurs at beginnings of syllables
j	*y*ou	*ci*elo (sky) Often substitute /dʒ/	*y*eu (to love)	*j*au (worry)
k	*k*ite Aspirated at the start of a word or stressed syllable	*c*asa (house) Never aspirated	*c*om (rice) Never aspirated	*kʰ*a (family) Distinguishes aspirated and non-aspirated
g	*g*oat	*g*ato (cat)	**NO EQUIVALENT** Substitute /k/	**NO EQUIVALENT** Substitute /k/
ŋ	*king*	*mango* (mango)	*Ngũyen* (proper last name)	*phang* (to cook)
h	*h*ope	*g*ente (people) Sometimes substitute sound with friction higher in the vocal tract as velar /x/ or uvular /χ/	*h*oa (flower)	*h*a (shrimp)

HMONG	FILIPINO	KOREAN	MANDARIN
NO EQUIVALENT Substitute /l/	**NO EQUIVALENT** Substitute the tap /ɾ/	**NO EQUIVALENT** Substitute the tap or /ɾ/ confused with /l/	*r*an (caterpillar) Tongue tip curled further backward than for English /r/
*s*au (to write)	*s*iya (s/he)	Only occurs before /i/; Considered an /s/ sound	*sh*i (wet)
*z*os (village)	**NO EQUIVALENT** Learners can use correct sound	**NO EQUIVALENT**	**NO EQUIVALENT** Substitute palatal affricate /tɕ/
*ch*eb (to sweep)	*ts*a (tea)	*c*ʰal (kicking)	*ch*eng (red)
NO EQUIVALENT Substitute *ch* sound	*D*ios (God)	**NO EQUIVALENT** Substitute *ch* sound	**NO EQUIVALENT** Substitute /ts/
*Y*aj (Yang, clan name)	ta*y*o (we)	*j*e:zan (budget)	*y*an (eye)
*K*oo (Kong, clan name) Distinguishes aspirated and non-aspirated	*k*alian (when) Never aspirated	*k*al (spreading)	*k*e (nest) Distinguishes aspirated and non-aspirated
NO EQUIVALENT Substitute /k/	*g*ulay (vegetable)	**NO EQUIVALENT** Substitute /k/ Learners use correct sound between two vowels	**NO EQUIVALENT** Substitute /k/
*g*us (goose)	an*g*aw (one million)	ba*ŋ* (room)	tan*g* (gong) Sometimes add /k/ sound to the end
*h*ais (to speak)	*h*indi (no)	*h*al (doing)	**NO EQUIVALENT** Substitute velar fricative /x/

Linguistic Contrastive Analysis Chart

CALIFORNIA

The Vowels of English

IPA	ENGLISH	SPANISH	VIETNAMESE	CANTONESE
i	*beat*	*hijo* (son)	*di* (to go)	*si* (silk)
ɪ	*bit* Rare in other languages Usually confused with /i/ (*meat* vs. *mit*)	NO EQUIVALENT Substitute /i/	NO EQUIVALENT Substitute /i/	*sik* (color) Only occurs before velars Substitute /i/
e	*bait* End of vowel diphthongized—tongue moves up to /i/ or /ɪ/ position	*eco* (echo)	*kê* (millet)	*se* (to lend)
ɛ	*bet* Rare in other languages Learners may have difficulty distinguishing /e/ and /ɛ/: pain vs. pen	NO EQUIVALENT Substitute /e/	NO EQUIVALENT Substitute /e/	*seŋ* (sound) Only occurs before velars; difficult to distinguish from /e/ in all positions
æ	*bat* Rare in other languages Learners may have trouble getting the tongue farther forward in the mouth	NO EQUIVALENT Substitute mid central /ʌ/ or low front tense /a/	*ghe* (boat)	NO EQUIVALENT Hard to distinguish between /æ/ and /e/
u	*boot*	*uva* (grape)	*mua* (to buy)	*fu* (husband)
ʊ	*could* Rare in other languages Learners may have difficulty distinguishing /u/ and /ʊ/; *wooed* vs. *wood*	NO EQUIVALENT Substitute /ù/	NO EQUIVALENT Substitute u' (high back unrounded)	*suk* (uncle) Only occurs before velars Difficult to distinguish from /u/ in all positions
o	*boat* End of vowel diphthongized – tongue moves up to /u/ or /ʊ/ position	*ojo* (eye)	*cô* (aunt)	*so* (comb)
ɔ	*law*	NO EQUIVALENT Substitute /o/ or /ɑ/ Substituting /o/ will cause confusion (*low* vs. *law*); substituting /ɑ/ will not	*cá* (fish)	*hok* (shell) Only occurs before velars Difficult to distinguish from /o/ in all positions
ɑ	*hot*	*mal* (bad)	*con* (child)	*sa* (sand)
ɑʊ	*house* Diphthong starts /ɑ/ and moves to /ʊ/	*pauta*	*dao* (knife)	*sau* (basket)
ɔɪ	*boy* Diphthong starts at /ɔ/ and moves to /ɪ/	*hoy* (today)	*rồi* (already)	*soi* (grill)
ɑɪ	*bite* Diphthong starts at /ɑ/ and moves to /ɪ/	*baile* (dance)	*hai* (two)	*sai* (to waste)
ə	*about* Most common vowel in English; only in unstressed syllables Learners may have difficulty keeping it very short	NO EQUIVALENT Substitute /ʌ/ or the full vowel from the word's spelling	*mua* (to buy)	NO EQUIVALENT
ʌ	*cut* very similar to schwa /ə/	NO EQUIVALENT Substitute /a/	*giờ* (time)	*san* (new)
ɝ	*bird* Difficult articulation, unusual in the world but common in American English Learners must bunch the tongue and constrict the throat	NO EQUIVALENT Substitute /ʌ/ or /eɪ/ with trill	NO EQUIVALENT Substitute /ɨ/	*hæ* (boot)

HMONG	FILIPINO	KOREAN	MANDARIN
ib (one)	ʑɯːʃaŋ (market)	ʑɯːʃaŋ (market)	*ti* (ladder) Sometimes English /i/ can be produced shorter
NO EQUIVALENT Substitute /i/	*limampu* (fifty) This vowel is interchangeable with /i/; hard for speakers to distinguish these	**NO EQUIVALENT** Substitute /i/	**NO EQUIVALENT**
tes (hand)	*sero* (zero)	*be:da* (to cut)	*te* (nervous) Sometimes substitute English schwa /ə/
NO EQUIVALENT Substitute /e/	*sero* (zero) This vowel interchanges with /e/ like *bait*; not difficult for speakers to learn	*thɛ:do* (attitude)	**NO EQUIVALENT**
NO EQUIVALENT Substitute /ɛ/	**NO EQUIVALENT** Substitute /ɑ/ as in *hot*	**NO EQUIVALENT**	**NO EQUIVALENT** Substitute /ə/ or /ʌ/
kub (hot or gold)	*tunay* (actual) This vowel interchanges with /ʊ/ like *could*; not difficult for speakers to learn	*zu:bag* (watermelon)	*lu* (hut) Sometimes English /u/ can be produced shorter
NO EQUIVALENT Substitute /ɨ/ (mid central with lips slightly rounded)	*gumawa* (act) This vowel interchanges with /u/ like *boot*; not difficult for speakers to learn	**NO EQUIVALENT**	**NO EQUIVALENT**
NO EQUIVALENT	*ubo* (cough)	*bo:zu* (salary)	*mo* (sword) This vowel is a little lower than English vowel
Yaj (Yang, clan name)	**NO EQUIVALENT** Spoken as /ɑ/ as in *hot*	**NO EQUIVALENT**	**NO EQUIVALENT** Substitute /o/
mov (cooked rice)	*ikaw* (you)	*ma:l* (speech)	*ta* (he/she) Sometimes substitute back /o/ or /u/
plaub (four)	*apoy* (fire)	**NO EQUIVALENT**	**NO EQUIVALENT**
NO EQUIVALENT	*himatay* (faint)	**NO EQUIVALENT**	**NO EQUIVALENT**
qaib (chicken)	**NO EQUIVALENT** Spoken as /ɑ/ as in *hot*	**NO EQUIVALENT**	**NO EQUIVALENT**
NO EQUIVALENT	*rin/din* (too) Variant of the /d/ sound	**NO EQUIVALENT** Difficult sound for learners	**NO EQUIVALENT**
NO EQUIVALENT	**NO EQUIVALENT** Spoken as /ɑ/ as in *hot*	**NO EQUIVALENT**	**NO EQUIVALENT**
NO EQUIVALENT Substitute diphthong /əɨ/	**NO EQUIVALENT** Spoken as many different vowels (depending on English spelling) plus tongue tap /ɾ/	**NO EQUIVALENT**	**NO EQUIVALENT**

How do we live, work, and play together?

Discuss the Big Question

Read and discuss the unit question. Introduce the word *cooperate.* When we cooperate, we work together with our friends or family to do something. What have you done this week to cooperate with others?

Have children use the pictures along the side of the page to preview the weekly concepts for this unit. Read the weekly questions together. Discuss the weekly questions and how they relate to the big question.

Get Online! www.pearsonsuccessnet.com

• Unit 1 Big Question Video

CONCEPT/ LANGUAGE GOALS

Use the Concept and Language Goals throughout the unit to develop the big idea.

Children develop concepts and language as they talk about, use, and practice:

• Concept Vocabulary
• Academic Language
• Language Forms and Functions
• Category Words
• High Frequency Words

Get Online!
PearsonSuccessNet.com

Hear it! See it! Do it!

• Big Idea Video
• Concept Talk Video
• Background Building Audio Slideshow
• eBooks

Cooperation— All Together Now

THE BIG ? How do we live, work, and play together?

6

Unit 1

We Come to School
How do we get to school?

Helping Out
How do people help each other?

Families Help Each Other
How do families cooperate?

Working Together
How do people in a community cooperate?

Fun with Friends
What do you like to do with your friends?

Machines
How do machines help people work together?

Cooperation—All Together Now

7

Read Aloud

Read the **Big Book** *Getting Along.* Prompt discussion about the book.

• How do the children in the book play together?

• How do the children in the book work together?

• How are the children in this book like the children in our school?

For more read alouds related to the theme, see the Big Book Anthology.

Unit Project: Cooperation

After discussing the unit question, provide children with paper, art supplies, and magazines. We will be creating a mural of how people play, work, and live together. To start, draw a picture of a time when you worked together with your family to do something. You will also look through magazines to find pictures of people playing, working, and living together.

After children have drawn their pictures and looked through magazines, display their work on a mural titled, "People Play, Work, and Live." Pair children of mixed abilities and encourage them to add words to describe the pictures. Then have children share their ideas and discuss the pictures. Children can add new ideas to the mural as you progress through the unit.

Question of the Week: How do we get to school?

Instructional Plan and Materials

- **Word Cards** 1–4

- **Big Book** Getting Along

- **Poster** Poster 1 can be used at beginning or end of day.

- **Song Book**, p. 1

Transparencies Explore content and vocabulary and model fluent reading.

For further information about using these components, see pages x–xv.

CALIFORNIA Standards

GK Sci 4.e Communicate observations orally and through drawings.

Academic Language

DAY 1 Get Ready to Read	**DAY 2** Read and Comprehend
Build Background	**Language: Category Words**

Preteach/Review 10–15 min
Poster, Song Book, Big Book
  Leveled Support Preteach
  Practice Stations Preteach
	Preteach/Review 10–15 min
	Poster
	  Leveled Support Preteach
	  Practice Stations Review

Teach 35–45 min
  Concept Talk
  Oral Vocabulary Routine
    Word Cards
  Build Concept Vocabulary
  Daily Table Talk
	Teach 35–45 min
	  Category Words
	  Letter Recognition
	  Daily Table Talk

Check/Reteach 5–10 min
Poster, Word Cards
  Leveled Support Reteach
	Check/Reteach 5–10 min
	Poster, Word Cards
	  Leveled Support Reteach

	Fluency: Writing or Speaking
ELA R 1.1 Identify the front cover, back cover, and title page of a book. **ELA R 1.18** Describe common objects and events in both general and specific language.	**ELA R 1.17** Identify and sort common words in basic categories (e.g., colors, shapes, foods).
Vocabulary: school	**Category Words:** coat, dress, hat, pants, shirt, shoes
Concept Talk Video	**Background Building Audio Slideshow**

This Week
Unit 1, Week 1

We Come to School

Next Week
Unit 1, Week 2
Helping Out

DAY 3 FORM & FUNCTION Read and Comprehend	**DAY 4** FORM & FUNCTION Language Arts	**DAY 5** Language Arts
Language: High Frequency Words	**Letter Recognition and Phonics**	**Think, Talk, and Recognize**

Preteach/Review 10–15 min
Poster
    Leveled Support Preteach
    Practice Stations Review
 	
Teach 35–45 min
    High Frequency Words
    Letter Recognition
    Daily Table Talk
 	
Check/Reteach 5–10 min
Poster, Word Cards
    Leveled Support Reteach
	Preteach/Review 10–15 min
	Poster
	    Leveled Support Preteach
	    Practice Stations Review
	
	Teach 35–45 min
	    Letter Recognition
	    Phonemic Awareness
	    Daily Table Talk
	
	Check/Reteach 5–10 min
	Poster, Word Cards
	    Leveled Support Reteach
		Preteach/Review 10–15 min
		Poster
		    Leveled Support Preteach
		    Practice Stations Review
		
		Teach 15–20 min
		    Think, Talk, and Recognize
		    Concept Wrap Up
		
		Check/Reteach 30–40 min
		Poster, Word Cards, Song Book
		    Leveled Support Reteach
		
		Fluency: Writing or Speaking

ELA R 1.15 Read simple one-syllable and high frequency words (i.e., sight words).	ELA R 1.6 Recognize and name all uppercase and lowercase letters of the alphabet.	ELA LS 1.2 Share information and ideas, speaking audibly in complete, coherent sentences.
High Frequency Words: I, am	**Letters** Aa, Bb, Cc, Dd, Ee	

Practice Stations

Materials and Activity

DAY 1 — Get Ready to Read

masking tape, three sheets of paper, each with one of the following sentences written on it: I ride a bus to school. I ride a car to school. I walk to school.

How We Go to School

Tape each statement to the wall. Have children line up under the statement that shows how they get to school. Have them ask their classmates how they go to school, and to find one person for each of the ways shown. Children can take turns introducing one person and telling how they get to school.

DAY 2 — Read and Comprehend

stack of cards with the following words and picture shown on them: *bus driver, school, store, park;* three large signs with the words and pictures *school, store, park* shown on them.

Bus Stop

Designate a bus route and post the three large signs at intervals to represent bus stops. Place cards in a stack and have each child pick one. The person with the driver card becomes the bus driver and forms the head of a line-to-be. Children line up under the signs. Have the driver move around the room to pick up the children. Continue until all children who wish to have been the driver.

Preteach/Reteach

Transfer and Common Misconceptions

/är/ Diphthong

Many English language learners have difficulty pronouncing diphthongs because the sounds do not exist in their native languages. Listen carefully and provide assistance to children as necessary.

/ou/ Diphthong

Children may confuse *coat* and *caught.* Model saying each word, and provide assistance as necessary.

Produce Language

Weekly Concept and Language Goal

CONCEPT GOALS

- name ways in which children come to school
- recognize that not all children can walk or ride the bus to school
- understand that children can come to school with different people

By Day 5, children should be able to gesture to an item in the drawing and talk about it.

Daily Table Talk

❶ **Beginning**

Children pantomins while you provide the language.

❷ ❸ **Early Intermediate/Intermediate**

Children pantomime and say a word or phrase.

❹ ❺ **Intermediate/Early Advanced**

Children say a sentence while pantomiming.

Daily Table Talk

❶ **Beginning**

Children talk about their drawings.

❷ ❸ **Early Intermediate/Intermediate**

Children write one-word labels.

❹ ❺ **Intermediate/Early Advanced**

Children write a phrase or sentence.

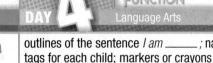

DAY 3 — Read and Comprehend

six large poster boards or paper with one of the following words written: *coat, hat, shoes, shirt, pants, dress;* pictures of clothing (from magazines, catalogs, etc.); scissors, glue

Clothing Word Wall (👥)

Have children work with a partner and find pictures of each of the category words, cut them out, and paste them on the corresponding poster board or paper to make a class word wall.

Letter/Sound Discrimination

Some children may pronounce *p* as /b/. Model saying *pants* and use exaggerated lip movements to show how to pronounce /p/.

DAY 4 — Language Arts

outlines of the sentence *I am _____;* name tags for each child; markers or crayons

I Am (👥)

Give each child a sentence strip. Have them write their name in the blank. They can copy the name tag if they need help. Children can color the words and decorate the sentence. Each child can say the sentence and introduce themselves to their neighbor. Attach the sentences to each child's desk.

High Frequency Words

Many words in English do not follow common pronunciation rules. Give children multiple opportunities to see and use these words.

DAY 5 — Language Arts

sets of index cards cut in half with one of the following letters written on each: *A, a, B, b, C, C, D, d, E,* and *e*; posterboard game boards for each player with 9 letters written in a 3 x 3 grid

Cover a Row (🧍) (👥)

Give each pair a set of index cards and two game boards. Have children take turns picking a card. If the letter shown on the card is on their gameboard, they place the card face down on the gameboard, covering the letter. The first player to cover three places in a row wins. Reshuffle and play again.

A	e	D
c	B	E
a	d	C

The Alphabet

Children should understand that in English, meaning is conveyed through words made up of letters. Some children may be more familiar with character writing, where each character represents a concept or idea.

Daily Table Talk (Day 3)

1 Beginning
> Children can say walk or ride as you display a corresponding picture.

2 3 Early Intermediate/Intermediate
> Phrase: live by school, walk to school.

4 5 Intermediate/Early Advanced
> Sentence: Children who live near the school can walk to it.

Daily Table Talk (Day 4)

1 Beginning
> Children raise their hands as you provide sample answers, such as My mother comes with me to school.

2 3 Early Intermediate/Intermediate
> One or two word: my brother, my mother

4 5 Intermediate/Early Advanced
> Sentence: My father walk me to school.

Daily Table Talk (Day 5)

1 Beginning Child draws with support.

2 3 Early Intermediate/Intermediate Child draws and speaks about the drawing using at least one concept vocabulary word.

4 5 Intermediate/Early Advanced Child draws and provides a label for the drawing.

Build Background Get **Ready** to **Read!**

Question of the Week How do we get to school?
www.pearsonsuccessnet.com

Concept Talk

Use the Big Book Connect the Big Book to the unit theme, Cooperation—All Together Now. Display and discuss the cover. Then read the book aloud.

Introduce the Weekly Concept Tell children that today, they will talk about the ways that people can come to school. Ask the weekly question: How do we get to school?

Use the Poster Direct children's attention to the weekly poster. Use the Day 1 teaching notes at the bottom of the poster.

Sing the Song Use the song **Go to School** to reinforce children's understanding of the weekly concept. Have the children sing or simply chant the words with you.

Use a Transparency Use the Realistic Fiction Transparency (Transparency 19) to share with children a story about the first day at a new school.

We Come to School

Vocabulary

bus

bus stop

driver

school

How do we get to school?

8

Vocabulary

* **Academic Vocabulary**

bus a large vehicle that people travel in

bus stop a place at the side of a road, marked with a sign, where buses stop for passengers

driver someone who drives a vehicle

* **school** a place where children are taught

SCHOOL BUS

9

Introduce Concept Vocabulary

1. Say the Word Display the Word Card as you say *bus.* Separate and then recombine the phonemes. Have children repeat after you.

2. Introduce Word Meaning Ask questions about the word. Where do you go on a bus? How many people can ride on a bus?

3. Demonstrate Have children role play getting on a bus, sitting down, and riding.

4. Apply Have children demonstrate their understanding.

Repeat with other vocabulary words.

Corrective Feedback If children have difficulty pronouncing the words, separate the phonemes again as children repeat after you. Combine them to form the word.

Concept Work

Name each kind of transportation, having children point to it. Then point to transportation methods as children name them. Children can color the picture that shows how they get to school.

The Letter Aa

 Aa Introduce the letter, using an Alphabet Card.

Write and Say the Letter Write the uppercase letter *A* on the board. Have children say the name of the letter. Repeat for the lowercase letter *a.*

Identify the Letter Write *A, B, C,* and *D.* Have children identify each letter by calling out "yes" or "no" as you point to each. Repeat with lowercase letters.

Leveled Support Vocabulary in Context

Preteach / Reteach

① **Beginning** Have children point to the bus, the bus stop sign, and the driver on the Worktext page. Say the word for each picture as children point, and have them echo read each word.

② ③ **Early Intermediate/Intermediate** Do the Beginning activity, but have children say the words themselves, giving help only if needed.

④ ⑤ **Early Advanced/Advanced** Ask children to draw a picture that shows how they get to school. Then have them describe what is happening in their pictures. Encourage them to use complete sentences.

Wrap Up **DAY** 1

 Table Talk How do we get to school? Have children answer the question, using the vocabulary words.

Produce Language Play charades. Ask each child to act out how she or he gets to school and then say a sentence.

Today children should have:

☑ **Learned** and applied vocabulary related to coming to school.

☑ **Spoken** complete sentences about coming to school.

☑ **Recognized** the letter *Aa.*

 ELA R1.18 Describe common objects and events in both general and specific language. (R B6)

9

To discuss why children ride a bus to school; to introduce category words for clothing; to recognize the letter *Bb*.

Concept Talk

Connect to Day 1 How do we get to school?

Introduce the Daily Question Why do children ride a bus to school? Have children answer orally.

Use the Poster Use the Day 2 teaching notes.

Introduce Category Words

1. **Say the Word** Point to the coat as you say the word. Have children repeat the word. Show children an actual coat if one is hanging in the classroom.

2. **Introduce Word Meaning** Relate the meaning to children's experiences. When it is cold outside, we wear coats. Role play shivering from the cold and putting on a coat.

3. **Demonstrate** Have children role play putting on their coats.

4. **Apply** Repeat with other vocabulary words and elicit that they all belong to the category "clothing."

Have children draw what they wore to school today.

The Letter Bb

B b	Introduce the letter using an Alphabet Card.

Write and Say the Letter Follow the routine for both uppercase and lowercase *B*.

Identify the Letter Children can use the routine to identify both upper and lowercase *B* from letters you write on the board.

Wrap Up   DAY 2

Table Talk Have children pretend to get on and ride a bus. Then discuss why children ride buses to school.

Produce Language To build fluency, encourage children to label or write a sentence about their drawings. They can share their writing with partners.

Today children should have:

☑ **Learned** and applied vocabulary related to things we wear.

☑ **Spoken** complete sentences about why some children ride a bus to school.

☑ **Recognized** the letter *Bb*.

ELA R 1.17 Identify and sort common words in basic categories (e.g., colors, shapes, foods). (R B4)

Things I Wear

Picture Dictionary

coat

dress

hat

pants

shirt

shoes

 Draw Draw things you wear.

coat	hat	shoes
shirt	pants	dress

10   **ELA R1.17** Identify and sort common words in basic categories (e.g., colors, shapes, foods). (ELD RB4)

Leveled Support   Category Words

Preteach / Reteach

❶ **Beginning** Have children point to each piece of clothing on the Worktext page. Say the word and have children repeat it.

❷ ❸ **Early Intermediate/Intermediate** Say the name of a piece of clothing. Have children point to it. Then reverse the activity.

❹ ❺ **Early Advanced/Advanced** Have children talk with partners. Have them tell each other what they are wearing.

How do we get to school?

✎ **Circle** Circle *I.*

I am on the bus.

✎ **Circle** Circle *am.*

I am walking.

ELA R1.15 Read simple one-syllable and high-frequency words (i.e., sight words). (ELD R.B2)

11

OBJECTIVE

To discuss walking to school; to introduce the high frequency words *I* and *am*; to recognize *Cc.*

Concept Talk

FORM & FUNCTION

Connect to Day 2 Why do children ride a bus to school?

Introduce the Daily Question Can all children walk to school? Discuss reasons children may not be able to walk to school.

Use the Poster Use the Day 3 teaching notes.

Review Concept Vocabulary Review words introduced on Day 1.

Introduce High Frequency Words

Introduce *I* and *am* by role playing sentences such as *I am walking.* Have children circle the words.

Phonemic Awareness

Read sentences on the Worktext page, having children clap once for each word.

Corrective Feedback For children who have difficulty, read the sentences one word at a time so children can listen for the words *I* and *am*. Cue them when to circle.

The Letter Cc

Introduce the letter, using an Alphabet Card.

Write and Say the Letter Follow the routine for both uppercase and lowercase *C.*

Identify the Letter Children can use the routine to identify both upper and lowercase *C* from letters you write on the board.

Wrap Up   DAY 3

Table Talk *Daily* Children can pretend to walk to school, then discuss why some children cannot walk to school.

Produce Language Have each child tell why about some children walk to school and some children ride.

Today children should have:

☑ **Learned** and applied the high frequency words *I* and *am.*

☑ **Spoken** complete sentences about why some children walk to school.

☑ **Recognized** the letter *Cc.*

 ELA R 1.15 Read simple one-syllable and high-frequency words (i.e., sight words). (R B2)

11

Preteach / Reteach

LS Leveled Support High Frequency Words

❶ **Beginning** Model the word *I* for children. Say something to yourself and point. I am wearing glasses. Continue with other sentences, modeling for children.

❷ ❸ **Early Intermediate/Intermediate** Write the words *I* and *am* on index cards, one word on each card. Give each child a set of cards. Say simple sentences, modeling how you hold up the correct card when you say each word. Have children listen as you speak, holding up the corresponding cards.

❹ ❺ **Early Advanced/Advanced** Write cloze sentences that are missing the word *I* or *am*. Say the sentences and have children say the word that belongs in the sentence. Children can then read the whole sentence with you. Repeat with several sentences.

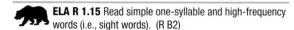

OBJECTIVE

To discuss who comes to school with children; to recognize letters *Aa* through *Ee*.

Concept Talk

 FORM & FUNCTION

Connect to Day 3 Can all children walk to school?

Introduce the Daily Question Ask: Who comes with you to school? Ask children who come to school with their parents to raise their hands. Continue with other options, such as siblings, grandparents, sitters, bus drivers, or alone.

Use the Poster Use the Day 4 teaching notes.

The Letters
Dd and Ee

Introduce the letters using an Alphabet Cards.

Write and Say the Letters Identify the letters *Dd* and *Ee* for children. Have children complete the activity in the Worktext.

Corrective Feedback If children have difficulty matching the letters correctly, write the upper- and lowercase letters on the board and point out how each pair looks alike and different.

Wrap Up   **DAY 4**

 Daily **Table Talk** Who comes to school with you? Have children discuss the question.

Produce Language Have each child say a sentence to tell who comes to school with them.

Today children should have:

☑ **Learned** and applied vocabulary related to who comes to school with children.

☑ **Spoken** complete sentences about who comes to school with children.

☑ **Recognized** the letters *Aa* through *Ee*.

ELA R 1.6 Recognize and name all uppercase and lowercase letters of the alphabet. (R B10)

 **Letter Match**

✏ **Circle** Circle the letters.

 **B**   E   **B**   **B**   C

 **D**   A   **D**   C   **D**

 **E**   **E**   C   D   **E**

 **a**   **a**   b   **a**   c

 **c**   d   e   **c**   **c**

 **e**   **e**   a   d   **e**

12 🐻 **ELA R1.6** Recognize and name all uppercase and lowercase letters of the alphabet. (ELD R.B10)

Preteach / Reteach **LS** **Leveled Support** **Letter Recognition**

① **Beginning** Hold up an alphabet card for *A*. Say the letter name and have children repeat it. Continue with *a, B, b, C, c, D, d, E, e*.

② ③ **Early Intermediate/ Intermediate** Write the letters *A – E* on a sheet of tagboard. Give children letter tiles for *A – E* and have them match the letter tiles to the written letters. Then ask them to name each letter.

④ ⑤ **Early Advanced/Advanced** Write each child's first and last name. Ask children to circle the letters *Aa, Bb,Cc, Dd,* and/or *Ee* in their names.

How do you get to school?

 Draw

OBJECTIVE

To guide children to express their understanding of weekly concepts and vocabulary.

Think, Talk, and Recognize!

Concept Talk

Connect to Day 4 Who comes to school with you? Model how to answer yesterday's question with a sentence.

Review the Weekly Question Ask: How do you get to school? Have children line up depending on how they get to school: bus, car, or walk. After children have answered, they can figure out which group of children is the largest.

Use the Poster Use the Day 5 teaching notes at the bottom of the poster.

Review Concept Vocabulary Review the vocabulary introduced on Day 1.

Concept Wrap-Up

Have children draw to answer the question: How do you get to school? They can talk about their pictures as they share them with friends.

Corrective Feedback If children have difficulty deciding on ideas for their pictures, draw their attention to the photograph. Ask How does this child get to school? Do you get to school the same way or a different way?

Preteach LS Reteach Leveled Support   Concept Vocabulary

① **Beginning** Display the Word Cards for *bus, driver, bus stop,* and *school.* Say each word. Ask children to repeat and point to the matching card.

② ③ **Early Intermediate/Intermediate** Draw a large picture of a school bus. Ask children to identify it and describe it. Then ask a volunteer to draw a bus driver by the bus. Continue with a bus stop. After the picture is completed, ask: Where is the bus going? Draw a simple picture of a school in the background. Ask volunteers to tell a story about the picture.

④ ⑤ **Early Advanced/Advanced** Display the Word Cards for *bus, bus stop,* and *school.* Say the word *bus* and ask children to say words that rhyme with *bus.* Accept real words and nonsense words. Continue with *stop* and *school.*

Wrap Up   **DAY 5**

Daily **Table Talk** How do we get to school? Children can discuss, using vocabulary words they learned this week.

Produce Language To build fluency, children can label, write about, or speak about their drawings. Ask children to respond to what they have heard or read.

Today children should have:

☑ **Reviewed** the weekly concept and concept vocabulary.

☑ **Spoken** about how they get to school.

☑ **Drawn or Written** to show how they get to school.

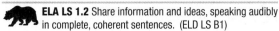 **ELA LS 1.2** Share information and ideas, speaking audibly in complete, coherent sentences. (ELD LS B1)

13

Question of the Week

How do people help each other?

DAY 1 — Get Ready to Read

Build Background

Preteach/Review 10–15 min
Poster, Song Book, Big Book

Leveled Support Preteach
Practice Stations Preteach

Teach 35–45 min

Concept Talk
Oral Vocabulary Routine
Word Cards
Build Concept Vocabulary
Letter Recognition
Daily Table Talk

Check/Reteach 5–10 min
Poster, Word Cards

Leveled Support Reteach

DAY 2 — Read and Comprehend

Language: Category Words

Preteach/Review 10–15 min
Poster

Leveled Support Preteach
Practice Stations Review

Teach 35–45 min

Category Words
Letter Recognition
Daily Table Talk

Check/Reteach 5–10 min
Poster, Word Cards

Leveled Support Reteach

Fluency: Writing or Speaking

Instructional Plan and Materials

- **Word Cards**
  5–8

- **Poster**
  Poster 2 can be used at beginning or end of day.

- **Big Book**
  Getting Along

- **Song Book**, p. 2

Transparencies Explore content and vocabulary and model fluent reading.

For further information about using these components, see pages x–xv.

ELA R 1.18 Describe common objects and events in both general and specific language.

ELA R 1.17 Identify and sort common words in basic categories (e.g., colors, shapes, foods).

CALIFORNIA Standards

GK Sci 1.a Students know objects can be described in terms of the materials they are made of (e.g., clay, cloth, paper) and their physical properties (e.g., color, size, shape, weight, texture, flexibility, attraction to magnets, floating, sinking).

GK Sci 4.e Communicate observations orally and through drawings.

Academic Language

Category Words: blue, green, orange, purple, red

www.pearsonsuccessnet.com

Concept Talk Video

Background Building Audio Slideshow

This Week
Unit 1, Week 2

Helping Out

Next Week
Unit 1, Week 3
Families Help
Each Other

FORM & FUNCTION DAY 3 Read and Comprehend	**FORM & FUNCTION** DAY 4 Language Arts	DAY 5 Language Arts
Language: High Frequency Words	**Letter Recognition and Phonics**	**Think, Talk, and Recognize**
Preteach/Review 10–15 min	**Preteach/Review** 10–15 min	**Preteach/Review** 10–15 min
Poster	Poster	Poster
Leveled Support Preteach	**Leveled Support Preteach**	**Leveled Support Preteach**
Practice Stations Review	**Practice Stations Review**	**Practice Stations Review**
Teach 35–45 min	**Teach** 35–45 min	**Teach** 15–20 min
High Frequency Words	**Letter Recognition**	**Think, Talk, and Recognize**
Letter Recognition	**Daily Table Talk**	**Concept Wrap Up**
Phonemic Awareness		
Daily Table Talk	**Check/Reteach** 5–10 min	**Check/Reteach** 30–40 min
	Poster, Word Cards	Poster, Word Cards, Song Book
Check/Reteach 5–10 min	**Leveled Support Reteach**	**Leveled Support Reteach**
Poster, Word Cards		
Leveled Support Reteach		
		Fluency: Writing or Speaking
ELA R 1.15 Read simple one-syllable and high frequency words (i.e., sight words).	**ELA R 1.6** Recognize and name all uppercase and lowercase letters of the alphabet.	**ELA LS 1.2** Share information and ideas, speaking audibly in complete, coherent sentences.
High Frequency Words: I, am	**Letters** Ff, Gg, Hh, Ii, Jj, Kk, Ll, Mm, Nn	

Practice Stations

Materials and Activity

DAY 1 Get Ready to Read	DAY 2 Read and Comprehend
booklets made of two sheets of 11 x 17 or construction paper folded and stapled in the center; pictures of people (from magazines, etc.); crayons, colored pencils, scissors, glue	none

People Helping People Booklet

Give each pair a booklet. Have children find pictures of people helping each other, cut them out, and paste them in the booklets. Have children tell their partners a story about one of the pictures.

Duck Duck Goose

Have children play Duck Duck Goose. All the children but one sit in a circle. The child outside the circle moves around the circle, taps each child and says *duck*. The tapper taps one person and says *goose*. The tagged child (the "goose") gets up, chases after the tapper (the "duck"). The goose tries to catch the duck before it can take the tagged child's place. If successful, the duck becomes the tapper. If not, the tapper continues circling the group.

Preteach/Reteach

Transfer and Common Misconceptions

Initial /sh/ Sound

Some children may have difficulty with /sh/ as this phoneme is not used in Spanish. Have children practice saying /sh/ alone and in *sheep*.

Word Order: Adjectives

In Spanish, many modifiers, such as colors, come after the noun (for example, "ball red"). Use phrases such as "red ball" and "yellow crayon" to familiarize children with word order in English.

Produce Language

Weekly Concept and Language Goal

CONCEPT GOALS

• understand the concept of helping others
• name ways that friends can help each other

By Day 5, children should be able to gesture to an item in the drawing and talk about it.

 Daily Table Talk

❶ **Beginning**
Children pantomime while you provide the language.

❷ ❸ **Early Intermediate/Intermediate**
Children pantomime and say a word or phrase.

❹ ❺ **Early Advanced/Advanced**
Children say a sentence while pantomiming.

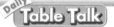 **Daily Table Talk**

❶ **Beginning**
Children talk about their drawings.

❷ ❸ **Early Intermediate/Intermediate**
Children write one-word labels.

❹ ❺ **Early Advanced/Advanced**
Children write a phrase or sentence.

DAY 3 FORM & FUNCTION — Read and Comprehend

 DAY 4 FORM & FUNCTION — Language Arts

DAY 5 Language Arts

---

index cards with one of the category words and colors shown on each (red, blue, orange, yellow, green, purple); a set of cards for each group

masking tape, a set of colored paper for each group with these sentences written on them: *I am five, I am six, I am seven; I am a girl, I am a boy; I am happy, I am sad.* Use the same color paper for sentences within a group.

name tags, highlighters

I See

Give each group a set of Category Word cards. Have children put cards face down in a pile. One child picks a card and says, "I see something _____ [color]." The other children take turns guessing what it is. Repeat so each child has a turn saying "I see _____ ."

"I Am" Lineup

Tape one set of sentences to the wall. Read the sentences with children. Children should line up under the appropriate one. Repeat for each group of sentences.

Letters in Our Names

Have children find their name tag. Then they highlight the letters *F, f, G, g, H, h, I, i, J, j, K, k, L, l, M, m, N,* and *n.* If children do not have one of these letters in their first name, write their last names on the name tag.

Subject Pronoun *I*

In some languages, such as Spanish, subject pronouns are not needed. Model sentences staring with *I.* Give examples of sentences with and without *I* and have students say yes or no to show correct usage.

Letter/Sound Correlation

Some children may pronounce /j/ in *orange* as /ch/, like in *chalk.* Point out that in English, *g* can sound like /g/ as in *game* or /j/ as in *jump.*

Letter/Sound Correlation

The letter *h* is always silent in Spanish. The /h/ sound is written as *j* and *g.* Give an example of a name (Jose) and ask students for more examples of names starting with /h/. Write each on board and point to the corresponding letter.

Daily Table Talk

① **Beginning**
> Children can say help or friend as you display a corresponding picture.

②③ **Early Intermediate/Intermediate**
> Phrase: help friend; do things

④⑤ **Early Advanced/Advanced**
> Sentence: I help [friend's name] feed ducks.

Daily Table Talk

① **Beginning**
> Children raise their hands as you provide sample answers, such as They tie my shoes and They help me get on my bicycle.

②③ **Early Intermediate/Intermediate**
> One or two-word response: pick up, hold hand

④⑤ **Early Advanced/Advanced**
> Sentence: [Friend's name] walks to school with me.

Daily Table Talk

① **Beginning** Child draws with support.

②③ **Early Intermediate/Intermediate** Child draws and speaks about the drawing using at least one concept vocabulary word

④⑤ **Intermediate/Early Advanced** Child draws and provides a label for the drawing.

OBJECTIVE

To introduce and discuss concepts and vocabulary relating to people helping each other; to recognize the letter *Ff*.

Build Background Get **Ready** to **Read!**

Question of the Week

How do people help each other?

www.pearsonsuccessnet.com

Concept Talk   5min

(**Use the Big Book**) If you haven't introduced the Big Book, consider reading it to children. Connect to the unit theme, Cooperation—All Together Now.   5min

(**Introduce the Weekly Concept**) Tell children that today they will talk about ways people help each other. Ask the weekly question: How do people help each other?

Use the Poster Direct children's attention to the weekly poster. Use the Day 1 teaching notes at the bottom of the poster.

Sing the Song Use the song **The Farmer Likes to Help** to reinforce children's understanding of the weekly concept. Have the children sing or simply chant the words with you.

Use a Transparency Use the Cause and Effect Map (Transparency 1) to record children's ideas about what might happen when we help other people.

Helping Out

Vocabulary

duck

frog

goat

sheep

14

How do people help each other?

Vocabulary

* **Academic Vocabulary**

duck a common water bird with short legs and a wide beak

frog a small animal with smooth skin that lives in or near water, makes a deep sound, and has long legs for jumping

goat a common farm animal with horns and with long hair under its chin

sheep a farm animal that is kept for its wool

ELA R1.18 Describe common objects and events in both general and specific language. (ELD R.B6)

15

 Leveled Support **Vocabulary in Context**

❶ ❷ Beginning/Early Intermediate Have children point to the duck, frog, goat, and sheep on the Worktext page. Say the word for each picture as children point, and have them echo read each word.

❸ Intermediate Say the vocabulary words, one word at a time, and have children point to the animals in the illustrations. Children can make the animals' sounds to help reinforce the word meanings.

❹ ❺ Early Advanced/Advanced Ask children to describe one of the animals without naming it. Others can guess what animal is being described.

Introduce Concept Vocabulary

1. **Say the Word** Display the Word Card as you separate the phonemes and then combine them to say *duck.* Have children repeat the word.

2. **Introduce Word Meaning** Ask questions about the word *duck.* What noise do ducks make?

3. **Demonstrate** Have children make sounds like a duck to show that they know what a duck is.

4. **Apply** Have children demonstrate their understanding. Have them point to a duck in the illustrations.

Repeat with other vocabulary words.

Corrective Feedback If children have difficulty with the vocabulary words, say the words again as you point to each photo. Have children point and say the words after you.

Concept Work

Ask children how people in the illustrations are helping each other. Prompt with a sentence frame if necessary: In this picture, people help each other by _____. Have children circle parts of the illustrations that show people helping each other.

The Letter Ff   5 min (letter A)

| Ff | Introduce the letter using an Alphabet Card. |

Write and Say the Letter Write the uppercase letter *F* on the board. Have children say the name of the letter. Repeat for the lowercase letter *f.*

Identify the Letter Write the letters *C, D, E,* and *F.* Have children identify the letter *F* by calling out "yes" or "no" as you point to each letter. Repeat, using lowercase letters.

Wrap Up   DAY **1**

Table Talk How do people help each other? Have children answer the question, using the vocabulary words.

Produce Language Have children role play helping each other feed an animal. Have children say sentences about what they are doing.

Today children should have:

☑ **Learned** and applied vocabulary related to how people help each other.

☑ **Spoken** complete sentences about helping other people.

☑ **Recognized** the letter *Ff.*

 ELA R1.18 Describe common objects and events in both general and specific language. (ELD R.B6)

15

OBJECTIVE

To discuss how children can help their families; to introduce category words for colors; to recognize *Gg* and *Hh.*

Concept Talk

Connect to Day 1 Recall with children that yesterday they talked about how people help each other.

Introduce the Daily Question How am I going to help my family? Have children answer orally.

Use the Poster Use the Day 2 teaching notes.

Corrective Feedback: If children have difficulty answering the question, provide a sentence frame: I help at home by _____ .

Introduce Category Words

1. **Say the Word** Point to the word *red* as you say the word. Have children repeat after you.

2. **Introduce Word Meaning** Point at both red and non-red objects and ask: Is this red?

3. **Demonstrate** Have children hold up a red crayon or point to a red object in the room.

4. **Apply** Repeat with other vocabulary words and elicit that they all belong to the category "colors."

Have children complete the Worktext page.

Letters Gg and Hh

Gg

Introduce the letters using Alphabet Cards.

Write and say the letter Follow the routine for uppercase and lowercase *G* and *H*.

Identify the letter Children can use the routine to identify both upper- and lowercase *G* and *H* from other letters.

Wrap Up   DAY 2

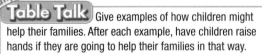 Give examples of how children might help their families. After each example, have children raise hands if they are going to help their families in that way.

Produce Language To build fluency, encourage children to label the colors of the items. They can share their writing with partners.

Today children should have:

☑ **Learned** and applied vocabulary related to color.

☑ **Spoken** complete sentences about how they are going to help their families.

☑ **Recognized** the letters *Gg* and *Hh.*

ELA R1.17 Identify and sort common words in basic categories (e.g., colors, shapes, foods). (ELD R.B4)

Colors

Picture Dictionary

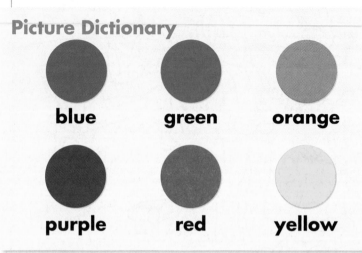

blue   green   orange

purple   red   yellow

 Circle Circle red.

 Circle Circle green.

16 **ELA R1.17** Identify and sort common words in basic categories (e.g., colors, shapes, foods). (ELD R.B4)

Leveled Support **Category Words**

❶ ❷ **Beginning/Early Intermediate** Point to a color on the Worktext page. Ask children to point to other items in the room that are the same color. They can say the color names as they point.

❸ **Intermediate** Say the name of a color. Have children point to the color on the Worktext page. Then reverse the activity.

❹ ❺ **Early Advanced/Advanced** Provide sentence frames with the color word missing, such as *I see a _____ apple.* Children supply the missing color word, then repeat the sentences.

How do you help your friends?

✎ **Circle** Circle *I.*

I show how to do things.

✎ **Circle** Circle *am.*

I am sharing.

ELA R1.15 Read simple one-syllable and high-frequency words (i.e., sight words). (ELD R.B2)

17

To discuss how they help their friends; to review the high-frequency words *I* and *am;* to identify syllables in a word; to recognize the letters *Ii, Jj,* and *Kk.*

Concept Talk ‒10min   FORM & FUNCTION

Connect to Day 2 Recall with children that yesterday they talked about how they are going to help their family.

Introduce the Daily Question How do you help your friends? Have children answer orally.

Use the Poster Use the Day 3 teaching notes.

Corrective Feedback If children have difficulty answering the question, describe how friends are helping each other in the photos. Model sentences based on the pictures.

Introduce High Frequency Words 15

Write "I am six" on the board. Point to each word and have children identify *I* by saying "yes" or "no." Circle *I.* Repeat for *am.* Help children complete the Worktext page.

Phonemic Awareness 15

Segmentation Read words on the Worktext page. Segment the words into syllables, clapping once for each syllable. Have children clap wth you after modeling.

The Letters Ii, Jj, and Kk 5
Introduce letters using Alphabet Cards.

Write and say the letters Follow the routine for upper- and lowercase *Ii, Jj,* and *Kk.*

Identify the letters Children can identify the letters from others that you write.

Table Talk How do you help your friends? Have children pantomime answers and discuss them.

Produce Language Have each child tell about a time they helped a friend.

Today children should have:

☑ **Learned** and applied the high-frequency words *I* and *am.*

☑ **Spoken** complete sentences about how they can help friends.

☑ **Recognized** the letters *Ii, Jj,* and *Kk,* and syllables in words.

 ELA R1.15 Read simple one-syllable and high-frequency words (i.e., sight words). (ELD R.B2)

Leveled Support **High-Frequency Words**

➊ ➋ **Beginning/Early Intermediate** Point at yourself and say *I am [name].* Have each child point to self and say *I am [name].*

➌ **Intermediate** Say *I am* statements such as "I am a girl." Children who match the statement move to a designated location such as the center of a circle.

➍ ➎ **Early Advanced/Advanced** Have children work with partners and say *I am* sentences such as "I am a book." Partners respond to each sentence by saying "yes" or "no."

OBJECTIVE

To discuss how their friends help them; to recognize letters *Ll*, *Mm*, and *Nn*.

Concept Talk

 FORM & FUNCTION

Connect to Day 3 Recall with children that yesterday they talked about how they help their friends.

Introduce the Daily Question How do your friends help you? Have children answer orally. Make a list of children's responses and read them back to children. Have children raise their hands each time they hear a way that a friend has helped them.

Use the Poster Use the Day 4 teaching notes.

The Letters Ll, Mm, and Nn

| Ll | Introduce the letters using Alphabet Cards. |

Write and say the letters Identify the letter *Ll*. Repeat for the other letters. Have children complete the activity in the Worktext.

Corrective Feedback If children have difficulty matching the letters, write the upper- and lowercase letters on the board. Identify the letters and then work with children through the Worktext, one line at a time.

Wrap Up   DAY 4

Table Talk How do your friends help you? Have children discuss the question.

Produce Language Have each say a sentence to tell how a friend helps them.

Today children should have:

☑ **Learned** and applied vocabulary related to how friends help them.

☑ **Spoken** complete sentences about how friends help them.

☑ **Recognized** the letters *Ff* through *Nn*.

ELA R1.6 Recognize and name all uppercase and lowercase letters of the alphabet. (ELD R.B10)

Letter Match

✏ **Circle** Circle the letter.

G	J	**G**	N	**G**
L	I	**L**	**L**	K
J	**J**	N	G	**J**
F	K	**F**	**F**	G
i	i	l	j	i
k	g	k	m	g
h	h	j	h	f

Leveled Support Letter Recognition

1 2 Beginning/Early Intermediate Write the letters *F* through *N* on index cards, one letter per card. Say the names of the letters as you hold up the cards. Then display a card and ask Is this *G*? Children can use "thumbs up" or "thumbs down" to answer. Repeat with other letters.

3 Intermediate Write the letters *F* – *N* on a sheet of tagboard. Give children index cards with *F* – *N* and have them match the letter cards to the written letters. Then ask them to name each letter.

4 5 Early Advanced/Advanced Write each child's first and last name. Ask children to circle the letters *Ff, Gg, Hh, Ii, Jj, Kk, Ll, Mm,* and *Nn* in their names.

How do people help each other?

 Draw

OBJECTIVE
To guide children to express their understanding of weekly concepts and vocabulary.

Think, Talk, and Recognize!

Concept Talk

Connect to Day 4 Recall with children that yesterday they talked about how friends help them.

Review the Weekly Question How do people help each other? Have children stand. Ask yes-no questions about how people help each other using children's examples or questions such as "Do you help your friends?" and "Do you help set the table at home?" Children answer "yes" or "no" and move forward one step for every yes answer.

Use the Poster Use the Day 5 teaching notes.

Review Concept Vocabulary Review the vocabulary introduced on Day 1.

Concept Wrap-Up

Have children draw to answer the question: *How do you help other people?* Write "I am helping."

Corrective Feedback If children have difficulty, point out the photo. Ask: How is the child in this photograph helping? Elicit other ways children help each other to prompt children's thinking.

Leveled Support Concept Vocabulary

① ② **Beginning/Early Intermediate** Display the Word Cards for *duck, frog, goat,* and *sheep.* Say each word. Ask children to repeat and point to the matching card.

③ **Intermediate** Display the Word Cards for *duck, frog, goat,* and *sheep.* Describe one of the words, asking children to choose the word that matches your description. As children choose the card, they should pronounce the word.

④ ⑤ **Early Advanced/Advanced** Ask children to choose a card and say a detail about the word. Then children can use the words in spoken sentences.

Wrap Up   DAY

Daily Table Talk How do people help each other? Have children discuss the question, using the vocabulary words they learned this week.

Produce Language To build fluency, children can label, write about, or speak about their drawings. Ask children to respond to what they read or heard.

Today, children should have:

☑ **Reviewed** the weekly concept and concept vocabulary.

☑ **Spoke** about how people help each other.

☑ **Drawn or written** to show how people help each other.

 ELA LS1.2 Share information and ideas, speaking audibly in complete, coherent sentences. (ELD LS.B1)

19

WEEK 3

CALIFORNIA

Weekly Lesson Plan

Last Week
Unit 1, Week 2
Helping Out

Question of the Week How do families cooperate?

	DAY 1 Get Ready to Read	**DAY 2** Read and Comprehend
	Build Background	**Language: Category Words**

Instructional Plan and Materials

- **Word Cards**
  9–11

- **Big Book**
  Getting Along

- **Poster**
  Poster 3 can be used at beginning or end of day.

- **Song Book**, p. 3

Transparencies Explore content and vocabulary and model fluent reading.

For further information about using these components, see pages x–xv.

DAY 1 — Build Background

Preteach/Review 10–15 min
Poster, Song Book, Big Book
- **Leveled Support Preteach**
- **Practice Stations Preteach**

Teach 35–45 min
- **Concept Talk**
- **Oral Vocabulary Routine**
  Word Cards
- **Build Concept Vocabulary**
- **Letter Recognition**
- **Daily Table Talk**

Check/Reteach 5–10 min
Poster, Word Cards
- **Leveled Support Reteach**

DAY 2 — Language: Category Words

Preteach/Review 10–15 min
Poster
- **Leveled Support Preteach**
- **Practice Stations Review**

Teach 35–45 min
- **Category Words**
- **Letter Recognition**
- **Daily Table Talk**

Check/Reteach 5–10 min
Poster, Word Cards
- **Leveled Support Reteach**

Fluency: Writing or Speaking

ELA R 1.18 Describe common objects and events in both general and specific language.

ELA R 1.17 Identify and sort common words in basic categories (e.g., colors, shapes, foods).

CALIFORNIA Standards

GK His-Soc Sci K.4.1 Determine the relative locations of objects using the terms near/far, left/right, and behind/in front.

GK Sci 4.c Describe the relative position of objects by using one reference (e.g., above or below).

GK Sci 4.e Communicate observations orally and through drawings.

Academic Language

Vocabulary: grandma

Category Words: up, down, in, out

Get Online! www.pearsonsuccessnet.com

Concept Talk Video

Background Building Audio Slideshow

Families Help Each Other

DAY 3 — Read and Comprehend	DAY 4 — Language Arts	DAY 5 — Language Arts
FORM & FUNCTION	FORM & FUNCTION	
Language: High Frequency Words	**Letter Recognition and Phonics**	**Think, Talk, and Recognize**
Preteach/Review 10–15 min Poster **Leveled Support Preteach** **Practice Stations Review**	**Preteach/Review** 10–15 min Poster **Leveled Support Preteach** **Practice Stations Review**	**Preteach/Review** 10–15 min Poster **Leveled Support Preteach** **Practice Stations Review**
Teach 35–45 min **High Frequency Words** **Phonemic Awareness** **Letter Recognition** **Daily Table Talk**	**Teach** 35–45 min **Letter Recognition** **Daily Table Talk**	**Teach** 15–20 min **Think, Talk, and Recognize** **Concept Wrap Up**
Check/Reteach 5–10 min Poster, Word Cards **Leveled Support Reteach**	**Check/Reteach** 5–10 min Poster, Word Cards **Leveled Support Reteach**	**Check/Reteach** 30–40 min Poster, Word Cards, Song Book **Leveled Support Reteach**
		Fluency: Writing or Speaking
ELA R 1.15 Read simple one-syllable and high frequency words (i.e., sight words).	**ELA R 1.6** Recognize and name all uppercase and lowercase letters of the alphabet.	**ELA LS 1.2** Share information and ideas, speaking audibly in complete, coherent sentences.
High Frequency Words: the, little	**Letters** Oo, Pp. Qq, Rr, Ss	

Practice Stations

Materials and Activity

DAY 1

crayons, colored pencils, paper

My Family
Have children draw a picture of the people in their family and tell a partner a story about them.

DAY 2

photocopies of the outlines of a girl or boy (similar to a paper doll); paper cutouts of different styles of shirts (for example, T-shirt, button-down, polo); crayons, colored paper, glue, glitter, ribbons, buttons, and so on

Create a Shirt
Give each child a paper with the outline of a boy or girl. Tell children to choose a shirt cutout and decorate it by coloring and pasting objects on it. Have children paste the shirt on their figure outlines and color the rest of the figure.

Preteach/Reteach

Transfer and Common Misconceptions

Family Members

Encourage children to share names that they have for their family members.

Prepositions

Demonstrate each using common objects.

Produce Language

Weekly Concept and Language Goal

CONCEPT GOALS

• recognize that family members often cooperate
• name ways that children can help parents
By Day 5, children should be able to gesture to an item in the drawing and talk about it.

Daily Table Talk

❶ **Beginning**
Children pantomime while you provide the language.

❷ ❸ **Early Intermediate/Intermediate**
Children pantomime and say a word or phrase.

❹ ❺ **Early Advanced/Advanced**
Children say a sentence while pantomiming.

Daily Table Talk

❶ **Beginning**
Children talk about their drawings.

❷ ❸ **Early Intermediate/Intermediate**
Children write one-word labels.

❹ ❺ **Early Advanced/Advanced**
Children write a phrase or sentence.

DAY 3 — Read and Comprehend
FORM & FUNCTION

one set of index cards with the category words written and pictures shown on them (up, down, in, out).

Which Way?

Post Category Word cards in a visible spot and read each one with children. Have children line up in two rows facing each other. Take turns giving each row commands with the words *up, down, in* or *out*. If children in the row complete the command, give another command to the opposite row. If the initial command is not completed, have the opposite row try to complete it.

Up

In

The Word *little*

Some children may be confused by the short vowel sounds in English, which don't always appear in other languages, and may pronounce *little* as leetle.

Daily Table Talk

❶ Beginning
Children can say grandma or brother as you display a corresponding picture.

❷ ❸ Early Intermediate/Intermediate
Phrase: wake my dad

❹ ❺ Early Advanced/Advanced
Sentence: I sing to my sister.

DAY 4 — Language Arts
FORM & FUNCTION

four large sheets of paper with one of the following sentences written on each: *I have a little sister. I have a little brother. I have a little sister and little brother. I do not have a little sister or brother.*

I Have a Little _____ ✤

Post the four pieces of paper on the wall. Have children line up under the matching statement. Children then play a game. Each take turns completing the sentence I have a little _____ (eg, car, bedroom, dog) and children who share that trait raise their hands and can say, "I do, too."

I have a little sister.

Letter/Sound Correlation

In the Spanish language, the letter *s* is pronounced /s/ like in *sun*. It does not use s for the /z/ sound heard in *please* or *cans*.

Daily Table Talk

❶ Beginning
Children raise their hands as you provide sample answers, such as I watch my brother and I find grandma's keys.

❷ ❸ Early Intermediate/Intermediate
One or two-word response: get things

❹ ❺ Early Advanced/Advanced
Sentence: I pick up my room.

DAY 5 — Language Arts

sticky notes with the letters *O, P, Q, R,* and *S* written on them

Find the Letters 👥

Give pairs of children a set of sticky notes. Have them work together to find the letters around the room. Encourage them to look on walls, desks, or books. Tell children that more than one group can add their sticky notes to letters.

Tactile Learners

Some children may have trouble recognizing letters. Show them how to write them in sand or using finger paint. Physically writing each letter can help some children remember them.

Daily Table Talk

❶ Beginning Child draws with support.

❷ ❸ Early Intermediate/Intermediate Child draws and speaks about the drawing using at least one concept vocabulary word.

❹ ❺ Early Advanced/Advanced Child draws and provides a label for the drawing.

OBJECTIVE

To introduce and discuss concepts and vocabulary related to ways that families cooperate; to recognize the letter *Oo.*

Build Background Get Ready to Read!

Question of the Week How do families cooperate?
www.pearsonsuccessnet.com

Concept Talk + Poster (10m)

Use the Big Book If you haven't introduced the Big Book, consider reading it to children. Connect to the unit theme, Cooperation—All Together Now.

Introduce the Weekly Concept Tell children that today they will talk about ways families cooperate. Ask the weekly question: How do families cooperate?

Use the Poster Direct children's attention to the weekly poster. Use the Day 1 teaching notes at the bottom of the poster.

Sing the Song Use the song **Help at Home** to reinforce children's understanding of the weekly concept. Have the children sing or simply chant the words with you.

Use a Transparency Use the Classification Map (Transparency 3) to help children classify different ways in which families cooperate.

Families Help Each Other
Vocabulary

grandma

shirt

swing

20

How do families cooperate?

Vocabulary + Activity (10m)

* Academic Language Vocabulary
* **grandma** your grandmother

shirt a piece of clothing that covers the upper part of your body and your arms

swing a seat hanging from ropes or chains, on which children swing

ELA R1.18 Describe common objects and events in both general and specific language. (ELD R.B6)

21

Introduce Concept Vocabulary

1. **Say the Word** Display the Word Card as you say *grandma.* Have children repeat the word.

2. **Introduce Word Meaning** Say: A grandma is your mom or dad's mom. Do you have a grandma? What do you and your grandma do together?

3. **Demonstrate** Show a picture of a man. Explain why this person could not be a grandma.

4. **Apply** Have children demonstrate their understanding.

Repeat with other vocabulary words.

Corrective Feedback If children have difficulty pronouncing the words, model saying the initial phonemes followed by the whole world.

Concept Work

Ask children questions about what the people in the pictures are doing. Have children talk about each picture and relate to their own experiences. Have children color the pictures.

The Letter Oo +5

 Introduce the letter using an Alphabet Card.

Write and Say the Letter Write the uppercase letter *O* on the board. Have children say the name of the letter. Repeat for the lowercase letter *o.*

Identify the Letter Write the letters *C, D, G,* and *O.* Have children identify the letter *O* by calling out "yes" or "no" as you point to each one. Repeat, using lowercase letters.

Leveled Support   Vocabulary in Context

① ② Beginning/Early Intermediate Have children point to the grandma, shirt, and swing on the Worktext page. Say the word for each picture as children point and have them echo each word.

③ Intermediate Place the Word Cards on the table. As you say the word, children point to the correct card. Then point to the words pictured in the illustrations. Children point to the card that matches.

④ ⑤ Early Advanced/Advanced Say a simple phrase or sentence that describes one of the words. Have children point to the word card and say the word. Children can also describe the words themselves for partners to guess.

Wrap Up   DAY 1

Table Talk How do families cooperate? Have children answer the question, using the vocabulary words.

Produce Language Have children role play how family members help each other. They can talk about what they are doing.

Today children should have:

☑ **Learned** and applied vocabulary related to how families cooperate.

☑ **Spoken** complete sentences about how families cooperate.

☑ **Recognized** the letter *Oo.*

 ELA R1.18 Describe common objects and events in both general and specific language. (ELD R.B6)

To discuss how children can help their parents; to introduce category words for position; to recognize the letter *Pp*.

Concept Talk + Poster (10 m)

Connect to Day 1 Recall with children that yesterday they talked about how families cooperate.

Introduce the Daily Question How can I help my parents? Have children answer orally.

Use the Poster Use the Day 2 teaching notes.

+Activity
(10 m)

Introduce Category Words

1. Say the Word Hold something up as you say the word *up*.

2. Introduce the meaning Show children that the dad in the photograph is holding the baby up.

3. Demonstrate Look up at the ceiling, point, and ask Is this up? Look down, point, and ask Is this up?

4. Apply Have children draw an up arrow. Have children label the picture with the word *up*. Repeat with other category words.

Corrective Feedback If children have difficulty understanding the meaning of the category words, have them play a modified game of "hokey pokey." Form a circle. Give a command to move a body part for each position, such as "Put your hands in the circle."

The Letter Pp (5)

 Pp   Introduce the letter\ using an Alphabet Card.

Write and say the letter Follow the routine for both uppercase and lowercase *P*.

Identify the letter Children can identify both upper- and lowercase *P* from letters you write.

Wrap Up
DAY 2

Table Talk Ask children how they can help their parents. Have each child say a phrase or sentence.

Produce Language To build fluency, encourage children to label or write a sentence about items in the closet. They can share their writing with partners.

Today children should have:

☑ **Learned** and applied vocabulary related to positions.

☑ **Spoken** complete sentences about how they help their parents.

☑ **Recognized** the letter *Pp*.

ELA R1.17 Identify and sort common words in basic categories (e.g., colors, shapes, foods). (ELD R.B4)

Where is it?

Picture Dictionary

up

down

in

out

 Circle Circle a thing in the closet.

Leveled Support   **Category Words**
Preteach / Reteach

❶ ❷ **Beginning/Early Intermediate** Hold up an item and ask: Is this up? Children can nod their heads to respond. Repeat with the other position words.

❸ **Intermediate** Create a circle on the floor with yarn or draw a circle with chalk outside. Practice the words *in* and *out*. Give children objects and ask them to place the objects in the circle. Then have them move certain objects out of the circle. Children can also hold items up and down.

❹ ❺ **Early Advanced/Advanced** Children can play "Simon Says." Say: Simon says hold your hand up. Simon says put your pencil down. Give similar commands. Then allow children to command, using *in, out, up,* and *down*.

How do you help family members?

✏️ **Circle** Circle *the*.

I help with the dishes.

✏️ **Circle** Circle *little*.

I help my little sister.

ELA R1.15 Read simple one-syllable and high-frequency words (i.e., sight words). (ELD R.B2)

23

Leveled Support High Frequency Words

① ② **Beginning/Early Intermediate** Display the word *the*. Have children use their fingers to write *the* on their desks. Repeat for *little*.

③ **Intermediate** Write *the* and *little* on tagboard cards. Give each child a card. Have children move around the room and find a person with the same word.

④ ⑤ **Early Advanced/Advanced** Display the word *the*. Write the letters *t, h,* and *e* on tagboard cards. Give each child a card. Have children move around room and find others with missing letters to spell *the*. Have children line up in order to spell *the*. Repeat for *little*, using *lit* and *tle* on tagboards.

CALIFORNIA   DAY 3

OBJECTIVE

To discuss how children help family members; to introduce high frequency words *the* and *little;* to discriminate initial /d/ and /s/; to recognize the letter *Qq.*

Concept Talk + Poster (10) 🔵 FORM & FUNCTION

Connect to Day 2 Recall with children that yesterday they talked about how they can help their families.

Introduce the Daily Question How do you help family members? Have children answer orally.

Use the Poster Use the Day 3 teaching notes.

Review Concept Vocabulary Review words introduced on Day 1.

+Activity (10)

Introduce High Frequency Words

Introduce by pointing at a familiar object and saying the [object]. Introduce *little* by pointing at a little object and saying little [object]. Help children circle the words in the Worktext.

Phonemic Awareness (+5)

Sound Discrimination Read dishes and emphasize the initial /d/. Say other words with initial /d/. Name words and have children say "yes" or "no" for each word with the initial /d/. Repeat for initial /s/ in *sister.*

The Letter Qq (5) | Qq | Introduce the letter using the Alphabet Card.

Write and say the letter Follow the routine for both uppercase and lowercase *Q.*

Identify the letter Children can use the routine to identify both upper- and lowercase *Q* from letters you write on the board.

Wrap Up   DAY 3

Table Talk Children can role-play things they do to help family members. Discuss their ideas.

Produce Language Have each child say a sentence about how they help family members.

Today children should have:

☑ **Learned** and applied the high frequency words *the* and *little.*

☑ **Spoken** complete sentences about how they help family members.

☑ **Recognized** the letter *Qq* and initial /d/ and /s/ sounds.

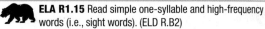 **ELA R1.15** Read simple one-syllable and high-frequency words (i.e., sight words). (ELD R.B2)

To discuss how children help at home; to recognize *Rr* and *Ss*.

Concept Talk + Poster (10)

Connect to Day 3 Recall with children that yesterday they talked about how they help family members.

Introduce the Daily Question How do you help at home? Have children answer orally.

Use the Poster Use the Day 4 teaching notes.

The Letters Rr and Ss

 10m   Rr   Introduce the letters, using Alphabet Cards.

Write and say the letters Identify the letters *Rr* and *Ss*. Have children complete the activity in the Worktext.

Corrective Feedback If children have difficulty matching the letters correctly, write the upper- and lowercase letters on the board. Print the letters on index cards, one letter per card. Have children match the index cards to the letters on the board.

Letter Match

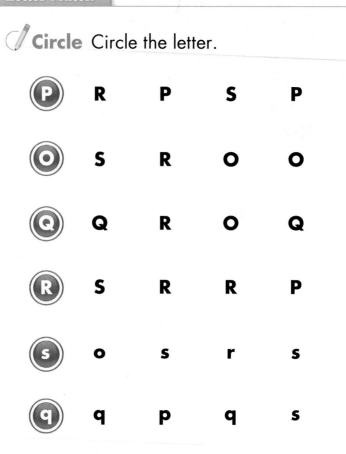

✏ **Circle** Circle the letter.

P	R	**P**	S	**P**
O	S	R	**O**	**O**
Q	**Q**	R	O	**Q**
R	S	**R**	**R**	P
s	o	**s**	r	**s**
q	**q**	p	**q**	s
r	s	**r**	**r**	o

24   🐻   **ELA R1.6** Recognize and name all uppercase and lowercase letters of the alphabet. (ELD R.B10)

Wrap Up   DAY 4

 **Table Talk** How do you help at home? Have children discuss the question.

Produce Language Have each child say a sentence about how he or she helps at home.

Today children should have:

☑ **Learned** and applied vocabulary related to how they help at home.

☑ **Spoken** complete sentences about how they help at home.

☑ **Recognized** the letters *Rr* and *Ss*.

ELA R1.6 Recognize and name all uppercase and lowercase letters of the alphabet. (ELD R.B10)

Leveled Support   Phonics

1 2 Beginning/Early Intermediate Hold up an alphabet card for *O*. Say the letter name and have children repeat it. Continue with *o*, *P*, *p*, *Q*, *q*, *R*, *r*, *S*, and *s*.

3 Intermediate Write the letters *O – S* on a sheet of tagboard. Give children letter tiles for *O – S* and have them match the letter tiles to the written letters. Then ask them to name each letter.

4 5 Early Advanced/Advanced Write each child's first and last name. Ask children to circle the letters *Oo*, *Pp*, *Qq*, *Rr*, and *Ss* in their names or in other words that you write.

How do families cooperate?

Draw

ELA LS1.2 Share information and ideas, speaking audibly in complete, coherent sentences. (ELD LS.B1)

25

Think, Talk, and Recognize!

Concept Talk ＋ Poster (10)

Connect to Day 4 Recall that yesterday children talked about how they help at home.

Review the Weekly Question How do families cooperate? Have children stand. Ask yes-no questions about how families cooperate such as "Do you help your parents?" and "Do you help a little brother [or sister]?" Children answer "yes" or "no" and move forward one step for every "yes" answer.

Use the Poster Use the Day 5 teaching notes.

Review Concept Vocabulary Review the vocabulary introduced on Day 1.

Concept Wrap-Up Act. (10)

Have children draw to answer the question: *How do families cooperate?* Help children to write a label for each person in their drawings. Use the photo to prompt discussion before drawing: What are the family members doing here? How is each person helping?

Leveled Support Concept Vocabulary (5)

Preteach / Reteach LS

① ② **Beginning/Early Intermediate** Display the Word Cards for *grandma*, *shirt*, and *swing*. Say each word. Ask children to repeat and point to the matching card.

③ **Intermediate** Display the Word Cards for *grandma*, *shirt*, and *swing*. Ask children to say a detail about each picture. Model: The shirt is red.

④ ⑤ **Early Advanced/Advanced** Display the Word Cards for *grandma*, *shirt*, and *swing*. Have each child tell a story about his or her family using one or more words.

Wrap Up **DAY** 5

Daily Table Talk How do families cooperate? Have children discuss the question, using the vocabulary words they learned this week.

Produce Language To build fluency, children can label, write about, or speak about their drawings. Ask children to respond to what they heard or read.

Today, children should have:

☑ **Reviewed** the weekly concept and concept vocabulary.

☑ **Spoken** about how families cooperate.

☑ **Drawn or written** to show how they help their families.

 ELA LS1.2 Share information and ideas, speaking audibly in complete, coherent sentences. (ELD LS.B1)

Question of the Week How do people in a community cooperate?

Instructional Plan and Materials

- **Word Cards**
  12–15

- **Poster**
  Poster 4 can be used at beginning or end of day.

- **Big Book**
  Getting Along

- **Song Book**, p. 4

Transparencies Explore content and vocabulary and model fluent reading.

For further information about using these components, see pages x–xv.

CALIFORNIA Standards

GK Sci 4.e Communicate observations orally and through drawings.

Academic Language

DAY 1 — Get Ready to Read

Build Background

Preteach/Review 10–15 min
Poster, Song Book, Big Book

- **Leveled Support Preteach**
- **Practice Stations Preteach**

Teach 35–45 min
- **Concept Talk**
- **Oral Vocabulary Routine**
  Word Cards
- **Build Concept Vocabulary**
- **Daily Table Talk**

Check/Reteach 5–10 min
Poster, Word Cards

- **Leveled Support Reteach**

ELA R 1.18 Describe common objects and events in both general and specific language.

Vocabulary: children, parents

Concept Talk Video

DAY 2 — Read and Comprehend

Language: Category Words

Preteach/Review 10–15 min
Poster

- **Leveled Support Preteach**
- **Practice Stations Review**

Teach 35–45 min
- **Category Words**
- **Letter Recognition**
- **Daily Table Talk**

Check/Reteach 5–10 min
Poster, Word Cards

- **Leveled Support Reteach**

Fluency: Writing or Speaking

ELA R 1.17 Identify and sort common words in basic categories (e.g., colors, shapes, foods).

Category Words: circle, oval, square, triangle

Background Building Audio Slideshow

Working Together

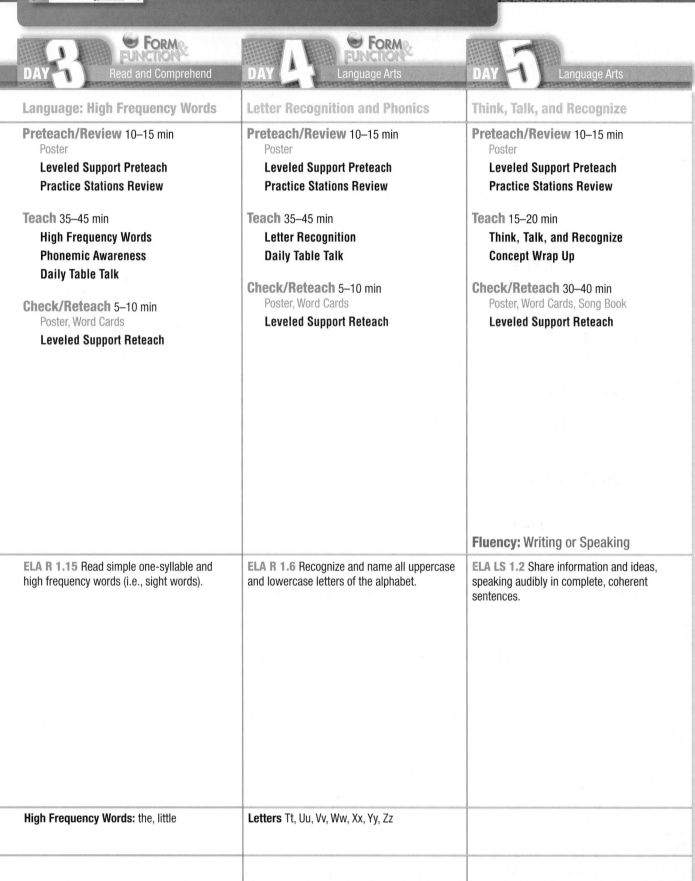

DAY 3 Read and Comprehend	**DAY 4** Language Arts	**DAY 5** Language Arts
Language: High Frequency Words	**Letter Recognition and Phonics**	**Think, Talk, and Recognize**
Preteach/Review 10–15 min Poster **Leveled Support Preteach** **Practice Stations Review**	**Preteach/Review** 10–15 min Poster **Leveled Support Preteach** **Practice Stations Review**	**Preteach/Review** 10–15 min Poster **Leveled Support Preteach** **Practice Stations Review**
Teach 35–45 min **High Frequency Words** **Phonemic Awareness** **Daily Table Talk**	**Teach** 35–45 min **Letter Recognition** **Daily Table Talk**	**Teach** 15–20 min **Think, Talk, and Recognize** **Concept Wrap Up**
Check/Reteach 5–10 min Poster, Word Cards **Leveled Support Reteach**	**Check/Reteach** 5–10 min Poster, Word Cards **Leveled Support Reteach**	**Check/Reteach** 30–40 min Poster, Word Cards, Song Book **Leveled Support Reteach**
		Fluency: Writing or Speaking
ELA R 1.15 Read simple one-syllable and high frequency words (i.e., sight words).	**ELA R 1.6** Recognize and name all uppercase and lowercase letters of the alphabet.	**ELA LS 1.2** Share information and ideas, speaking audibly in complete, coherent sentences.
High Frequency Words: the, little	**Letters** Tt, Uu, Vv, Ww, Xx, Yy, Zz	

Practice Stations

Materials and Activity

DAY 1   Get ready to Read

large sheet of blank newsprint, drawing paper, crayons, colored pencils, colored markers, tape

Community Mural (♣)

Tape a large sheet of blank newsprint to a wall. Write "The People in Our Community" across the top. Have children draw a picture of a person in their community who helps other people (for example, bus driver, fire fighter, crossing guard). Have students post their pictures on the paper to create a mural.

DAY 2   Read and Comprehend

large sheets of drawing paper with lines dividing paper into four squares, crayons, colored pencils

My Kindergarten Day (♣)

Have children draw one picture in each section of the drawing paper about what they do in Kindergarten. Have children tell a partner about their drawings.

Preteach/Reteach

Transfer and Common Misconceptions

Letter/Sound Correlation

Some many children will read *ch* as /tch/. Have practice saying *children* and *teachers.* ✓

Sound Discrimination

Some children may pronounce the v in *oval* as /f/ or /b/. Model saying the /v/ in *oval* and have children repeat and practice.

Produce Language

Weekly Concept and Language Goal

CONCEPT GOALS

- recognize that people who live in a community cooperate with each other
- name ways in which adults and children work together
- describe ways in which people cooperate at school

By Day 5, children should be able to gesture to an item in the drawing and talk about it.

Daily Table Talk

❶ Beginning
> Children pantomime while you provide the language.

❷ ❸ Early Intermediate/Intermediate
> Children pantomime and say a word or phrase.

❹ ❺ Early Advanced/Advanced
> Children say a sentence while pantomiming.

Daily Table Talk

❶ Beginning
> Children talk about their drawings.

❷ ❸ Early Intermediate/Intermediate
> Children write one-word labels.

❹ ❺ Early Advanced/Advanced
> Children write a phrase or sentence.

FORM & FUNCTION

DAY 3 Read and Comprehend

  FORM & FUNCTION

DAY 4 Language Arts

  FORM & FUNCTION

DAY 5 Language Arts

index cards with one of the category words and shapes shown on each (square, triangle, circle, oval); mural paper, markers, crayons	shallow trays of salt	four sets of index cards for each group; write one of the following letters on each card: *T, t, U, u, V, v, W, w, X, x, Y, y, Z, z*

Draw a Shape

Post Category Word cards at intervals along the mural paper. Have partners take turns drawing shapes on the mural paper and guessing the shape.

Salt Writing

Give each pair of children a shallow tray of salt. Have them take turns writing *the* and *little* in the salt.

Go Fish

Have children form groups of three. Give each group four sets of cards mixed together. Each child should draw four cards. They take turns trying to match the letters in their hands. One big letter should go with a small letter of the same type to make a match. If yes, the player must give the card to the asking player. If no, the player says, "Go fish!" and the asking child draws a new card from the pile. When children have a match, they place the pair of cards face up on the table or floor. Play until the first player has all of his or her cards in pairs face up.

Definite Article

The article *the* often is challenging to Spanish-speaking children. In Spanish, four words are used to represent the English *the*.

Letter/Sound Correlation

In Spanish, *z* may sound like /s/ in *sun* or /th/ in *thing*. Many children merge /s/ and /z/. Point out that in English, the letter *z* sounds like /z/ as in *buzz*.

Silent Letter

Because the *h* is always silent in Spanish, some children may pronounce *the* as /te/.

Daily Table Talk

① **Beginning**
> Children can say *play* or *game* as you display a corresponding picture.

② ③ **Early Intermediate/Intermediate**
> Phrase: take turns, share toys

④ ⑤ **Early Advanced/Advanced**
> Sentence: I let [friend's name] play with *my* toys.

Daily Table Talk

① **Beginning**
> Children raise their hands as you provide sample answers, such as *I line up* and *I use a quiet voice.*

② ③ **Early Intermediate/Intermediate**
> One or two-word response: work together; don't hit

④ ⑤ **Early Advanced/Advanced**
> Sentence: I take turns on the playground.

Daily Table Talk

① **Beginning** Child draws with support

② ③ **Early Intermediate/Intermediate** Child draws and speaks about the drawing using at least one concept vocabulary word.

④ ⑤ **Early Advanced/Advanced** Child draws and provides a label for the drawing.

Build Background Get Ready to Read!

Question of the Week

How do people in a community cooperate?

www.pearsonsuccessnet.com

Concept Talk

Use the Big Book If you haven't introduced the Big Book, consider reading it to children. Connect to the unit theme, Cooperation—All Together Now.

Introduce the Weekly Concept Tell children that today they will talk about how people in a community cooperate. Let children know that *cooperate* means to get along well and work together. Ask the weekly question: How do people in a community cooperate?

Use the Poster Direct children's attention to the weekly poster. Use the Day 1 teaching notes at the bottom of the poster.

Sing the Song Use the song **Help in School** to reinforce children's understanding of the weekly concept. Have the children sing or simply chant the words with you.

Use a Transparency Use the Central Concept Map (Transparency 2) to collect children's ideas about helping in different communities: their families, their school community, and their neighborhoods.

Working Together

Vocabulary

children

kindergarten

parents

teacher

26

How do people in a community cooperate?

Vocabulary

* Academic Vocabulary

* **children** more than one child

* **kindergarten** a school class for young children who are about five years old

* **parents** the father and mother of a person or animal

teacher someone whose job is to teach

 ELA R1.18 Describe common objects and events in both general and specific language. (ELD R.B6)

27

Introduce Concept Vocabulary

1. Say the Word Display the Word Card as you say *children.* Have children repeat the word.

2. Introduce Word Meaning Ask questions about children. Are there children in this room? How old are children? How big are children?

3. Demonstrate Have each join hands with another child, raise hands, and say "children."

4. Apply Have children demonstrate their understanding.

Repeat with other vocabulary words.

Corrective Feedback If children have difficulty pronouncing the words, separate the phonemes. Combine to form the word.

Concept Work

Talk about the different communities shown. A family is a community. So is a class full of children. Discuss how the people work together. Have children choose a picture to color. They can explain to partners how the picture shows cooperation.

The Letter Tt

T t

Introduce the letter using an Alphabet Card.

Write and Say the Letter Write *Tt* as you name the letter.

Identify the Letter Write other letters so that children can distinguish between them and *Tt.*

Preteach / Reteach — Leveled Support Vocabulary in Context

① ② Beginning/Early Intermediate Have children point to children, kindergarten, parents, and teachers on the Worktext page. Say the word for each picture as children point, and have them echo each word.

③ Intermediate Do the Beginning activity, but have children say the words themselves, giving help only if needed.

④ ⑤ Early Advanced/Advanced Have children do the Beginning activity with a partner. Give help only if needed.

Wrap Up   DAY 1

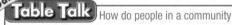

Daily Table Talk How do people in a community cooperate? Have children answer the question, using the vocabulary words.

Produce Language Have children play school or house. Have children say sentences about how they cooperate as they play.

Today children should have:

☑ **Learned** and applied vocabulary related to how people in a community cooperate.

☑ **Spoken** complete sentences about how people in a community cooperate.

☑ **Recognized** the letter *Tt.*

 ELA R1.18 Describe common objects and events in both general and specific language. (ELD R.B6)

27

To discuss how children and adults work together; to introduce category words for shape; to recognize *Uu* and *Vv*.

Concept Talk

Connect to Day 1 Recall with children that yesterday they talked about how people in a community cooperate.

Introduce the Daily Question How do children and adults work together? Have children answer orally.

Use the Poster Use the Day 2 teaching notes.

Introduce Category Words

1. **Say the Word** Have children point to the square. Say the word and have children repeat.

2. **Introduce Word the Meaning** Draw a square and circle on the board. Point at each and say: Is this a square?

3. **Demonstrate** Have children draw a square in the air with their fingers.

4. **Apply** Repeat with other vocabulary words and elicit that they all belong to the category "shapes."

Have children draw shapes on the Worktext page.

The Letters
Uu and Vv

 Introduce letters using Alphabet Cards.

Write and Say the Letter Follow the routine for both upper- and lowercase *Uu* and *Vv*.

Identify the Letters Children can use the routine to distinguish *Uu*, *Vv* from other letters.

 Wrap Up DAY **2**

Table Talk How do children and adults work together? Discuss with children ways that they help adults.

Produce Language To build fluency, encourage children to label or write a sentence about the shapes they drew. They can share their writing with partners.

Today children should have:

☑ **Learned** and applied vocabulary related to shapes.

☑ **Spoken** complete sentences about how children and adults work together.

☑ **Recognized** the letters *Uu* and *Vv*.

 ELA R1.17 Identify and sort common words in basic categories (e.g., colors, shapes, foods). (ELD R.B4)

Shapes

Picture Dictionary

circle

oval

square

triangle

 **Draw** Draw shapes.

Preteach **LS** **Leveled Support** **Category Words**
Reteach

① ② **Beginning/Early Intermediate** Have children point to each shape on the Worktext page. Say the word. Have children repeat.

③ **Intermediate** Say the name of a shape. Have children point to the picture on the Worktext page. Then point to an object in the room. Ask: Is this object a square? Children respond by nodding yes or no. Repeat with other shapes.

④ ⑤ **Early Advanced/Advanced** Have children work with partners. Have each draw a shape. Partners can name the shapes.

How do we cooperate with each other?

✏ **Circle** Circle *the*.

We share the crayons.

✏ **Circle** Circle *little*.

I listen to my little brother.

🐻 ELA R1.15 Read simple one-syllable and high-frequency words (i.e., sight words). (ELD R.B2)   29

Preteach **Reteach** **LS** **Leveled Support** **High Frequency Words**

❶ ❷ **Beginning/Early Intermediate** Display the word *the*. Write sentences on the board. Say *the* and have children point to *the* in each sentence. Repeat for *little*.

❸ **Intermediate** Display the word *the*. Write sets of sentences on board. Have children work with partners. Have one child in each group point at a word and partners say "yes" or "no" if the word is *the*. Repeat for *little*.

❹ ❺ **Early Advanced/Advanced** Have children work with partners. Write the following words on sets of eight tagboard cards: *the, the, little, little, it, teacher, I, am.* Give each group a set of tagboard cards. Have children place the cards face down and take turns turning two cards over to find the matching cards for *the* and *little*.

To discuss how we cooperate with other children; to review the high frequency words *the* and *little;* to discriminate the initial /sh/ and /s/ sounds; to recognize the letters *Ww* and *Xx*.

Concept Talk

Connect to Day 2 Recall with children that yesterday they talked about how children and adults work together.

Introduce the Daily Question How do we cooperate with other children? Have children answer orally.

Use the Poster Use the Day 3 teaching notes.

Introduce High Frequency Words

Display the words *the* and *little.* Write sentences on the board, read them aloud, and have children clap when you say the word *the* or *little.* Help children complete the Worktext page.

Phonemic Awareness

Sound Discrimination Read the sentences on the Worktext page. Emphasize the initial /sh/ in *share.* Say other words with initial /sh/. Name words and ask children to say "yes" or "no" for each word with initial /sh/. Say: The little boy is talking to his sister. Repeat for initial /s/ in *sister.*

The Letters Ww and Xx

 Introduce the letters using the Alphabet Cards.

Write and Say the Letters Follow the routine for the letters *Ww, Xx*.

Identify the Letters Children can use the routine to distinguish *Ww, Xx* from other letters.

Wrap Up **DAY 3**

Daily Table Talk How do we cooperate with other children? Have children discuss the question.

Produce Language Have each child say a sentence about how he or she cooperates with other children.

Today children should have:

☑ **Learned** and applied the high frequency words *the* and *little.*

☑ **Spoken** complete sentences about how they cooperate with other children.

☑ **Recognized** the letters *Ww* and *Xx* and initial /sh/ and /s/ sounds.

 ELA R1.15 Read simple one-syllable and high-frequency words (i.e., sight words). (ELD R.B2)

29

OBJECTIVE

To discuss how we cooperate at school; to recognize the letters *Tt* through *Zz*.

Concept Talk

 FORM & FUNCTION

Connect to Day 3 Recall with children that yesterday they talked about how they cooperate with other children.

Introduce the Daily Question How do we cooperate at school? Have children answer orally.

Use the Poster Use the Day 4 teaching notes.

The Letters Yy and Zz

 Yy   Introduce the letters using Alphabet Cards.

Write and Say the Letters Identify the letters *Yy* and *Zz*. Have children complete the activity in the Worktext.

Corrective Feedback If children have difficulty matching the letters correctly, pair children of mixed abilities to complete the activity. Allow children to match letters with index cards on which you have written the letters before they circle their answers in the Worktext.

Wrap Up   DAY 4

 Daily Table Talk How do we cooperate at school? Have children discuss the question.

Produce Language Have each child say a sentence about how they cooperate at school.

Today children should have:

- ☑ **Learned** and applied vocabulary related to how they cooperate at school.

- ☑ **Spoken** complete sentences about how they cooperate at school.

- ☑ **Recognized** the letters *Yy* and *Zz*.

ELA R1.6 Recognize and name all uppercase and lowercase letters of the alphabet. (ELD R.B10)

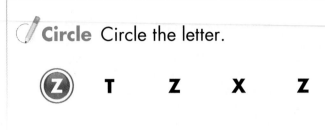

Letter Match

 **Circle** Circle the letter.

Z	T	Z	X	Z
W	W	U	W	Y
T	V	T	T	X
y	w	y	t	y
u	u	u	x	z
v	y	v	w	v

Preteach / Reteach LS **Leveled Support** Letter Recognition

① ② **Beginning/Early Intermediate** Hold up an alphabet card for *T*. Say the letter name and have children repeat it. Continue with *t, U, u, V, v, W, w, X, x, Y, y, Z,* and *z*.

③ **Intermediate** Write the letters *T – Z* on a sheet of tagboard. Give children letter tiles for *T – Z* and have them match the letter tiles to the written letters. Then ask them to name each letter.

④ ⑤ **Early Advanced/Advanced** Write each child's first and last name. Ask children to circle the letters *Tt, Uu, Vv, Ww, Xx, Yy,* and *Zz* in their names. Include other words if necessary.

How do people in a community cooperate?

 Draw

31

Think, Talk, and Recognize!

Concept Talk

Connect to Day 4 Recall that yesterday they talked about how we cooperate at school.

Review the Weekly Question How do people in a community cooperate? Tell children they are going to make a chart about how people in a community cooperate. Draw a T-chart on the board. Write *grandma, bus driver, children, parents,* and *teacher* in the left column. Say each word. These are people in a community. Ask children to give examples of how these people in a community cooperate. Write each across the top of the right column and add vertical lines. Complete the chart by asking questions such as "Does grandma take children to school?" and marking yes answers with an "x."

Use the Poster Use the Day 5 teaching notes.

Review Concept Vocabulary Review the vocabulary introduced on Day 1.

Concept Wrap-Up

Have children draw to answer the question: *How do people in a community cooperate?* Prompt discussion about the photograph: The teachers and children are working together to hold up a parachute. What are other ways teachers and children work together?

Wrap Up DAY 5

Table Talk *Daily* How do people in a community cooperate? Have children discuss the question, using the vocabulary words they learned this week.

Produce Language To build fluency, children can label, write about, or speak about their drawings. Ask children to respond to what they read or heard.

Today, children should have:

☑ **Reviewed** the weekly concept and concept vocabulary.

☑ **Spoken** about how people in communities cooperate.

☑ **Drawn or written** to show how people in communities cooperate.

31

Leveled Support — Concept Vocabulary

① ② Beginning/Early Intermediate Display the Word Cards for *children, kindergarten, parents,* and *teacher.* Say each word. Ask children to repeat and point to the matching card.

③ Intermediate Display the Word Cards for *children, kindergarten, parents,* and *teachers.* Ask children to say a detail about each picture. Model: The parents hold a baby.

④ ⑤ Early Advanced/Advanced Display the Word Cards for *children, kindergarten, parents,* and *teachers.* Ask children to tell a partner a story about one or more of the words.

Weekly Lesson Plan

Last Week
Unit 1, Week 4
Working Together

 Question of the Week What do you like to do with your friends?

	DAY 1 Get Ready to Read	**DAY 2** Read and Comprehend
	Build Background	**Language: Category Words**

Instructional Plan and Materials

	Preteach/Review 10–15 min	**Preteach/Review** 10–15 min
	Poster, Song Book, Big Book	Poster
	Leveled Support Preteach	**Leveled Support Preteach**
	Practice Stations Preteach	**Practice Stations Review**
	Teach 35–45 min	**Teach** 35–45 min
	Concept Talk	**Category Words**
	Oral Vocabulary Routine	**Daily Table Talk**
	Word Cards	
	Build Concept Vocabulary	**Check/Reteach** 5–10 min
	Daily Table Talk	Poster, Word Cards
		Leveled Support Reteach
	Check/Reteach 5–10 min	
	Poster, Word Cards	
	Leveled Support Reteach	

find

- **Word Cards**
  16–19

- **Big Book**
  Getting Along

- **Poster**
  Poster 5 can be
  used at beginning
  or end of day.

- **Song Book**, p. 5

Transparencies Explore content and
vocabulary and model fluent reading.

For further information about using these
components, see pages x–xv.

		Fluency: Writing or Speaking

CALIFORNIA Standards

GK Sci 4.e Communicate observations orally
and through drawings.

	ELA R 1.18 Describe common objects and events in both general and specific language.	**ELA R 1.17** Identify and sort common words in basic categories (e.g., colors, shapes, foods).

Academic Language

	Vocabulary: morning, night	**Category Words:** drum, flute, guitar, piano, trumpet, violin

Get Online! www.pearsonsuccessnet.com

	Concept Talk Video	**Background Building Audio Slideshow**

Fun with Friends

DAY 3 FORM & FUNCTION Read and Comprehend	**DAY 4** FORM & FUNCTION Language Arts	**DAY 5** Language Arts
Language: High Frequency Words	**Letter Recognition and Phonics**	**Think, Talk, and Recognize**
Preteach/Review 10–15 min Poster **Leveled Support Preteach** **Practice Stations Review**	**Preteach/Review** 10–15 min Poster **Leveled Support Preteach** **Practice Stations Review**	**Preteach/Review** 10–15 min Poster **Leveled Support Preteach** **Practice Stations Review**
Teach 35–45 min **High Frequency Words** **Phonemic Awareness** **Daily Table Talk**	**Teach** 35–45 min **Phonemic Awareness/Phonics** **Daily Table Talk**	**Teach** 15–20 min **Think, Talk, and Recognize** **Concept Wrap Up**
Check/Reteach 5–10 min Poster, Word Cards **Leveled Support Reteach**	**Check/Reteach** 5–10 min Poster, Word Cards **Leveled Support Reteach**	**Check/Reteach** 30–40 min Poster, Word Cards, Song Book **Leveled Support Reteach**
		Fluency: Writing or Speaking
ELA R 1.15 Read simple one-syllable and high frequency words (i.e., sight words).	**ELA R 1.14** Match all consonant and short-vowel sounds to appropriate letters.	**ELA LS 2.3** Relate an experience or creative story in a logical sequence.
High Frequency Words: a, to		

Practice Stations

Materials and Activity

large sheet of paper with the following written on it: *I like to _____ with my friends. Do you?*

I Like to _____

Post the paper in a prominent spot. Have children sit in a circle. The first player completes this sentence: "I like to _____ with my friends." Have children demonstrate what they like to do. The child then turns to the next child and asks, "Do you?" That child answers yes or no. If yes, the two children complete the action together. Repeat until every child has had a turn.

> I like to _____ with my friends.
> Do you?

large colored button or similar object

Find the Button

Give the children a button. One player (the "looker") leaves the area and the other children hide the button. When the looker returns, the group calls out, "What are you looking for?" The looker responds by saying, "I am looking for a button." Children can give clues to the player until the button has been found. Continue playing until all children who wish to have been given a chance to look for the button.

Preteach/Reteach

Transfer and Common Misconceptions

Syllable Stress

Some children may say *morning* and *looking* with the stress on the last syllable. Model each word and have students repeat and practice.

Aspirated Sound

Children may have difficulty with the initial /p/ sound in *piano.* In English, this sound is produced with an extra puff of air at the end when the sound occurs at the beginning of a word or stressed syllable.

Produce Language

Weekly Concept and Language Goal

CONCEPT GOALS

- recognize that friends are people who like to do things together
- provide examples of things that friends can do at school
- name different things that friends can do outside and on rainy days

By Day 5, children should be able to gesture to an item in the drawing and talk about it.

Daily Table Talk

1 Beginning
> Children pantomime while you provide the language.

2 3 Early Intermediate/Intermediate
> Children pantomime and say a word or phrase.

4 5 Early Advanced/Advanced
> Children say a sentence while pantomiming.

Daily Table Talk

1 Beginning
> Children talk about their drawings.

2 3 Early Intermediate/Intermediate
> Children write one-word labels.

4 5 Early Advanced/Advanced
> Children write a phrase or sentence.

DAY 3 **FORM & FUNCTION** Read and Comprehend

DAY **3** **FORM & FUNCTION** Read and Comprehend

index cards with one of the category words and picture of musical instruments shown on each, paper, crayons, markers, tongue depressors or sticks, glue

Our Band

Show children the category words. Have them pretend that they will play one of those instruments in the class band. They can draw the instrument they would like to play and label it. Have them attach each picture to a stick. When all children have finished, have them line up and march around the room holding their pictures and making noises for their instruments.

A as a Preposition

In Spanish, *a* is a preposition meaning *to, at, from,* or *by.* It also may be used as a personal preposition before people's names.

DAY **4** **FORM & FUNCTION** Language Arts

two papers, each with one of the following sentences written on it: *Go to _____ .* *Touch a _____ .*

Follow the Directions

Post the papers in a visible spot and read each sentence with children. Give children commands using the sentences. Have children follow them. Encourage children to use the sentence frames to come up with their own commands such as: *Go to [the door, the wall, the front]. Touch a [blue crayon, book, table].*

Articles

Unlike English, in Spanish articles are often used before subjects. Using articles as often as possible can help children become more familiar with their correct usage.

DAY **5** Language Arts

pictures from magazines, some of which begin with /m/; outline of a mouth for each child; glue

Find the /m/ Words

Give each pair a stack of picture cards. Have children hold up each word card and say its name. Children decide together if the word begins with /m/. If so, children glue the picture on the mouth. Continue until all children have several pictures on their papers. Children may wish to color their mouths.

Pictures

Children may not be familiar with all of the pictures from magazines or on the word cards. Review the names for all pictures before children complete an activity.

Daily Table Talk

① **Beginning**
> Children can say outside or play as you display a corresponding picture.

② ③ **Early Intermediate/Intermediate**
> Phrase: play on swing, throw ball

④ ⑤ **Early Advanced/Advanced**
> Sentence: I like to jump rope.

Daily Table Talk

① **Beginning**
> Children raise their hands as you provide sample answers, such as I like to play games and I like to paint.

② ③ **Early Intermediate/Intermediate**
> One or two words: make things, watch movie

④ ⑤ **Early Advanced/Advanced**
> Sentence: I play inside.

Daily Table Talk

① **Beginning** Child draws with support.

② ③ **Early Intermediate/Intermediate** Child draws and speaks about the drawing using at least one concept vocabulary word.

④ ⑤ **Early Advanced/Advanced** Child draws and provides a label for the drawing.

Build Background Get Ready to Read!

Question of the Week

What do you like to do with your friends?
www.pearsonsuccessnet.com

Concept Talk

Use the Big Book If you haven't introduced the Big Book, consider reading it to children. Connect to the unit theme, Cooperation—All Together Now.

Introduce the Weekly Concept Tell children that today they will talk about things they like to do with their friends. Ask the weekly question: What do you like to do with your friends?

Use the Poster Direct children's attention to the weekly poster. Use the Day 1 teaching notes at the bottom of the poster.

Sing the Song Use the song **Fun with Friends** to reinforce children's understanding of the weekly concept. Have the children sing or simply chant the words with you.

Use a Transparency Use the Description Map (Transparency 4) to capture children's ideas about "Fun with Friends."

Fun with Friends

Vocabulary

looking

morning

night

find

What do you like to do with your friends?

32

Vocabulary

* **Academic Vocabulary**
   looking turning your eyes toward something so you can see it

* **morning** the early part of the day

* **night** the dark patch of each day, when the sun cannot be seen

   find to discover and get something that you have been looking for

ELA R1.18 Describe common objects and events in both general and specific language. (ELD R.B6)

33

Introduce Concept Vocabulary

1. Say the Word Display the Word Card as you separate and then combine the phonemes for the word *find*.

2. Introduce Word Meaning Pantomime looking for a lost pencil. I am looking for my pencil. I cannot find it. Then "find" your pencil as you say the word.

3. Demonstrate Have children role play looking for something—and finding it.

4. Apply Have children demonstrate their understanding.

Repeat with other vocabulary words.

Corrective Feedback If children have difficulty distinguishing between morning and night, show pictures of morning and night scenes. Point out differences, such as sun versus moon, people waking up versus going to sleep, eating breakfast versus eating dinner.

Concept Work

Direct children to the first picture. What are the children doing in this picture? Discuss. Ask children to raise their hands if they have played with blocks with a friend. Repeat for each picture. Have children color the pictures.

Leveled Support Vocabulary in Context

❶ ❷ Beginning/Early Intermediate Have children point to each picture on the Worktext page. Say the word for each picture as children point, and have them echo each word.

❸ Intermediate Do the Beginning activity, but have children say the words themselves, giving help only if needed.

❹ ❺ Early Advanced/Advanced Have children do the Beginning activity with a partner. Give help only if needed.

Wrap Up   **DAY** 1

Table Talk What do you like to do with your friends? Have children answer the question, using the vocabulary words.

Produce Language Have children work in small groups. Each says a sentence about what they like to do with their friends. Children respond by saying "Me too" and raising their hands if they also like to do that activity with friends.

Today children should have:

☑ **Learned** and applied vocabulary related to what they like to do with their friends.

☑ **Spoken** complete sentences about what they like to do with their friends.

☑ **Recognized** concept vocabulary words.

 ELA R1.18 Describe common objects and events in both general and specific language. (ELD R.B6)

OBJECTIVE

To discuss what children like to do with their friends at school; to introduce category words for musical instruments.

Concept Talk

Connect to Day 1 Recall with children that yesterday they talked about what they like to do with their friends.

Introduce the Daily Question What do you like to do with your friends at school? Have children answer orally.

Use the Poster Use the Day 2 teaching notes.

Introduce Category Words

1. Say the Word Have children point to the trumpet. Say the word and ask children to repeat.

2. Introduce the Meaning Demonstrate how to hold and play a trumpet. If you can, play a recording of a trumpet.

3. Demonstrate Have children role play holding and playing a trumpet.

4. Apply Repeat with the other vocabulary words. Elicit that all belong to the category of things that can make music.

Have children circle the musical instruments on the Worktext page.

Corrective Feedback If children are having difficulty understanding the word concepts, assign groups of children an instrument. Call out an instrument and have children in that group pantomime playing that instrument. Repeat for each instrument.

Wrap Up   DAY 2

Daily Table Talk What do you like to do with your friends at school? Have children answer the question, using the vocabulary words.

Produce Language To build fluency, encourage children to label or write sentences about the musical instruments on the Worktext page. They can share their writing with partners.

Today children should have:

☑ **Learned** and applied vocabulary related to musical instruments.

☑ **Spoken** complete sentences about what they like do with their friends at school.

☑ **Recognized** words that belong in the same category.

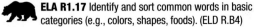 **ELA R1.17** Identify and sort common words in basic categories (e.g., colors, shapes, foods). (ELD R.B4)

34 Fun with Friends • Unit 1, Week 5

Picture Dictionary

drum   flute   guitar

piano   trumpet   violin

✏ **Circle** Circle musical instruments.

34 🐻 **ELA R1.17** Identify and sort common words in basic categories (e.g., colors, shapes, foods). (ELD R.B4)

Preteach LS Reteach Leveled Support Category Words

① ② **Beginning/Early Intermediate** Have children point to each musical instrument on the Worktext page. Say the word. Have children repeat.

③ **Intermediate** Say the name of a musical instrument. Have children point to the picture on the Worktext page.

④ ⑤ **Early Advanced/Advanced** Have children work with partners. Have each role play playing an instrument as the partner names it.

What do you do outside with friends?

✏️ **Circle** Circle *a*.

We fly a kite.

✏️ **Circle** Circle *to*.

We go to the park.

🐻 **ELA R1.15** Read simple one-syllable and high-frequency words (i.e., sight words). (ELD R.B2)

35

CALIFORNIA   DAY 3

OBJECTIVE

To discuss what children like to do outside with their friends; to introduce the high frequency words *a* and *to*; to discriminate initial /m/.

Concept Talk

Connect to Day 2 Recall with children that yesterday they talked about what they like to do with their friends at school.

Introduce the Daily Question What do you like to do outside with your friends? Discuss children's ideas.

Use the Poster Use the Day 3 teaching notes.

Introduce High Frequency Words

Display the word *a*. Say *a*. Slowly say short sentences with *a* such as "I ate a banana" and "I drive a car." Have children sway to the right every time they hear *a*. Repeat for *to*. Help children complete the Worktext page.

Phonological Awareness

Discriminate Initial /m/ Say words with initial /m/ such as children's names, *mud, messy*. Ask children to say words with initial /m/. Say several words and have children say "yes" or "no" after each word to identify whether the word has initial /m/.

Corrective Feedback If children are having trouble discriminating initial /m/, say an initial /m/ word and use exaggerated mouth movement for /m/. Have children repeat and imitate mouth movement. Say the initial /m/ sound several times. Ask children to say it for 10 seconds without stopping.

Wrap Up   DAY 3

Table Talk What do you like to do outside with your friends? Have children answer the question, using the vocabulary words.

Produce Language Have each child say a sentence about what he or she likes do outside with friends.

Today children should have:

☑ **Learned** and applied the high frequency words *a* and *to*.

☑ **Spoken** complete sentences about what they like do outside with their friends.

☑ **Recognized** the initial /m/ and the high frequency words *a* and *to*.

🐻 **ELA R1.15** Read simple one-syllable and high-frequency words (i.e., sight words). (ELD R.B2)

35

Preteach **LS** **Reteach** **Leveled Support** **High Frequency Words**

① ② **Beginning/Early Intermediate** Display the word *a*. Have children use their fingers to write *a* on their desks. Repeat for *to*.

③ **Intermediate** Write *a* and *to* on tagboard cards. Give each child a card. Have children move around the room and find a person with the same word. They should read the words together and use them in sentences.

④ ⑤ **Early Advanced/Advanced** Display the word *to*. Write the letters *t* and *o* on tagboard cards. Give each child a card. Have children move around the room and find others with the missing letter to spell *to*. Have pairs stand together to spell *to*. Display *a*. Have children air write *a*.

To discuss what children like to do on rainy days; to connect m to /m/.

Concept Talk

Connect to Day 3 Recall with children that yesterday they talked about how they cooperate with other children.

Introduce the Daily Question What do you like to do on a rainy day? Discuss that some activities they like to do outside cannot be done on rainy days. Why does rain make a difference? Have children answer orally.

Use the Poster Use the Day 4 teaching notes.

Phonemic Awareness/Phonics

Connect m to /m/ Display a card on which you have written *Mm*. Say words with initial /m/ such as children's names, *mud, messy*. Ask children to say words with initial /m/. Write each on the board. Point to each letter and have children identify the *m*. Circle the *m*.

Have children complete the Worktext activity by coloring pictures that show items beginning with *m*.

Corrective Feedback If children have difficulty coloring the correct pictures, say each of the words with children, exaggerating the beginning sounds. Children can point to pictures that show words beginning with *m* before they color. Children may have trouble with the names of the pictures. Read them with children.

Wrap Up — DAY 4

 Table Talk What do you like to do on a rainy day? Have children answer the question, using the vocabulary words.

Produce Language Have each say a sentence about what he or she likes to do on a rainy day.

Today children should have:

- ☑ **Learned** and applied vocabulary related to what they like to do on a rainy day.

- ☑ **Spoken** complete sentences about what they like to do on a rainy day.

- ☑ **Recognized** the letter *m* and initial /m/.

ELA R1.14 Match all consonant and short-vowel sounds to appropriate letters. (ELD R.B1)

Identify Sound Mm

 **Draw** Color pictures with *m*.

36 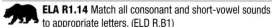 **ELA R1.14** Match sounds to letters. (ELD R.B1)

Leveled Support Phonics

❶ ❷ **Beginning/Early Intermediate** Display an index card on which you have written *Mm*. Point to lowercase *m*. This letter is *m*. Say /m/. Have children repeat.

❸ **Intermediate** Display Alphabet card *Mm*. Point to lowercase *m*. What letter is this? What sound does *m* make? Have children say /m/. Trace shape of lowercase *m* as you say /m/. Have children write *m* on their desks with their fingers as they say /m/.

❹ ❺ **Early Advanced/Advanced** Do the Intermediate activity, but have children say words starting with *m*.

What do you like to do with your friends?

 Draw

To guide children to express their understanding of weekly concepts and vocabulary.concepts and vocabulary.

Think, Talk, and Recognize!

Concept Talk

Connect to Day 4 Recall that yesterday children talked about what they like to do on a rainy day.

Review the Weekly Question What do you like to do with your friends? Have children give examples. Write examples on the board. After each child has given an example, read the examples and have children show hands if they like to do that activity with their friends.

Use the Poster Use the Day 5 teaching notes.

Review Concept Vocabulary Review the vocabulary introduced on Day 1.

Concept Wrap Up

Have children draw to answer the question: *What do you like to do with your friends?* Prompt discussion with the photograph. These friends are swinging at the park. What other things can you do with friends at the park?

Leveled Support   Concept Vocabulary

① ② **Beginning/Early Intermediate** Display the Word Cards for *looking, morning, night,* and *find.* Say each word. Ask children to repeat and point to the matching card.

③ **Intermediate** Display the Word Cards for *looking, morning, night,* and *find.* Ask children to say a detail about each picture. Model: The [boy] is looking for [object].

④ ⑤ **Early Advanced/Advanced** Display the Word Cards for *looking, morning, night,* and *find.* Ask children to play charades and role play the words.

Wrap Up   DAY 5

 Table Talk What do you like to do with your friends? Have children brainstorm as many examples as possible, using the vocabulary words they learned this week.

Produce Language To build fluency, children can label, write about, or speak about their drawings. Ask children to respond to what they read or heard.

Today, children should have:

☑ **Reviewed** the weekly concept and concept vocabulary.

☑ **Spoken** about what they like to do with friends.

☑ **Drawn or written** to show what they like to do with friends.

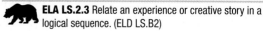 **ELA LS.2.3** Relate an experience or creative story in a logical sequence. (ELD LS.B2)

Question of the Week

How do machines help people work together?

	DAY 1 Get Ready to Read	**DAY 2** Read and Comprehend
	Build Background	**Language: Category Words**

Instructional Plan and Materials

- **Word Cards** 20–23

- **Big Book** Getting Along

- **Poster** Poster 6 can be used at beginning or end of day.

- **Song Book**, p. 6

Transparencies Explore content and vocabulary and model fluent reading.

For further information about using these components, see pages x–xv.

DAY 1 — Build Background

Preteach/Review 10–15 min
Poster, Song Book, Big Book

Leveled Support Preteach
Practice Stations Preteach

Teach 35–45 min
Concept Talk
Oral Vocabulary Routine
Word Cards
Build Concept Vocabulary
Daily Table Talk

Check/Reteach 5–10 min
Poster, Word Cards
Leveled Support Reteach

DAY 2 — Language: Category Words

Preteach/Review 10–15 min
Poster

Leveled Support Preteach
Practice Stations Review

Teach 35–45 min
Category Words
Daily Table Talk

Check/Reteach 5–10 min
Poster, Word Cards
Leveled Support Reteach

Fluency: Writing or Speaking

CALIFORNIA Standards

GK Sci 4.e Communicate observations orally and through drawings.

ELA R 1.18 Describe common objects and events in both general and specific language.

ELA R 1.17 Identify and sort common words in basic categories (e.g., colors, shapes, foods).

Academic Language

Vocabulary: machines

Category Words: crane, dump truck, road roller, tractor

www.pearsonsuccessnet.com

Concept Talk Video

Background Building Audio Slideshow

This Week
Unit 1, Week 6

Machines

Next Week
Unit 2, Week 1
Flowers

DAY 3 Read and Comprehend	**DAY 4** Language Arts	**DAY 5** Language Arts
Language: High Frequency Words	**Phonics**	**Think, Talk, and Recognize**
Preteach/Review 10–15 min	**Preteach/Review** 10–15 min	**Preteach/Review** 10–15 min
Poster	Poster	Poster
Leveled Support Preteach	**Leveled Support Preteach**	**Leveled Support Preteach**
Practice Stations Review	**Practice Stations Review**	**Practice Stations Review**
Teach 35–45 min	**Teach** 35–45 min	**Teach** 15–20 min
High Frequency Words	**Phonemic Awareness**	**Think, Talk, and Recognize**
Phonemic Awareness	**Daily Table Talk**	**Concept Wrap Up**
Daily Table Talk		
	Check/Reteach 5–10 min	**Check/Reteach** 30–40 min
Check/Reteach 5–10 min	Poster, Word Cards	Poster, Word Cards, Song Book
Poster, Word Cards	**Leveled Support Reteach**	**Leveled Support Reteach**
Leveled Support Reteach		
		Fluency: Writing or Speaking
ELA R 1.15 Read simple one-syllable and high frequency words (i.e., sight words).	**ELA R 1.14** Match all consonant and short-vowel sounds to appropriate letters.	**ELA LS 1.2** Share information and ideas, speaking audibly in complete, coherent sentences.
High Frequency Words: a, to		

Practice Stations

Materials and Activity

pictures of machines (from magazines, catalogs, etc.); large drawing paper; crayons, colored pencils, scissors, glue

Machine Collage

Have each child find pictures of machines that help people, cut them out, and paste them on a large sheet of paper. Have children tell their partners a story about the pictures in their collage.

papers with the following questions written: *Who uses the machines? Where do the machines go? How do the machines move?*

Machine Role Play

Post and read the following questions: Who uses the machines? Where do the machines go? How do the machines move? Have children discuss the questions with a partner and then role play situations involving the machines. For example, children may role play being a helicopter pilot looking for people lost in the mountains, or fire fighters riding on a fire engine as it rushes to a fire.

Preteach/Reteach

Transfer and Common Misconceptions

The Word *machine*

Some children may have difficulty with the word *machine* because they are used to the letters *ch* having a /ch/ sound.

The Letters *ll*

In Spanish, the letters *ll* have a sound similar to /y/. Children may have difficulty with the word *road roller*.

Produce Language

Weekly Concept and Language Goal

CONCEPT GOALS

- understand concepts about machines and how they make work easier
- describe how machines help people do things
- name machines that help people on farms and in schools

By Day 5, children should be able to gesture to an item in the drawing and talk about it.

Daily Table Talk

❶ **Beginning**
> Children pantomime while you provide the language.

❷ ❸ **Early Intermediate/Intermediate**
> Children pantomime and say a word or phrase.

❹ ❺ **Early Advanced/Advanced**
> Children say a sentence while pantomiming.

Daily Table Talk

❶ **Beginning**
> Children talk about their drawings.

❷ ❸ **Early Intermediate/Intermediate**
> Children write one-word labels.

❹ ❺ **Early Advanced/Advanced**
> Children write a phrase or sentence.

index cards with the word and picture of a category word on each (crane, tractor, dump truck, road roller); two sets of cards for each pair

index cards with *a* and *to*, paper, pencils

picture cards (category words, vocabulary words, etc.)

Guess the Machine 👥

Give each pair two sets of category word cards. Have one child take a card from the pile. The other player asks up to three questions and tries to guess the machine. If Player 2 is correct, then the card is put on the table face up. If the guess is not correct, the card goes back on the pile. Continue until all cards are face up.

A and to 👥

Have children fold their pieces of paper in half. On one side they should glue the words *a* and *to.* They write the words on the other side.

Find the /t/ Words 👥

Give each pair a stack of picture cards. Have children sort through the cards and select words starting with /t/. They should say each word with /t/.

Articles

Russian and many Asian languages do not use articles.

The /t/ Sound

In Spanish, the /t/ sound is produced by the tongue touching the back of the teeth. Point out how to make the /t/ sound by using the tip of the tongue to touch the ridge behind the teeth.

The /d/ Sound

Like the Spanish *t,* in Spanish the *d* is produced by the tongue touching the back of the teeth. Point out how to make the /d/ sound by using the tip of the tongue to touch the ridge behind the teeth.

Daily Table Talk

❶ **Beginning**
Children can say truck or store as you display a corresponding picture.

❷ ❸ **Early Intermediate/Intermediate**
Phrase: take to store

❹ ❺ **Early Advanced/Advanced**
Sentence: The truck takes food to the store.

Daily Table Talk

❶ **Beginning**
Children raise their hands as you provide sample answers.

❷ ❸ **Early Intermediate/Intermediate**
One or two word: computer, bus

❹ ❺ **Early Advanced/Advanced**
Sentence: The bus takes us on trips.

Daily Table Talk

❶ **Beginning** Child draws with support.

❷ ❸ **Early Intermediate/Intermediate** Child draws and speaks about the drawing using at least one concept vocabulary word.

❹ ❺ **Early Advanced/Advanced** Child draws and provides a label for the drawing.

To introduce and discuss how machines help people work together and related concept vocabulary.

Build Background Get Ready to Read!

Question of the Week

How do machines help people work together?

www.pearsonsuccessnet.com

Concept Talk

Use the Big Book If you haven't introduced the Big Book, consider reading it to children. Connect to the unit theme, Cooperation—All Together Now.

Introduce the Weekly Concept Tell children that today they will talk about how machines help people work together. Give examples of machines in the classroom and school to help children understand the concept. Ask the weekly question: How do machines help people work together?

Use the Poster Direct children's attention to the weekly poster. Use the Day 1 teaching notes at the bottom of the poster.

Sing the Song Use the song **Machines We Use** to reinforce children's understanding of the weekly concept. Have the children sing or simply chant the words with you.

Use a Transparency Use the Relationship Map (Transparency 6) to help children connect the machines to the jobs that they help people do.

Machines
....
Vocabulary

fire engines

helicopters

machines

trucks

38

How do machines help people work together?

Vocabulary

* **Academic Vocabulary**

fire engines special large vehicles that carry people and equipment to stop fires from burning

helicopters types of aircraft with metal blades on top of them that spin very fast

* **machines** equipment that uses power such as electricity to do a particular job

trucks large road vehicles that carry heavy loads

39

Introduce Concept Vocabulary

1. **Say the Word** Display the Word Card as you say *fire engines*. Point out that the word is made up of two words: *fire* and *engines*. Say each word slowly. Have children repeat the word.

2. **Introduce Word Meaning** Ask questions about fire engines. Who has seen a fire engine? What color is a fire engine? What sound does a fire engine make?

3. **Demonstrate** Have children role play fire engines racing to a fire or making the noise that fire engines make.

4. **Apply** Have children draw a picture of a fire engine. Have children label their pictures with the words *fire engine.*

Repeat with other vocabulary words.

Corrective Feedback If children have difficulty with the words, find other photographs of machines to help children understand the concept.

Concept Work

Direct children to each picture. What machine is in this picture? Help children identify the fire truck, bulldozer, and helicopter. Have children describe what is happening in each picture and relate to their personal experiences. Have children circle the machine in each picture. Children can color the pictures.

Leveled Support   Vocabulary in Context

Preteach LS Reteach

❶ ❷ **Beginning/Early Intermediate** Have children point to the fire engines, helicopters, machines, and trucks on the Worktext page. Say the word for each picture as children point, and have them echo each word.

❸ **Intermediate** Do the Beginning activity, but have children say the words themselves, giving help only if needed.

❹ ❺ **Early Advanced/Advanced** Ask children to draw a picture of a fire engine, helicopter, machine, or truck. Have children describe their pictures to partners.

Table Talk *Daily* How do machines help people work together? Have children answer the question, using the vocabulary words.

Produce Language Have each child role play a machine or using a machine and say a sentence about how machines help people work together.

Today children should have:

☑ **Learned** and applied vocabulary related to how machines help people work together.

☑ **Spoken** complete sentences about how machines help people work together.

☑ **Recognized** concept vocabulary words.

 ELA R1.18 Describe common objects and events in both general and specific language. (ELD R.B6)

39

OBJECTIVE

To discuss how machines help people do things; to introduce category words for machines.

Concept Talk

Connect to Day 1 Recall with children that yesterday they talked about how machines help people work together.

Introduce the Daily Question How do machines help people do things? Have children answer orally.

Use the Poster Use the Day 2 teaching notes.

Introduce Category Words

1. **Say the Word** Have children point to the crane. Say the word and have children repeat after you.

2. **Introduce the Meaning** Describe what a crane can do. A crane can lift very heavy objects, such as big piles of wood or bricks. People cannot lift these things on their own. Then the cranes move the objects from one place to another.

3. **Demonstrate** Have children role play the action a crane makes. Their arms can be the cranes, and they can use their hands to pick up objects such as piles of blocks and move them from place to place.

4. **Apply** Repeat with other vocabulary words and elicit that all the words belong to the category "machines."

Have children draw machines on their Worktext pages.

Corrective Feedback If children have difficulty understanding the meaning of the category words, use a physical action related to each word to demonstrate meaning; for example, act out dumping items from a dump truck, or the wheels of a road roller rolling down a road.

Wrap Up   DAY 2

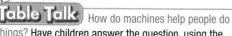 **Table Talk** How do machines help people do things? Have children answer the question, using the vocabulary words.

Produce Language To build fluency, encourage children to label or write a sentence about their drawings. They can share their writing with partners.

Today children should have:

☑ **Learned** and applied vocabulary related to machines.

☑ **Spoken** complete sentences about how machines help people do things.

☑ **Recognized** words that belong in the same category.

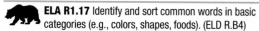 **ELA R1.17** Identify and sort common words in basic categories (e.g., colors, shapes, foods). (ELD R.B4)

Machines

Picture Dictionary

crane

dump truck

road roller

tractor

 Draw Draw a machine.

40   ELA R1.17 Identify and sort common words in basic categories (e.g., colors, shapes, foods). (ELD R.B4)

Preteach Reteach LS Leveled Support   Category Words

①②Beginning/Early Intermediate Have children point to each machine on the Worktext page. Say each word. Have children repeat.

③ Intermediate Describe what one of the machines does. Children say or point to the machine based on your description.

④⑤ Early Advanced/Advanced Have children work with partners. Have each point at a picture on the Worktext page and the partner name it. Then reverse. Have each say a word and the partner point at a picture. Partners choose a picture and say a sentence describing it.

What machine takes food from farms to stores?

✏️ **Circle** Circle *a*.

Food grows on a farm.

✏️ **Circle** Circle *to*.

Trucks take the food to a store.

🐻 **ELA R1.15** Read simple one-syllable and high-frequency words (i.e., sight words). (ELD R.B2)

41

OBJECTIVE

To discuss machines that take food from farms to stores; to introduce the high frequency words *a* and *to*; to discriminate initial /t/.

Concept Talk

🔵 **FORM & FUNCTION**

Connect to Day 2 Recall with children that yesterday they talked about how machines help people do things.

Introduce the Daily Question What machines take food from farms to stores?

Use the Poster Use the Day 3 teaching notes.

Introduce High Frequency Words

Display the word *a*. Write phrases on the board such as "a cat" and "the dog." Read each phrase slowly and point at each word. Have children clap when you say the word *a*. Repeat for the word *to*. Help children complete the Worktext page.

Phonemic Awareness

Discriminate Initial /t/ Say words with initial /t/ such as children's names, *toy*, and *two*. Ask children to say words with initial /t/. Say several words and have children say "yes" or "no" after each word to identify if it has initial /t/.

Corrective Feedback If children are having trouble discriminating initial /t/, say an initial /t/ word and use exaggerated mouth movement for /t/. Have children repeat and imitate mouth movement.

Wrap Up **DAY 3**

Table Talk *Daily* What machines take food from farms to stores? Have children answer the question, using the vocabulary words.

Produce Language Tell half the children they are a food, such as corn. Tell the other children they are a machine. Have children role play a machine taking food from a farm to stores. Say a sentence. Then have children reverse roles and repeat.

Today children should have:

☑ **Learned** and applied the high frequency words *a* and *to*.

☑ **Spoken** complete sentences about machines that take food from farms to stores.

☑ **Recognized** the initial /t/ and the high frequency words *a* and *to*.

🐻 **ELA R1.15** Read simple one-syllable and high-frequency words (i.e., sight words). (ELD R.B2)

LS **Leveled Support** **High Frequency Words**
Preteach / Reteach

1 **2** **Beginning/Early Intermediate** Display the word *a*. Write sentences on the board. Say *a* and have children point to *a* in each sentence. Repeat for *to*.

3 **Intermediate** Display the word *a*. Write sets of sentences on board. Have children work with partners. Have one child in each pair point at a word and partners say "yes" if the word is *a* and or "no" if the word is not *a*. Repeat for *to*.

4 **5** **Early Advanced/Advanced** Have children work with partners. Write the following words on sets of eight tagboard cards: *a, a, to, to, the, little, I, night*. Give each group a set of tagboard cards. Have children place the cards face down and take turns turning two cards over to find the matching cards for *a* and *to*.

41

OBJECTIVE

To discuss what kinds of machines help us at school; to connect *t* to /t/.

Concept Talk

 FORM & FUNCTION

Connect to Day 3 Recall with children that yesterday they talked about what machines take food from farms to stores.

Introduce the Daily Question What kinds of machines help us at school? Give examples of machines, such as computers, that children might use at school. Have children answer orally.

Use the Poster Use the Day 4 teaching notes.

Phonological Awareness

Connect *t* to /t/ Display an index card on which you have written *Tt*. Say words with initial /t/ such as children's names, *toes, tomato.* Ask children to say words starting with /t/. Write each on the board. Point to each letter and have children identify *t*. Circle the *t*.

Have children complete the activity on the Worktext page by coloring all items that begin with *t*.

Corrective Feedback If children have difficulty with the activity, say the words for each picture: *truck, toaster, tractor, bus, train, car.* Exaggerate the beginning sounds and have children repeat after you.

Wrap Up   DAY 4

Table Talk What kinds of machines help us at school? Have children answer the question, using the vocabulary words.

Produce Language Have each child say a sentence about what kinds of machines help us at school.

Today children should have:

☑ **Learned** and applied vocabulary related to what kinds of machines help us at school.

☑ **Spoken** complete sentences about what kinds of machines help us at school.

☑ **Recognized** the letter *t* and initial /t/.

 ELA Match all consonant and short-vowel sounds to appropriate letters. (ELD R.B1)

Identify Sound Tt

✏ **Draw** Color pictures with *t*.

42   **ELA R1.14** Match sounds to letters. (ELD R.B1)

Leveled Support Phonemic Awareness/Phonics

①② **Beginning/Early Intermediate** Display a card on which you have written *Tt*. Point to lower-case t. This letter is *t*. Say /t/. Have children repeat.

③ **Intermediate** Display a card on which you have written *Tt*. Point to lowercase *t*. What letter is this? What sound does this letter make? Have children say /t/. Trace the shape of lowercase *t* as you say /t/. Have children write *t* on their desks with their fingers as they say /t/.

④⑤ **Early Advanced/Advanced** Ask children to work with partners to find objects in the room that start with the sound /t/. Have them sort objects based on their beginning sounds. Children can say the names of the objects they identify.

How do machines help people work together?

✏ Draw

ELA LS. 1.2 Share information and ideas, speaking audibly in complete, coherent sentences. (ELD LS.B1)

43

① ② **Beginning/Early Intermediate** Display the Word Cards for *fire engines, helicopters, machines,* and *trucks.* Say each word. Ask children to repeat and point to the matching card.

③ **Intermediate** Display the Word Cards for *fire engines, helicopters, machines,* and *trucks.* Ask children to say a detail about each picture. Model: The fire engine has a ladder.

④ ⑤ **Early Advanced/Advanced** Display the Word Cards for *fire engines, helicopters, machines,* and *trucks.* Have children describe each picture to a partner.

To guide children to express their understanding of weekly concepts and vocabulary.

Think, Talk, and Recognize!

Concept Talk

Connect to Day 4 Recall that yesterday children talked about what kinds of machines help us at school.

Review the Weekly Question How do machines help people work together? Ask silly questions such as "Does a fire engine take children to school?" and "Does a helicopter take food to stores?" Follow with questions such as "What machines help children get to school?" and "What machines take food to stores?" Discuss other examples.

Use the Poster Use the Day 5 teaching notes.

Review Concept Vocabulary Review the vocabulary introduced on Day 1.

Concept Wrap Up

Have children draw to answer the question: *How do machines help people work together?* Prompt ideas by discussing the photograph. These children are working together on a computer. What other machines help people work together?

Daily Table Talk How do machines help people work together? Have children brainstorm as many examples as possible, using the vocabulary words they learned this week.

Produce Language To build fluency, children can label, write about, or speak about their drawings. Ask children to respond to what they read or heard.

This week children should have:

☑ **Reviewed** the weekly concept and concept vocabulary.

☑ **Spoken** about how machines help people work together.

☑ **Drawn or written** to show how machines help people work together.

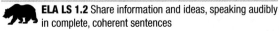 **ELA LS 1.2** Share information and ideas, speaking audibly in complete, coherent sentences

43

How are animals and plants unique?

Discuss the Big Question

Read and discuss the unit question. Introduce the word *unique*. When something is unique, that means it is special. What is something that is unique about yourself? What is something that is unique about your family? Why do you think we can call animals and plants unique? What makes them special?

Have children use the pictures along the side of the page to preview the weekly concepts for this unit. Read the weekly questions together. Discuss the weekly questions and how they relate to the big question.

 **Get Online!** www.pearsonsuccessnet.com
• Unit 2 Big Question Video

CONCEPT/ LANGUAGE GOALS

Use the Concept and Language Goals throughout the unit to develop the big idea.

Children develop concepts and language as they talk about, use, and practice:

• Concept Vocabulary
• Academic Language
• Language Forms and Functions
• Category Words
• High Frequency Words

 **Get Online!**
PearsonSuccessNet.com
Hear it!
See it!
Do it!

• Big Idea Video
• Concept Talk Video
• Background Building Audio Slideshow
• Comprehension Think Aloud Video
• eBooks

Animal and Plant Characteristics — Look at Us!

How are animals and plants unique?

44

Unit 2

Flowers
How are flowers unique?

Animals Dig
Why do animals dig?

Animals in the Grasslands
Who lives in the grasslands?

Bears Hibernate
Where does a bear hibernate?

Animal Homes
What kind of home does an animal need?

Animals Move
How do animals move?

Animal and Plant Characteristics—Look at Us!

45

Read Aloud

Read the **Big Book** *The Rainforest.* Prompt discussion about the book.

• What is unique about the monkey?

• What is unique about the sloth?

• What do you think is the most unique animal or plant in this book? Tell why you think so.

For more read alouds related to the theme, see the Big Book Anthology.

Unit Project: Animals and Plants

After discussing the unit question, provide children with paper and art supplies such as paints, crayons, and modeling clay. Also provide children with books or magazines with pictures of plants and animals from around the world. We will create a classroom zoo of unique plants and animals. You will draw, paint, or make a model of an animal or a plant that you think is unique. You can use any art supplies you wish. Then, as each new animal or plant is added to the zoo, we will talk about the plants and animals and how they are unique.

Have children add to the zoo by displaying their drawings, paintings, or models. Be sure all children contribute to the corner and encourage them to describe and discuss their art work. As children learn about plants and animals throughout the unit, they may wish to add more pieces to the zoo.

Question of the Week   How are flowers unique?

Instructional Plan and Materials

- **Word Cards**
  24–27

- **Big Book**
  The Rain Forest

- **Poster**
  Poster 7 can be used at beginning or end of day.

- **Song Book**, p. 7

Transparencies Explore content and vocabulary and model fluent reading.

For further information about using these components, see pages x–xv.

CALIFORNIA Standards

GK Sci 2.a Students know how to observe and describe similarities and differences in the appearance and behavior of plants and animals (e.g., seed-bearing plants, birds, fish, insects).

GK Sci 1.a Students know objects can be described in terms of the materials they are made of (e.g., clay, cloth, paper) and their physical properties (e.g., color, size, shape, weight).

Academic Language

Online! www.pearsonsuccessnet.com

DAY 1   Get Ready to Read

Build Background

Preteach/Review 10–15 min
Poster, Song Book, Big Book
- **Leveled Support Preteach**
- **Practice Stations Preteach**

Teach 35–45 min
- **Concept Talk**
- **Oral Vocabulary Routine**
  Word Cards
- **Build Concept Vocabulary**
- **Daily Table Talk**

Check/Reteach 5–10 min
Poster, Word Cards
- **Leveled Support Reteach**

ELA R 1.18 Describe common objects and events in both general and specific language.

Vocabulary: flowers, plants, grow

Concept Talk Video

DAY 2   Read and Comprehend

Language: Category Words

Preteach/Review 10–15 min
Poster
- **Leveled Support Preteach**
- **Practice Stations Review**

Teach 35–45 min
- **Category Words**
- **Daily Table Talk**

Check/Reteach 5–10 min
Poster, Word Cards
- **Leveled Support Reteach**

Fluency: Writing or Speaking

ELA R 1.17 Identify and sort common words in basic categories (e.g., colors, shapes, foods).

Category Words: carnation, daisy, lily, rose, sunflower, tulip

Background Building Audio Slideshow

This Week
Unit 2, Week 1

Flowers

Next Week
Unit 2, Week 2
Animals Dig

FORM & FUNCTION	**FORM & FUNCTION**	
DAY 3 Read and Comprehend	**DAY 4** Language Arts	**DAY 5** Language Arts
Language: High Frequency Words	**Phonics**	**Think, Talk, and Recognize**
Preteach/Review 10–15 min Poster **Leveled Support Preteach** **Practice Stations Review**	**Preteach/Review** 10–15 min Poster **Leveled Support Preteach** **Practice Stations Review**	**Preteach/Review** 10–15 min Poster **Leveled Support Preteach** **Practice Stations Review**
Teach 35–45 min **High Frequency Words** **Daily Table Talk**	**Teach** 35–45 min **Phonics** **Daily Table Talk**	**Teach** 15–20 min **Think, Talk, and Recognize** **Concept Wrap Up**
Check/Reteach 5–10 min Poster, Word Cards **Leveled Support Reteach**	**Check/Reteach** 5–10 min Poster, Word Cards **Leveled Support Reteach**	**Check/Reteach** 30–40 min Poster, Word Cards, Song Book **Leveled Support Reteach**
		Fluency: Writing or Speaking
ELA R 1.15 Read simple one-syllable and high frequency words (i.e., sight words).	**ELA R 1.14** Match all consonant and short-vowel sounds to appropriate letters.	**ELA LS 1.2** Share information and ideas, speaking audibly in complete, coherent sentences.
High Frequency Words: have, is		

Practice Stations

Materials and Activity

DAY 1 — Get Ready to Read

construction paper, flower catalogues or magazines, scissors, glue

Flower Garden Collage ✶ ✶✶

Have children create a flower garden collage. Give them a large piece of construction paper. Have children cut out pictures of different flowers and arrange them on the construction paper to make a flower garden.

DAY 2 — Read and Comprehend

index cards with the vocabulary words written on them

Use the Word ✶✶ ✶✶✶

Read the vocabulary words with children. One child chooses a card and says a sentence with that vocabulary word. The next child chooses a card and says a sentence with that word. Children continue to choose cards and say sentences. When all of the words have been used, children can reshuffle the cards and start again.

"plants"

"The plants will grow tall."

Preteach/Reteach

Transfer and Common Misconceptions

ow Pronounced as Long *o*

Although the long *o* sound exists in Spanish, some children may have difficulty matching the letters *ow* to the long *o* sound.

/z/ Sound

Some children may want to pronounce the s in *rose* and *daisy* as /s/. In English an *s* can often be pronounced /z/ in the middle or end of a word.

Produce Language

Weekly Concept and Language Goal

CONCEPT GOALS

• understand that flowers are unique plants
• name some of the parts of flowers
• describe things that flowers do, such as grow

By Day 5, children should be able to gesture to an item in the drawing and talk about it.

Daily Table Talk

❶ **Beginning**
Children pantomime while you provide the language.

❷ ❸ **Early Intermediate/Intermediate**
Children pantomime and say a word or phrase.

❹ ❺ **Early Advanced/Advanced**
Children say a sentence while pantomiming.

Daily Table Talk

❶ **Beginning**
Children talk about their drawings.

❷ ❸ **Early Intermediate/Intermediate**
one or two word response: stem petal

❹ ❺ **Early Advanced/Advanced**
Children write a phrase or sentence.

DAY 3 — **FORM & FUNCTION** Read and Comprehend

DAY 4 — **FORM & FUNCTION** Language Arts

DAY 5 — **Language Arts**

index cards with category words written on them, pictures of the following flowers pasted onto index cards: *rose, tulip, daisy, carnation, sunflower, lily*

index cards with the high frequency words written on them, letter tiles, paper

picture cards, an apple

Flower Match Game

Have word cards in one pile and picture cards in another. A child chooses a card from each pile. If the picture matches the word, the child keeps both cards. If they don't match, the cards go under each pile. Children take turns until all the cards have been matched.

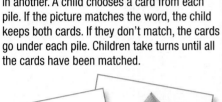

"rose"

Letter Tiles

Use Word Cards and Letter Tiles to spell high frequency words. Make placemats with two columns. Have them place the Word Card in the first column. Have them use the Letter Tiles to spell the word in the second column.

have

A is for Apple

A child chooses a picture card and says the word out loud. If the card has the same beginning sound as "apple," the child places the card next to the apple. Children choose cards until they have all been used.

ant

The Word *have*

Children may be confused by the word *have* and pronounce it with a long *a* sound because it ends with an *e.*

The /a/ Sound

Many children will find this sound easy to pronounce as it is found in a number of other languages.

Plurals

Children may forget to add *s* when using the plural form of a noun. Some languages, including Cantonese, Hmong, and Korean, do not use a plural marker.

Daily

❶ **Beginning** Name things about flowers and have children answer same or different.

❷ ❸ **Early Intermediate/Intermediate** Phrase: different colors

❹ ❺ **Early Advanced/Advanced** Sentence: Flowers can be different colors.

Daily Table Talk

❶ **Beginning** Name things flowers can and can't do and have children answer yes or no.

❷ ❸ **Early Intermediate/Intermediate** Phrase: smell nice

❹ ❺ **Early Advanced/Advanced** Sentence: Flowers can smell nice.

Daily Table Talk

❶ **Beginning** Child draws with support.

❷ ❸ **Early Intermediate/Intermediate** Child draws and speaks about the drawing using at least one concept vocabulary word.

❹ ❺ **Early Advanced/Advanced** Child draws and provides a label for the drawing.

OBJECTIVE

To introduce and discuss concepts and vocabulary related to what makes flowers unique.

Build Background Get Ready to Read!

Question of the Week How are flowers unique?
www.pearsonsuccessnet.com

Concept Talk 75min

Use the Big Book Connect the Big Book to the unit theme, Animal and Plant Characteristics—Look at Us! Display and discuss the cover. Then read the book aloud.

Introduce the Weekly Concept Tell children that today they will talk about things that make flowers unique. Tell children that *unique* is another word for *special*. Ask the weekly question: How are flowers unique?

Use the Poster Direct children's attention to the weekly poster. Use the Day 1 teaching notes at the bottom of the poster.

Sing the Song Use the song **Pretty Flowers** to reinforce children's understanding of the weekly concept. Have children sing or simply chant the words with you.

Flowers

Vocabulary

flowers

plants

grow
inside

46

How are flowers unique?

Vocabulary

* **Academic Vocabulary**
* **flowers** the brightly colored parts of plants
* **grow** to develop and become bigger over a period of time

  inside in or into a container, room, or building
* **plants** living things that have leaves and roots and grow in the ground

Introduce Concept Vocabulary

1. Say the Word Display the Picture Card as you say *flowers*. Have children repeat the word.

2. Introduce Word Meaning Show pictures of other flowers or point out flowers in the classroom or outside the window. Ask questions about the flowers. *What are your favorite flowers?*

3. Demonstrate Lead children to role play picking flowers and smelling them.

4. Apply Have children demonstrate their understanding.

Repeat with other vocabulary words.

Corrective Feedback If children have difficulty with the vocabulary words, demonstrate them again for children. Pantomime picking flowers, show with motions how things grow, place something inside a desk or cabinet, and show classroom plants. Have children say the words and follow your movements to build understanding of the words.

Concept Work

Discuss the illustrations with children. Ask them what makes flowers special. Have children circle the flowers in each illustration. Point out the pot and use the word *grow* as you explain that a flower will grow out of the pot. Children can color the pictures.

Leveled Support   Vocabulary in Context

Preteach / Reteach

❶ **Beginning** Point to the pictures for flowers, plant, grow, and inside on the Worktext page. Say the word for each picture as children point, and have them echo each word.

❷ ❸ **Early Intermediate/Intermediate** Have children point to each picture and say the word. Prompt children to give one- or two-word descriptions of the photographs.

❹ ❺ **Early Advanced/Advanced** Ask children to draw pictures of flower gardens. Then ask them to use vocabulary words to label their drawings.

Wrap Up   DAY 1

Daily Table Talk What makes flowers unique? Have children answer the question, using the vocabulary words.

Produce Language Ask each child to talk about a flower that they like. Have them say a sentence about the flower.

Today children should have:

☑ **Learned** and applied vocabulary related to what makes flowers unique.

☑ **Spoken** complete sentences about what makes flowers unique.

☑ **Recognized** concept vocabulary words.

ELA R 1.18 Describe common objects and events in general and specific language. (ELD R.B3)

To discuss the parts of flowers; to introduce category words for types of flowers.

Concept Talk

Connect to Day 1 How are flowers unique?

Introduce the Daily Question What parts do flowers have? Use the illustration in the Worktext to point out the petals and the stem of the sunflower. Have children answer orally.

Use the Poster Use the Day 2 teaching notes.

Introduce the Category Words

1. **Say the Word** Have children point to the rose. Say the word and have children repeat.

2. **Introduce Word Meaning** Ask questions: Do you like roses? What color roses do you like? Do you like red ones? Pink ones?

3. **Demonstrate** Pretend to pick and smell a rose.

4. **Apply** Repeat with other vocabulary words and elicit that they all belong to the category "types of flowers."

Have children draw their favorite flowers on the Worktext page.

Flowers

Picture Dictionary

carnation   **daisy**   **lily**

rose   **sunflower**   **tulip**

✎ **Draw** Draw a flower.

48 🐻 ELA R1.17 Identify and sort common words in basic categories (e.g., colors, shapes, foods). (ELD R.B4)

Wrap Up   DAY 2

Daily

Table Talk Have children discuss the different parts of a flower.

Produce Language To build fluency, encourage children to label or write a sentence about their drawings. They can share their writing with partners.

Today children should have:

☑ **Learned** and applied vocabulary related to types of flowers.

☑ **Spoken** complete sentences about the parts of a flower.

☑ **Recognized** words that belong in the same category.

🐻 **ELA R1.17** Identify and sort common words in basic categories (e.g., colors, shapes, foods). (ELD R.B4)

48 Flowers • Unit 2, Week 1

LS **Preteach Reteach** **Leveled Support** **Category Words**

❶ **Beginning** Have children point to each flower on the Worktext page as you say the names. Have children echo the word.

❷ ❸ **Early Intermediate/Intermediate** Say the name of a flower. Have children point to it. Then reverse the activity.

❹ ❺ **Early Advanced/Advanced** Have children point to and name each flower. Have children say one detail to describe each flower, such as its color or shape.

How can flowers be the same or different?

✏️ **Circle** Circle *have.*
Flowers have petals.

✏️ **Circle** Circle *is.*
This rose is red.

🐻 **ELA R1.15** Read simple one-syllable and high-frequency words (i.e., sight words). (ELD R.B2)

49

OBJECTIVE

To discuss how flowers can be the same or different; to introduce the high frequency words *have* and *is.*

Concept Talk

🔵 **FORM & FUNCTION**

Connect to Day 2 What parts do flowers have?

Introduce the Daily Question How can flowers be the same or different? Use the flowers on the category words page as an example.

Use the Poster Use the Day 3 teaching notes.

Review Concept Vocabulary Review the words introduced on Day 1.

Introduce the High Frequency Words

Introduce *have* and *is* by role playing sentences such as, *I have a pencil. This is a book.* Help children complete the Worktext page.

Corrective Feedback If children have difficulty identifying the high frequency words in the sentences, have them look for the first letter *h* to find *have* and *i* to find *is.*

Preteach **LS** **Leveled Support** **High Frequency Words**
Reteach

① **Beginning** Write the word *have.* Say: *This is the word have.* Point to the word and have children repeat the word after you. Continue with *is.*

② ③ **Early Intermediate/Intermediate** Write *have* and *is.* Say a sentence and have children raise their hands when they hear the words. Then give them each a set of index cards, with one word written on each card. Children can hold up the corresponding cards when they hear the words.

④ ⑤ **Early Advanced/Advanced** Have children look for the words *have* and *is* in classroom books.

Wrap Up **DAY** 3

Daily **Table Talk** Have children discuss things that make flowers the same and things that make flowers different.

Produce Language Have each child say a sentence about something that is the same about all flowers and something that makes them different.

Today children should have:

☑ **Learned** and applied the high frequency words *have* and *is.*

☑ **Spoken** complete sentences about how flowers can be the same or different.

☑ **Recognized** that flowers can be the same and different.

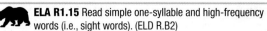

To discuss what flowers can do; to identify initial and medial /a/.

Concept Talk

 FORM & FUNCTION

Connect to Day 3 How can flowers be the same or different?

Introduce the Daily Question What can flowers do? Discuss possible answers, such as grow, bloom, and so on.

Use the Poster Use the Day 4 teaching notes.

Phonological Awareness

Identify Sound /a/ Have children point to each picture as you name it. Say: Listen for the /a/ sound in the words. The /a/ sound can be in the beginning of a word, like *apple*. It can be in the middle of a word, like *hat*. Which word has the /a/ sound, *sun* or *apple*? Continue with remaining pairs of words: *ant, bus; dog, cat*.

Corrective Feedback If children have difficulty identifying the initial or medial sound /a/, read each word again, separating the phonemes and emphasizing the initial or medial phoneme in each word.

Wrap Up
DAY **4**

Table Talk What can flowers do? Have children discuss different things that flowers can do.

Produce Language Have each child say a sentence about something a flower can do.

Today children should have:

☑ **Learned** and applied vocabulary related to what flowers can do.

☑ **Spoken** complete sentences about what flowers can do.

☑ **Recognized** words with initial and medial /a/.

 ELA R 1.14 Match all consonant and short-vowel sounds to appropriate letters. (ELD R. B10)

Identify Sound Aa

 **Color** Color things with a.

50  **ELA R1.14** Match sounds to letters. (ELD R.B10)

Preteach **Reteach** Leveled Support **Phonics**

❶ **Beginning** Hold up an index card on which you have written the letter *A*. Say: The name of this letter is *a*. The sound for this letter is /a/. Have children echo you.

❷ ❸ **Early Intermediate/Intermediate** Hold up a card on which you have printed the letter *A*. Say: What letter is this? What sound does it make? Guide children if necessary.

❹ ❺ **Early Advanced/Advanced** Have children identify the letter that makes /a/. Ask children to name other words that have the /a/ sound in the beginning or middle of the word.

How are flowers unique?

✎ Draw

OBJECTIVE

To guide children to express their understanding of weekly concepts and vocabulary.

Think, Talk, and Recognize!

Concept Talk

Connect to Day 4 What can flowers do? Model how to answer yesterday's question with a sentence.

Review the Weekly Question Ask: What makes flowers unique? Have children talk about what makes flowers unique. After children have answered, they can compare flowers to other plants.

Use the Poster Use the Day 5 teaching notes.

Review Concept Vocabulary Review the vocabulary introduced on Day 1.

Concept Wrap Up

Have children draw to answer the question: What makes flowers unique?

Leveled Support   Concept Vocabulary

① **Beginning** Display the Picture Cards for *flowers, plants, grow,* and *inside.* Say each word. Ask children to repeat and point to the matching card.

② ③ **Early Intermediate/Intermediate** Display the Picture Cards for *flowers, plants, grow,* and *inside.* Ask children to say each word and point to the matching card.

④ ⑤ **Early Advanced/Advanced** Display the Picture Cards for *flowers, plants, grow,* and *inside.* Ask children to talk about a garden using the words.

Wrap Up   DAY 5

Daily Table Talk What makes flowers unique? Have children discuss the question, using the vocabulary words they have learned this week.

Produce Language To build fluency, children can label, write about, or speak about their drawings. Ask children to respond to what they read or heard.

Today children should have:

☑ **Reviewed** the weekly concept and concept vocabulary.

☑ **Spoken** about what makes flowers unique.

☑ **Drawn or written** to show what makes flowers unique.

ELA LS 1.2 Share information and ideas, speaking audibly in complete, coherent sentences. (ELD LS.B3)

51

WEEK **2**

CALIFORNIA

Weekly Lesson Plan

Last Week
Unit 2, Week 1
Flowers

Question of the Week Why do animals dig?

Instructional Plan and Materials

- **Word Cards**
  28–31

- **Big Book**
  The Rain Forest

- **Poster**
  Poster 8 can be used at beginning or end of day.

- **Song Book**, p. 8

Transparencies Explore content and vocabulary and model fluent reading.

For further information about using these components, see pages x–xv.

CALIFORNIA Standards

GK Sci 2.a Students know how to observe and describe similarities and differences in the appearance and behavior of plants and animals (e.g., seed-bearing plants, birds, fish, insects).

Academic Language

DAY **1** Get Ready to Read

Build Background

Preteach/Review 10–15 min
Poster, Song Book, Big Book
- **Leveled Support Preteach**
- **Practice Stations Preteach**

Teach 35–45 min
- **Concept Talk**
- **Oral Vocabulary Routine**
  Word Cards
- **Build Concept Vocabulary**
- **Daily Table Talk**

Check/Reteach 5–10 min
Poster, Word Cards
- **Leveled Support Reteach**

ELA R 1.18 Describe common objects and events in both general and specific language.

Vocabulary: home, neighbors

Concept Talk Video

DAY **2** Read and Comprehend

Language: Category Words

Preteach/Review 10–15 min
Poster
- **Leveled Support Preteach**
- **Practice Stations Review**

Teach 35–45 min
- **Category Words**
- **Daily Table Talk**

Check/Reteach 5–10 min
Poster, Word Cards
- **Leveled Support Reteach**

Fluency: Writing or Speaking

ELA R 1.17 Identify and sort common words in basic categories (e.g., colors, shapes, foods).

Category Words: apple, banana, grapes, orange, pear, watermelon

Background Building Audio Slideshow

Animals Dig

DAY 3 FORM & FUNCTION Read and Comprehend	**DAY 4** FORM & FUNCTION Language Arts	**DAY 5** Language Arts
Language: High Frequency Words	**Phonics**	**Think, Talk, and Recognize**
Preteach/Review 10–15 min Poster **Leveled Support Preteach** **Practice Stations Review**	**Preteach/Review** 10–15 min Poster **Leveled Support Preteach** **Practice Stations Review**	**Preteach/Review** 10–15 min Poster **Leveled Support Preteach** **Practice Stations Review**
Teach 35–45 min **High Frequency Words** **Daily Table Talk**	**Teach** 35–45 min **Phonics** **Daily Table Talk**	**Teach** 15–20 min **Think, Talk, and Recognize** **Concept Wrap Up**
Check/Reteach 5–10 min Poster, Word Cards **Leveled Support Reteach**	**Check/Reteach** 5–10 min Poster, Word Cards **Leveled Support Reteach**	**Check/Reteach** 30–40 min Poster, Word Cards, Song Book **Leveled Support Reteach**
		Fluency: Writing or Speaking
ELA R 1.15 Read simple one-syllable and high frequency words (i.e., sight words).	**ELA R 1.14** Match all consonant and short-vowel sounds to appropriate letters.	**ELA LS 1.2** Share information and ideas, speaking audibly in complete, coherent sentences.
High Frequency Words: have, is		

Practice Stations

Materials and Activity

DAY 1 — Get Ready to Read

container with sand or rice, various small ojects buried inside (such as stones or tiny plastic animals), digging utensils, such as spoons and shovels

I Like to Dig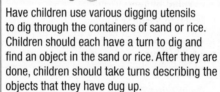

Have children use various digging utensils to dig through the containers of sand or rice. Children should each have a turn to dig and find an object in the sand or rice. After they are done, children should take turns describing the objects that they have dug up.

DAY 2 — Read and Comprehend

vocabulary words written on index cards

Match Game

Say the meaning of one of the vocabulary words aloud and the first letter in that word. Children work together to find the correct vocabulary word card to the definition. Continue until children have matched all words.

home

Preteach/Reteach

Transfer and Common Misconceptions

Compound Words

Speakers of languages such as Cantonese, Hmong, and Vietnamese, in which words consist of one syllable, may need extra practice with compound words.

Unstressed Syllables

Many syllables in English are pronounced with a short unstressed vowel sound. The words *apple* and *banana* contain unstressed syllables and may be difficult for some children to pronounce.

Produce Language

Weekly Concept and Language Goal

CONCEPT GOALS

• recognize that some animals dig
• name some animals that live underground
• describe how animals find their way home

By Day 5, children should be able to gesture to an item in the drawing and talk about it.

Daily Table Talk

❶ **Beginning**
Children pantomime while you provide the language.

❷ ❸ **Early Intermediate/Intermediate**
Children pantomime and say a word or phrase.

❹ ❺ **Early Advanced/Advanced**
Children say a sentence while pantomiming.

Daily Table Talk

❶ **Beginning**
Children talk about their drawings.

❷ ❸ **Early Intermediate/Intermediate**
Children write one-word labels.

❹ ❺ **Early Advanced/Advanced**
Children write a phrase or sentence.

DAY 3 FORM & FUNCTION Read and Comprehend	**DAY 4** FORM & FUNCTION Language Arts	**DAY 5** Language Arts

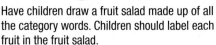

paper, crayons, colored pencils | sentence strips, various classroom objects | paper, crayons, colored pencils

Fruit Salad

Have children draw a fruit salad made up of all the category words. Children should label each fruit in the fruit salad.

What Do You Have?

Write these sentences on the strips: *I have a _____. This is a _____.* Have children pick up an object and one of the sentence strips. Children complete either sentence strip with the name of the object. Children take turns.

> I have a _____.
>
> This is a _____.

Special Soup

Have children draw a large bowl of soup. Have them fill the bowl with drawings of objects that begin with /s/.

The Word *have*

Children may be confused by this word. It is one that does not follow common pronunciation rules and must be memorized.

Sound /s/

Children will likely find this sound easy to pronounce as it is found in many different languages.

Present-Tense Verbs

Some children may have difficulty using the correct verb form when speaking in the first person.

Daily Table Talk

① Beginning
> Say dig in the ground, fly in the air, and sit in a tree and have children answer yes or no.

② ③ Early Intermediate/Intermediate
> Phrase: dig in the ground

④ ⑤ Early Advanced/Advanced
> Sentence: Armadillos dig in the ground.

Daily Table Talk

① Beginning
> Children raise their hands as you provide sample answers, such as sniffing the ground..

② ③ Early Intermediate/Intermediate
> Phrase: sniff the ground

④ ⑤ Early Advanced/Advanced
> Sentence: Animals sniff the ground to find their way back home.

Daily Table Talk

① Beginning Child draws with support.

② ③ Early Intermediate/Intermediate Child draws and speaks about the drawing using at least one concept vocabulary word.

④ ⑤ Early Advanced/Advanced Child draws and provides a label for the drawing.

OBJECTIVE

To introduce and discuss concepts and vocabulary related to animals and how they dig.

Build Background   Get **Ready** to **Read!**

Question of the Week   **Why do animals dig?**

www.pearsonsuccessnet.com

Concept Talk

Use the Big Book If you haven't introduced the Big Book, consider reading it to children. Connect to the unit theme, Animal and Plant Characteristics —Look at Us!

Introduce the Weekly Concept Tell children that today, they will talk about why animals dig. Ask the weekly question: Why do animals dig?

Use the Poster Direct children's attention to the weekly poster. Use the Day 1 teaching notes at the bottom of the poster.

Sing the Song Use the song **Animal Homes** to reinforce children's understanding of the weekly concept. Have children sing or simply chant the words with you.

Use a Transparency Use the Cause and Effect Map (Transparency 1) to record children's ideas about the reasons that animals dig.

Animals Dig

Vocabulary

home

honeybees

neighbors

orange

52

Why do animals dig?

Vocabulary

* Academic Vocabulary

* **home** the place where you usually live, especially with your family

  honeybees yellow and black insects that fly, make honey, and can sting you

* **neighbors** people who live very near your home

  orange a round fruit that has sweet juice and thick skin

 ELA R1.18 Describe common objects and events in both general and specific language. (ELD R.B3)

53

Introduce Concept Vocabulary

1. **Say the Word** Display the Word Card as you say *orange.* Have children repeat the word.

2. **Introduce Word Meaning** Show children an orange. Peel and slice it. Describe it to children: The orange is round. It is juicy. Ask questions about oranges. Do you like to eat oranges?

3. **Demonstrate** Have children role play peeling and eating an orange.

4. **Apply** Have children demonstrate their understanding.

Repeat with other vocabulary words.

Corrective Feedback If children have difficulty pronouncing a vocabulary word, repeat the word again, separating it into phonemes. Have the children repeat the word after you, blending the phonemes.

Concept Work

Tell children that the animal in the top illustration is an armadillo. Armadillos dig in the ground. Discuss the other vocabulary words and ask children to find them in the illustrations. Tell children that animals dig with their feet. Ask children to circle the feet of the digging animals. Then children can color the pictures.

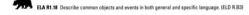

Leveled Support   Vocabulary in Context

Preteach Reteach

❶ **Beginning** Point to the home, honeybees, neighbor, and orange on the Worktext page. Say the word for each picture as children point and have them echo each word.

❷ ❸ **Early Intermediate/Intermediate** Do the Beginning activity, but have children say the words themselves, providing help if needed.

❹ ❺ **Early Advanced/Advanced** Ask children to draw a picture of an animal digging outside. Have children use vocabulary words to label their drawings. They can describe their work to partners.

Wrap Up   **DAY** 1

Table Talk   Why do animals dig? **Have children** answer the question, using the vocabulary words.

Produce Language Play charades. Ask each child to act out being an animal that digs and say a sentence about it.

Today children should have:

☑ **Learned** and applied vocabulary related to animals that dig.

☑ **Spoken** complete sentences about animals that dig.

☑ **Recognized** concept vocabulary words.

 ELA R 1.18 Describe common objects and events in both general and specific language. (ELD R.B3)

DAY 2

OBJECTIVE

To discuss animals that live underground; to introduce category words for fruit.

Concept Talk

Connect to Day 1 Why do animals dig?

Introduce the Daily Question What kinds of animals live underground? Have children answer orally.

Use the Poster Use the Day 2 teaching notes.

Introduce Category Words

1. **Say the Word** Have children point to the apple. Say the word and have children repeat after you.

2. **Introduce Word Meaning** Show an apple and cut it in half, showing the seeds inside. Describe the apple as you examine it. Ask questions: Do you like apples? Do you like red apples or green apples?

3. **Demonstrate** Have children role play biting into and chewing on an apple with you.

4. **Apply** Repeat with other vocabulary words and elicit that they all belong to the category "fruits."

Have children point to items as you name them. Then have them draw their favorite fruits.

Corrective Feedback If children have difficulty with category words for fruit, supply pictures of fruit and other objects. Have children sort the pictures into categories: fruit and other objects.

Wrap Up — DAY 2

Table Talk Have children pretend to be an animal living underground. Then have them each say a sentence about what kinds of animals live underground.

Produce Language To build fluency, encourage children to label or write a sentence about the fruit that they draw. They can share their writing with partners.

Today children should have:

☑ **Learned** and applied vocabulary related to fruits.

☑ **Spoken** complete sentences about animals that live underground.

☑ **Recognized** words that belong in the same category.

ELA R1 1.7 Identify and sort common words in basic categories (e.g., colors, shapes, foods). (ELD R.B4)

Fruits

Picture Dictionary

apple   banana   grapes

orange   pear   watermelon

 Draw Draw fruit.

54 ELA R1.17 Identify and sort common words in basic categories (e.g., colors, shapes, foods). (ELD R.B4)

Leveled Support — Category Words

Preteach / Reteach

① **Beginning** Have children point to each fruit on the Worktext page as you say it. Have children echo the word.

② ③ **Early Intermediate/Intermediate** Describe a fruit by color and shape. Have children say the name of the fruit you are describing or point to its picture.

④ ⑤ **Early Advanced/Advanced** Have children tell a partner which fruits they have tried and which fruits are their favorites.

How does an armadillo find its food?

✏️ **Circle** Circle *have*.
Armadillos have claws to dig.

✏️ **Circle** Circle *is*.
An armadillo is digging.

🐻 **ELA R1.15** Read simple one-syllable and high-frequency words (i.e., sight words). (ELD R.B2)

55

To discuss how armadillos find food; to introduce the high frequency words *have* and *is*.

Concept Talk

FORM & FUNCTION

Connect to Day 2 What kinds of animals live underground?

Introduce the Daily Question How does an armadillo find its food? Use the photographs in the Worktext to explain. Introduce words like *claws* and *digs*.

Use the Poster Use the Day 3 teaching notes.

Review Concept Vocabulary Review the words introduced on Day 1.

Introduce High Frequency Words

Guide children to point to the word *have* in the direction line. Say: This is the word *have*. Let's say the word together. Now point to the word *have* in the sentence. Circle it. Help children complete the Worktext page.

Corrective Feedback If children have difficulty reading the high frequency words, provide many opportunities for children to identify the words in short sentences. Write the words on sticky notes so children can place the notes near the words in the sentences.

Preteach / Reteach **LS** **Leveled Support** **High Frequency Words**

① **Beginning** Ask children to listen for the word *have* as you say a sentence. They can raise their hands when they hear the word. Repeat with the word *is*.

②③ **Early Intermediate/Intermediate** Repeat the Beginning Activity, but provide index cards with one word on the back and one on the front. Have children hold up the correct side of the card when they hear the words.

④⑤ **Early Advanced/Advanced** Write the words *have* and *is*. Have the children say sentences using these words. Write their sentences. Have children circle the high frequency word in each of their sentences.

Wrap Up

DAY 3

Daily **Table Talk** Children can pretend to be an armadillo looking for food and then talk about how armadillos find food.

Produce Language Have each child say a sentence about how armadillos find food.

Today children should have:

☑ **Learned** and applied the high frequency words *have* and *is*.

☑ **Spoken** complete sentences about how armadillos find food.

☑ **Recognized** that armadillos can find food by digging.

 ELA R1.15 Read simple one-syllable and high-frequency words (i.e., sight words). (ELD R.B2)

55

To discuss how animals find their way back home; to identify the sound /s/.

Concept Talk

FORM & FUNCTION

Connect to Day 3 How does an armadillo find its food?

Introduce the Daily Question How does an animal find its way back home? Provide an example that children will understand, such as a bird flying away from its nest but finding the same nest after looking for food. How do children think that animals can find their way home?

Use the Poster Use the Day 4 teaching notes.

Phonics Awareness

Identify Sound /s/ Have children point to each picture as you name it. Say: Now I'm going to read the words again. Listen for /s/ at the beginning of each word. Which word begins with /s/, *sun* or *apple*? Continue with remaining pairs of words: *bicycle, socks; snake, cat.*

Corrective Feedback If children have difficulty identifying the initial sound /s/, read each word again, separating the phonemes and emphasizing the initial phoneme in each word. Say the words, exaggerating the initial sound for children. Children can say the words with you, emphasizing /s/.

Identify Sound Ss

Draw Color pictures with *s*.

56 ELA R1.11 Distinguish orally stated one-syllable words and separate into beginning or ending sounds. (ELD R.B10)

Leveled Support Phonics

Preteach / Reteach

① **Beginning** Hold up an alphabet card for *S*. Say: The name of this letter is *s*. The sound for this letter is /s/. Have children echo you. Say the sound, exaggerating it.

② ③ **Early Intermediate/Intermediate** Tell children you will say several words and they should listen for /s/. When you say a word that begins with /s/, children should clap and repeat the word. Say: sad, ant, fox, sock, nut, six.

④ ⑤ **Early Advanced/Advanced** Have children identify the letter that makes the /s/ sound. Ask children to name words that being with /s/.

Wrap Up DAY

Table Talk Daily How does an animal find its way back home? Have children discuss the question.

Produce Language Have each child say a sentence to tell how animals find their way back home.

Today children should have:

- ☑ **Learned** and applied vocabulary related to how animals find their way back home.

- ☑ **Spoken** complete sentences about how animals find their way back home.

- ☑ **Recognized** words with the sound /s/.

ELA R1.14 Match all consonant and short-vowel sounds to appropriate letters. (ELD R B10)

Why do animals dig?

✏ **Draw**

To guide children to express their understanding of weekly concepts and vocabulary.

Think, Talk, and Recognize!

Concept Talk

Connect to Day 4 How does an animal find its way back home? Model how to answer yesterday's question with a sentence.

Review the Weekly Question Ask: Why do animals dig? Have children pretend to dig like an animal and explain why they are doing it.

Use the Poster Use the Day 5 teaching notes.

Review Concept Vocabulary Review the vocabulary introduced on Day 1.

Concept Wrap Up

Have children draw to answer the question: Why do animals dig? Prompt discussion with the photo: This badger looks too big to live in this hole, so it must be digging for food. What other reasons do animals have for digging?

Preteach / Reteach

ⓁⓈ Leveled Support   Concept Vocabulary

① **Beginning** Display the Word Cards for *home, honeybees, neighbors,* and *orange.* Say each word. Ask children to repeat and point to the matching card.

② ③ **Early Intermediate/Intermediate** Display the Word Cards for *home, honeybees, neighbors,* and *orange.* Ask children questions about the words, such as: Where do neighbors live? Which word is a fruit? Children can ask questions of their own.

④ ⑤ **Early Advanced/Advanced** Display the Word Cards for *home, honeybees, neighbors,* and *orange.* Ask children to work with partners to tell stories about animals using the words.

Daily Table Talk Why do animals dig? Have children discuss the question, using the vocabulary words they have learned this week.

Produce Language To build fluency, children can label, write about, or speak about their drawings. Ask children to respond to what they heard or read.

Today, children should have:

☑ **Reviewed** the weekly concept and concept vocabulary.

☑ **Spoken** about why animals dig.

☑ **Drawn or written** to show why animals dig.

 ELA LS 1.2 Share information and ideas, speaking audibly in complete, coherent sentences. (ELD LS.B3)

Question of the Week Who lives in the grasslands?

DAY 1 Get Ready to Read

DAY 2 Read and Comprehend

Instructional Plan and Materials

- **Word Cards**
  32–35

- **Big Book**
  The Rain Forest

- **Poster**
  Poster 9 can be used at beginning or end of day.

- **Song Book**, p. 9

Transparencies Explore content and vocabulary and model fluent reading.

For further information about using these components, see pages x–xv.

Build Background

Preteach/Review 10–15 min
Poster, Song Book, Big Book

   Leveled Support Preteach

   Practice Stations Preteach

Teach 35–45 min

   Concept Talk

   Oral Vocabulary Routine
     Word Cards

   Build Concept Vocabulary

   Daily Table Talk

Check/Reteach 5–10 min
Poster, Word Cards

   Leveled Support Reteach

Language: Category Words

Preteach/Review 10–15 min
Poster

   Leveled Support Preteach

   Practice Stations Review

Teach 35–45 min

   Category Words

   Daily Table Talk

Check/Reteach 5–10 min
Poster, Word Cards

   Leveled Support Reteach

Fluency: Writing or Speaking

CALIFORNIA Standards

G1 Sci 2.a Students know different plants and animals inhabit different kinds of environments and have external features that help them thrive in different kinds of places.

ELA LS 2.1 Describe people, places, things (e.g., size, color, shape), locations, and actions.

ELA R 1.17 Identify and sort common words in basic categories (e.g., colors, shapes, foods).

Academic Language

Category Words: chick, colt, kitten, lamb, piglet, puppy

 Get Online! www.pearsonsuccessnet.com

Concept Talk Video

Background Building Audio Slideshow

Animals in the Grasslands

DAY 3 — FORM FUNCTION — Read and Comprehend	**DAY 4** — FORM FUNCTION — Language Arts	**DAY 5** — Language Arts
Language: High Frequency Words	**Phonics**	**Think, Talk, and Recognize**
Preteach/Review 10–15 min Poster **Leveled Support Preteach** **Practice Stations Review**	**Preteach/Review** 10–15 min Poster **Leveled Support Preteach** **Practice Stations Review**	**Preteach/Review** 10–15 min Poster **Leveled Support Preteach** **Practice Stations Review**
Teach 35–45 min **High Frequency Words** **Daily Table Talk**	**Teach** 35–45 min **Phonics** **Daily Table Talk**	**Teach** 15–20 min **Think, Talk, and Recognize** **Concept Wrap Up**
Check/Reteach 5–10 min Poster, Word Cards **Leveled Support Reteach**	**Check/Reteach** 5–10 min Poster, Word Cards **Leveled Support Reteach**	**Check/Reteach** 30–40 min Poster, Word Cards, Song Book **Leveled Support Reteach**
		Fluency: Writing or Speaking
ELA R 1.15 Read simple one-syllable and high frequency words (i.e., sight words).	**ELA R 1.14** Match all consonant and short-vowel sounds to appropriate letters.	**ELA LS 1.2** Share information and ideas, speaking audibly in complete, coherent sentences.
High Frequency Words: we, my, like		

Practice Stations

Materials and Activity

mural paper, cut-out magazine pictures of grasslands animals, crayons

Animals in the Grasslands ✹

Have children create a mural of grassland animals. They can draw grass along the bottom of the paper and then paste pictures of grassland animals in the grass.

clay, colored construction paper, crayons, colored pencils, glue, tape, paint

Animal Art ✹✹

Have children design and create vocabulary animals. Provide children with various art supplies. Display animals in a table grasslands habitat.

Preteach/Reteach

Transfer and Common Misconceptions

g Pronounced /j/

Children may want to say /g/ at the beginning of *giraffe. G* can often make the /j/ sound at the beginning of words.

/ch/ Sound

The /ch/ sound, or an approximate sound, is common in many languages, including Spanish, Cantonese, Hmong, and Korean.

Produce Language

Weekly Concept and Language Goal

CONCEPT GOALS

- recognize that some animals live in grasslands
- understand that animal babies need to stay with their mothers
- describe ways in which young animals play

By Day 5, children should be able to gesture to an item in the drawing and talk about it.

Daily Table Talk

❶ **Beginning**

Children pantomime while you provide the language.

❷ ❸ **Early Intermediate/Intermediate**

Children pantomime and say a word or phrase.

❹ ❺ **Early Advanced/Advanced**

Children say a sentence while pantomiming.

Daily Table Talk

❶ **Beginning**

Children talk about their drawings.

❷ ❸ **Early Intermediate/Intermediate**

Children write one-word labels.

❹ ❺ **Early Advanced/Advanced**

Children write a phrase or sentence.

DAY 3 — FORM & FUNCTION — Read and Comprehend

index cards with the following words written on them: *lamb, chick, colt, kitten, puppy, piglet;* pictures of each animal baby pasted onto index cards

Animal Babies Concentration

Put cards facedown in two rows: the top row should be the word cards, and the bottom row should be the pictures. Have children turn over a card from each row. The child should say the word aloud. If the picture matches the word, the child keeps the card. If not, both cards are turned facedown again.

chick

DAY 4 — FORM & FUNCTION — Language Arts

sentence strips, various classroom objects

What Do You Have?

Write these sentences on the strips: *I have a _____ . This is a _____ .* Have children pick up an object and one of the sentence strips. Children complete either sentence strip with the name of the object. Children take turns.

I have a _____ .

This is a _____ .

DAY 5 — Language Arts

stack of picture cards, should include many words that begin with *p*, pie tins

Put It in the Pie!

Children choose a picture card from the stack and say the word aloud. If it has the same beginning sound as *pie,* they put the card in the pie tin. Other cards go in a pile. Children should continue until all the cards have been categorized correctly.

The Word *my*

Children may be confused by the word *my* and its long *i* sound spelled with a *y.* However, most students will have no trouble pronouncing the long *i* sound.

Sound /p/

Children will likely find this sound easy to pronounce as it is found in many different languages.

Articles

Some children may omit articles, such as *a* and *the,* when speaking about the grasslands or a particular animal. Languages such as Cantonese, Hmong, Korean, and Vietnamese either have no articles or do not differentiate between *a* and *the.*

 Table Talk

❶ **Beginning** Children can pantomime while you provide the language.

❷ ❸ **Early Intermediate/Intermediate** Phrase: run and roll

❹ ❺ **Early Advanced/Advanced** Sentence: Prairie dog pups run and roll together.

Table Talk

❶ **Beginning** Children raise their hands when they hear their favorite as you name each grassland anima.l.

❷ ❸ **Early Intermediate/Intermediate** One or two words: a lion, zebra

❹ ❺ **Early Advanced/Advanced** Sentence: My favorite grassland animal is a lion.

 **Table Talk**

❶ **Beginning** Child draws with support.

❷ ❸ **Early Intermediate/Intermediate** Child draws and speaks about the drawing using at least one concept vocabulary word.

❹ ❺ **Early Advanced/Advanced** Child draws and provides a label for the drawing.

Build Background Get **Ready** to **Read!**

? Question of the Week

Who lives in the grasslands?

www.pearsonsuccessnet.com

Concept Talk

Use the Big Book If you haven't introduced the Big Book, consider reading it to children. Connect to the unit theme, Animal and Plant Characteristics—Look at Us!

Introduce the Weekly Concept Tell children that today, they will talk about animals that live in the grasslands. Explain that grasslands are a special place where special plants and animals live. Ask the weekly question: Who lives in the grasslands?

Use the Poster Direct children's attention to the weekly poster. Use the Day 1 teaching notes at the bottom of the poster.

Sing the Song Use the song **Animals Far Away** to reinforce children's understanding of the weekly concept. Have children sing or simply chant the words with you.

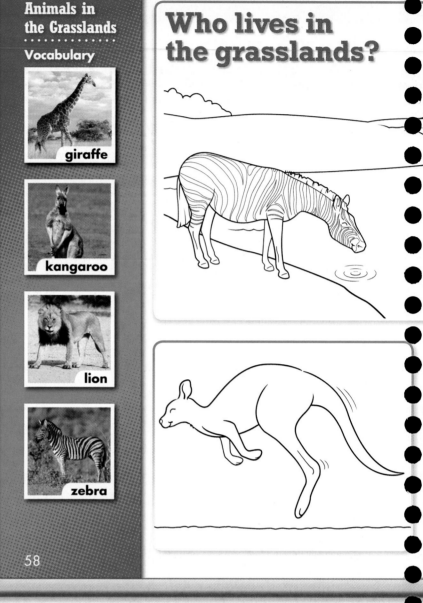

Animals in the Grasslands
Vocabulary

giraffe

kangaroo

lion

zebra

Who lives in the grasslands?

58

Vocabulary

giraffe a tall African animal with a very long neck and legs and dark spots on its yellow-brown hair

kangaroo an Australian animal that has strong back legs for jumping and carries its babies in a pocket of skin on its stomach

lion a large African and Asian wild cat, the male of which has long thick hair around his neck

zebra a wild African animal like a horse, that has black and white bands on its body

 ELA LS 2.1 Describe people, places, things (e.g., size, color, shape), locations, and actions. (ELD R.B2)

59

Introduce Concept Vocabulary

1. **Say the Word** Display the Picture Card as you say *zebra.* Have children repeat the word.

2. **Introduce Word Meaning** Show that a zebra looks like a horse, except that it has stripes. Zebra's stripes are not all the same. Ask questions about zebras. What colors are zebras? Do they have stripes or spots?

3. **Demonstrate** Partners can tell how zebras and horses are alike and different. Have children role play galloping like a zebra.

4. **Apply** Have children demonstrate their understanding.

Repeat with other vocabulary words.

Corrective Feedback If children have difficulty identifying the names of the animals, show additional pictures of the animals in magazines or books. As you say the animal names, separate the phonemes and then blend the sounds together.

Concept Work

Name each animal, having children point to it. Then point to the animals as children name them. Have children color the pictures.

Leveled Support Vocabulary in Context

Preteach / Reteach

① **Beginning** Point to the giraffe, kangaroo, lion, and zebra on the Worktext page. Say the word for each picture as children point, and have them echo each word.

② ③ **Early Intermediate/Intermediate** Describe an animal in simple terms: This animal has stripes. This animal has a lot of hair on its neck. Children can point to or name the animal you describe.

④ ⑤ **Early Advanced/Advanced** Ask children to draw a picture of animals in the grasslands. Then have them label the pictures with the vocabulary words.

Wrap Up   DAY 1

Daily Table Talk Who lives in the grasslands? Have children answer the question, using the vocabulary words.

Produce Language Play charades. Ask each child to act out one of the animals that lives in the grasslands.

Today children should have:

☑ **Learned** and applied vocabulary related to animals that live in the grasslands.

☑ **Spoken** complete sentences about animals that lives in the grasslands.

☑ **Recognized** concept vocabulary words.

 ELA LS 2.1 Describe people, places, things (e.g. size, color, shape, locations, and actions.) (ELD R.B2)

59

OBJECTIVE

To discuss why animal babies stay with their mothers; to introduce category words for animal babies.

Concept Talk

Connect to Day 1 Who lives in the grasslands?

Introduce the Daily Question Why do animal babies stay with their mothers? Have children answer orally.

Use the Poster Use the Day 2 teaching notes.

Introduce the Category Words

1. Say the Word Have children point to the chick. Say the word and have children repeat.

2. Introduce Word Meaning Say: A hen is a grown-up chicken. A chick is a baby. It hatches from an egg.

3. Demonstrate Ask questions to demonstrate meaning: Is a chick a baby hen? Is a chick a baby dog?

4. Apply Repeat with other vocabulary words and elicit that they all belong to the category "animal babies."

Have children point to items as you name them. Have children draw lines to match babies and their parents on the Worktext page.

Corrective Feedback If children have difficulty matching the babies with their parents, help them name each of the pictures.

Wrap Up   DAY 2

Daily Table Talk Discuss why animal babies stay with their mothers. Children can each say a sentence about baby animals and their mothers.

Produce Language To build fluency, encourage children to label or write a sentence about their drawings. They can share their writing with partners.

Today children should have:

☑ **Learned** and applied vocabulary related to animal babies.

☑ **Spoken** complete sentences about why animal babies live with their mothers.

☑ **Recognized** words that belong in the same category.

ELA R1.17 Identify and sort common words in basic categories (e.g., colors, shapes, foods). (ELD R.B4)

Animal Babies

Picture Dictionary

chick **colt** **kitten**

lamb **piglet** **puppy**

 Match Match babies with adults.

60 ELA R1.17 Identify and sort common words in basic categories (e.g., colors, shapes, foods). (ELD R.B4)

Preteach Reteach LS Leveled Support Category Words

① **Beginning** Have children point to each baby animal on the Worktext page as you say it. Have children echo the word.

② ③ **Early Intermediate/Intermediate** Say the name of a baby animal. Have children point to it. Then reverse the activity.

④ ⑤ **Early Advanced/Advanced** Have children talk in pairs. Have them tell each other what baby animals they have seen and which one is their favorite.

How do you think a prairie dog pup would play?

🖊 **Circle** Circle *We.*
We saw the pups play.

🖊 **Circle** Circle *my.*
Prairie dogs are my favorite animal.

🖊 **Circle** Circle *like.*
I like prairie dogs.

ELA R1.15 Read simple one-syllable and high-frequency words (i.e., sight words). (ELD R.B2)

61

To discuss how prairie dog pups play; to introduce the high frequency words *we, my,* and *like.*

Concept Talk

Connect to Day 2 Why do animal babies stay with their mothers?

Introduce the Daily Question How do you think a prairie dog pup would play? Link children's experiences with puppies they know to the question. How do puppies play? How might puppies on the prairie play?

Use the Poster Use the Day 3 teaching notes.

Review Concept Vocabulary Review the words introduced on Day 1.

Introduce the High Frequency Words

Introduce *we, my,* and *like* by role playing sentences such as: *We like to dance. This is my friend.* Help children complete the Worktext page.

Wrap Up   DAY 3

Daily Table Talk Children can pretend to play like prairie dog pups and talk about what they are doing.

Produce Language Have each child say a sentence about how they think prairie dog pups would play.

Today children should have:

☑ **Learned** and applied the high frequency words *we, my,* and *like.*

☑ **Spoken** complete sentences about how prairie dog pups might play.

☑ **Recognized** ways in which wild animals might play.

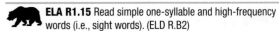

ELA R1.15 Read simple one-syllable and high-frequency words (i.e., sight words). (ELD R.B2)

61

Preteach / Reteach Leveled Support High Frequency Words

❶ **Beginning** Write the word *we.* Say This is the word *we.* We use the word *we* to talk about ourselves and other people. Demonstrate the meaning by gathering several children around you and saying *we* as you gesture toward yourself and the group. Continue explaining *my* and *like* with physical gestures.

❷ ❸ **Early Intermediate/Intermediate** Write *we, my,* and *like* on index cards. Give the cards to children. Say a sentence with one of the words and have children hold up the correct word.

❹ ❺ **Early Advanced/Advanced** Write sentences with the words *we, my,* and *like.* Have children find and circle the words.

OBJECTIVE

To discuss children's favorite grasslands animal; to identify the sound /p/.

Concept Talk

 FORM & FUNCTION

Connect to Day 3 How do you think a prairie dog pup would play?

Introduce the Daily Question Which grassland animal is your favorite? List the animals children have studied this week. Have them pick out a favorite.

Use the Poster Use the Day 4 teaching notes.

Phonological Awareness

Identify Sound /p/ Write the word *pig* on the board. Say: Say this word with me: *pig.* What sound do you hear at the beginning of the word? What letter makes the sound /p/? Tell children they are going to be listening for the sound /p/ in the beginning of words. Help children complete the Worktext page.

Corrective Feedback If children have difficulty identifying the initial sound /p/, saying the name of each animal, separating the phonemes and emphasizing the initial phoneme in each word.

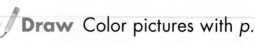

Identify Sound Pp

 **Draw** Color pictures with *p.*

62 ![bear] ELA R1.14 Match all consonant and short-vowel sounds to appropriate letters. (ELD R.B10)

Leveled Support **Phonics**
Preteach / Reteach **LS**

① **Beginning** Hold up a card on which you have written the letter *p.* Say: This letter is *p.* The letter *p* makes the sound /p/. Have children repeat after you: *p,* /p/.

② ③ **Early Intermediate/Intermediate** Give each child an index card on which you have written the letter *p.* Say words, some that begin with *p* and some that do not. When you say a word that begins with the sound /p/, children should hold up their cards.

④ ⑤ **Early Advanced/Advanced** Chidlren can work with partners to draw pictures of words that start with the sound /p/. Encourage them when possible to label their pictures.

Wrap Up DAY **4**

 Daily **Table Talk** Which grassland animal is your favorite? Have children discuss the question.

Produce Language Have each child say a sentence about their favorite grassland animal.

Today children should have:

☑ **Learned** and applied vocabulary related to grassland animals.

☑ **Spoken** complete sentences about which grassland animal is their favorite.

☑ **Recognized** words with the sound /p/.

![bear] **ELA R1.14** Match all consonant and short-vowel sounds to appropriate letters. (ELD R.B10)

Who lives in the grasslands?

✏️ **Draw**

 ELA LS. 1.2 Share information and ideas, speaking audibly in complete, coherent sentences. (ELD LS.B1)

63

 Preteach Reteach **Leveled Support** **Concept Vocabulary**

① **Beginning** Display the Word Cards for *giraffe, kangaroo, lion,* and *zebra.* Say each word. Ask children to repeat and point to the matching card.

② ③ **Early Intermediate/Intermediate** Display the Word Cards for *giraffe, kangaroo, lion,* and *zebra.* Ask children to each take one card and name and describe the animal on the card.

④ ⑤ **Early Advanced/Advanced** Display the Word Cards for *giraffe, kangaroo, lion,* and *zebra.* Ask children to tell a story set in the grasslands using these words.

OBJECTIVE

To guide children to express their understanding of weekly concepts and vocabulary.

Think, Talk, and Recognize!

Concept Talk

Connect to Day 4 Which grassland animal is your favorite? Model how to answer yesterday's question with a sentence.

Review the Weekly Question Ask: Who lives in the grasslands? Have children name a grassland animal. After children have answered, they can talk about which ones are their favorites.

Use the Poster Use the Day 5 teaching notes.

Review Concept Vocabulary Review the vocabulary introduced on Day 1.

Concept Wrap Up

Have children draw to answer the question: Who lives in the grasslands? They can talk about their pictures as they share them with friends.

Wrap Up **DAY** 5

Table Talk Who lives in the grasslands? Have children discuss the question, using the vocabulary words they have learned this week.

Produce Language To build fluency, children can label, write about, or speak about their drawings. Ask children to respond to what they read or heard.

Today, children should have:

☑ **Reviewed** the weekly concept and concept vocabulary.

☑ **Spoken** about animals that live in the grasslands.

☑ **Drawn or written** about animals that live in the grasslands.

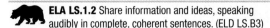 **ELA LS.1.2** Share information and ideas, speaking audibly in complete, coherent sentences. (ELD LS.B3)

63

Where does a bear hibernate?

Instructional Plan and Materials

snores

• **Word Cards**
36–37

The Rain Forest

• **Big Book**
The Rain Forest

• **Poster**
Poster 10 can be used at beginning or end of day.

• **Song Book**, p. 10

Transparencies Explore content and vocabulary and model fluent reading.

For further information about using these components, see pages x–xv.

CALIFORNIA Standards

G1 Sci 2.a Students know different plants and animals inhabit different kinds of environments and have external features that help them thrive in different kinds of places.

Academic Language

DAY 1 — Get Ready to Read

Build Background

Preteach/Review 10–15 min
Poster, Song Book, Big Book
- **Leveled Support Preteach**
- **Practice Stations Preteach**

Teach 35–45 min
- **Concept Talk**
- **Oral Vocabulary Routine**
  Word Cards
- **Build Concept Vocabulary**
- **Daily Table Talk**

Check/Reteach 5–10 min
Poster, Word Cards
- **Leveled Support Reteach**

ELA LS 2.1 Describe people, places, things (e.g., size, color, shape), locations, and actions.

Concept Talk Video

DAY 2 — Read and Comprehend

Language: Category Words

Preteach/Review 10–15 min
Poster
- **Leveled Support Preteach**
- **Practice Stations Review**

Teach 35–45 min
- **Category Words**
- **Daily Table Talk**

Check/Reteach 5–10 min
Poster, Word Cards
- **Leveled Support Reteach**

Fluency: Writing or Speaking

ELA R 1.17 Identify and sort common words in basic categories (e.g., colors, shapes, foods).

Category Words: den, hive, hole, log, nest, tree

Background Building Audio Slideshow

This Week
Unit 2, Week 4

Bears Hibernate

Next Week
Unit 2, Week 5
Animal Homes

FORM & FUNCTION

DAY 3   Read and Comprehend

DAY 4   Language Arts

DAY 5   Language Arts

Language: High Frequency Words	Phonics	Think, Talk, and Recognize
Preteach/Review 10–15 min Poster **Leveled Support Preteach** **Practice Stations Review**	**Preteach/Review** 10–15 min Poster **Leveled Support Preteach** **Practice Stations Review**	**Preteach/Review** 10–15 min Poster **Leveled Support Preteach** **Practice Stations Review**
Teach 35–45 min **High Frequency Words** **Daily Table Talk**	**Teach** 35–45 min **Phonics** **Daily Table Talk**	**Teach** 15–20 min **Think, Talk, and Recognize** **Concept Wrap Up**
Check/Reteach 5–10 min Poster, Word Cards **Leveled Support Reteach**	**Check/Reteach** 5–10 min Poster, Word Cards **Leveled Support Reteach**	**Check/Reteach** 30–40 min Poster, Word Cards, Song Book **Leveled Support Reteach**
		Fluency: Writing or Speaking
ELA R 1.15 Read simple one-syllable and high frequency words (i.e., sight words).	ELA R 1.14 Match all consonant and short-vowel sounds to appropriate letters.	ELA LS 1.2 Share information and ideas, speaking audibly in complete, coherent sentences.
High Frequency Words: we, my		

Practice Stations

Materials and Activity

picture of a bear hibernating, drawing paper, crayons

Sleeping Bear

Draw a simple outline of a bear sleeping in a cave on drawing paper for each child. Show children the picture of a bear hibernating. Have children talk about what it looks like. Then have them complete the picture by drawing eyes, ears, and mouth. Have them color the picture.

vocabulary words written on index cards

Picture Dictionary

Read each word with children. Have children create a picture dictionary for each vocabulary word. Children can work together, or use the pictures in their work texts to help them find meanings for each word.

bear

Preteach/Reteach

Transfer and Common Misconceptions

The Letters *ea*

Because vowels in Spanish are never silent, Spanish speakers may pronounce the *ea* in *bear* with two vowel sounds. Spanish also does not include *r*-controlled vowel sounds.

Long Vowels

Children are likely to be familiar with the long vowel sounds in *hole*, *tree*, and *hive*.

Produce Language

Weekly Concept and Language Goal

CONCEPT GOALS

- understand that some animals, such as bears, hibernate
- describe where and when bears hibernate

By Day 5, children should be able to gesture to an item in the drawing and talk about it.

Daily Table Talk

❶ **Beginning**
| Children pantomime while you provide the language. |

❷ ❸ **Early Intermediate/Intermediate**
| Children pantomime and say a word or phrase. |

❹ ❺ **Early Advanced/Advanced**
| Children say a sentence while pantomiming. |

Daily Table Talk

❶ **Beginning**
| Children talk about their drawings. |

❷ ❸ **Early Intermediate/Intermediate**
| Children write one-word labels. |

❹ ❺ **Early Advanced/Advanced**
| Children write a phrase or sentence. |

DAY 3 FORM & FUNCTION — Read and Comprehend

index cards with the words *log, den, hole, tree, nest, hive;* picture cards of various animals

Where Do I Live? 👥

Mix up all index cards into one pile. Mix up the pictures cards into another pile. One partner chooses a card from each pile. If the animal can live in the type of home listed on the index card, a match is made and the child keeps both cards. If the animal can not live in the home, both cards go under the bottom of each pile. Partners should take turns until all the cards are matched.

The Word *we*

Speakers of Spanish should have no trouble pronouncing this word as both sounds exist in Spanish.

DAY 4 FORM & FUNCTION — Language Arts

cut-out paragraphs from children's magazines, word cards for *we, my*

Word Search 👥

Give partners a set of word cards and have them read the words. Then have them look for the words in paragraphs and circle the words that they find.

Sound /k/

Children will likely find this sound easy to pronounce as it is found in many different languages.

DAY 5 — Language Arts

stack of picture cards, should include many words that begin with /k/

Find the /k/ Words 🧍 👥

Give each pair a stack of picture cards. Have children look through the cards and find words that begin with /k/. Have them say the words aloud.

Pronouns

Speakers of Spanish may use inappropriate pronouns, particularly with neutal nouns, because all nouns in Spanish are either masculine or feminine.

Daily Table Talk

❶ **Beginning**
Have children respond yes or no.

❷ ❸ **Early Intermediate/Intermediate**
Phrase: never saw one

❹ ❺ **Early Advanced/Advanced**
Sentence: I never saw a cave.

Daily Table Talk

❶ **Beginning**
Children raise their hands as you provide sample answers, such as spring, summer, winter, fall.

❷ ❸ **Early Intermediate/Intermediate**
Phrase: in the winter

❹ ❺ **Early Advanced/Advanced**
Sentence: A bear hibernates in the winter.

Daily Table Talk

❶ **Beginning** Child draws with support.

❷ ❸ **Early Intermediate/Intermediate** Child draws and speaks about the drawing using at least one concept vocabulary word.

❹ ❺ **Early Advanced/Advanced** Child draws and provides a label for the drawing.

64d

OBJECTIVE

To introduce and discuss concepts and vocabulary related to bears' hibernating.

Build Background Get Ready to Read!

Question of the Week

Where does a bear hibernate?

www.pearsonsuccessnet.com

Concept Talk

Use the Big Book If you haven't introduced the Big Book, consider reading it to children. Connect to the unit theme, Animal and Plant Characteristics—Look at Us!

Introduce the Weekly Concept Tell children that today, they will talk about where bears hibernate. Let children know that hibernating is sleeping for a long time. Bears hibernate all winter. Ask the weekly question: Where does a bear hibernate?

Use the Poster Direct children's attention to the weekly poster. Use the Day 1 teaching notes at the bottom of the poster.

Sing the Song Use the song **Bear Is Sleeping** to reinforce children's understanding of the weekly concept. Have children sing or simply chant the words with you.

Bears Hibernate
. . . .
Vocabulary

bear

snores

Where does a bear hibernate?

64

Vocabulary

bear a large, strong animal with thick fur

snores makes a loud noise while sleeping

 ELA LS. 2.1 Describe people, places, things (e.g., size, color, shape), locations, and actions. (ELD LS.B3)

65

Introduce Concept Vocabulary

1. **Say the Word** Display the Word Card as you say *bear.* Have children repeat the word.

2. **Introduce Word Meaning** Ask questions about bears. Have you ever seen a bear? Are they big or small? What color are they?

3. **Demonstrate** Have children role play acting like a bear.

4. **Apply** Have children demonstrate their knowledge.

Repeat with other vocabulary words.

Corrective Feedback If children have difficulty pronouncing the words, separate the phonemes. Combine them to form the words.

Concept Talk

Let children know that the illustrations are in sequence, or in order. First, the bear eats a lot to get ready to sleep. Then the bear makes a comfortable bed. Finally, the bear can go to sleep. Ask children to point to what the bear does first. Ask children to point to what the bear does last. Children can color the pictures. They can use their colored pictures to narrate what the bear does first, second, and last.

 Leveled Support **Vocabulary in Context**

① **Beginning** Point to the pictures for *bear* and *snores* on the Worktext page. Say the word for each picture as children point, and have them echo each word.

② ③ **Early Intermediate/Intermediate** Ask children to pantomime the words as you say them. Children can describe what classmates are doing as they pantomime.

④ ⑤ **Early Advanced/Advanced** Ask children to draw pictures of bears snoring in caves. Then ask them to use the vocabulary words to dictate or write labels for their pictures.

Wrap Up   DAY **1**

 Table Talk Where does a bear hibernate? Have children answer the question, using the vocabulary words.

Produce Language Play charades. Ask children to act like a bear snoring in a cave and say a sentence about what they are doing.

Today children should have:

☑ **Learned** and applied vocabulary related to bears and hibernation.

☑ **Spoken** complete sentences about bears and hibernation.

☑ **Recognized** concept vocabulary words.

 ELA LS 2.1 Describe people, places, things (e.g., size, color, shape), locations, and actions. (ELD LS.B3)

65

To discuss why bears hibernate in a covered place; to introduce category words for places animals live.

Concept Talk

Connect to Day 1 Where does a bear hibernate?

Introduce the Daily Question Why does a bear hibernate in a covered place? Have children answer orally.

Use the Poster Use the Day 2 teaching notes.

Introduce the Category Words

1. **Say the Word** Have children point to the den. Say the word and have children repeat.

2. **Introduce Word Meaning** Ask questions: Who lives in a den? Where would you find a den?

3. **Demonstrate** Have children role play an animal in a den by using stuffed animals in the classroom. What in the classroom looks like a den for an animal?

4. **Apply** Repeat with other vocabulary words and elicit that they all belong to the category "places animals live."

Have children point to items as you name them. Then have them draw a picture of an animal in its home.

Places Animals Live

Picture Dictionary

den

hive

hole

log

nest

tree

✏️ **Draw** Draw an animal home.

Leveled Support Category Words

Preteach / Reteach

① **Beginning** Have children point to each animal home on the Worktext page as you say it. Have children echo each word.

② ③ **Early Intermediate/Intermediate** Say the name of an animal home. Have children point to it. Then reverse the activity.

④ ⑤ **Early Advanced/Advanced** Have children talk in pairs. Have them discuss what animal lives in each animal home. They should use the names of the animal homes as they speak with partners.

Wrap Up | DAY 2

Daily Table Talk Have children pretend to be a bear in a cave. Then discuss why bears hibernate in a covered place.

Produce Language To build fluency, encourage children to label or write a sentence about their drawings. They can share their writing with partners.

Today children should have:

☑ **Learned** and applied vocabulary related to places animals live.

☑ **Spoken** complete sentences about why bears hibernate in a covered place.

ELA R1.17 Identify and sort common words in basic categories (e.g., colors, shapes, foods). (ELD R.B4)

Have you ever seen a real cave?

✏️ **Circle** Circle *We.*

We saw a bear in a cave.

✏️ **Circle** Circle *my.*

Bears are my favorite animal.

ELA R1.15 Read simple one-syllable and high-frequency words (i.e., sight words). (ELD R.B2)

67

To discuss if children have ever seen a real cave; to introduce the high frequency words *we* and *my*.

Concept Talk

Connect to Day 2 Why does a bear hibernate in a covered place?

Introduce the Daily Question Have you ever seen a real cave? Discuss children's ideas about caves.

Use the Poster Use the Day 3 teaching notes.

Review Concept Vocabulary Review the words introduced on Day 1.

Introduce the High Frequency Words

Introduce *we* and *my* by saying sentences, such as: We are in the classroom. This is my desk. Use gestures to indicate *we* and *my* as you say the words. Help children complete the Worktext page.

Corrective Feedback If children have difficulty finding the high-frequency words in the sentences, highlight each word in the direction line and have children look for it in the sentence.

Preteach LS Leveled Support High Frequency Words
Reteach

① **Beginning** Display the word *we.* Say the word and have children echo. Repeat with the word *my.* Show the meanings of the words with simple gestures, such as gathering a group around you as you say *we* and holding up something that belongs to you and saying *my pencil.*

② ③ **Early Intermediate/Intermediate** Have children write *we* and *my* on index cards. Have children listen as you say sentences. When they hear the words, they should raise their cards and say the words.

④ ⑤ **Early Advanced/Advanced** Provide cloze sentences that could be completed with *we* or *my.* Read the sentences and work with children to choose the correct high frequency words to place in the sentences.

Wrap Up **DAY 3**

Daily **Table Talk** Children can pretend to walk into a cave and talk about what they see.

Produce Language Have each child tell if they have ever seen a real cave. If they have, children should talk about what the cave was like.

Today children should have:

☑ **Learned** and applied the high frequency words *we* and *my.*

☑ **Spoken** complete sentences about real caves they may have seen.

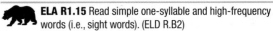 **ELA R1.15** Read simple one-syllable and high-frequency words (i.e., sight words). (ELD R.B2)

67

Concept Talk

 FORM & FUNCTION

Connect to Day 3 Have you ever seen a real cave?

Introduce the Daily Question When does a bear hibernate?

Use the Poster Use the Day 4 teaching notes.

Phonological Awareness

Identify Sound Cc Write the word *cat*. Say: Say this word with me: *cat*. What sound do you hear at the beginning of *cat?* What letter makes the /k/ sound in this word? Yes, *c* makes the /k/ sound in many words. Now listen for the /k/ sound in other words. Help children complete the Worktext page.

Corrective Feedback If children have difficulty identifying the initial sound /k/, say the word for each picture, separating the phonemes and emphasizing the initial phoneme in each word.

Identify Sound Cc

 Circle Circle things with *c*.

68 ELA R1.14 Match all consonant and short-vowel sounds to appropriate letters. (ELD R.B10)

Wrap Up DAY 4

Table Talk When does a bear hibernate? Have children discuss the question.

Produce Language Have each child say a sentence about when bears hibernate.

Today children should have:

☑ **Learned** and applied vocabulary related to when bears hibernate.

☑ **Spoken** complete sentences about when bears hibernate.

☑ **Recognized** words with the sound /k/.

 ELA R1.14 Match all consonant and short-vowel sounds to appropriate letters. (ELD R B10)

Preteach LS Reteach Leveled Support **Phonemic Awareness/Phonics**

① **Beginning** Hold up an alphabet card for *C*. Say: The name of this letter is *c*. One sound for this letter is /k/. Have children echo you.

② ③ **Early Intermediate/Intermediate** Tell children you will read several words and they should listen for /k/. When you say a word that begins with /k/, children should raise their hands and repeat the word. Say: The cat can jump. The cat can nap. The cat can eat cake.

④ ⑤ **Early Advanced/Advanced** Write the word *cat* and have children identify the first sound in the word. Ask children to name other words that begin with the /k/ sound spelled *c*.

Where does a bear hibernate?

Draw

ELA LS. 1.2 Share information and ideas, speaking audibly in complete, coherent sentences. (ELD LS.B1)

69

To guide children to express their understanding of weekly concepts and vocabulary.

Think, Talk, and Recognize!

Concept Talk

Connect to Day 4 When does a bear hibernate? Model how to answer yesterday's question with a sentence.

Review the Weekly Question Ask: Where does a bear hibernate? Have children describe where bears hibernate.

Use the Poster Use the Day 5 teaching notes.

Review Concept Vocabulary Review the vocabulary introduced on Day 1.

Concept Wrap Up

Have children draw to answer the question: Where does a bear hibernate? They can talk about their pictures as they share them with friends.

Preteach LS Reteach Leveled Support Concept Vocabulary

① **Beginning** Display the Word Cards for *bear* and *snores*. Say each word. Ask children to repeat and point to the matching card.

② ③ **Early Intermediate/Intermediate** Display the Word Cards for *bear* and *snores*. Ask children to say each word and point to the matching card.

④ ⑤ **Early Advanced/Advanced** Give children index cards with the vocabulary words on them. Have them create a story using the words. As they tell their stories, they can hold up the cards to show the words.

Wrap Up   **DAY 5**

Daily Table Talk Where does a bear hibernate? Have children discuss the question, using the vocabulary words they have learned this week.

Produce Language To build fluency, children can label, write about, or speak about their drawings. Ask children to respond to what they read or heard.

Today, children should have:

☑ **Reviewed** the weekly concept and concept vocabulary.

☑ **Spoken** about where bears hibernate.

☑ **Drawn or written** to show where bears hibernate.

 ELA LS 1.2 Share information and ideas, speaking audibly in complete, coherent sentences. (ELD LS.B3)

WEEK 5

CALIFORNIA

Weekly Lesson Plan

Last Week
Unit 2, Week 4
Bears Hibernate

Question of the Week What kind of home does an animal need?

Instructional Plan and Materials

- **Word Cards** 38–41

- **Big Book** The Rain Forest

- **Poster** Poster 11 can be used at beginning or end of day.

- **Song Book**, p. 11

Transparencies Explore content and vocabulary and model fluent reading.

For further information about using these components, see pages x–xv.

CALIFORNIA Standards

G1 Sci 2.a Students know different plants and animals inhabit different kinds of environments.

GK Sci 4.c Describe the relative position of objects by using one reference (e.g., above or below).

GK His-Soc Sci K.4.1 Determine the relative locations of objects using the terms near/far, left/right, and behind/in front.

Academic Language

DAY 1 — Get Ready to Read

Build Background

Preteach/Review 10–15 min
Poster, Song Book, Big Book
- **Leveled Support Preteach**
- **Practice Stations Preteach**

Teach 35–45 min
- **Concept Talk**
- **Oral Vocabulary Routine**
  Word Cards
- **Build Concept Vocabulary**
- **Daily Table Talk**

Check/Reteach 5–10 min
Poster, Word Cards
- **Leveled Support Reteach**

ELA LS 2.1 Describe people, places, things (e.g., size, color, shape), locations, and actions.

Vocabulary: cave, winter

Concept Talk Video

DAY 2 — Read and Comprehend

Language: Category Words

Preteach/Review 10–15 min
Poster
- **Leveled Support Preteach**
- **Practice Stations Review**

Teach 35–45 min
- **Category Words**
- **Daily Table Talk**

Check/Reteach 5–10 min
Poster, Word Cards
- **Leveled Support Reteach**

Fluency: Writing or Speaking

ELA R 1.17 Identify and sort common words in basic categories (e.g., colors, shapes, foods).

Category Words: top, over, bottom, under

Background Building Audio Slideshow

Online! www.pearsonsuccessnet.com

This Week
Unit 2, Week 5

Animal Homes

Next Week
Unit 2, Week 6
Animals Move

DAY 3 Read and Comprehend	**DAY 4** Language Arts	**DAY 5** Language Arts
Language: High Frequency Words	**Phonics**	**Think, Talk, and Recognize**
Preteach/Review 10–15 min Poster **Leveled Support Preteach** **Practice Stations Review**	**Preteach/Review** 10–15 min Poster **Leveled Support Preteach** **Practice Stations Review**	**Preteach/Review** 10–15 min Poster **Leveled Support Preteach** **Practice Stations Review**
Teach 35–45 min **High Frequency Words** **Daily Table Talk**	**Teach** 35–45 min **Phonics** **Daily Table Talk**	**Teach** 15–20 min **Think, Talk, and Recognize** **Concept Wrap Up**
Check/Reteach 5–10 min Poster, Word Cards **Leveled Support Reteach**	**Check/Reteach** 5–10 min Poster, Word Cards **Leveled Support Reteach**	**Check/Reteach** 30–40 min Poster, Word Cards, Song Book **Leveled Support Reteach**
		Fluency: Writing or Speaking
ELA R 1.15 Read simple one-syllable and high frequency words (i.e., sight words).	**ELA R 1.14** Match all consonant and short-vowel sounds to appropriate letters.	**ELA LS 1.2** Share information and ideas, speaking audibly in complete, coherent sentences.
High Frequency Words: he, for		

Practice Stations

Materials and Activity

crayons, colored pencils, paper

Animals In Their Homes 🏃

Have children draw pictures of animals in their homes. Children can include pets or other animals they are familiar with.

plain paper, pencils, crayons, markers, vocabulary word list

Illustrate a Word 🏃

Have children choose one vocabulary word to illustrate. Children should write a label for their drawings that include the vocabulary word.

Preteach/Reteach

Transfer and Common Misconceptions

The Letters *rr*

Speakers of Spanish may roll their *r*'s when reading two *r*'s together. In Spanish, *rr* is a separate letter and is pronounced differently than one *r*.

The Word *bottom*

This word may confuse children as the two *o*'s in the word are pronounced differently. The second syllable in the word is unstressed and the *o* does not make the /o/ sound.

Produce Language

Weekly Concept and Language Goal

CONCEPT GOALS

- recognize that wild animals need places to live
- understand why animals may need different homes in the winter
- describe the characteristics of good homes for animals

By Day 5, children should be able to gesture to an item in the drawing and talk about it.

Daily Table Talk

❶ **Beginning**
> Children pantomime while you provide the language.

❷ ❸ **Early Intermediate/Intermediate**
> Children pantomime and say a word or phrase.

❹ ❺ **Early Advanced/Advanced**
> Children say a sentence whhile pantomiming.

Daily Table Talk

❶ **Beginning**
> Children talk about their drawings.

❷ ❸ **Early Intermediate/Intermediate**
> Children write one-word labels.

❹ ❺ **Early Advanced/Advanced**
> Children write a phrase or sentence.

DAY 3 **FORM & FUNCTION** Read and Comprehend

 DAY 4 **FORM & FUNCTION** Language Arts

 DAY 5 Language Arts

index cards with these words written on them: *top, bottom, over, under*; two simple classroom objects

children's magazine, highlighter pens

picture cards for various words, especially words beginning with /i/

Where Does It Go?

Mix up all index cards into one pile. A child chooses a card and reads it aloud. Then the child uses the two objects to demonstrate the word. For example, the child can place one object over another object. Children take turns until every child has a chance to demonstrate each word.

Find the Words

Give children an article from a children's magazine and looks for the high frequency words (*he* and *for*). Have children locate and highlight these words in the article.

Interesting /i/ Words

A child chooses a card from the pile. The child says the word aloud. If the word begins with /i/, the child places it one pile. If the word does not begin with /i/, the card goes in another pile. Continue until all cards have been used.

The Word *for*

Children may have difficulty pronouncing this word, although there is an approximate *r*-controlled *or* sound in Spanish.

Sound /i/

Children may have trouble producing the sound /i/, though there is an approximate /i/ sound in Spanish.

Adjectives

Speakers of Spanish may place adjectives after the noun when describing animal homes. In Spanish, adjectives usually follow nouns, while in English, it is the reverse.

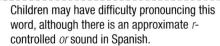 **Daily Table Talk**

❶ **Beginning** Give different reasons that animals might need homes in the winter and have children answer yes or no.

❷ ❸ **Early Intermediate/Intermediate**
Phrase: because it is cold

❹ ❺ **Early Advanced/Advanced**
Sentence: Animals need homes in the winter because it is cold.

 Daily Table Talk

❶ **Beginning** Children raise their hands as you provide sample answers, such as cave, grocery store, nest.

❷ ❸ **Early Intermediate/Intermediate**
One or two words: cave, a nest

❹ ❺ **Early Advanced/Advanced**
Sentence: A cave makes a good home for an animal.

 **Daily Table Talk**

❶ **Beginning** Child draws with support.

❷ ❸ **Early Intermediate/Intermediate** Child draws and speaks about the drawing using at least one concept vocabulary word

❹ ❺ **Early Advanced/Advanced** Child draws and provides a label for the drawing.

To introduce and discuss concepts and vocabulary related to animals' homes.

Build Background Get **Ready** to **Read!**

Question of the Week What kind of home does an animal need?
www.pearsonsuccessnet.com

Concept Talk

Use the Big Book If you haven't introduced the Big Book, consider reading it to children. Connect to the unit theme, Animal and Plant Characteristics —Look at Us!

Introduce the Weekly Concept Tell children that today, they will talk about the kinds of homes animals need. Ask the weekly question: What kind of home does an animal need?

Use the Poster Direct children's attention to the weekly poster. Use the Day 1 teaching notes at the bottom of the poster.

Sing the Song Use the song **Good Homes** to reinforce children's understanding of the weekly concept. Have children sing or simply chant the words with you.

Use a Transparency Use the Shared Description Map (Transparency 8) to help children compare and contrast animals' homes.

Animal Homes

Vocabulary

bed

burrow

cave

winter

70

What kind of home does an animal need?

Vocabulary

* **Academic Vocabulary**
  bed a piece of furniture for sleeping on

  burrow a hole or passage an animal makes in the ground

* **cave** a large natural hole in the side of a cliff or under the ground

* **winter** the season between fall and spring, when the weather is coldest

 ELA LS 2.1 Describe people, places, things (e.g., size, color, shape), locations, and actions. (ELD LS.B3)

71

Introduce Concept Vocabulary

1. **Say the Word** Display the Word Card as you say *bed*. Have children repeat the word.

2. **Introduce Word Meaning** Ask children where they sleep. Tell children that animals have different beds than people, but some animals have special beds. Pets may have pet beds. Wild animals have different kinds of homes. Ask questions about beds. What does your bed look like?

3. **Demonstrate** Have children role play getting into a bed and going to sleep.

4. **Apply** Have children demonstrate their understanding.

Repeat with other vocabulary words.

Corrective Feedback If children have difficulty with the words, show photographs of the various animal homes, labeling the photos for children to help them learn the words.

Concept Work

Tell children that animals need homes to be safe. They have different kinds of homes. Some have burrows, some live in trees, some live in nests, and so on. Point out the different homes in the illustrations. A fox can live in a cave. A badger can live in a burrow. A mouse can curl up and make its bed in leaves or twigs. **Have children circle the animal homes. Then they can color the pictures.**

 Leveled Support **Vocabulary in Context**

① **Beginning** Point to the pictures for *bed, burrow, cave,* and *winter* on the Worktext page. Say the word for each picture as children point and have them echo each word.

② ③ **Early Intermediate/Intermediate** Ask questions to elicit yes/no responses, such as: Does an elephant live in a burrow? Could a dog live in a cave? Children can nod their heads to respond.

④ ⑤ **Early Advanced/Advanced** Have children draw a picture of an animal home in the winter. Then ask them to dictate or write a label for their pictures.

Wrap Up **DAY** 1

Table Talk What kind of home does an animal need? Have children answer the question, using the vocabulary words.

Produce Language Play charades. Ask each child to act like an animal curled up in its home and say a sentence about an animal home.

Today children should have:

☑ **Learned** and applied vocabulary related to animal homes.

☑ **Spoken** complete sentences about animal homes.

☑ **Recognized** concept vocabulary words.

 ELA LS 2.1 Describe people, places, things (e.g., size, color, shape), locations, and actions. (ELD LS.B3)

To discuss what kind of home a dormouse needs for winter; to introduce category words for position words.

Concept Talk

Connect to Day 1 What kind of home does an animal need?

Introduce the Daily Question What kind of home does a dormouse need for winter? Discuss with children why an animal might need different homes in the summer and winter. Have children answer orally.

Use the Poster Use the Day 2 teaching notes.

Introduce Category Words

1. **Say the Word** Have children point to the top of the tree. Say the word and have children repeat.

2. **Introduce Word Meaning** Point to the top of an object in class. Then relate to the photograph. Ask: Where is the top of the tree?

3. **Demonstrate** Have children point to the top of various objects.

4. **Apply** Repeat with other vocabulary words and elicit that they all belong to the category "position words." Point out that position words tell us where things are.

Help children complete the activity on the Worktext page.

Corrective Feedback If children have difficulty understanding position words, use various classroom objects to demonstrate *top, bottom, over,* and *under.* As you demonstrate, say the position word and have children repeat.

Wrap Up   DAY 2

Table Talk *Daily* Have children pretend to be a dormouse in its home. Then discuss the kind of home a dormouse needs for winter.

Produce Language To build fluency, encourage children to label or write a sentence about the illustrations in the Worktext. They can share their writing with partners.

Today children should have:

☑ **Learned** and applied vocabulary related to position words.

☑ **Spoken** complete sentences about the kind of home a dormouse needs for winter.

☑ **Recognized** words that belong in the same category.

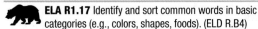 **ELA R1.17** Identify and sort common words in basic categories (e.g., colors, shapes, foods). (ELD R.B4)

72 Animal Homes • Unit 2, Week 5

Words that Tell Where

Picture Dictionary

 top ➡

over ⬇

bottom ➡

under ⬆

✏ **Circle** Circle the top of the cave.

✏ **Circle** Circle the thing over the log.

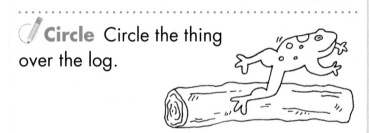

72 🐻 **ELA R1.17** Identify and sort common words in basic categories (e.g., colors, shapes, foods). (ELD R.B4)

Preteach LS Reteach **Leveled Support** **Category Words**

❶ **Beginning** Have children point to each position word on the Worktext page as you say it. Have children echo the words.

❷ ❸ **Early Intermediate/Intermediate** Hold objects or point to objects in various positions in the classroom. Ask: Is this on the top? Is this over or under? Children can respond with gestures, such as nods or "thumbs up."

❹ ❺ **Early Advanced/Advanced** Hold up an object. Have children point to the top and bottom of the object. Then have them place another object over and under the object. As they place the objects, they should describe what they are doing.

Why do animals need homes for winter?

✏️ **Circle** Circle *He.*

He saw a dormouse sleeping.

✏️ **Circle** Circle *for.*

Chipmunks build homes for winter.

🐻 **ELA R1.15** Read simple one-syllable and high-frequency words (i.e., sight words). (ELD R.B2)

73

OBJECTIVE

To discuss why animals need homes for winter; to introduce the high frequency words *he* and *for.*

Concept Talk 🌐 FORM & FUNCTION

Connect to Day 2 What kind of home does a dormouse need for winter?

Introduce the Daily Question Why do animals need homes for winter? Discuss with children. Remind them that in some places in the world, it is very cold in the winter.

Use the Poster Use the Day 3 teaching notes.

Review Concept Vocabulary Review the words introduced on Day 1.

Introduce High Frequency Words

Introduce *he* and *for* by using gestures while saying sentences such as: *He* is [child's name]. This is *for* you. Help children complete the Worktext page.

Corrective Feedback If children have difficulty circling the high frequency words, read the sentences aloud, giving special emphasis to the high frequency words as you read.

LS Leveled Support   High Frequency Words

① **Beginning** Write the words *he* and *for.* Read the words and have children repeat after you. Say sentences containing the words aloud, and ask children to raise their hands when they hear the high frequency words.

②③ **Early Intermediate/Intermediate** Write the high frequency words on index cards, one word on each side of the card. Give the cards to children. Say sentences aloud, and have children hold up the correct side of the card when they hear the high frequency word.

④⑤ **Early Advanced/Advanced** Write the words *he* and *for.* Have the children say sentences using these words. Write their sentences. Have children circle the words *he* and *for* in each of their sentences.

Wrap Up   DAY

Table Talk *Daily* Have children talk about what happens in the winter and why animals would need homes.

Produce Language Have each child say a sentence about why animals need homes for winter.

Today children should have:

☑ **Learned** and applied the high frequency words *he* and *for.*

☑ **Spoken** complete sentences about why animals need homes for winter.

🐻 **ELA R1.15** Read simple one-syllable and high-frequency words (i.e., sight words). (ELD R.B2)

73

OBJECTIVE

To discuss what makes a good home for an animal; to identify the sound /i/.

Concept Talk

FORM & FUNCTION

Connect to Day 3 Why do animals need homes for winter?

Introduce the Daily Question Ask: What makes a good home for an animal? Discuss, reminding children of some of the homes they talked about on Day 1.

Use the Poster Use the Day 4 teaching notes.

Phonics

Identify Sound /i/ Have children point to each picture as you name it. Say: Now I'm going to read the words again. Listen for the sound /i/ at the beginning of the word. Which word begins with /i/, *igloo* or *tree?* Continue with remaining pairs of words: *cow, iguana; insect, mouse.*

Corrective Feedback If children have difficulty completing the Worktext page, say the word for each picture slowly, emphasizing the initial sound in each.

Wrap Up   DAY 4

Daily Table Talk What makes a good home for an animal? Have children discuss the question.

Produce Language Have each child say a sentence about what makes a good home for an animal.

Today children should have:

☑ **Learned** and applied vocabulary related to what makes a good home for an animal.

☑ **Spoken** complete sentences about what makes a good home for an animal.

☑ **Recognized** words with sound /i/.

ELA R1.14 Match all consonant and short-vowel sounds to appropriate letters. (ELD R.B10)

Sound Ii

✏ **Circle** Circle things with *i.*

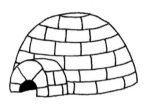

Preteach LS Reteach **Leveled Support** **Phonemic Awareness/Phonics**

❶ **Beginning** Hold up an index card on which you have printed *i*. Say: This letter is *i*. One sound for this letter is /i/. Have children echo you.

❷ ❸ **Early Intermediate/Intermediate** Tell children you will read several words and they should listen for /i/. When you say a word that begins with /i/, children should clap and repeat the word. Say: itch, house, ant, inchworm, igloo, apple.

❹ ❺ **Early Advanced/Advanced** Have children name other words that begin with /i/. Partners can work together to draw pictures and label some of the items.

What kind of home does an animal need?

 Draw

ELA LS. 1.2 Share information and ideas, speaking audibly in complete, coherent sentences. (ELD LS.B1)

75

To guide children to express their understanding of weekly concepts and vocabulary.

Think, Talk, and Recognize!

Concept Talk

Connect to Day 4 What makes a good home for an animal? Model how to answer yesterday's question with a sentence.

Review the Weekly Question Ask: What kind of home does an animal need? Have children talk about the different animal homes that they have learned about.

Use the Poster Use the Day 5 teaching notes.

Review Concept Vocabulary Review the vocabulary introduced on Day 1.

Concept Wrap Up

Have children draw to answer the question: What kind of home does an animal need? They can talk about their pictures as they share them with friends.

Leveled Support Concept Vocabulary

Preteach LS Reteach

① **Beginning** Display the Word Cards for *bed, burrow, cave,* and *winter.* Say each word. Ask children to repeat and point to the matching card.

② ③ **Early Intermediate/Intermediate** Ask questions about the words, such as: Which word is a hole in the side of a hill? Children can point to the Word Card that answers the question.

④ ⑤ **Early Advanced/Advanced** Pair children and give each pair a Word Card. Have partners work together to create a sentence that tells more about the word.

Wrap Up DAY 5

Daily **Table Talk** What kind of home does an animal need? Have children discuss the question, using the vocabulary words they have learned this week.

Produce Language To build fluency, children can label, write about, or speak about their drawings. Ask children to respond to what they read or heard.

Today, children should have:

☑ **Reviewed** the weekly concept and concept vocabulary.

☑ **Spoken** about animals' homes.

☑ **Drawn or written** to show what kinds of homes animals need.

 ELA LS 1.2 Share information and ideas, speaking audibly in complete, coherent sentences. (ELD LS.B3)

75

Question of the Week How do animals move?

	DAY **1** Get Ready to Read	DAY **2** Read and Comprehend

Instructional Plan and Materials

- **Word Cards**
  42–43

- **Big Book**
  The Rain Forest

- **Poster**
  Poster 12 can be used at beginning or end of day.

- **Song Book**, p. 12

Transparencies Explore content and vocabulary and model fluent reading.

For further information about using these components, see pages x–xv.

DAY 1 — Build Background

Preteach/Review 10–15 min
Poster, Song Book, Big Book
- **Leveled Support Preteach**
- **Practice Stations Preteach**

Teach 35–45 min
- **Concept Talk**
- **Oral Vocabulary Routine**
  Word Cards
- **Build Concept Vocabulary**
- **Daily Table Talk**

Check/Reteach 5–10 min
Poster, Word Cards
- **Leveled Support Reteach**

DAY 2 — Language: Category Words

Preteach/Review 10–15 min
Poster
- **Leveled Support Preteach**
- **Practice Stations Review**

Teach 35–45 min
- **Category Words**
- **Daily Table Talk**

Check/Reteach 5–10 min
Poster, Word Cards
- **Leveled Support Reteach**

Fluency: Writing or Speaking

	ELA LS 2.1 Describe people, places, things (e.g., size, color, shape), locations, and actions.	ELA R 1.17 Identify and sort common words in basic categories (e.g., colors, shapes, foods).

CALIFORNIA Standards

G1 Sci 2.a Students know different plants and animals inhabit different kinds of environments and have external features that help them thrive in different kinds of places.

GK Sci 2.a Students know how to observe and describe similarities and differences in the appearance and behavior of plants and animals (e.g., seed-bearing plants, birds, fish, insects).

Academic Language

		Category Words: climb, hop, jump, run, skip, walk
Get Online! www.pearsonsuccessnet.com	**Concept Talk Video**	**Background Building Audio Slideshow**

This Week
Unit 2, Week 6

Animals Move

Next Week
Unit 3, Week 1
Moving Away

FORM & FUNCTION

DAY 3 Read and Comprehend	**DAY 4** Language Arts	**DAY 5** Language Arts
Language: High Frequency Words	**Phonics**	**Think, Talk, and Recognize**
Preteach/Review 10–15 min Poster **Leveled Support Preteach** **Practice Stations Review**	**Preteach/Review** 10–15 min Poster **Leveled Support Preteach** **Practice Stations Review**	**Preteach/Review** 10–15 min Poster **Leveled Support Preteach** **Practice Stations Review**
Teach 35–45 min **High Frequency Words** **Daily Table Talk**	**Teach** 35–45 min **Phonics** **Daily Table Talk**	**Teach** 15–20 min **Think, Talk, and Recognize** **Concept Wrap Up**
Check/Reteach 5–10 min Poster, Word Cards **Leveled Support Reteach**	**Check/Reteach** 5–10 min Poster, Word Cards **Leveled Support Reteach**	**Check/Reteach** 30–40 min Poster, Word Cards, Song Book **Leveled Support Reteach**
		Fluency: Writing or Speaking
ELA R 1.15 Read simple one-syllable and high frequency words (i.e., sight words).	**ELA R 1.14** Match all consonant and short-vowel sounds to appropriate letters.	**ELA LS 1.2** Share information and ideas, speaking audibly in complete, coherent sentences.
High Frequency Words: he, for		

Practice Stations

Materials and Activity

DAY **1** Get Ready to Read

booklets made of construction paper folded and stapled in the center; animal magazine pictures of various animals moving (running, leaping, swimming, etc.); crayons; colored pencils; scissors; glue

Animals Move Booklet 👥

Give each pair a booklet. Have children find pictures of different animals moving and paste them in the booklets. Have children describe to their partner what each animal is doing in the pictures.

DAY **2** Read and Comprehend

picture cards for *swim, swing;* drawing paper; crayons; colored markers

Swim and Swing 👥

Have partners look at each picture, say the word, and describe what they see. Have partners work together to draw a picture of themselves either swimming or swinging.

Preteach/Reteach

Transfer and Common Misconceptions

The *sw* Blend

Some children may find this sound difficult to pronounce. Spanish does not have *s* blends, so pronouncing *sw* can be challenging.

Silent *b*

Children may pronounce the *b* in *climb.* However, Spanish does have some silent letters, such as *h.* This can be pointed out to help children understand silent letters in English.

Produce Language

Weekly Concept and Language Goal

CONCEPT GOALS

• recognize that animals have different ways of moving
• describe animals that use their tails for moving
• name animals that move by digging and climbing

By Day 5, children should be able to gesture to an item in the drawing and talk about it.

Daily Table Talk

❶ Beginning
> Children pantomime while you provide the language.

❷ ❸ Early Intermediate/Intermediate
> Children pantomime and say a word or phrase.

❹ ❺ Early Advanced/Advanced
> Children say a sentence while pantomiming.

Daily Table Talk

❶ Beginning
> Children talk about their drawings.

❷ ❸ Early Intermediate/Intermediate
> Children write one-word labels.

❹ ❺ Early Advanced/Advanced
> Children write a phrase or sentence.

DAY 3 **FORM & FUNCTION**
Read and Comprehend

index cards with these words written on them: *run, walk, skip, swim, hop, jump, climb*

How Can I Move?

Mix up all index cards into one pile. One partner chooses a card. The child silently reads the card. Then he or she demonstrates the action on the card while the other child guesses what the card says. After the first partner demonstrates all the cards, children should switch roles and repeat.

skip

The Word *he*

Children may have difficulty pronouncing this as the *e* can stand for a short *a* sound in some languages.

Daily **Table Talk**

① **Beginning**

Name an animal and have children answer yes or no.

② ③ **Early Intermediate/Intermediate**

One or two-words: a fox, meerkat

④ ⑤ **Early Advanced/Advanced**

Sentence: A fox digs.

DAY 4 **FORM & FUNCTION**
Language Arts

index cards with *he* and *for* written on them, large index cards, pencils, colored marker

Letter Jigsaw Puzzles

Have partners copy each high-frequency word from the Word Cards onto index cards in pencil. Then have children trace over the letters in colored markers. Next have children cut the words on the cards into letters. Then have them mix up the letters. Partners should put the letters together to spell each word correctly.

Picture Cards

Some picture cards may not be familiar to children. Be sure to review all the picture words used in an activity before beginning the activity to give all students an opportunity to review the picture names.

Daily **Table Talk**

① **Beginning**

Children raise their hands as you provide sample answers, such as bear, catfish, dolphin.

② ③ **Early Intermediate/Intermediate**

One or two words: cats, a bear

④ ⑤ **Early Advanced/Advanced**

Sentence: Cats can climb.

DAY 5
Language Arts

picture cards for various three letter words with and without the middle /i/ sound, a small bin

Words in the Bin ⊛ ⊛⊛

A child chooses a card from the pile. The child says the word aloud. If the word has a the sound /i/ in the middle, the child puts the word in the bin. Words that have a different middle sound are placed in a pile outside the bin. Children take turns until all the cards have been sorted.

The Verbs *have* and *be*

Spanish and English have different uses for the words *have* and *be*. Children might use these words incorrectly in English. For example, they may say, *I have hungry.*

Daily **Table Talk**

① **Beginning** Child draws with support.

② ③ **Early Intermediate/Intermediate** Child draws and speaks about the drawing using at least one concept vocabulary word.

④ ⑤ **Early Advanced/Advanced** Child draws and provides a label for the drawing.

OBJECTIVE

To introduce and discuss how animals move and related concept vocabulary

Build Background **Get Ready to Read!**

Question of the Week How do animals move?

www.pearsonsuccessnet.com

Concept Talk

Use the Big Book If you haven't introduced the Big Book, consider reading it to children. Connect to the unit theme, Animal and Plant Characteristics—Look at Us!

Introduce the Weekly Concept Tell children that today, they will talk about how animals move. Ask the weekly question: How do animals move?

Use the Poster Direct children's attention to the weekly poster. Use the Day 1 teaching notes at the bottom of the poster.

Sing the Song Use the song **Animals Move** to reinforce children's understanding of the weekly concept. Have children sing or simply chant the words with you.

Use a Transparency Use the Classification Map (Transparency 3) to help children classify the ways in which various animals move.

Animals Move

Vocabulary

swim

swing

How do animals move?

76

Vocabulary

swim to move through the water, using your arms and legs

swing to move from side to side or backward and forward from a fixed place

ELA LS 2.1 Describe people, places, things (e.g., size, color, shape), locations, and actions. (ELD LS.B3)

77

Introduce Concept Vocabulary

1. Say the Word Display the Word Card as you say *swim*. Have children repeat the word.

2. Introduce Word Meaning Ask questions about swimming: Do you like to swim? Where do you go swimming?

3. Demonstrate Have children role play swimming.

4. Apply Have children demonstrate their understanding.

Repeat with other vocabulary words.

Corrective Feedback If children have difficulty understanding the vocabulary words, demonstrate each action for children as you say the word.

Concept Work

Ask children to look at the illustrations. Talk about how each animal moves. Ask children to point to the animal that swings and point to the animals that swim. Then ask children how the horse moves. Children can choose one way animals move and color the picture. Have them describe the animal's movement to partners.

Preteach LS Reteach **Leveled Support** **Vocabulary in Context**

❶ **Beginning** Point to the picture for *swim* and *swing* on the Worktext page. Say the word for each picture as children point and have them echo each word.

❷ ❸ **Early Intermediate/Intermediate** Show a picture of an animal and ask: Does this animal swim? Children can nod yes or no to respond. Repeat with other animals and with animals that swing rather than swim.

❹ ❺ **Early Advanced/Advanced** Have children draw a picture for each word and label the pictures "swim" and "swing." They can describe their work to partners.

Wrap Up   DAY

Daily **Table Talk** How do animals move? Have children answer the question, using the vocabulary words.

Produce Language Play charades. Ask each child to act like an animal that swims or swings. Then they tell a sentence about their animals.

Today children should have:

☑ **Learned** and applied vocabulary related to how animals move.

☑ **Spoken** complete sentences about how animals move.

☑ **Recognized** concept vocabulary words.

 ELA LS 2.1 Describe people, places, things (e.g., size, color, shape), locations, and actions. (ELD LS.B3)

OBJECTIVE

To discuss which animals use their tails for moving; to introduce category words for ways to move.

Concept Talk

Connect to Day 1 How do animals move?

Introduce the Daily Question Which animals use their tails for moving? Have children answer orally.

Use the Poster Use the Day 2 teaching notes.

Introduce Category Words

1. **Say the Word** Have children point to the child running. Say the word *run* and have children repeat.

2. **Introduce Word Meaning** Ask questions: Do you like to run? Can you run fast?

3. **Demonstrate** Role play running around the room. Children can follow your lead.

4. **Apply** Repeat with other vocabulary words and elicit that they all belong to the category "ways to move."

Have children point to items as you name them. Then have them draw a picture of themselves moving in one of the ways they learned about.

Corrective Feedback If children have difficulty identifying ways to move, demonstrate each action for children and say the word as you are demonstrating. Children should then do the action and say the word.

Ways to Move

Picture Dictionary

climb

hop

jump

run

skip

walk

✏ **Draw** Draw a way to move.

78 ELA R1.17 Identify and sort common words in basic categories (e.g., colors, shapes, foods). (ELD R.B4)

Leveled Support — Category Words

Preteach / Reteach

❶ **Beginning** Have children point to each action on the Worktext page as you say it. Have children echo the word.

❷ ❸ **Early Intermediate/Intermediate** Say the name of an action. Have children demonstrate the action.

❹ ❺ **Early Advanced/Advanced** Have children talk in pairs. Have one demonstrate a way to move and have the other child guess what they are doing. Have children switch roles and repeat the activity.

Wrap Up — DAY 2

Daily Table Talk Have children pretend to be a monkey swinging by its tail. Then discuss which animals use their tails for moving.

Produce Language To build fluency, encourage children to label or write a sentence about their drawings. They can share their writing with partners.

Today children should have:

☑ **Learned** and applied vocabulary related to ways to move.

☑ **Spoken** complete sentences about which animals use their tails for moving.

☑ **Recognized** words that belong in the same category.

 ELA R1.17 Identify and sort common words in basic categories (e.g., colors, shapes, foods). (ELD R.B4)

What are some animals that dig?

✏️ **Circle** Circle *He.*

He saw a fox dig a hole.

✏️ **Circle** Circle *for.*

Meerkats dig for food.

🐻 **ELA R1.15** Read simple one-syllable and high-frequency words (i.e., sight words). (ELD R.B2)

79

To discuss animals that dig; to introduce the high frequency words *he* and *for*

Concept Talk

🔵 **FORM & FUNCTION**

Connect to Day 2 Which animals use their tails for moving?

Introduce the Daily Question What are some animals that dig? Discuss ideas children might remember from Week 2.

Use the Poster Use the Day 3 teaching notes.

Review Concept Vocabulary Review the words introduced on Day 1.

Introduce High Frequency Words

Introduce *he* and *for* by using gestures while saying sentences such as: *He is my friend. This is for [child's name].* Help children complete the Worktext page.

Corrective Feedback If children have difficulty circling the high frequency words, give them index cards with the words written on them so they can match the words to words in the sentences.

Preteach / Reteach **LS** **Leveled Support** **High Frequency Words**

❶ **Beginning** Write the word *he.* Say *This is the word he.* We use the word *he* to talk about a boy or a man. He is my brother. **Continue with** *for.*

❷ ❸ **Early Intermediate/Intermediate** Give children index cards with *he* on one side and *for* on the other. Say sentences with the words. When children hear the words, they should hold up their cards.

❹ ❺ **Early Advanced/Advanced** Have children find and circle the words *he* and *for* in newspapers.

Wrap Up **DAY**

Daily **Table Talk** Children can pretend to be an animal digging for food.

Produce Language Have each child say a sentence about animals that dig.

Today children should have:

☑ **Learned** and applied the high frequency words *he* and *for.*

☑ **Spoken** complete sentences about animals that dig.

☑ **Recognized** that some animals dig.

 ELA R1.15 Read simple one-syllable and high-frequency words (i.e., sight words). (ELD R.B2)

79

OBJECTIVE

To discuss animals that climb; to identify the sound /i/

Concept Talk

FORM& FUNCTION

Connect to Day 3 What are some animals that dig?

Introduce the Daily Question What kind of animals climb? Discuss with children.

Use the Poster Use the Day 4 teaching notes.

Phonics

Identify Sound /i/ Write the word *big*. Say: What sounds are in this word? /b/ /i/ /g/ Listen to the middle sound in the word: /biiiig/, big. What sound is the middle of the word? Tell children they are going to be listening for the sound /i/ in words. Help children complete Worktext page.

Corrective Feedback If children have difficulty completing the Worktext page, say the word for each picture very slowly, emphasizing both initial and medial sounds.

Identify Sound Ii

 Draw Color things with *i*.

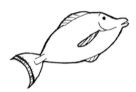

80 ELA R1.14 Match all consonant and short-vowel sounds to appropriate letters. (ELD R.B1)

Wrap Up   DAY 4

 Table Talk What kind of animals climb? Have children discuss the question.

Produce Language Have each child say a sentence about animals that climb.

Today children should have:

☑ **Learned** and applied vocabulary related to animals that climb.

☑ **Spoken** complete sentences about animals that climb.

☑ **Recognized** words with the sound /i/.

ELA R1 1.14 Match all consonant and short-vowel sounds to appropriate letters. (ELD R.B10)

Preteach Reteach Leveled Support **Phonics**

① ② **Beginning** Display a card on which you have written *i*. Say: This letter is *i*. One sound that it can make is /i/. Have children repeat after you: *i*, /i/.

③ **Early Intermediate/Intermediate** Say words that have the sound /i/ both in the initial and medial positions of the word. Have children raise their hands when they hear the sound. Have them repeat the words after you.

④ ⑤ **Early Advanced/Advanced** Have children think of words that have the /i/ sound at the beginning and in the middle. They can draw and label pictures of the words.

How do animals move?

✏️ **Draw**

OBJECTIVE

To guide children to express their understanding of weekly concepts and vocabulary.

Think, Talk, and Recognize!

Concept Talk

Connect to Day 4 What kind of animals climb? Model how to answer yesterday's question with a sentence.

Review the Weekly Question Ask: How do animals move? Have children talk about one way that animals move.

Use the Poster Use the Day 5 teaching notes.

Review Concept Vocabulary Review the vocabulary introduced on Day 1.

Concept Wrap Up

Have children draw to answer the question: How do animals move? Use the photograph to prompt discussion. This cheetah is running. The way its feet are moving show me that the animal runs very quickly. What other animals run?

 Leveled Support **Concept Vocabulary**

① **Beginning** Display the Word Cards for *swim* and *swing.* Say each word. Ask children to repeat and point to the matching card.

② ③ **Early Intermediate/Intermediate** Show children pictures of various animals. Have them classify the animals as animals that swim or animals that swing.

④ ⑤ **Early Advanced/Advanced** Display the Word Cards for *swim* and *swing.* Ask children to use each word in a sentence about an animal.

Wrap Up **DAY 5**

Table Talk How do animals move? Have children discuss the question, using the vocabulary words they have learned this week.

Produce Language Have children ask a partner the question, "How do animals move?" Have children answer in complete sentences.

Today, children should have:

☑ **Reviewed** the weekly concept and concept vocabulary.

☑ **Spoken** about how animals move.

☑ **Drawn or written** to show how animals move.

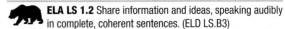 **ELA LS 1.2** Share information and ideas, speaking audibly in complete, coherent sentences. (ELD LS.B3)

81

How do changes affect us?

Discuss the Big Question

Read and discuss the unit question. Introduce the word *change*. When something changes, it becomes different from what it was before. A baby changes when it grows up. Many things change as we grow and learn. What is something that changed in your life during this school year?

Have children use the pictures along the side of the page to preview the weekly concepts for this unit. Read the weekly questions together. Discuss the weekly questions and how they relate to the big question.

Get Online! www.pearsonsuccessnet.com

• Unit 3 Big Question Video

CONCEPT/ LANGUAGE GOALS

Use the Concept and Language Goals throughout the unit to develop the big idea.

Children develop concepts and language as they talk about, use, and practice:

• Concept Vocabulary
• Academic Language
• Language Forms and Functions
• Category Words
• High Frequency Words

Get Online!
PearsonSuccessNet.com

Hear it!
See it!
Do it!

• Big Idea Video
• Concept Talk Video
• Background Building Audio Slideshow
• Comprehension Think Aloud Video
• eBooks

Changes–Changes All Around Us

How do changes affect us?

82

Unit 3

Moving Away
What happens when a friend moves away?

Getting Older
What new things can you do as you get older?

American Heroes
What can we learn from people in the past?

Friends Change
How do friendships change?

Things Change
How was the past different from today?

Feelings Change
How can we change the way we feel?

Changes—Changes All Around Us

83

Read Aloud

Read the **Big Book** *Life Long Ago.* Prompt discussion about the book.

- How have our clothes changed from what people wore in the past?
- What things did people make with their hands in the past? How do we make those things today?
- How have the ways people got from one place to another changed?

For more read alouds related to the theme, see the Big Book Anthology.

Unit Project: Changes

After discussing the unit question, provide children with paper and art supplies. Ask children to bring in or draw pictures of themselves as babies. This week we will each make a poster of how we have changed. You will draw or show a picture of yourself as a baby. Then you will draw or show a picture of yourself now.

Have children display their posters on a bulletin board titled, "We Have Changed!" Have children add to their posters pictures, drawings, or words describing things they have learned as they have grown. Encourage children to discuss and share their ideas.

Question of the Week
What happens when a friend moves away?

	DAY **1** Get Ready to Read	DAY **2** Read and Comprehend

Instructional Plan and Materials

• **Word Cards**
44–47

• **Big Book**
Life Long Ago

• **Poster**
Poster 13 can be used at beginning or end of day.

• **Song Book**, p. 13

Transparencies Explore content and vocabulary and model fluent reading.

For further information about using these components, see pages x–xv.

Build Background

Preteach/Review 10–15 min
Poster, Song Book, Big Book
Leveled Support Preteach
Practice Stations Preteach

Teach 35–45 min
Concept Talk
Oral Vocabulary Routine
Word Cards
Build Concept Vocabulary
Daily Table Talk

Check/Reteach 5–10 min
Poster, Word Cards
Leveled Support Reteach

Language: Category Words

Preteach/Review 10–15 min
Poster
Leveled Support Preteach
Practice Stations Review

Teach 35–45 min
Category Words
Daily Table Talk

Check/Reteach 5–10 min
Poster, Word Cards
Leveled Support Reteach

Fluency: Writing or Speaking

CALIFORNIA Standards

GK Sci 4.e Communicate observations orally and through drawings.

ELA LS 2.3 Relate an experience or creative story in a logical sequence.

ELA R 1.17 Identify and sort common words in basic categories (e.g., colors, shapes, foods).

Academic Language

Academic Words: word

Category Words: grandma, grandpa, father, mother, sister, brother

---

Get Online! www.pearsonsuccessnet.com

Concept Talk Video

Background Building Audio Slideshow

This Week
Unit 3, Week 1

Moving Away

Next Week
Unit 3, Week 2
Getting Older

FORM & FUNCTION

DAY 3 Read and Comprehend

DAY 4 Language Arts

DAY 5 Language Arts

Language: High Frequency Words	**Phonics**	**Think, Talk, and Recognize**
Preteach/Review 10–15 min	**Preteach/Review** 10–15 min	**Preteach/Review** 10–15 min
Poster	Poster	Poster
Leveled Support Preteach	**Leveled Support Preteach**	**Leveled Support Preteach**
Practice Stations Review	**Practice Stations Review**	**Practice Stations Review**
Teach 35–45 min	**Teach** 35–45 min	**Teach** 15–20 min
High Frequency Words	**Phonics**	**Think, Talk, and Recognize**
Daily Table Talk	**Daily Table Talk**	**Concept Wrap Up**
Check/Reteach 5–10 min	**Check/Reteach** 5–10 min	**Check/Reteach** 30–40 min
Poster, Word Cards	Poster, Word Cards	Poster, Word Cards, Song Book
Leveled Support Reteach	**Leveled Support Reteach**	**Leveled Support Reteach**
		Fluency: Writing or Speaking
ELA R 1.15 Read simple one-syllable and high frequency words (i.e., sight words).	ELA R 1.14 Match all consonant and short-vowel sounds to appropriate letters.	ELA LS 1.2 Share information and ideas, speaking audibly in complete, coherent sentences.
High Frequency Words: she, me, with		

Practice Stations

Materials and Activity

a cardboard box decorated as a mailbox, crayons, colored pencils, paper

Staying in Touch

Tell children to think of how they would feel if a friend moved away. Pair children. Tell children to draw pictures that they would mail to each other if they moved away. Have children copy their friends' names on the drawings. Have children place their drawings in the mail box. Deliver the mail to the children.

note cards with picture words for different toys, games, food, school supplies, people; index cards with color words; vocabulary word cards

Use the Word

Set the four vocabulary word cards across the table. Place the note cards in a pile in the center. One child chooses a card. That child decides if the picture card or word card shows something that you play with, something you can share, someone you can call, or a word. He places it under the correct vocabulary card and tells why he put it there. Play continues until all cards have been played.

Preteach/Reteach

Transfer and Common Misconceptions

Prepositions

Some children may have a hard time understanding the preposition *away* without an object of the preposition. Explain the meaning of the sentence *My friend moved away.* Explain that what is actually meant is *My friend moved away to a new house.*

/w/ in Words

Some children may have a difficult time with the word *word,* as *w* is not found by itself in Spanish.

Produce Language

Weekly Concept and Language Goal

CONCEPT GOALS

- understand the concept of moving from one place to another
- name things that would be important to bring during a move
- describe why moving might be a sad experience

By Day 5, children should be able to talk about their drawings and write a one-word label.

Daily Table Talk

❶ **Beginning**
> Children pantomime saying good-bye to a friend who is moving.

❷ ❸ **Early Intermediate/Intermediate**
> Children pantomime and say a word or phrase.

❹ ❺ **Early Advanced/Advanced**
> Children say a sentence while pantomiming.

Daily Table Talk

❶ **Beginning**
> Children talk about their drawings.

❷ ❸ **Early Intermediate/Intermediate**
> Children write one-word labels.

❹ ❺ **Early Advanced/Advanced**
> Children write a phrase or sentence.

DAY 3 Read and Comprehend

DAY 4 Language Arts

DAY 5 Language Arts

paper with outline of a house, paper, pencils, crayons, scissors, glue

one set of word cards with these words for each child: *me, with, she;* sentence strips with sentences like: *She plays with me. She is my friend. Mary shares with me. Do you like me? She ate with me.*

stack of index cards face down with these picture words: *boy, tub, bat, blue, brown, cub, crib, nut, sun, bun, nose, net, man, nine*

My Family 🚶

Have children cut out the outline of the house. Have children draw the members of their family. Have children cut them out and glue onto the house. Have them decorate the house as one of the rooms in their own home. Have children name each of the members of their family.

Find the Word 🚶🚶

Pile the sentence strips face down on the table. One child chooses a sentence strip. The child matches any of the high-frequency cards with those in the sentence. The partner checks if he is correct. If he is correct, he takes the sentence strip. If not, the strip is returned to the bottom of the pile. Continue until all sentence strips are gone.

> Do you like me?

Listen for the Sound 🚶 🚶🚶

A child chooses one card from the pile. The child tells if he or she hears the /b/ or /n/ sound in the word. Then the child tells if the sound is at the beginning or end of the word. The player keeps the card if correct. If not, he or she returns it to the bottom of the pile. Play continues until all of the cards are gone.

Family Members

Children may have a hard time understanding that family members do not necessarily have to live in the same house that they do. Explain the concepts of aunt, uncle, cousins, and other relatives to children.

Using the Words *Me* and *She*

Children may be confused when to use the word *me* and *she* when speaking. Model using *me* and *she* correctly in sentences.

Words with the Letter *b*

Children who speak Spanish, Japanese, or Korean may have problems pronouncing any of the words with the sound /b/ as they can easily be confused with the sounds of the letters *v* and *w*.

Daily Table Talk

① **Beginning**
> Children make a sad face when you name things they would be sad to leave.

② ③ **Early Intermediate/Intermediate**
> Phrase: *my friends, my school*

④ ⑤ **Early Advanced/Advanced**
> Sentence: *I would be sad to leave all of my friends.*

Daily Table Talk

① **Beginning**
> Children pantomime how they would keep in touch with a faraway friend.

② ③ **Early Intermediate/Intermediate**
> Phrase: *write a letter, call on phone*

④ ⑤ **Early Advanced/Advanced**
> Sentence: *I could write a letter to my friend.*

Daily Table Talk

① **Beginning** Child draws and speaks about the drawing.

② ③ **Early Intermediate/Intermediate** Child draws and speaks about the drawing using at least one concept vocabulary word.

④ ⑤ **Early Advanced/ Advanced** Child draws and provides a label for the drawing that includes a vocabulary word.

Build Background Get Ready to Read!

Question of the Week

What happens when a friend moves away?

www.pearsonsuccessnet.com

Concept Talk

Use the Big Book Connect the Big Book to the unit theme, Changes—Changes All Around Us. Display and discuss the cover. Then read the book aloud.

Introduce the Weekly Concept Tell children that today they will talk about how people feel when someone special moves away. Ask the weekly question: What happens when a friend moves away?

Use the Poster Direct children's attention to the weekly poster. Use the Day 1 teaching notes at the bottom of the poster.

Sing the Song Use the song **My Friend Has Gone** to reinforce children's understanding of the weekly concept. Have the children sing or simply chant the words with you.

Use a Transparency Use the Friendly Letter Transparency (Transparency 14) to model a friendly letter. Children can discuss what they would write to a friend or family member who moved away.

Moving Away

Vocabulary

called

play

shared

word

What happens when a friend moves away?

Vocabulary

* **Academic Vocabulary**

called telephoned someone

play to do things that you enjoy, especially to pretend or to use toys

shared had or used something with other people

* **word** a group of sounds or letters that have a particular meaning

ELA LS 2.3 Relate an experience or creative story in a logical sequence. (ELD LS.B3)

85

Introduce Concept Vocabulary

1. **Say the Word** Display the Word Card as you say *play.* Have children repeat the word.
2. **Introduce Word Meaning** Ask questions about play. *What do you like to play? Who do you like to play with?*
3. **Demonstrate** Have children role play how they would play with blocks: picking up the blocks, stacking them up one on top of another.
4. **Apply** Have children demonstrate their understanding.

Repeat with other vocabulary words.

Corrective Feedback If children have difficulty with the words, demonstrate their meanings with gestures that children can repeat.

Concept Work

Discuss the illustrations with children. Point out that they show a sequence, or order of events. In one illustration, the friends play together. In the next, one friend moves. In the last illustration, one friend calls another. Have children talk with partners about the illustrations. Then have children color the picture that shows someone moving away.

 Leveled Support **Vocabulary in Context**

❶ **Beginning** Have children point to the friends, the girl, the boy, the toys, the mother, the father, the boxes, and the phone in the pictures on the Student Worktext page. Say the word for each picture as children point and have them echo each word.

❷ ❸ **Early Intermediate/Intermediate** Do the Beginning activity, but have children say the words themselves, giving help only if needed.

❹ ❺ **Early Advanced/Advanced** Ask children to draw a picture of themselves and a friend playing. Then ask them to use a sentence to tell how they would feel if their friend moved away.

Wrap Up **DAY** 1

 Table Talk What happens when a friend moves away? Have children answer the question, using the vocabulary words.

Produce Language Have children role play. Have them pretend that one of them is moving away. Have them say good-bye to each other, with one child leaving. Have the children say a sentence that tells how they would feel if this happened.

Today children should have:

☑ **Learned** and applied vocabulary related to moving away.

☑ **Spoken** complete sentences about moving away.

☑ **Recognized** concept vocabulary words.

ELA LS 2.3 Relate an experience or creative story in a logical sequence. (ELD LS.B3)

To discuss what children would bring with them if they moved; to discuss members of families.

Concept Talk

Connect to Day 1 Recall with children that yesterday they talked about how they would feel when a friend moves away. What else makes you sad?

Introduce the Daily Question What would you bring with you if you moved? Have children answer orally.

Use the Poster Use the Day 2 teaching notes at the bottom of the poster.

Introduce Category Words

1. **Say the Word** Have children point to the mother. Say the word and have children repeat it.

2. **Introduce the Meaning** Ask questions: Is a mother a boy or a girl? How is she related to the children? How is she related to the grandma and grandpa?

3. **Demonstrate** Point to the father. Explain why he is a father and not a mother.

4. **Apply** Repeat with other vocabulary words and elicit that they all belong to the category "family members."

Have children point to items as you name them. Then have them draw members of their own families.

Wrap Up DAY 2

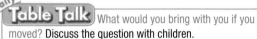 What would you bring with you if you moved? Discuss the question with children.

Produce Language To build fluency, encourage children to label or write a sentence about their drawings. They can share their writing with partners.

Today children should have:

☑ **Learned** and applied vocabulary related to family members.

☑ **Spoken** complete sentences about who they would bring with them if they moved.

☑ **Recognized** words that belong in the same category.

 ELA R1.17 Identify and sort common words in basic categories (e.g., colors, shapes, foods). (ELD R.B4)

Family Members

Picture Dictionary

grandpa   father

grandma →   ← mother

sister   brother

✏ **Draw** Draw your family.

86 🐻 **ELA R1.17** Identify and sort common words in basic categories (e.g., colors, shapes, foods). (ELD R.B4)

Leveled Support **Category Words**

❶ **Beginning** Have children point to each family member on the Worktext page. Say the word for each picture. Then have children repeat the word.

❷ ❸ **Early Intermediate/Intermediate** Say the name of a family member on the Worktext page. Have children point to the picture. Then reverse the activity as you point to a picture and ask children to name the family member.

❹ ❺ **Early Advanced/Advanced** Have children talk with partners. Have them tell each other the names of all of the people in their families. Have them tell what they like to do with their families.

What can be sad about moving?

✏ **Circle** Circle *She*. Circle *me*.

She told me goodbye.

✏ **Circle** Circle *with*.

I can not play with my friend.

ELA R1.15 Read simple one-syllable and high-frequency words (i.e., sight words). (ELD R.B2)   87

Leveled Support High Frequency Words

① **Beginning** Write the words *me*, *with*, and *she*. Read the words. Have the children repeat the words. Write sentences like: *She will eat with me. She will read with me.* Circle each of the high frequency words in the sentence.

② ③ **Early Intermediate/Intermediate** Do the beginning activity, but have the children circle the high frequency words themselves.

④ ⑤ **Early Advanced/Advanced** Write the words *me*, *with*, and *she*. Have the children say sentences using these words. Write their sentences. Have children circle the high frequency word in each of their sentences.

To discuss feeling sad about moving; to introduce the high-frequency words *me, with,* and *she;* to recognize the final /n/ and /b/; to blend onset and rime initial and final /b/ and /n/ words.

Concept Talk

Connect to Day 2 What else would you bring along if you moved?

Introduce the Daily Question Ask: What can be sad about moving?

Use the Poster Use the Day 3 teaching notes at the bottom of the poster.

Review Concept Vocabulary Review the words introduced on Day 1.

Introduce High Frequency Words

Introduce *me, with,* and *she* by role playing and speaking with sentences such as *Will you dance with me?* Help children complete the Worktext page.

Corrective Feedback If children have difficulty with high frequency words, write each on a sticky note. List the words on chart paper and have children match them.

Phonemic Awareness

Phoneme Isolation/Oral Blending Say *man* and *sun,* emphasizing ending sounds. Ask children to identify the letter sound they hear at the end of each word. Then do the same for *cab* and *tub.* Have them change /m/ in *man* to /p/, /s/ in *sun* to /b/, /k/ in *cab* to /t/, and /t/ in *tub* to /r/.

Wrap Up   DAY **3**

Table Talk

What are some things you would miss if you moved? Have children discuss the question.

Produce Language Have children draw pictures of things they would be sad to leave. They can describe their pictures.

Today children should have:

☑ **Learned** and applied the high frequency words *me, with,* and *she.*

☑ **Spoken** complete sentences about how they would feel if they moved.

☑ **Recognized** the ending sounds of *n* and *b.*

 ELA R.1.15 Read simple one-syllable and high-frequency words (i.e., sight words). (ELD R.B2)

OBJECTIVE
To discuss how we can stay in touch with faraway friends; to recognize the beginning and ending sounds of *n* /n/ and *b* /b/.

Concept Talk

 FORM & FUNCTION

Connect to Day 3 Elicit from children that yesterday they talked about what can be sad about moving.

Introduce the Daily Question Ask: How can we stay in touch with faraway friends? Ask children if they have ever received a letter or card from anyone who lives far away.

Use the Poster Use the Day 4 teaching notes at the bottom of the poster.

Phonics

Identify the Sounds /n/ and /b/ Introduce the sound /n/. Read each picture word and have children repeat the words. Have them complete the exercise on the Worktext page. Do the same for the sound /b/.

Corrective Feedback For children having difficulty recognizing the /n/ and /b/ sounds in the Worktext, isolate the phonemes in each word, emphasizing the /n/ and /b/.

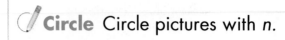
 Circle Circle pictures with *n*.

 Circle Circle pictures with *b*.

88 🐻 **ELA R1.14** Match all consonant and short-vowel sounds to appropriate letters. (ELD R.B10)

 **Leveled Support** **Phonics**

① **Beginning** Say the words *nut*, *nest*, and *nose*, emphasizing the sound /n/ at the beginning of each. I hear /n/ at the beginning of each of these words. Raise your hand if you hear /n/ at the beginning of each word I say: *neck, nap, mitt, night*. Do the same with words that begin with the letter *b*.

② ③ **Early Intermediate/Intermediate** Review the sound of the letter *n*. Raise your hand if you hear the sound of the letter *n* in these words: *nut, nose, fun, neck, fan, nap, night, bun*. Review the sound of the letter *b*. Follow the same format for words that have the initial or ending sound of the letter *b*.

④ ⑤ **Early Advanced/Advanced** Review the sound of the letter *n*. Have children say words that begin or end with the sound of the letter *n*. Write the words that they say. Read these words and have children repeat them. Do the same for the letter *b*.

 Wrap Up DAY **4**

Daily **Table Talk** How can you stay in touch with faraway friends? Have children discuss the question.

Produce Language Have children draw a picture that they would send to a friend or relative who lives faraway. They can tell about their pictures.

Today children should have:

☑ **Learned** and applied vocabulary related to staying in touch with faraway friends.

☑ **Spoken** complete sentences about staying in touch with faraway friends.

☑ **Recognized** the sounds of /n/ and /b/ in words.

 ELA R.1.14 Match all consonant and short-vowel sounds to appropriate letters. (ELD R.B10)

What happens when a friend moves away?

 Draw

ELA LS. 1.2 Share information and ideas, speaking audibly in complete, coherent sentences. (ELD LS.B1)   89

To guide children to express their understanding of weekly concepts and vocabulary.

Think, Talk, and Recognize!

Concept Talk

Connect to Day 4 Remind children that yesterday they discussed how we can stay in touch with faraway friends. Model how to answer yesterday's question with a sentence.

Review the Weekly Question Ask: What happens when a friend moves away? Have children talk about how they would feel if their friends moved away. Have them talk about how they could keep in touch with their faraway friends.

Use the Poster Use the Day 5 teaching notes at the bottom of the poster.

Review Concept Vocabulary Review the vocabulary introduced on Day 1.

Concept Wrap Up

Have children draw in the Worktext to answer the question: What happens when a friend moves away? Discuss the picture of the young child making a card and putting a letter in a mailbox. How is the child staying in touch with someone who lives faraway? Can you think of any other ways to keep in touch with someone who lives faraway?

Wrap Up   DAY 5

Table Talk Have children turn to the weekly question and discuss it. They can say a sentence about what happens when a friend moves away.

Produce Language To build fluency, children can label, write about, or speak about their drawings. Ask children to respond to what they read or heard.

Today children should have:

☑ **Reviewed** the weekly concept and concept vocabulary.

☑ **Spoken** about how what happens when a friend moves away.

☑ **Drawn or written** to show what happens when a friend moves away.

 ELA LS. 1.2 Share information and ideas, speaking audibly in complete, coherent sentences. (ELD LS.B1)

Leveled Support   Concept Vocabulary
Preteach / Reteach

① **Beginning** Display the Word Cards for *called, play, share,* and *word.* Say each word. Ask children to repeat and point to the matching card.

②③ **Early Intermediate/Intermediate** Draw a picture of two children playing together. After the picture is completed, ask: What is happening in this picture? What should children do when they play together? Have children role play how they play well with others.

④⑤ **Early Advanced/Advanced** Display the Word Cards for *called, play,* and *share.* Have children name someone who has called them on the telephone. Have them name a toy they like to play with. Have them name a person they like to share with. Write the answers they give in lists under the picture cards. Read the lists when they are complete.

Question of the Week

What new things can you do as you get older?

Instructional Plan and Materials

- **Word Cards** 48–49

- **Big Book** Life Long Ago

- **Poster** Poster 14 can be used at beginning or end of day.

- **Song Book**, p. 14

Transparencies Explore content and vocabulary and model fluent reading.

For further information about using these components, see pages x–xv.

CALIFORNIA Standards

GK Sci 4.e Communicate observations orally and through drawings.

Academic Language

DAY 1 — Get Ready to Read

Build Background

Preteach/Review 10–15 min
Poster, Song Book, Big Book
- **Leveled Support Preteach**
- **Practice Stations Preteach**

Teach 35–45 min
- **Concept Talk**
- **Oral Vocabulary Routine**
  Word Cards
- **Build Concept Vocabulary**
- **Daily Table Talk**

Check/Reteach 5–10 min
Poster, Word Cards
- **Leveled Support Reteach**

ELA LS 2.3 Relate an experience or creative story in a logical sequence.

Concept Talk Video

DAY 2 — Read and Comprehend

Language: Category Words

Preteach/Review 10–15 min
Poster
- **Leveled Support Preteach**
- **Practice Stations Review**

Teach 35–45 min
- **Category Words**
- **Daily Table Talk**

Check/Reteach 5–10 min
Poster, Word Cards
- **Leveled Support Reteach**

Fluency: Writing or Speaking

ELA R 1.17 Identify and sort common words in basic categories (e.g., colors, shapes, foods).

Category Words: happy, scared, excited, sad

Background Building Audio Slideshow

Get Online! www.pearsonsuccessnet.com

This Week
Unit 3, Week 2

Getting Older

Next Week
Unit 3, Week 3
American Heroes

DAY 3 Read and Comprehend	**DAY 4** Language Arts	**DAY 5** Language Arts
Language: High Frequency Words	**Phonics**	**Think, Talk, and Recognize**
Preteach/Review 10–15 min Poster **Leveled Support Preteach** **Practice Stations Review**	**Preteach/Review** 10–15 min Poster **Leveled Support Preteach** **Practice Stations Review**	**Preteach/Review** 10–15 min Poster **Leveled Support Preteach** **Practice Stations Review**
Teach 35–45 min **High Frequency Words** **Phonemic Awareness** **Daily Table Talk**	**Teach** 35–45 min **Phonics** **Daily Table Talk**	**Teach** 15–20 min **Think, Talk, and Recognize** **Concept Wrap Up**
Check/Reteach 5–10 min Poster, Word Cards **Leveled Support Reteach**	**Check/Reteach** 5–10 min Poster, Word Cards **Leveled Support Reteach**	**Check/Reteach** 30–40 min Poster, Word Cards, Song Book **Leveled Support Reteach**
		Fluency: Writing or Speaking
ELA R 1.15 Read simple one-syllable and high frequency words (i.e., sight words).	**ELA R 1.14** Match all consonant and short-vowel sounds to appropriate letters.	**ELA LS 1.2** Share information and ideas, speaking audibly in complete, coherent sentences.
High Frequency Words: she, me, with		

Practice Stations

Materials and Activity

---

strips of paper folded in thirds, crayons, colored pencils

I Am Growing

Have children draw a picture of themselves in each of the three frames—one when they were a baby, one when they were two or three, and one as they are now. Have each child include in the drawing something that they did at each age. Have them dictate a caption for each of their drawings, telling what they are doing in each picture.

---

photos of scenes of a lake; large paper for a mural; blue paint, crayons, markers

Life Near the Water

Show children photos of areas near a lake. Have children work together to paint a lake on the large paper. Have them draw things that are found in and around the water with their crayons and markers. Have children say the names of the things they have drawn. Label their drawings.

Preteach/Reteach

Transfer and Common Misconceptions

Present and Past Tense

Many children have difficulty using the correct tense of a verb. Remind children that we use different words for things that happened already and things that are happening right now.

/w/ Sound

Some children may have a hard time with the initial /w/ sound in *water.* Model other words that have the initial /w/ sound for them.

Produce Language

Weekly Concept and Language Goal

CONCEPT GOALS

- understand the concept of growing up
- describe how babies play
- name things that children can do as they grow up

By Day 5, children should be able to talk about their drawings and write a one-word label.

Daily **Table Talk**

❶ **Beginning**
Children pantomime something they could do that they could not do before while you provide the language.

❷ ❸ **Early Intermediate/Intermediate**
Children pantomime and say a word or phrase: tie my shoes

❹ ❺ **Early Advanced/Advanced**
Children say a sentence while pantomiming: I can tie my shoes now.

Daily **Table Talk**

❶ **Beginning**
Children talk about their drawings.

❷ ❸ **Early Intermediate/Intermediate**
Children write one-word labels.

❹ ❺ **Early Advanced/Advanced**
Children write a phrase or sentence.

DAY 3 · FORM & FUNCTION · Read and Comprehend

DAY 4 · FORM & FUNCTION · Language Arts

DAY 5 · Language Arts

index cards with faces that show the feelings *happy, sad, scared, excited;* small sheets of paper, pencils, crayons

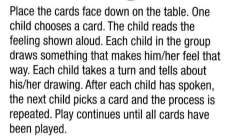

a copy of this verse on drawing paper for each child: *My friend Anne plays with me. She draws with me. She runs with me. She is a good friend to me.;* colored pencils, crayons, markers

stack of index cards face down with these picture words: *rug, rope, red, ribbon, rock, radio, raccoon, rainbow, banana, block, fish, duck, cupcake, candle, dog, cat, bed;* a grid with four boxes and the letter *r* as the heading

How Do You Feel?

Place the cards face down on the table. One child chooses a card. The child reads the feeling shown aloud. Each child in the group draws something that makes him/her feel that way. Each child takes a turn and tells about his/her drawing. After each child has spoken, the next child picks a card and the process is repeated. Play continues until all cards have been played.

Things Friends Do

Read the verse. Have children repeat after you. Have each child circle the high frequency words *me, with,* and *she.* Have children illustrate the verse. Have them draw other things that friends can do together. Have them tell about their drawings by saying: My friend _____ with me.

Beginning /r/

Stack the word cards face down. The first child takes a card and reads the picture word. If it begins with /r/, he or she places it on the grid. If it does not, the card is returned to the bottom of the pile. The partner does the same. Play continues until one of the child's grids is filled.

Synonyms

Children may have a problem distinguishing the meaning of words that are similar, such as *happy* and *excited* or *sad* and *scared.* Give children examples that distinguish the words from each other.

Consistency in Tense

Children may want to change the tense of the verb when they speak their own sentences. If they do this, model the sentence using the same tense that is used in the verse for consistency.

The /r/ Sound

Some children may have a problem pronouncing the initial /r/ in the words. Model the correct pronunciation for them. Have them repeat the words after you.

Daily Table Talk

❶ **Beginning**

Children can say *ride a two-wheeler* or *skate* as you display a corresponding picture.

❷ ❸ **Early Intermediate/Intermediate**

Phrase: *ride a two-wheeler; roller skate*

❹ ❺ **Early Advanced/Advanced**

Sentence: *I want to learn to ride a two-wheeler.*

Daily Table Talk

❶ **Beginning**

Children raise their hands as you provide sample answers, such as *Did you go to Kindergarten before? Could you zipper your coat by yourself?*

❷ ❸ **Early Intermediate/Intermediate**

Phrase: *zipper my coat, go to Kindergarten*

❹ ❺ **Early Advanced/Advanced**

Sentence: *I can zipper my coat now.*

Daily Table Talk

❶ **Beginning** Child draws and speaks about the drawing.

❷ ❸ **Early Intermediate/Intermediate** Child draws and speaks about the drawing using at least one concept vocabulary word.

❹ ❺ **Early Advanced/Advanced** Child draws and provides a label for the drawing that includes a vocabulary word.

Build Background Get Ready to Read!

Question of the Week

What new things can you do as you get older?

www.pearsonsuccessnet.com

Concept Talk

Use the Big Book If you haven't introduced the Big Book, consider reading it to children. Connect to the unit theme, Changes—Changes All Around Us.

Introduce the Weekly Concept Tell children that today they will talk about new things that they can do as they get older. Ask the weekly question: What new things can you do as you get older?

Use the Poster Direct children's attention to the weekly poster. Use the Day 1 teaching notes at the bottom of the poster.

Sing the Song Use the song **Growing Up** to reinforce children's understanding of the weekly concept. Have the children sing or simply chant the words with you.

Use a Transparency Use the Sequence Map (Transparency 7) to help children organize ways that they have changed as they have grown.

Getting Older

Vocabulary

duck

water

What new things can you do as you get older?

90

Vocabulary

duck a common water bird with short legs and a wide beak

water the clear, colorless liquid that falls from the sky as rain; forms lakes, river, and oceans; and is used for drinking and washing

Introduce Concept Vocabulary

1. Say the Word Display the Word Card as you say *duck*. Have children repeat the word.

2. Introduce the Meaning Ask questions about a duck. What kind of sound does a duck make? Demonstrate if necessary, having children follow your lead.

3. Demonstrate Have children role play how a duck would walk around, flapping its wings and quacking.

4. Apply Have children demonstrate their understanding.

Repeat with other vocabulary words.

Corrective Feedback If children have difficulty pronouncing a vocabulary word, repeat the word again, separating it into phonemes. Have the children repeat the word, blending the phonemes.

Concept Work

Discuss the pictures, relating them to the concept. Ask: What is the girl doing with her father? Is this something a young child should do alone? Explain why or why not. Discuss how the illustrations show the idea of growing and changing. Have children choose an illustration that shows a way in which they have grown. Have them color the picture and talk about it with a partner.

Preteach LS Reteach Leveled Support   Vocabulary in Context

1 Beginning Have children point to the ducks and the water in the pictures on the Worktext page. Say the word for each picture as children point, and have them echo each word.

2 3 Early Intermediate/Intermediate Do the Beginning activity, but have children say the words themselves, giving help only if needed.

4 5 Early Advanced/Advanced Ask children to draw a picture of themselves feeding a mother duck and her babies. Then ask them to use a sentence to tell about feeding the ducks. They should use both vocabulary words as they speak.

Wrap Up   DAY 1

Daily **Table Talk** What new things can you do as you get older? Have children answer the question, using the vocabulary words.

Produce Language Have each child say a sentence about something they can do all by themselves that they could not do before.

Today children should have:

☑ **Learned** and applied vocabulary related to new things they can do as they get older.

☑ **Spoken** complete sentences about something they can do all by themselves.

☑ **Recognized** concept vocabulary words.

 ELA LS 2.3 Relate an experience or creative story in a logical sequence. (ELD LS.B3)

91

OBJECTIVE

To discuss how babies play; to discuss different kinds of feelings.

Concept Talk

Connect to Day 1 Recall with children that yesterday they talked about new things they can do as they get older. What other things can you do all by yourself?

Introduce the Daily Question How do babies play? Have children answer orally.

Use the Poster Use the Day 2 teaching notes at the bottom of the poster.

Introduce Category Words

1. Say the Word Have children point to the girl smiling. Say the word and have children repeat it. Make a happy face as you say the word.

2. Introduce Word Meaning Ask questions: What makes you happy? What do you do when you feel happy?

3. Demonstrate Role play opening a present. How do you feel when you get a present?

4. Apply Repeat with other vocabulary words and elicit that they all belong to the category "feelings."

Have children draw a person who is happy and a person who is sad.

Corrective Feedback For children having difficulty, model the feelings for them with facial expressions and gestures. Have children repeat with gestures or expressions of their own.

Wrap Up DAY **2**

Daily
Table Talk How do babies play? What kinds of toys do babies play with? Have them discuss the questions. Have children draw a picture of a baby playing with a baby toy.

Produce Language To build fluency, encourage children to label or write sentences about the pictures they drew of happy and sad people. They can share their writing with partners.

Today children should have:

☑ **Learned** and applied vocabulary related to feelings.

☑ **Spoken** complete sentences about what babies play with.

☑ **Recognized** words that belong in the same category.

ELA R1.17 Identify and sort common words in basic categories (e.g., colors, shapes, foods). (ELD R.B4)

Feelings

Picture Dictionary

happy

sad

scared

excited

✏ **Draw** Draw feelings.

happy	sad

92 🐻 **ELA R1.17** Identify and sort common words in basic categories (e.g., colors, shapes, foods). (ELD R.B4)

Preteach
LS **Leveled Support** **Category Words**
Reteach

❶ **Beginning** Have children point to each feeling on the Worktext page. Say the word for each picture. Then have children repeat the word.

❷ ❸ **Early Intermediate/Intermediate** Say the name of a feeling on the Worktext page. Have children point to the picture. Then reverse the activity as you point to a picture and ask children to name the feeling shown in the picture. Have children name things that make them feel happy, sad, scared, and excited.

❹ ❺ **Early Advanced/Advanced** Have children talk with partners. Have them take turns naming the feelings in the pictures. Have them tell each other what makes them happy, sad, scared, and excited.

What can an older friend do?

✏️ **Circle** Circle *with*. Circle *me*.
You ride with me.

✏️ **Circle** Circle *She*.
She rides without help.

🐻 ELA R1.15 Read simple one-syllable and high-frequency words (i.e., sight words). (ELD R.B2)　　93

Preteach / Reteach LS Leveled Support High Frequency Words

① **Beginning** Write the words *me, with,* and *she*. Read the words. Have the children repeat the words. Write sentences like: *She will play a game with me. She will run with me.* Circle each of the high frequency words in the sentence.

② ③ **Early Intermediate/Intermediate** Do the beginning activity, but have the children circle the high frequency words themselves.

④ ⑤ **Early Advanced/Advanced** Write the words *me, with,* and *she*. Have the children say sentences using these words. Write their sentences. Have children circle the high frequency word in each of their sentences. Have them point to the words they circle and read them.

OBJECTIVE

To discuss feeling sad about moving; to introduce high frequency words *me, with,* and *she;* to distinguish initial sound /r/; to delete individual sounds in words to make new words.

Concept Talk　🌐 FORM & FUNCTION

Connect to Day 2 How do babies play?

Introduce the Daily Question Ask: What can an older friend do that you cannot do yet? Discuss things that children still cannot do.

Use the Poster Use the Day 3 teaching notes at the bottom of the poster.

Review Concept Vocabulary Review the words introduced on Day 1.

Introduce High Frequency Words

Introduce *me, with,* and *she* by role playing and speaking with sentences such as *She plays ball with me.* Help children circle the words on the Worktext page.

Phonemic Awareness

Phoneme Isolation/Segmentation Say the words *rag* and *rain,* emphasizing the beginning sounds. Have children repeat. Ask children to identify the letter sound that they hear at the beginning of each word. Do the same for *red* and *rat.* Have chidlren change the /r/ in *rag* to /b/, the /r/ in *rain* to /p/, the /r/ in *red* to /b/, and the /r/ in *rat* to /k/.

Corrective Feedback For children who have difficulty identifying the beginning sounds, review the sound /r/. Then repeat the words.

Wrap Up　　DAY 3

Daily Table Talk What are some things that you cannot do yet? Who will teach you to do these things? Have children discuss these questions.

Produce Language Have children draw a picture of something they still want to learn how to do. Have them tell about their picture.

Today children should have:

☑ **Learned** and applied the high frequency words *me, with,* and *she.*

☑ **Spoken** complete sentences about things that they are still not able to do.

☑ **Recognized** the beginning sound of /r/.

 ELA R.1.15 Read simple one-syllable and high-frequency words (i.e., sight words). (ELD R.B2)

To discuss what children can do now that they could not do before; to connect /r/ to *r*.

Concept Talk

FORM&
FUNCTION

Connect to Day 3 What can an older friend do that you cannot do yet?

Introduce the Daily Question Ask: What can you do now that you could not do before? **Ask children what are some things that they can do that babies cannot.** How did you learn to do these things?

Use the Poster Use the Day 4 teaching notes at the bottom of the poster.

Phonics

Identifying the Sound /r/ Introduce the sound /r/. Read each picture word and have children repeat the words. Have them complete the exercise on the Worktext page.

Corrective Feedback For children having difficulty recognizing the sound /r/ in words, repeat the sound that the letter *r* makes. Then say each word, emphazing /r/. Have children repeat the words, also emphasizing /r/.

Wrap Up

DAY 4

 Daily

Table Talk What can you do now that you could not do before? Have children discuss the question.

Produce Language Have children draw a picture of something they can do now that they could not do before. Have them say a sentence about their picture.

Today children should have:

- ☑ **Learned** and applied vocabulary related to things they can do now that they could not do before.

- ☑ **Spoken** complete sentences about things they can do now that they could not do before.

- ☑ **Recognized** the sound /r/ in words.

ELA R.1.14 Match all consonant and short-vowel sounds to appropriate letters. (ELD R.B1)

Identify Sound Rr

✏ **Draw** Color pictures with *r*.

94  **ELA R1.14** Match all consonant and short-vowel sounds to appropriate letters. (ELD R.B1)

Preteach / Reteach LS Leveled Support Phonics

① **Beginning** Say the words *run, rope,* and *rose,* emphasizing the /r/ at the beginning of each. I hear the sound /r/ at the beginning of each of these words. Here are some more words that begin with /r/: *ran, rocket, right.* Have children repeat the words after you.

② ③ **Early Intermediate/Intermediate** Review the sound of the letter *r*. Raise your hand if you hear the sound of the letter *r* in these words: *run, dog, rope, rose, ten, ran, sun, rocket, right.*

④ ⑤ **Early Advanced/Advanced** Review the sound of the letter *r*. Say *rope.* The word *rope* begins with the sound of the letter *r*. Have children say other words that begin with the sound of the letter *r*. Write the words that they say. Read these words and have children repeat them.

What new things can you do as you get older?

✏️ **Draw**

🐻 **ELA LS. 1.2** Share information and ideas, speaking audibly in complete, coherent sentences. (ELD LS.B1)

95

OBJECTIVE

To guide children to express their understanding of weekly concepts and vocabulary.

Think, Talk, and Recognize!

Concept Talk

Connect to Day 4 Remind children that yesterday they discussed what they can do now that they could not do before. Model how to answer yesterday's question with a sentence.

Review the Weekly Question Ask: What new things can you do as you get older? Have children talk about things they can do now that they could not do before. Have them talk about other things that they still want to learn how to do.

Use the Poster Use the Day 5 teaching notes at the bottom of the poster.

Review Concept Vocabulary Review the vocabulary introduced on Day 1.

Concept Wrap Up

Have children draw to answer the question: What new things can you do as you get older? Discuss the picture of the girl jumping off the diving board into the pool. Can you do that yet? If not, when do you think you will be able to jump off the diving board?

Wrap Up   **DAY 5**

Daily Table Talk What new things can you do as you get older? Have children discuss the question, using the vocabulary words they have learned this week.

Produce Language To build fluency, children can label, write about, or speak about their drawings. Ask children to respond to what they read or heard.

Today children should have:

☑ **Reviewed** the weekly concept and concpet vocabulary.

☑ **Spoken** about things that they can do now that they are older.

☑ **Drawn or written** to show what they can do now that they are older

 ELA LS. 1.2 Share information and ideas, speaking audibly in complete, coherent sentences. (ELD LS.B1)

95

 Leveled Support **Concept Vocabulary**

① **Beginning** Display the Word Cards for *duck* and *water.* Say each word. Ask children to repeat and point to the matching card.

② ③ **Early Intermediate/Intermediate** Draw pictures of other animals that live in or near the water. Have children say the name of each animal. Have children draw an animal that lives in or near the water.

④ ⑤ **Early Advanced/Advanced** Have children draw pictures of other ways we use water. Have children say sentences about their pictures.

Question of the Week

What can we learn from people in the past?

DAY 1 — Get Ready to Read

DAY 2 — Read and Comprehend

Instructional Plan and Materials

- **Word Cards**
  50–53

- **Big Book**
  Life Long Ago

- **Poster**
  Poster 15 can be used at beginning or end of day.

- **Song Book**, p. 15

Transparencies Explore content and vocabulary and model fluent reading.

For further information about using these components, see pages x–xv.

DAY 1 — Get Ready to Read	DAY 2 — Read and Comprehend
Build Background	**Language: Category Words**
Preteach/Review 10–15 min Poster, Song Book, Big Book **Leveled Support Preteach** **Practice Stations Preteach**	**Preteach/Review** 10–15 min Poster **Leveled Support Preteach** **Practice Stations Review**
Teach 35–45 min **Concept Talk** **Oral Vocabulary Routine** Word Cards **Build Concept Vocabulary** **Daily Table Talk**	**Teach** 35–45 min **Category Words** **Daily Table Talk**
Check/Reteach 5–10 min Poster, Word Cards **Leveled Support Reteach**	**Check/Reteach** 5–10 min Poster, Word Cards **Leveled Support Reteach**
	Fluency: Writing or Speaking

CALIFORNIA Standards

GK His-Soc Sci K.6.2 Know the triumphs in American legends and historical accounts through the stories of such people as Pocahontas, George Washington, Booker T. Washington, Daniel Boone, and Benjamin Franklin.

ELA LS 2.1 Describe people, places, things (e.g., size, color, shape), locations and actions.	**ELA R 1.17** Identify and sort common words in basic categories (e.g., colors, shapes, foods).

Academic Language

Vocabulary: storm	**Category Words:** bell, blacksmith, cottage, horse

Get Online! www.pearsonsuccessnet.com

Concept Talk Video	**Background Building Audio Slideshow**

This Week
Unit 3, Week 3
American Heroes

Next Week
Unit 3, Week 4
Friends Change

DAY 3 Read and Comprehend	**DAY 4** Language Arts	**DAY 5** Language Arts
Language: High Frequency Words	**Phonics**	**Think, Talk, and Recognize**
Preteach/Review 10–15 min Poster **Leveled Support Preteach** **Practice Stations Review**	**Preteach/Review** 10–15 min Poster **Leveled Support Preteach** **Practice Stations Review**	**Preteach/Review** 10–15 min Poster **Leveled Support Preteach** **Practice Stations Review**
Teach 35–45 min **High Frequency Words** **Daily Table Talk**	**Teach** 35–45 min **Phonics** **Daily Table Talk**	**Teach** 15–20 min **Think, Talk, and Recognize** **Concept Wrap Up**
Check/Reteach 5–10 min Poster, Word Cards **Leveled Support Reteach**	**Check/Reteach** 5–10 min Poster, Word Cards **Leveled Support Reteach**	**Check/Reteach** 30–40 min Poster, Word Cards, Song Book **Leveled Support Reteach**
		Fluency: Writing or Speaking
ELA R 1.15 Read simple one-syllable and high frequency words (i.e., sight words).	**ELA R 1.14** Match all consonant and short-vowel sounds to appropriate letters.	**ELA LS 1.2** Share information and ideas, speaking audibly in complete, coherent sentences.
High Frequency Words: see, look		

Practice Stations

Materials and Activity

several pictures of historical figures, paper, pencils, crayons

Our Heroes

Discuss famous people with children. Hold up pictures of the people and name them. Tell what they did that made them heroes. Children can cut out pictures of famous people and pin them to a bulletin board.

one paper for each child with the words *My Hero* written (with letters that can be colored or traced) across the top, pencil, crayons, colored pencils

My Hero

Have each child color or trace the words *My Hero*. Have each child make a sign by drawing a picture of someone they think is a hero. Have them attach their heroes to the hero bulletin board.

Preteach/Reteach

Transfer and Common Misconceptions

Heroes

Children may be more familiar with heroes from their native countries. Encourage them to tell about them.

The Letter *H*

In Spanish, the letter *h* is always silent. Have children hold one hand in front of their mouths as they say *hat.* Tell them that they should feel a puff of air as they say the /h/ in *hat.*

Produce Language

Weekly Concept and Language Goal

CONCEPT GOALS

• understand the concept of learning from people who lived in the past
• describe how people can show respect for people who lived in the past
• explain why George Washington is an important person

By Day 5, children should be able to talk about their drawings and write a one-word label.

Daily **Table Talk**

❶ **Beginning**

Children point to the picture of the hero you are speaking about.

❷ ❸ **Early Intermediate/Intermediate**

Name what the hero did. Children name the hero. (Betsy Ross)

❹ ❺ **Early Advanced/Advanced**

Children say a sentence: Betsy Ross sewed the first flag.

Daily **Table Talk**

❶ **Beginning**

Children talk about their drawings.

❷ ❸ **Early Intermediate/Intermediate**

Children write one-word labels.

❹ ❺ **Early Advanced/Advanced**

Children write a phrase or sentence.

DAY 3 — FORM & FUNCTION — Read and Comprehend

index cards with word pictures showing activities people did long ago and activities people do today drawn on them, two large pieces of string or yarn

Long Ago or Today? 🚶🚶

Have children make two large circles with the string (or yarn). Have partners sort the pictures into the categories of *Long Ago* and *Today.* When all of the pictures have been categorized, have one partner name the things of long ago. Have the other name the things of today.

Past and Present Tense Verbs

Remind children that when we speak of the past we use different words than those we use when speaking of the present. Demonstrate changing verb tenses with sentences that talk about the past and present.

❶ **Beginning**
> Children can say yes or no as you say things that Washington was famous for.

❷ ❸ **Early Intermediate/Intermediate**
> Phrase: first president, war hero

❹ ❺ **Early Advanced/Advanced**
> Sentence: George Washington was our first president.

DAY 4 — FORM & FUNCTION — Language Arts

paper with these sentences written on it: *Look at the (insert picture). I see it!;* set of cards with *see* and *look* for each student; four small square sheets of paper for each child; crayons

Look and See 🚶🚶

Have partners take turns matching their high frequency word cards with the words in the sentences. Have each partner take turns drawing the things they need to do an activity on their four squares of paper. (Example: paint brush, jar of paint, paper, artist). When each child has finished their drawings, have partners take turns reading the sentences with their drawings placed over the pictures.

Exclamation Points

In Spanish, exclamation points are found at the beginning and end of exclamations. This is not true in English.

❶ **Beginning**
> Children raise their hands as you provide sample answers, such as Everyone is equal.

❷ ❸ **Early Intermediate/Intermediate**
> One or two word: free, equal

❹ ❺ **Early Advanced/Advanced**
> Sentence: It is important to be free.

DAY 5 — Language Arts

index cards with picture words starting with *k* and *d,* paper grid that measures 5 across and 2 down (/d/ written in first box of row 1, /k/ written in the first box of row 2)

What's the Beginning Sound? 🚶🚶

Stack the cards face down on the table. The first child takes a card and names the picture. If it begins with /d/, it is placed in the /d/ row. If it begins with /k/, it is placed in the /k/ row. If one row is already filled, he/she puts the card on the pile. The other partner takes a turn. Play continues until one child has filled both rows of the grid.

Initial /k/

Remind children that both letters *c* and *k* can sound like /k/. You may want to remind children that the letter *c* can also sound like /s/.

Table Talk

❶ **Beginning** Child draws and speaks about the drawing.

❷ ❸ **Early Intermediate/Intermediate** Child draws and speaks about the drawing using at least one concept vocabulary word.

❹ ❺ **Early Advanced/Advanced** Child draws and provides a label for the drawing that includes a vocabulary word.

To introduce and discuss vocabulary and concepts related to heroes from the past.

Build Background

Get Ready to Read!

Question of the Week What can we learn from people in the past?

www.pearsonsuccessnet.com

Concept Talk

Use the Big Book If you haven't introduced the Big Book, consider reading it to children. Connect to the unit theme, Changes—Changes All Around Us.

Introduce the Weekly Concept Tell children that today they will talk about the things we can learn from people who lived in the past. Ask the weekly question: What can we learn from people in the past?

Use the Poster Direct children's attention to the weekly poster. Use the Day 1 teaching notes at the bottom of the poster.

Sing the Song Use the song **A Hero** to reinforce children's understanding of the weekly concept. Have the children sing or simply chant the words with you.

Use a Transparency Use the Biography Transparency (Transparency 9) to share with children a biography of George Washington.

American Heroes

Vocabulary

crowds

hero

sign

storm

What can we learn from people in the past?

96

Vocabulary

* Academic Vocabulary

crowds large groups of people in one place

hero someone who is admired for doing something very brave or good

sign a piece of paper, metal, or the like with words or a picture that gives people information, warnings, or instructions

* **storm** a period of bad weather when there is a lot of wind, rain, or snow

Introduce Concept Vocabulary

1. **Say the Word** Display the Word Card as you say *sign*. Have children repeat the word.

2. **Introduce Word Meaning** Point out signs in the classroom or in the school. Ask questions about signs. *What kinds of signs have you seen before? How do signs help you?*

3. **Demonstrate** Draw a "no-swimming" sign (a circle with a person swimming in water with a diagonal line running through the circle). *What does this sign tell you?*

4. **Apply** Have children demonstrate their understanding.

Repeat with other vocabulary words.

Corrective Feedback If children have difficulty with the vocabulary words, say them more slowly, separating them into phonemes. Emphasize the initial phonemes and hold up the corresponding Word Cards.

Concept Work

Ask children to point to the drawings of the American heroes in the Worktext. *Have you ever seen pictures of any of these American heroes before?* If so, have them tell what they know about them. If not, tell children who they are and why they are American heroes. Have children choose a hero to color.

Table Talk *What can we learn from people who lived in the past?* Have children answer the question, using the vocabulary words.

Produce Language Have children say a sentence that tells about the things we learn from people who lived long ago.

Today children should have:

☑ **Learned** and applied vocabulary related to people we learn from who lived long ago.

☑ **Spoken** complete sentences about people we learn from who lived long ago.

☑ **Recognized** concept vocabulary words.

 ELA LS 2.1 Describe people, places, things (e.g., size, color, shape), locations, and actions.

Leveled Support **Vocabulary in Context**

Preteach LS Reteach

❶ **Beginning** Have children point to the drawings of George Washington, Betsy Ross, and Martin Luther King Jr. on the Worktext page. *Each of these people is a hero.* Have them repeat the word *hero.* Have them point to the other vocabulary words as they are pictured on the page. Have them repeat these words after you.

❷ ❸ **Early Intermediate/Intermediate** Point to items in the illustrations and ask questions about them, such as: *Is this person a hero? Are these people in a crowd?* Children can respond with gestures and add spoken details if they are able.

❹ ❺ **Early Advanced/Advanced** Ask children to name any heroes that they know. Then ask them to use a sentence to tell about a hero that they know. (Children may need prompting to think of a hero. If so, you can help them by suggesting the President, firefighters, police officers, and so on.)

OBJECTIVES

To discuss how we respect important people from the past; to discuss things that were in a colonial village.

Concept Talk

Connect to Day 1 Recall with children that yesterday they talked about heroes who lived long ago. What did some of these heroes do?

Introduce the Daily Question How do we show respect to important people from the past? Have children answer orally.

Use the Poster Use the Day 2 teaching notes at the bottom of the poster.

Introduce the Category Words

1. **Say the Word** Have children point to the horse. Say the word and have children repeat it.

2. **Introduce the Meaning** Ask questions: What is the horse doing? Why would people need a horse to pull a carriage? How is this different from today?

3. **Demonstrate** Role play a rider in a carriage holding the reigns of a horse, riding in a carriage.

4. **Apply** Repeat with other vocabulary words and elicit that they all belong to the category "things in a colonial village." Help children complete the Worktext page.

Have children point to items as you name them. Then have them circle the things that were present in colonial days.

Corrective Feedback If students have difficulty understanding the concept of how things were different in the past, discuss the items from today that are equivalent to the pictured items.

Wrap Up   DAY 2

 Daily **Table Talk** How do we show respect to important people from the past? Say a sentence to answer the question.

Produce Language To build fluency, encourage children to label or write a sentence about the items they circled on the Worktext page. They can share their writing with partners.

Today children should have:

☑ **Learned** and applied vocabulary related to things in a colonial village.

☑ **Spoken** complete sentences about ways that we show respect to important people from the past.

☑ **Recognized** words that belong in the same category.

 ELA R1.17 Identify and sort common words in basic categories (e.g., colors, shapes, foods). (ELD R.B4)

Things in a Colonial Village

Picture Dictionary

bell

blacksmith

cottage

horse

✏ **Circle** Circle things in a Colonial village.

98 🐻 **ELA R1.17** Identify and sort common words in basic categories (e.g., colors, shapes, foods). (ELD R.B4)

Leveled Support **Category Words**
Preteach / Reteach

① **Beginning** Have children point to each thing in a colonial village on the Worktext page. Say the word for each picture. Then have children repeat the word.

② ③ **Early Intermediate/Intermediate** Point to each picture of a thing in a colonial village on the Worktext page. Ask children to name each thing. Then give children a clue as to how each was used. Have children guess the thing you are describing.

④ ⑤ **Early Advanced/Advanced** Have children talk with partners. Have them tell each other the names of all of the things in a colonial village. Have them tell a partner how each thing was used in the colonial village.

Who is a good example for us from the past?

✏️ **Circle** Circle *see*.

I see Lincoln's hat.

✏️ **Circle** Circle *Look*.

Look at Ben Franklin work.

🐻 **ELA R1.15** Read simple one-syllable and high-frequency words (i.e., sight words). (ELD R.B2)

99

To discuss good examples for us from the past; to introduce the high frequency words *see* and *look*.

Concept Talk FORM& FUNCTION

Connect to Day 2 What were some ways that we honor these people from the past?

Introduce the Daily Question Ask: Who is a good example for us from the past? Discuss Abraham Lincoln and Ben Franklin. Why are these two people good examples for us? Have children answer the question.

Use the Poster Use the Day 3 teaching notes at the bottom of the poster.

Review Concept Vocabulary Review the words introduced on Day 1.

Introduce High Frequency Words

Introduce *see* and *look* by role playing and speaking with sentences such as *I see a book. What do you see?* Or *Look at the red crayon.* Help children circle the words on the Worktext page.

Leveled Support High Frequency Words

Preteach / Reteach

1 **Beginning** Write the words *see* and *look*. Read the words. Have the children repeat the words. Write sentences like: *I see the pencil. Look at the baby.* Circle each of the high frequency words in the sentences.

2 3 **Early Intermediate/Intermediate** Do the beginning activity, but have the children circle the high frequency words themselves. Have them read the words that they circle.

4 5 **Early Advanced/Advanced** Write the words *see* and *look*. Have the children say sentences using these words. Write their sentences. Have children circle the high-frequency word in each of their sentences.

Daily **Table Talk** Why are Abraham Lincoln and Ben Franklin good examples for us? What did they do? Have them discuss these questions.

Produce Language Have children draw a picture of one of the heroes they have learned about. Have them tell about their picture.

Today children should have:

☑ **Learned** and applied the high frequency words *see* and *look*.

☑ **Spoken** complete sentences about people in the past who were good examples for us.

☑ **Recognized** the qualities of a hero.

 ELA R.1.15 Read simple one-syllable and high-frequency words (i.e., sight words). (ELD R.B2)

99

OBJECTIVE

To discuss George Washington as an important person; to recognize the initial and ending /d/ and the initial /k/.

Concept Talk

 FORM & FUNCTION

Connect to Day 3 Elicit from children that yesterday they talked about people from the past who are good examples.

Introduce the Daily Question Ask: Why is George Washington an important person? Have students turn to the picture of George Washington in the Worktext. Ask children if they remember what they learned about George Washington. Have children tell why he was important.

Use the Poster: Use the Day 4 teaching notes at the bottom of the poster.

Phonics/Phonemic Awareness

Phoneme Isolation/Segmentation Say *mud* and *dad*, emphasizing ending sounds. Have children repeat the words and identify the letter sound at the end of each word. Then say the word *mud*. Demonstrate that when you change the /m/ sound to /b/, the word becomes *bud*. Have children try changing the /f/ sound in *fed* to /r/.

Corrective Feedback For children who have difficulty identifying the ending sounds, review the sound of the letter *d*. Then repeat the words, once again emphasizing the ending sound /d/.

Identifying /d/ and /k/ Remind children of the sound /d/. Read each pictured word and have children repeat the words. Have them complete the exercise on the Worktext page. Do the same for the sound /k/.

Wrap Up

DAY 4

 Table Talk Why is George Washington an important person? Have children discuss the question.

Produce Language Have children say a sentence about what George Washington did that made him important.

Today children should have:

☑ **Learned** and applied vocabulary related to George Washington.

☑ **Spoken** complete sentences about why George Washington is an important person.

☑ **Recognized** the sounds of /d/ and /k/ in words.

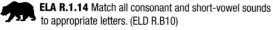 **ELA R.1.14** Match all consonant and short-vowel sounds to appropriate letters. (ELD R.B10)

Identify Sounds Dd and Kk

✏ **Circle** Circle pictures with *d*.

✏ **Circle** Circle pictures with *k*.

100 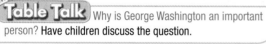 **ELA R1.14** Match all consonant and short-vowel sounds to appropriate letters. (ELD R.B10)

Preteach LS Reteach **Leveled Support** **Phonics**

① ② **Beginning** Remind children of the sound of the letter *d*. Say the words *den*, *dad*, and *dog*, emphasizing the sound /d/ at the beginning of each. I hear /d/ at the beginning of each of these words. Raise your hand if you hear /d/ at the beginning of the word I say: *desk, dot, dig.* Do the same with the sound of the letter *k* and words that begin with /k/.

③ **Early Intermediate/Intermediate** Review the sound of the letter *d*. Raise your hand if you hear the sound of the letter *d* in these words: *dad, dog, fed, desk, mad, dot, dig, bud.* Review the sound /k/. Follow the same format for words with the initial /k/.

④ ⑤ **Early Advanced/Advanced** Review the sound of the letter *d*. Have children say words that begin or end with /d/. Write the words that they say. Read these words and have children repeat them. Do the same for the letter *k* and words that begin with /k/.

What can we learn from people in the past?

 Draw

ELA LS. 1.2 Share information and ideas, speaking audibly in complete, coherent sentences. (ELD LS.B1)

101

OBJECTIVE
To guide children to express their understanding of weekly concepts and vocabulary.

Think, Talk, and Recognize!

Concept Talk

Connect to Day 4 Remind children that yesterday they discussed why George Washington was an important person. Model how to answer yesterday's question with a sentence.

Review the Weekly Question Ask: What can we learn from people who lived before us? Have children name some important people who lived long ago. Have them talk about things they have learned from these people.

Use the Poster Use the Day 5 teaching notes at the bottom of the poster.

Review Concept Vocabulary Review the vocabulary introduced on Day 1.

Concept Wrap Up

Have children draw to answer the question: What can we learn from people who lived before us? Discuss the illustration of George Washington. Why was George Washington important? What did we learn from him?

① **Beginning** Display the Word Cards for *crowds, hero, sign,* and *storm.* Say each word. Ask children to repeat and point to the matching card.

② ③ **Early Intermediate/Intermediate** Display the Word Cards for *crowds, hero, sign,* and *storm.* Give a definition or description for each word. Have children name the vocabulary word you are describing.

④ ⑤ **Early Advanced/Advanced** Display the Word Cards for *crowds, hero, sign,* and *storm.* Have children try to have a partner guess the vocabulary word by giving the definition or by telling something about the word.

Table Talk What can we learn from people in the past? Have children discuss the question, using the vocabulary words they have learned this week.

Produce Language To build fluency, children can label, write about, or speak about their drawings. Ask children to respond to what they read or heard.

Today children should have:

☑ **Reviewed** the weekly concept and concept vocabulary.

☑ **Spoken** about what we can learn from people in the past.

☑ **Drawn or written** to show what we can learn from people in the past.

ELA LS. 1.2 Share information and ideas, speaking audibly in complete, coherent sentences. (ELD LS.B1)

101

Question of the Week How do friendships change?

Instructional Plan and Materials

- **Word Cards**
  54–55

- **Poster**
  Poster 16 can be used at beginning or end of day.

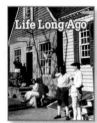

- **Big Book**
  Life Long Ago

- **Song Book**, p. 16

Transparencies Explore content and vocabulary and model fluent reading.

For further information about using these components, see pages x–xv.

CALIFORNIA Standards

GK Sci 4.e Communicate observations orally and through drawings.

Academic Language

DAY 1 — Get Ready to Read

Build Background

Preteach/Review 10–15 min
Poster, Song Book, Big Book
- **Leveled Support Preteach**
- **Practice Stations Preteach**

Teach 35–45 min
- **Concept Talk**
- **Oral Vocabulary Routine**
  Word Cards
- **Build Concept Vocabulary**
- **Daily Table Talk**

Check/Reteach 5–10 min
Poster, Word Cards
- **Leveled Support Reteach**

ELA LS 2.3 Relate an experience or creative story in a logical sequence.

Vocabulary: friends

Concept Talk Video

DAY 2 — Read and Comprehend

Language: Category Words

Preteach/Review 10–15 min
Poster
- **Leveled Support Preteach**
- **Practice Stations Review**

Teach 35–45 min
- **Category Words**
- **Daily Table Talk**

Check/Reteach 5–10 min
Poster, Word Cards
- **Leveled Support Reteach**

Fluency: Writing or Speaking

ELA R 1.17 Identify and sort common words in basic categories (e.g., colors, shapes, foods).

Category Words: feathers, fur, quills, scales, shell

Background Building Audio Slideshow

Friends Change

DAY 3 Read and Comprehend	**DAY 4** Language Arts	**DAY 5** Language Arts
FORM & FUNCTION	**FORM & FUNCTION**	
Language: High Frequency Words	**Phonics**	**Think, Talk, and Recognize**
Preteach/Review 10–15 min Poster **Leveled Support Preteach** **Practice Stations Review**	**Preteach/Review** 10–15 min Poster **Leveled Support Preteach** **Practice Stations Review**	**Preteach/Review** 10–15 min Poster **Leveled Support Preteach** **Practice Stations Review**
Teach 35–45 min **High Frequency Words** **Daily Table Talk**	**Teach** 35–45 min **Phonics** **Daily Table Talk**	**Teach** 15–20 min **Think, Talk, and Recognize** **Concept Wrap Up**
Check/Reteach 5–10 min Poster, Word Cards **Leveled Support Reteach**	**Check/Reteach** 5–10 min Poster, Word Cards **Leveled Support Reteach**	**Check/Reteach** 30–40 min Poster, Word Cards, Song Book **Leveled Support Reteach**
		Fluency: Writing or Speaking
ELA R 1.15 Read simple one-syllable and high frequency words (i.e., sight words).	**ELA R 1.14** Match all consonant and short-vowel sounds to appropriate letters.	**ELA LS 1.2** Share information and ideas, speaking audibly in complete, coherent sentences.
High Frequency Words: see, look		

Practice Stations

Materials and Activity

---

 photos of friends doing different things (such as playing, hugging, helping); crayons, colored pencils, paper

Playing with Friends

Have partners take turns telling about what the friends are doing in each picture. Have children fold a paper in half. Have them draw one thing they do with their friend. Have them tell what they are doing with their friends.

---

paper, markers, crayons, outlines of the letters in the words *OUR FRIENDS*

My Friends

Have children draw a picture of one of their friends. Then have them share with the group the name of their friend. Have children pin their pictures on a friendship wall. Then have children color the letters of the words "Our Friends." They can add them to the top of the bulletin board.

Preteach/Reteach

Transfer and Common Misconceptions

Word Meaning

Encourage children to talk about games they play at home. They can share the games that they played in their home countries.

Forming Plurals

Remind children that adding *s* to a word shows that it is more than one. Demonstrate with words like *game, friend, toy, doll, truck.*

Produce Language

Weekly Concept and Language Goal

CONCEPT GOALS

- understand how people change as they grow
- discuss things they have learned

By Day 5, children should be able to talk about their drawings and write a one-word label.

Daily Table Talk

❶ **Beginning**
> Children pantomime different things to do with a friend while you provide the language.

❷ ❸ **Early Intermediate/Intermediate**
> Children pantomime and say a word or phrase: play games, say goodbye, help them.

❹ ❺ **Early Advanced/Advanced**
> Children say a sentence while pantomiming: I have fun with a friend. I say "sorry" to a friend.

Daily Table Talk

❶ **Beginning**
> Children talk about their drawings.

❷ ❸ **Early Intermediate/Intermediate**
> Children write one-word labels.

❹ ❺ **Early Advanced/Advanced**
> Children write a phrase or sentence.

outlined drawings of a bird, a porcupine, and a rabbit; crayons; pipe cleaners; feathers; cotton balls

five small sheets of paper for each child, pencils, and crayons

index cards with pictures for words with and without /f/, two small pieces of thicker paper for each child, two popsicle sticks for each child

What's It Covered With?

Give children outline drawings of an animal. Have them add the feathers, cotton balls (as fur), or pipe cleaners (as quills) to their drawings. They can name their animals and what covers that animal.

Look and See

Have each child draw five things they see in the classroom. When they have finished drawing, the first partner picks up one of the drawings and says, "I see _____." The child places it in the space of the sentence *I see _____*. He/she reads the sentence. The partner looks around the room to find it. The game continues until all pictures have been found.

What Begins with /f/?

Each child makes a yes and no sign by writing each word on the paper and taping a popsicle to the back of it. Place the word cards face down on the table. The first child turns over the first card and says the word. That child counts to three. At the count of three each child holds up the *yes* or *no* sign, determining if the word begins with /f/ or not.

Naming Animals

Students can share names of animals common in their home countries.

Close Meanings

See and *look* have very similar meanings. Model using each of these words in sentences so that children can understand when to use each word.

The Sound /th/

Some children may have difficulty pronouncing words like *feather, father,* and *three* as the sound /th/ is rare in other languages. Model correct pronunciation with these words and other that have the sound of /th/.

Daily Table Talk

❶ **Beginning** Children can say happy or sad as you describe something between friends. (Examples: Your friend falls down. Your friend tells a funny story.)

❷ ❸ **Early Intermediate/Intermediate** Phrase: (happy) having fun, sharing; (sad) being selfish, calling names

❹ ❺ **Early Advanced/Advanced** Sentence: I am happy when my friend shares. I am sad when my friend is mean.

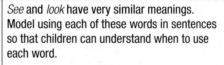

Daily Table Talk

❶ **Beginning** Children raise their hands if you describe a good friend: nice, kind, mean, selfish, helpful.

❷ ❸ **Early Intermediate/Intermediate** One or two words: nice, kind, helps me.

❹ ❺ **Early Advanced/Advanced** Sentence: My friend shares toys with me.

Daily Table Talk

❶ **Beginning** Child draws and speaks about the drawing.

❷ ❸ **Early Intermediate/Intermediate** Child draws and speaks about the drawing using at least one concept vocabulary word.

❹ ❺ **Early Advanced/Advanced** Child draws and provides a label for the drawing that includes a vocabulary word.

OBJECTIVE

To introduce and discuss concepts and vocabulary related to changes in friendships.

Build Background
Get Ready to Read!

Question of the Week

How do friendships change?

www.pearsonsuccessnet.com

Concept Talk

Use the Big Book If you haven't introduced the Big Book, consider reading it to children. Connect to the unit theme, Changes—Changes All Around Us.

Introduce the Weekly Concept Tell children that today they will talk about how friendships change. Ask the weekly question: How do friendships change?

Use the Poster Direct children's attention to the weekly poster. Use the Day 1 teaching notes at the bottom of the poster.

Sing the Song Use the song **Friends** to reinforce children's understanding of the weekly concept. Have the children sing or simply chant the words with you.

Use a Transparency Use the Play Transparency (Transparency 17) to spark children's ideas for a play about friendships and how they change.

Friends Change

Vocabulary

friends

game

How do friendships change?

102

Vocabulary

* Academic Vocabulary

* **friends** people whom you like very much and enjoy spending time with

game an activity or sport that people play for fun or in a competition

Introduce Concept Vocabulary

1. **Say the Word** Display the Word Card as you say *game.* Have children repeat the word.

2. **Introduce Word Meaning** Ask questions about games. *What games do you like to play?*

3. **Demonstrate** Collect games that you have in the classroom. *These are some of the games that we have in our classroom. But, you can also play a game of cards or a game of tag.*

4. **Apply** Have children demonstrate their understanding.

Repeat with other vocabulary words.

Corrective Feedback If children have difficulty pronouncing a vocabulary word, repeat the word again, separating it into phonemes. Have the children repeat the word after you, blending the phonemes.

Concept Work

Ask children to point to the pictures of the friends. Have children talk about each picture, telling what is happening in each picture and how the children feel when they are playing together. Have children color the pictures.

Preteach **LS** **Leveled Support** **Vocabulary in Context**
Reteach

① **Beginning** Have children point to the pictures of the friends and the game as you say the words. Then point to items in the illustrations and ask *Is this a game?* Children can nod their heads yes or no to respond. Repeat with the word *friends.*

② ③ **Early Intermediate/Intermediate** Have children name games they like to play with their friends. Write the names of the games. Read the names and have them echo each word.

④ ⑤ **Early Advanced/Advanced** Ask children to draw a picture of themselves and a friend playing a game. Then ask them to use a sentence to tell what game they are playing.

Wrap Up **DAY** 1

Table Talk How do friendships change? Have
Daily children answer the question, using the vocabulary words.

Produce Language What are some of the different things you can do with your friends? Have each child say a sentence about the different things they can do with their friends (playing, helping, talking, sharing).

Today children should have:

☑ **Learned** and applied vocabulary related to friendship.

☑ **Spoken** complete sentences about different things they do with their friends.

☑ **Recognized** concept vocabulary words.

 ELA LS 2.3 Relate an experience or creative story in a logical sequence. (ELD LS.B3)

OBJECTIVE

To discuss what children like to do with their friends; to learn about coverings on animal bodies.

Concept Talk

Connect to Day 1 Recall with children that yesterday they talked about different things they can do with their friends.

Introduce the Daily Question What do you like to do with your friends? Have children answer orally.

Use the Poster Use the Day 2 teaching notes at the bottom of the poster.

Introduce Category Words

1. **Say the Word** Have children point to the fur. Say the word and have children repeat it. Use a stuffed animal in the classroom to show children fur.

2. **Introduce the Meaning** Ask questions: What are some other animals that have fur?

3. **Demonstrate** Role play petting the fur on an animal. How does it feel when you pet the fur on a cat?

4. **Apply** Repeat with other vocabulary words and elicit that they all belong to the category "animal body coverings."

Have children name the animals on the Worktext page. Read the directions so that children can circle the correct animals.

Corrective Feedback If children have difficulty completing the exercise, have them work with partners to compare the photographs to the illustrations. Provide and model a sentence frame for discussing the animals: *This animal is a _____. It is covered with _____.*

Wrap Up   DAY **2**

 Table Talk *Daily* What do you like to do with your friends when you are at school? What do you like to do with your friends at your home? **Have children discuss the questions.**

Produce Language To build fluency, encourage chidlren to label or write a sentence about the animals they circled. They can share their writing with partners.

Today children should have:

☑ **Learned** and applied vocabulary related to animal body coverings.

☑ **Spoken** complete sentences about things they like to do with their friends.

☑ **Recognized** words that belong in the same category.

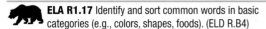 **ELA R1.17** Identify and sort common words in basic categories (e.g., colors, shapes, foods). (ELD R.B4)

104   Friends Change • Unit 3, Week 4

Animal Body Coverings

Picture Dictionary

feathers   **fur**   **quills**

scales   **shell**

 Circle Circle an animal with feathers.

 Circle Circle an animal with a shell.

104    **ELA R1.17** Identify and sort common words in basic categories (e.g., colors, shapes, foods). (ELD R.B4)

Leveled Support   Category Words

Preteach / Reteach

❶ **Beginning** Have children point to each animal body covering on the Worktext page. Say the word for the animal and body covering in each picture. Then have children repeat the word.

❷ ❸ **Early Intermediate/Intermediate** Say the name of one of the animals in the pictures on the Worktext page. Have children point to the animal. Have them name the body covering for that animal. Then reverse the activity as you say the body covering and they say the animal that has that body covering.

❹ ❺ **Early Advanced/Advanced** Have children talk with partners. Have them tell each other the names of the different kinds of body coverings. Have them name the animal in the picture with that body covering and another animal that has that same body covering.

Why might a friendship change?

✎ **Circle** Circle *see*.

I see my friend after school.

✎ **Circle** Circle *Look*.

Look at the friends playing.

ELA R1.15 Read simple one-syllable and high-frequency words (i.e., sight words). (ELD R.B2)

105

OBJECTIVE

To discuss why a friendship might change; to introduce the high frequency words *see* and *look*.

Concept Talk FORM & FUNCTION

Connect to Day 2 Remind children that yesterday they talked about things they like to do with their friends. What are some other things that you like to do with your friends?

Introduce the Daily Question Ask: Why might a friendship change? Discuss things that could happen to make a friendship change.

Use the Poster Use the Day 3 teaching notes at the bottom of the poster.

Review Concept Vocabulary Review the words introduced on Day 1.

Introduce High Frequency Words

Introduce *see* and *look* by role playing and speaking with sentences such as *I see a flag. What do you see?* Help children complete the Worktext page.

Corrective Feedback If children have difficulty finding the high frequency words in the sentences, highlight the word in the direction line and have the children look for it in the sentence.

Leveled Support **High Frequency Words**
Preteach / Reteach

❶ **Beginning** Write the words *see* and *look*. Read the words. Have the children repeat the words. Write sentences like: *I see a chair. Look at my friend.* Circle each of the high frequency words in the sentence.

❷ ❸ **Early Intermediate/Intermediate** Do the Beginning activity, but have the children circle the high frequency words themselves.

❹ ❺ **Early Advanced/Advanced** Write the words *see* and *look*. Have the children say sentences using these words. Write their sentences. Have children circle the high frequency word in each of their sentences.

Wrap Up **DAY** 3

Table Talk *Daily* What are some of the different things you do with your friends? How do these different things change your friendship? Have children discuss these questions.

Produce Language Have children fold a piece of drawing paper in half. On each side of the paper, have them draw themselves doing two different things with a friend. Have them tell about the different things they are doing.

Today children should have:

☑ **Learned** and applied the high frequency words *see* and *look*.

☑ **Spoken** complete sentences about how a friendship might change.

☑ **Recognized** ways in which friendships might change.

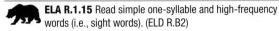 ELA R.1.15 Read simple one-syllable and high-frequency words (i.e., sight words). (ELD R.B2)

105

OBJECTIVE

To discuss how we feel when a friendship changes; to recognize final /f/; to practice initial /f/; to substitute medial and final sounds.

Concept Talk

FORM & FUNCTION

Connect to Day 3 Elicit from children that yesterday they talked about why a friendship might change.

Introduce the Daily Question Ask: How do you feel when a friendship changes? Ask children if there are times when they disagree with their friend. How is that different than when you are getting along? Children can tell about different feelings they have.

Use the Poster Use the Day 4 teaching notes at the bottom of the poster.

Phonemic Awareness/Phonics

Phoneme Isolation/Segmentation Say the words *puff* and *stiff*, emphasizing the ending sound in each. Have children repeat the words. Ask children to identify the letter sound that they hear at the end of each word. Then do the same for the words *off* and *if*. Review the initial /f/ sound by asking for the beginning sound in words like *family* and *fun*. Then have them change the /f/ in *stiff* to /k/, the /i/ in *stiff* to /u/. Substitute ending and medial sounds in other words as well.

Have children complete the Worktext page.

Corrective Feedback If children have difficulty choosing the correct pictures, say the words that name each picture. Emphasize the initial phonemes.

✏ **Color** Color pictures with *f*.

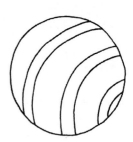

106 🐻 **ELA R1.14** Match all consonant and short-vowel sounds to appropriate letters. (ELD R.B10)

Wrap Up   DAY 4

Daily **Table Talk** What are some of the different feelings that you have when you are with your friends? Have children discuss the question.

Produce Language Have children draw a picture that shows how they might feel when they are with a friend. Have them tell about their drawing.

Today children should have:

☑ **Learned** and applied vocabulary related to feelings we have when a friendship changes.

☑ **Spoken** complete sentences about different feelings we have when a friendship changes.

☑ **Recognized** the initial /f/ in words.

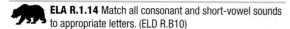 **ELA R.1.14** Match all consonant and short-vowel sounds to appropriate letters. (ELD R.B10)

106 Friends Change • Unit 3, Week 4

Preteach LS Reteach Leveled Support **Phonemic Awareness/Phonics**

① **Beginning** Say the words *fun, feather,* and *foot,* emphasizing the sound /f/ at the beginning of each. I hear /f/ at the beginning of each of these words. Here are other words that begin with /f/: *finger, father, fill, football, fan.* Have children repeat the words after you.

② ③ **Early Intermediate/Intermediate** Review the sound of the letter *f*. Raise your hand if you hear the sound of the letter *f* in these words: *fun, feather, foot, happy, finger, boy, hat, fill, nap, fan.*

④ ⑤ **Early Advanced/Advanced** Do the same as the Early Intermediate/Intermediate activity. Then have children say words that begin with /f/. Write the words that they say. Read these words and have children repeat them.

How do friendships change?

 Draw

Leveled Support — Concept Vocabulary

① Beginning Display the Word Cards for *friends* and *game*. Say each word. Ask children to repeat and point to the matching card. Have children name some of their friends. Say the names of games they play at school. Have them repeat the names.

② ③ Early Intermediate/Intermediate Draw a picture of two children playing a game together. After the picture is completed, ask: Who is playing in this picture? What are they playing? Have children role play playing a game with a friend. Have children guess the game they are playing.

④ ⑤ Early Advanced/Advanced Display the Word Cards for *friends* and *game*. Have children name some of their friends. Write these names under the title "Friends." Read the list of friends when it is complete. Do the same for games that they like to play.

OBJECTIVE

To guide children to express their understanding of weekly concepts and vocabulary.

Think, Talk, and Recognize!

Concept Talk

Connect to Day 4 How do you feel when a friendship changes? Model how to answer yesterday's question with a sentence.

Review the Weekly Question Ask: How do friendships change? Have children talk about different ways that their friendships change. Friends might move away or meet new friends. Friends might decide they like to do different things.

Use the Poster Use the Day 5 teaching notes at the bottom of the poster.

Review Concept Vocabulary Review the vocabulary introduced on Day 1.

Concept Wrap Up

Have children draw to answer the question: How do friendships change? Discuss the picture of the two friends having fun together. What other kinds of things can these friends do together?

Table Talk How do friendships change? Have children discuss the question, using the vocabulary words they have learned this week.

Produce Language To build fluency, children can label, write about, or speak about their drawings. Ask children to respond to what they have read or heard.

Today children should have:

☑ **Reviewed** the weekly concept and concept vocabulary.

☑ **Spoken** about how friendships can change.

☑ **Drawn or written** to show how friendships can change.

 ELA LS. 1.2 Share information and ideas, speaking audibly in complete, coherent sentences. (ELD LS.B1)

WEEK 5

CALIFORNIA

Weekly Lesson Plan

Last Week
Unit 3, Week 4
Friends Change

Question of the Week How was the past different from today?

DAY **1** Get Ready to Read	DAY **2** Read and Comprehend

Instructional Plan and Materials

- **Word Cards**
  56–57

- **Poster**
  Poster 17 can be used at beginning or end of day.

- **Big Book**
  Life Long Ago

- **Song Book**, p. 17

Transparencies Explore content and vocabulary and model fluent reading.

For further information about using these components, see pages x–xv.

Build Background	**Language: Category Words**

Preteach/Review 10–15 min
Poster, Song Book, Big Book
  Leveled Support Preteach
  Practice Stations Preteach
 	
Teach 35–45 min
  Concept Talk
  Oral Vocabulary Routine
    Word Cards
  Build Concept Vocabulary
  Daily Table Talk
 	
Check/Reteach 5–10 min
Poster, Word Cards
  Leveled Support Reteach
	Preteach/Review 10–15 min
	Poster
	  Leveled Support Preteach
	  Practice Stations Review
	
	Teach 35–45 min
	  Category Words
	  Daily Table Talk
	
	Check/Reteach 5–10 min
	Poster, Word Cards
	  Leveled Support Reteach

	Fluency: Writing or Speaking
ELA R 1.18 Describe common objects and events in both general and specific language.	ELA R 1.17 Identify and sort common words in basic categories (e.g., colors, shapes, foods).

CALIFORNIA Standards

GK His-Soc Sci K.6.3 Understand how people lived in earlier times and how their lives would be different today (e.g., getting water from a well, growing food, making clothing, having fun, forming organizations, living by rules and laws).

Academic Language

	Category Words: book, calendar, crayons, desk, paper, pencil

Get Online! www.pearsonsuccessnet.com

Concept Talk Video	**Background Building Audio Slideshow**

This Week

Unit 3, Week 5

Things Change

Next Week

Unit 3, Week 6

Feelings Change

DAY 3 Read and Comprehend	**DAY 4** Language Arts	**DAY 5** Language Arts
Language: High Frequency Words	**Phonics**	**Think, Talk, and Recognize**
Preteach/Review 10–15 min Poster **Leveled Support Preteach** **Practice Stations Review**	**Preteach/Review** 10–15 min Poster **Leveled Support Preteach** **Practice Stations Review**	**Preteach/Review** 10–15 min Poster **Leveled Support Preteach** **Practice Stations Review**
Teach 35–45 min **High Frequency Words** **Daily Table Talk**	**Teach** 35–45 min **Phonics** **Daily Table Talk**	**Teach** 15–20 min **Think, Talk, and Recognize** **Concept Wrap Up**
Check/Reteach 5–10 min Poster, Word Cards **Leveled Support Reteach**	**Check/Reteach** 5–10 min Poster, Word Cards **Leveled Support Reteach**	**Check/Reteach** 30–40 min Poster, Word Cards, Song Book **Leveled Support Reteach**
		Fluency: Writing or Speaking
ELA R 1.15 Read simple one-syllable and high frequency words (i.e., sight words).	**ELA R 1.14** Match all consonant and short-vowel sounds to appropriate letters.	**ELA LS 1.2** Share information and ideas, speaking audibly in complete, coherent sentences.
High Frequency Words: they, you, of		

Weekly Practice

Practice Stations

Materials and Activity

pictures of things from the past (old-time telephone, typewriter, refrigerator, horse and buggy, television, and so on); scissors

paper, markers, crayons, shoe box

Things Change Over Time

Have partners take turns telling what they know about the pictures of things from the past. Partners can add any extra information that they know. Have them take turns telling what is the same and different about each pair of illustrations.

Classroom Time Capsule

Explain that some people keep items in a special box and open it later to see how things have changed. Have children create their own time capsule. They can draw pictures of things they have done, or what they have learned in Kindergarten. Children can decorate the shoe box. Put all the drawings in the box and open it at the end of the year to see what has changed.

Preteach/Reteach

Transfer and Common Misconceptions

Comparisons

Some children may have difficulty verbalizing the differences or similarities between the old and modern machines. Model comparisons for them.

Words That are Plural

It may be difficult for some children to understand that news is the same whether singular or plural.

Produce Language

Weekly Concept and Language Goal

CONCEPT GOALS

- understand the difference between the past and the present
- tell how machines today make work easier
- compare and contrast schools in the past and the present

By Day 5, children should be able to talk about their drawings and write a one-word label.

Daily Table Talk

❶ **Beginning**

Children pantomime while you provide the language.

❷ ❸ **Early Intermediate/Intermediate**

Children pantomime and say a word or phrase: (horse and buggy) took longer or needed a horse.

❹ ❺ **Early Advanced/Advanced**

Children say a sentence while pantomiming: Cars are faster than horse and buggies.

Daily Table Talk

❶ **Beginning**

Children talk about their drawings.

❷ ❸ **Early Intermediate/Intermediate**

Children write one-word labels.

❹ ❺ **Early Advanced/Advanced**

Children write a phrase or sentence.

DAY 3 Read and Comprehend

 DAY 4 Language Arts

 DAY 5 Language Arts

two index cards with these word pictures on them: *desk, calendar, book, pencil, crayon, puzzle, chalk, CD player, marker, eraser, chair, stove,* and *refrigerator*

index cards with the high frequency words *they, you,* and *of;* letter tiles; paper for a placemat with two columns and these sentences at the bottom of the paper: *They gave you a box of crayons. You are a friend of mine. They sent you a letter.*

two sets of cards with picture words for: *octopus, on, off, ostrich, otter, ox, pot, bottle, cot, dot, hot, knot, top,* and *stop*

Match by Category

Mix up the cards and turn them face down on the table in rows. Partners take turns matching identical cards that show things that are found in a classroom. If a match is made, have the child keep the cards and play again. If the child does not make a match, the other partner takes a turn.

Copy the Word

Have children place the word card with the high frequency word in the first column. Have them use the Letter Tiles to spell the word in the second column. Have students circle all of the high frequency words in the sentences on the bottom of the page.

Go Fish

Each partner gets five cards. The rest are spread face down on the table. Partners take turns asking each other for a matching picture card: *Do you have an octopus?* If they do, they give it to their partner. If not, the partner picks a card from the center of the table. If he/she still does not make a match, it is the partner's turn.

Pronouncing /r/

The letter *r* can be a problem for many non-English speakers. Model pronouncing any of the words that contain an *r* in their spellings.

Sight Words

Characteristic of sight words, the words *of, you,* and *they* are not pronounced as they are spelled. Children will have to memorize them.

Short *o*, Long *o*

Children may be confused because words such as *orange, oar,* and *open* begin with the letter *o,* but have a different sound.

 Daily Table Talk

🔵 **Beginning**
> Name things in a classroom from long ago and in a classroom today. Have children respond by saying *long ago* or *today.*

🔵🔵 **Early Intermediate/Intermediate**
> Word or phrase: computer, calculator, videos

🔵🔵 **Early Advanced/Advanced**
> Sentence: Classrooms today have computers.

 Daily Table Talk

🔵 **Beginning**
> Children raise their hands as you mention things that people used to do for fun.

🔵🔵 **Early Intermediate/Intermediate**
> One or two word: listen to the radio, picnics, visit neighbors

🔵🔵 **Early Advanced/Advanced**
> Sentence: People long ago did not. They listened to their radios.

 **Daily Table Talk**

🔵 **Beginning** Child draws and speaks about the drawing.

🔵🔵 **Early Intermediate/Intermediate** Child draws and speaks about the drawing using at least one concept vocabulary word.

🔵🔵 **Early Advanced/Advanced** Child draws and provides a label for the drawing that includes a vocabulary word.

OBJECTIVE

To introduce and discuss concepts and vocabulary related to the ways in which things from the past change.

Build Background

Get Ready to Read!

Question of the Week

How was the past different from today?

www.pearsonsuccessnet.com

Concept Talk

Use the Big Book If you haven't introduced the Big Book, consider reading it to children. Connect to the unit theme, Changes—Changes All Around Us.

Introduce the Weekly Concept Tell children that today they will talk about how things of the past are different from things today. Ask the weekly question: How was the past different from today?

Use the Poster Direct children's attention to the weekly poster. Use the Day 1 teaching notes at the bottom of the poster.

Sing the Song Use the song **Fast and Slow News** to reinforce children's understanding of the weekly concept. Have the children sing or simply chant the words with you.

Use a Transparency Use the Shared Description Map (Transparency 8) to help children compare the present with the past.

Things Change

Vocabulary

cameras

news

How was the past different from today?

108

Vocabulary

cameras equipment used for taking photographs or for making movies or television

news information about something that has happened recently

ELA R 1.18 Describe common objects and events in both general and specific language. (ELD R.B4)

109

Introduce Concept Vocabulary

1. **Say the Word** Display the Word Card as you say *cameras.* Have children repeat the word.

2. **Introduce the Meaning** Show a camera or a photograph of one. Ask questions about a camera. Has anyone ever taken a picture of you? What did they use to take the picture?

3. **Demonstrate** Have children role play how they would use a camera to take a picture of someone or something in the classroom.

4. **Apply** Have children demonstrate their understanding. Repeat with other vocabulary words.

Corrective Feedback If children have difficulty with the words, show the actual items to children to further their understanding.

Concept Work

Have children look at the first picture. Tell them that the picture shows how things have changed. Today, people can get from place to place driving a car. Long ago, people could get from place to place in a horse-drawn buggy. Continue with the other illustrations. Have children choose a picture to color. They can talk about their pictures with partners, using the word *change* to tell how things are different than they were in the past.

Leveled Support Vocabulary in Context

❶ **Beginning** Have children point to the newspaper in the illustration as you say *news.* Children can repeat the word after you. Ask them if the television could also have news.

❷ ❸ **Early Intermediate/Intermediate** Have children place the Word Cards in categories: *long ago* and *today.* They may place the cards in both categories. Continue with the items pictured in the Worktext.

❹ ❺ **Early Advanced/Advanced** Do the same activity as Early Intermediate/ Intermediate, but have children work with partners to say a sentence using information from the chart you create. Provide a sentence frame: *Long ago _____. Today _____.*

Wrap Up   DAY 1

Table Talk *Daily* How are things from the past different from things today? Have children answer the question, using the vocabulary words.

Produce Language Have children explain in a sentence what is different about riding in a horse and buggy and riding in a car.

Today children should have:

☑ **Learned** and applied vocabulary related to how things from the past are different from things today.

☑ **Spoken** complete sentences about how things from the past are different from things today.

☑ **Recognized** concept vocabulary words.

 ELA R 1.18 Describe common objects and events in both general and specific language. (ELD R.B.4)

To discuss things that people used to do for fun; to to learn the sound /o/ and identify medial and initial /o/; to substitute medial sounds.

Concept Talk

 FORM & FUNCTION

Connect to Day 3 How are schools today different from those in the past?

Introduce the Daily Question Ask: What is something that people used to do for fun? Explain how children used to gather a group of friends on their block and play baseball in the street. Families would get in their horses and buggies and go for a ride. How is this different from the way people have fun today? Have children tell how people have fun today.

Use the Poster Use the Day 4 teaching notes at the bottom of the poster.

Phonological Awareness

Phoneme Isolation/Segmentation Teach children the /o/ sound. Say the words *mop, on* and *octopus*, emphasizing the /o/ in each. Have children repeat the words. Ask children to identify the letter sound that they hear at the beginning of each word. Then ask what vowel sound they hear in *pot* and *top.* Have them change the /o/ in *pot* to /e/ and the /o/ in *top* to /a/. Have children complete the activity in the Worktext. Have children circle the pictures with /o/.

Corrective Feedback For children who have difficulty identifying /o/, repeat the sound showing them how your mouth opens wide like the letter *o* when you make the sound. Emphasize this when saying words like *otter, hot,* and *mop.*

Wrap Up — DAY 4

Daily **Table Talk** What is something that people used to do for fun? Have children discuss the question.

Produce Language Have children talk about things from long ago that people still like to do for fun today.

Today children should have:

- ☑ **Learned** and applied vocabulary related to things that people used to do for fun.

- ☑ **Spoken** complete sentences about things people used to do for fun.

- ☑ **Recognized** the initial and medial /o/.

 ELA R 1.14 Match all consonant and short -vowel sounds to appropriate letters. (ELD R.B10)

Identify Sound Oo

✏ **Color** Color things with *o.*

112 **ELA R1.14** Match all consonant and short-vowel sounds to appropriate letters. (ELD R.B10)

 Leveled Support Phonemic Awareness

① **Beginning** Say the words *on, not,* and *job,* emphasizing the sound /o/ in each of the words. I hear the sound /o/ in each of these words. Repeat these words that have the /o/ sound: *otter, top, cot, job, octopus.*

② ③ **Early Intermediate/Intermediate** Review one of the sounds of the letter *o.* Raise your hand if you hear the sound /o/ in each word I say: *on, knot, jet, otter, top, fun, neck, hop, fan, nap, hot, night, job.*

④ ⑤ **Early Advanced/Advanced** Review the sound /o/. Have children say words that have the sound /o/. Write the words that they say. Read these words and have children repeat them.

How was the past different from today?

 Draw

OBJECTIVE

To guide children to express their understanding of weekly concepts and vocabulary.

Think, Talk, and Recognize!

Concept Talk

Connect to Day 4 Remind children that yesterday they discussed things that people used to do for fun. Model how to answer yesterday's question with a sentence.

Review the Weekly Question Ask: How was the past different from today? Have children talk about some of the things that people used in the past. Have them compare these things to today.

Use the Poster Use the Day 5 teaching notes at the bottom of the poster.

Review Concept Vocabulary Review the vocabulary introduced on Day 1.

Concept Wrap Up

Have children draw to answer the question: How was the past different from today? Discuss the picture of the people riding in the horse and buggy. What do we use today instead of the horse and buggy? How has that changed things today?

Leveled Support   Concept Vocabulary

(Preteach / Reteach)

① **Beginning** Display the Word Cards for *camera* and *news.* Say each word. Ask children to repeat and point to the matching card.

② ③ **Early Intermediate/Intermediate** Show children a newspaper. What is this called? What does it tell us? Show children pictures in the paper. What did the person use to take this picture?

④ ⑤ **Early Advanced/Advanced** Do the Early Intermediate/Intermediate activity. Have children say sentences telling where we can find the news and why we use a camera.

Wrap Up **DAY 5**

Table Talk (Daily) How was the past different from today? Have children discuss the question, using the vocabulary words they have learned this week.

Produce Language To build fluency, children can label, write about, or speak about their drawings. Ask children to respond to what they read or heard.

Today children should have:

☑ **Reviewed** the weekly concept and concept vocabulary.

☑ **Spoken** about how things from the past have changed.

☑ **Drawn or written** about how things have changed since the past.

ELA LS 1.2 Share information and ideas, speaking audibly in complete, coherent sentences. (ELD LS.B1)

113

WEEK **6**
CALIFORNIA

Weekly Lesson Plan

Last Week
Unit 3, Week 5
Things Change

Question of the Week How can we change the way we feel?

	DAY 1 Get Ready to Read	**DAY 2** Read and Comprehend
	Build Background	**Language: Category Words**

Instructional Plan and Materials

- **Word Cards** 58–59

Life Long Ago

- **Big Book** Life Long Ago

- **Poster** Poster 18 can be used at beginning or end of day.

- **Song Book**, p. 18

Transparencies Explore content and vocabulary and model fluent reading.

For further information about using these components, see pages x–xv.

DAY 1 — Build Background

Preteach/Review 10–15 min
Poster, Song Book, Big Book
- **Leveled Support Preteach**
- **Practice Stations Preteach**

Teach 35–45 min
- **Concept Talk**
- **Oral Vocabulary Routine**
  Word Cards
- **Build Concept Vocabulary**
- **Daily Table Talk**

Check/Reteach 5–10 min
Poster, Word Cards
- **Leveled Support Reteach**

DAY 2 — Language: Category Words

Preteach/Review 10–15 min
Poster
- **Leveled Support Preteach**
- **Practice Stations Review**

Teach 35–45 min
- **Category Words**
- **Daily Table Talk**

Check/Reteach 5–10 min
Poster, Word Cards
- **Leveled Support Reteach**

Fluency: Writing or Speaking

CALIFORNIA Standards

GK Sci 4.e Communicate observations orally and through drawings.

ELA LS 2.3 Relate an experience or creative story in a logical sequence.

ELA R 1.17 Identify and sort common words in basic categories (e.g., colors, shapes, foods).

Academic Language

Category Words: mouth, tail, legs, paws

This Week
Unit 3, Week 6

Feelings Change

Next Week
Unit 4, Week 1
A Day's Adventures

DAY 3 FORM & FUNCTION Read and Comprehend	**DAY 4** FORM & FUNCTION Language Arts	**DAY 5** Language Arts
Language: High Frequency Words	**Phonics**	**Think, Talk, and Recognize**
Preteach/Review 10–15 min Poster **Leveled Support Preteach** **Practice Stations Review**	**Preteach/Review** 10–15 min Poster **Leveled Support Preteach** **Practice Stations Review**	**Preteach/Review** 10–15 min Poster **Leveled Support Preteach** **Practice Stations Review**
Teach 35–45 min **High Frequency Words** **Daily Table Talk**	**Teach** 35–45 min **Phonics** **Daily Table Talk**	**Teach** 15–20 min **Think, Talk, and Recognize** **Concept Wrap Up**
Check/Reteach 5–10 min Poster, Word Cards **Leveled Support Reteach**	**Check/Reteach** 5–10 min Poster, Word Cards **Leveled Support Reteach**	**Check/Reteach** 30–40 min Poster, Word Cards, Song Book **Leveled Support Reteach**
		Fluency: Writing or Speaking
ELA R 1.15 Read simple one-syllable and high frequency words (i.e., sight words).	**ELA R 1.14** Match all consonant and short-vowel sounds to appropriate letters.	**ELA LS 1.2** Share information and ideas, speaking audibly in complete, coherent sentences.
High Frequency Words: they, you of		

Practice Stations

Materials and Activity

several books children are familiar with that evoke different emotions, crayons, colored pencils, paper

How I Feel

Have partners review each book by looking at the pictures. Have them tell each other how they felt when they read each book. Have students draw a picture of something that makes them happy, sad, excited, or worried. Have them tell about their drawings.

paper plates, markers, scissors, string

What Sound Do I Make?

Show children how to make a lion mask. Cut out the eye holes for children and have them color the paper plate to look like a lion. Attach string to each mask and have children tie them on each other. Children can take turns telling what sound they make as lions.

Preteach/Reteach

Transfer and Common Misconceptions

Naming Their Feelings

To help children name feelings, pantomime the feeling and name it. Children can repeat.

Three Consonant Syllable Structure

Some Japanese-speakers have a difficult time pronouncing words with three-consonant blends. Remind children to say the sound for each of the letters.

Produce Language

Weekly Concept and Language Goal

CONCEPT GOALS

- recognize that our feelings can change
- describe the characteristics of a good friend

By Day 5, children should be able to talk about their drawings and write a one-word label.

Daily Table Talk

❶ **Beginning**

Children pantomime feelings that they feel while you describe a situation.

❷ ❸ **Early Intermediate/Intermediate**

Describe a situation. Child says a word about feelings: happy, sad, afraid.

❹ ❺ **Early Advanced/Advanced**

Children say a sentence: I feel sad when I get hurt.

Daily Table Talk

❶ **Beginning**

Children talk about their drawings.

❷ ❸ **Early Intermediate/Intermediate**

Children write one-word labels.

❹ ❺ **Early Advanced/Advanced**

Children write a phrase or sentence.

DAY 3 · FORM & FUNCTION — Read and Comprehend

chart paper with a drawing of a pet with body parts labeled and a line connecting the label to the body part; paper, pencil, crayons

DAY 4 · FORM & FUNCTION — Language Arts

set of cards for each child with these high frequency words: *they, you,* and *of;* markers, sequins, macaroni or beads, glue

DAY 5 · Language Arts

index cards with 2 of each of these picture words (You can use the ones from Week 5): *octopus, on, off, ostrich, otter, ox, pot, bottle, cot, dot, hot, knot, top, stop;* one card with a picture of an "Old Maid"

Name the Body Parts

Have children draw a picture of an animal such as a dog, cat, or horse. Have them make labels for the body parts of their animal by copying your labels on the chart paper. Have them draw lines from their labels to the body parts, just like you did. Have them read their labels to their partners.

Write the Word

Have children copy the high frequency words from their word cards by using the provided materials. Have them cut up the words into letters. Have them put the letters together to spell the high frequency words.

Old Maid

Deal all of the cards. The first person picks a card from the hand of the child to the left. If it is a match, the child names the picture, puts the cards on the table, and picks again. If it is not a match, the next child has a turn. Play continues until one child is left with the "Old Maid."

Writing Plural Words

Be sure that children write the plural forms of any body part that numbers more than one. Point out that adding *s* to many words shows that there are more than one.

Prepositions

Children who speak Spanish will be familiar with prepositions. Build on what they already know about these words to boost their confidence using these words in English.

Naming the Pictures

Name all the pictures before playing the game so that children know the names for each.

 **Daily Table Talk**

① **Beginning** — Children pantomime feeling to your descriptions. (*Example:* How would you feel if your friend moved away?)

②③ **Early Intermediate/Intermediate** — Children respond to same questions with words or phrases: very sad, excited

④⑤ **Early Advanced/Advanced** — Sentence: I would feel sad.

 Daily Table Talk

① **Beginning** — Children raise their hands when you describe how a friend behaves: grabs toys away from you, shares his crayons, and so on.

②③ **Early Intermediate/Intermediate** — Responds to prompts with a word or phrase: a friend, not a friend or yes, no

④⑤ **Early Advanced/Advanced** — Sentence: My friend helps me clean up.

 **Daily Table Talk**

① **Beginning** Child draws and speaks about the drawing.

②③ **Early Intermediate/Intermediate** Child draws and speaks about the drawing using at least one concept vocabulary word.

④⑤ **Early Advanced/Advanced** Child draws and provides a label for the drawing that includes a vocabulary word.

To introduce concepts and vocabulary related to the way that people's feelings change.

Build Background Get Ready to Read!

Question of the Week How can we change the way we feel?

www.pearsonsuccessnet.com

Concept Talk

Use the Big Book If you haven't introduced the Big Book, consider reading it to children. Connect to the unit theme, Changes—Changes All Around Us.

Introduce the Weekly Concept Tell children that today they will talk about how we can change the way we feel. Ask the weekly question: How can we change the way we feel?

Use the Poster Direct children's attention to the weekly poster. Use the Day 1 teaching notes at the bottom of the poster.

Sing the Song Use the song **We Are Friends** to reinforce children's understanding of the weekly concept. Have the children sing or simply chant the words with you.

Use a Transparency Use the Cause and Effect Map (Transparency 1) to help children organize ideas about how we can change the way we feel.

Feelings Change

Vocabulary

roar

strong

How can we change the way we feel?

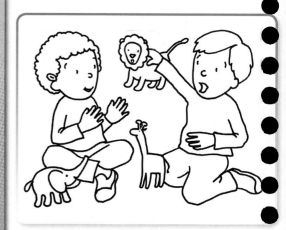

114

Vocabulary

roar to make a deep, very loud noise

strong having a lot of physical power

Introduce Concept Vocabulary

1. **Say the Word** Display the Word Card as you say *roar.* Have children repeat the word.

2. **Introduce Word Meaning** Ask questions about *roar.* Have you ever heard a lion roar? It opens its mouth and makes a very loud sound. It look like it is yawning, but the sound is much louder.

3. **Demonstrate** Have children role play how a lion roars.

4. **Apply** Have children demonstrate their understanding.

Repeat with other vocabulary words.

Corrective Feedback If children have difficulty understanding the words, physically demonstrate them for children. Have them follow your modeling.

Concept Work

Discuss the illustrations with children. For the first, ask what has happened, how feelings may have changed, and what friends are doing to help each other. Continue with the other illustrations. Then have children color the pictures.

Preteach / Reteach LS Leveled Support **Vocabulary in Context**

❶ **Beginning** Hold up the Word Cards as you say the words. Have children repeat after you. Make a physical gesture or pantomime for each word. Have children model your physical movements to remember the words.

❷ ❸ **Early Intermediate/Intermediate** Have children interact with the illustrations to understand the word meanings. **Ask:** Which child is playing with an animal that roars? Point to the animal. Which child might feel strong? Point to that child.

❹ ❺ **Early Advanced/Advanced** Have children look at each picture and tell the feeling that is demonstrated. Have children tell what makes them feel that same way.

Wrap Up   DAY

Daily **Table Talk** How can we change the way we feel? Have children answer the question, using the vocabulary words.

Produce Language Play charades. Have children pretend to be someone who is happy, sad, excited, or afraid. Have children say a sentence that tells about how the person feels.

Today children should have:

☑ **Learned** and applied vocabulary related to changing the way we feel.

☑ **Spoken** complete sentences about feelings.

☑ **Recognized** concept vocabulary words.

ELA LS 2.3 Relate an experience or creative story in a logical sequence. (ELD LS.B3)

115

OBJECTIVE

To discuss how friends are alike and different; to discuss animal body parts.

Concept Talk

Connect to Day 1 Recall with children that yesterday they talked about how they can change the way they feel. What can you do to make someone laugh?

Introduce the Daily Question How are friends alike and different? Have children answer orally.

Use the Poster Use the Day 2 teaching notes at the bottom of the poster.

Introduce Category Words

1. **Say the Word** Have children point to the paws. Say the word and have children repeat it.

2. **Introduce the Meaning** Ask questions: What animals have paws? How do animals use their paws?

3. **Demonstrate** Show the location of paws on a stuffed animal in the classroom. Role play how a cat would play with a ball of yarn with its paws.

4. **Apply** Repeat with other vocabulary words and elicit that they all belong to the category "animal body parts."

Have children point to items as you name them. Then have them complete the activity in the Worktext.

Wrap Up   DAY 2

Daily Table Talk How are friends alike and different? Have children talk about how the friends are alike and different.

Produce Language To build fluency, encourage children to label or write a sentence about the animals on the Worktext page. They can share their writing with partners.

Today children should have:

- ☑ **Learned** and applied vocabulary related to animal body parts.

- ☑ **Spoken** complete sentences about how friends are alike and different.

- ☑ **Recognized** words that belong in the same category.

 ELA R1.17 Identify and sort common words in basic categories (e.g., colors, shapes, foods). (ELD R.B4)

Animal Body Parts

Picture Dictionary

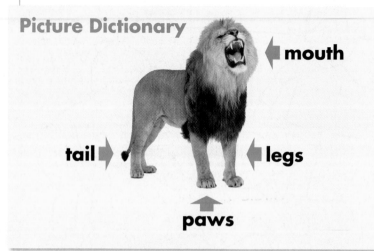

mouth

tail

legs

paws

✏️ **Circle** Circle the tail.

✏️ **Circle** Circle a paw.

116   **ELA R1.17** Identify and sort common words in basic categories (e.g., colors, shapes, foods). (ELD R.B4)

Leveled Support   Category Words

Preteach / Reteach

① **Beginning** Have children point to each animal body part on the Worktext page. Say the word for each picture. Then have children repeat the word.

②③ **Early Intermediate/Intermediate** Say the name of an animal body part on the Worktext page. Have children point to the picture. Then reverse the activity as you point to a picture and ask children to name the animal body part. Have children name different animals that have each of the body parts. Children can also identify body parts on stuffed animals in the room.

④⑤ **Early Advanced/Advanced** Have children draw their favorite animals. Have them tell a partner about the body parts of that animal.

How do friendships change?

✎ **Circle** Circle *They*.
They were good friends.

✎ **Circle** Circle *you*. Circle *of*.
Friends take care of you.

ELA R1.15 Read simple one-syllable and high-frequency words (i.e., sight words). (ELD R.B2)

117

To discuss how friendships change; to introduce the high-frequency words *they, you,* and *of.*

Concept Talk

 FORM & FUNCTION

Connect to Day 2 Remind children that yesterday they talked about how friends are alike and different. How are you like your friend? How are you different?

Introduce the Daily Question Ask: How do friendships change? Discuss the kinds of things that can change friendships. What would happen if your friend moved away? What would happen if your friend was in a different class?

Use the Poster Use the Day 3 teaching notes at the bottom of the poster.

Review Concept Vocabulary Review the words introduced on Day 1.

Introduce High Frequency Words

Introduce *they, you,* and *of* by role playing and speaking with sentences such as *You are my friend. They drew a picture of you.* Help children circle the words on the Worktext page.

Corrective Feedback If children have difficulty finding the high frequency words in the sentences, write the words on sticky notes so that children can place them near the words on the Worktext page.

Preteach / Reteach LS **Leveled Support** **High Frequency Words**

❶ **Beginning** Write the words *they, you,* and *of.* Read the words. Have the children repeat the words. Write sentences like: *You are a friend of mine. They know you.* Circle the high frequency words in each sentence.

❷ ❸ **Early Intermediate/Intermediate** Do the Beginning activity, but have the children circle the high frequency words themselves.

❹ ❺ **Early Advanced/Advanced** Write the words *they, you,* and *of.* Have the children say sentences using these words. Write their sentences. Have children circle the high frequency word in each of their sentences.

Wrap Up DAY 3

Daily Table Talk How do friendships change? How do you feel when these changes happen? Discuss these questions.

Produce Language Have children draw a picture of themselves showing how a friendship might change. Have them tell about their pictures.

Today children should have:

☑ **Learned** and applied the high frequency words *they, you,* and *of.*

☑ **Spoken** complete sentences about how friendships change.

☑ **Recognized** that friendships can change.

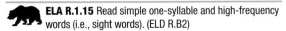 ELA R.1.15 Read simple one-syllable and high-frequency words (i.e., sight words). (ELD R.B2)

OBJECTIVE

To discuss what makes a good friend; to recognize /o/; to practice medial and initial /o/; to substitute medial sounds /o/, /a/, and /i/.

Concept Talk

 FORM & FUNCTION

Connect to Day 3 Elicit from children that yesterday they talked about how friendships change. What kinds of things can happen to make friendships change?

Introduce the Daily Question Ask: What makes a good friend? Ask children what they like about their friend. How does your friend treat you? How do you treat your friend?

Use the Poster Use the Day 4 teaching notes at the bottom of the poster.

Phonemic Awareness

Phoneme Isolation/Segmentation Review the sound /o/. Say the words *odd* and *on*, emphasizing the initial sound in each. Have children repeat the words. Ask children to identify the letter sound that they hear at the beginning of each word. Then do the same for the words *lot, top, cob,* emphasizing the medial sound in each. Then have them change the /o/ in *lot* to /i/, the /o/ in *top* to /a/, the /o/ in *cob* to /a/.

Have children complete the Worktext page.

Corrective Feedback If children have difficulty, remind them that the sound may be in the middle of the word or the beginning of the word. Say each pair of words: *fox/bee, clock/bed, cat/otter, octopus/duck.* Emphasize the vowel sounds.

Wrap Up   DAY 4

 Table Talk What makes a good friend? Have children discuss the question.

Produce Language Have children tell about a time that a friend helped them.

Today children should have:

☑ **Learned** and applied vocabulary related to being a good friend.

☑ **Spoken** complete sentences about being a good friend.

☑ **Recognized** initial and medial /o/.

ELA R.1.14 Match all consonant and short-vowel sounds to appropriate letters. (ELD R.B10)

Identify Sound Oo

 Circle Circle things with *o*.

Leveled Support **Phonemic Awareness**

Preteach LS Reteach

① **Beginning** Say the words *on, ox,* and *odd,* emphasizing the sound /o/ at the beginning of each. I hear the sound /o/ at the beginning of each of these words. Say *octopus* and *otter*. Have children repeat the words. Now listen to these words that have /o/ as the middle sound: *hot, rod, Tom.* Have children repeat these words.

② ③ **Early Intermediate/Intermediate** Review the sound /o/. Raise your hand if you hear /o/ in these words: *on, ox, add, odd, octopus, ham, hot, rod, bud.*

④ ⑤ **Early Advanced/Advanced** Review the sound of the letter *o*. Have children say a rhyming word for each of these words: *hot, rod, mob, tock, mom, top.*

How can we change the way we feel?

✎ Draw

OBJECTIVE

To guide children to express their understanding of weekly concepts and vocabulary.

Think, Talk, and Recognize!

Concept Talk

Connect to Day 4 Remind children that yesterday they discussed what makes a good friend. Model how to answer yesterday's question with a sentence.

Review the Weekly Question Ask: How can we change the way we feel? Have children talk about how they feel when a friend tells them a funny story.

Use the Poster Use the Day 5 teaching notes at the bottom of the poster.

Review Concept Vocabulary Review the vocabulary introduced on Day 1.

Concept Wrap Up

Have children draw to answer the question: *How can we change the way we feel?* Discuss the picture of the child comforting a friend. How is that child helping her friend? How will the friend feel now?

Preteach / Reteach
LS Leveled Support **Concept Vocabulary**

① **Beginning** Display the Word Cards for *strong* and *roar.* Say each word. Ask children to repeat and point to the matching card. Have them flex their muscles to show how strong they are. Have them roar like a lion.

② ③ **Early Intermediate/Intermediate** Play a guessing game with the children. Ask questions like: What is a strong animal that can climb a tree? What is a strong animal that can pull a buggy? What is a strong animal that can roar?

④ ⑤ **Early Advanced/Advanced** Write *strong.* Have children say things that a strong person can do. Write their answers. Read their answers and have them echo read them to you.

Wrap Up DAY 5

Daily Table Talk How can we change the way we feel? Have children discuss the question, using the vocabulary words they have learned this week.

Produce Language To build fluency, children can label, write about, or speak about their drawings. Ask children to respond to what they read or heard.

Today children should have:

☑ **Reviewed** the weekly concept and concept vocabulary.

☑ **Spoken** about how we can change the way we feel.

☑ **Drawn or written** to show how we can change the way we feel.

 ELA LS. 1.2 Share information and ideas, speaking audibly in complete, coherent sentences. (ELD LS.B1)

119

Where will our adventures take us?

Discuss the Big Question

Read and discuss the unit question. Introduce the word *adventure*. An adventure is when we go somewhere or do something that is very exciting. An adventure can take place anywhere, even in your town. Has anyone had an adventure they would like to tell about?

Have children use the pictures along the side of the page to preview the weekly concepts for this unit. Read the weekly questions together. Discuss the weekly questions and how they relate to the big question.

 www.pearsonsuccessnet.com

• Unit 4 Big Question Video

Use the Concept and Language Goals throughout the unit to develop the big idea.

Children develop concepts and language as they talk about, use, and practice:

• Concept Vocabulary
• Academic Language
• Language Forms and Functions
• Category Words
• High Frequency Words

Get Online!
PearsonSuccessNet.com
Hear it!
See it!
Do it!

• Big Idea Video
• Concept Talk Video
• Background Building Audio Slideshow
• eBooks

Adventures— Let's Go Exploring

Where will our adventures take us?

120

Unit 4

A Day's Adventures
What adventures can you have every day?

A Lucky Day
What adventures can you have on a lucky day?

Animal Adventures
What adventures can animals have?

Goldilocks's Adventures
What kind of adventures can a child have?

Cold Adventures
What is it like in the Antarctic?

City Adventures
What are some city adventures?

Adventures—Let's Go Exploring

121

Read Aloud

Read the **Big Book** *A Trip to Los Angeles.* Prompt discussion about the book.

• Where can a child go to have adventures in Los Angeles?

• What kinds of things do people do on their adventures in Los Angeles?

• Would you like to go on an adventure in Los Angeles? Which adventure would you like the best?

For more read alouds related to the theme, see the Big Book Anthology.

Unit Project: Adventures

After discussing the unit question, have children think about what it means to go on an adventure. Have a digital camera, tape recorder, or art supplies on hand. This week we are going to make recordings of an adventure we have gone on or an adventure we want to take. Think about an adventure you have had or one you would like to take.

Record children's adventures on camera, or on tape. Children can also draw pictures to show their adventures. Each day, play recordings of the children's adventures or display pictures. Pair children of mixed abilities and encourage them to share their adventure stories.

Question of the Week
What adventures can you have every day?

Instructional Plan and Materials

- **Word Cards**
  60–64

- **Big Book**
  A Trip to Los Angeles

- **Poster**
  Poster 19 can be used at beginning or end of day.

- **Song Book**, p. 19

Transparencies Explore content and vocabulary and model fluent reading.

For further information about using these components, see pages x–xv.

DAY 1 — Build Background

Preteach/Review 10–15 min
Poster, Song Book, Big Book
   Leveled Support Preteach
   Practice Stations Preteach

Teach 35–45 min
   Concept Talk
   Oral Vocabulary Routine
      Word Cards
   Build Concept Vocabulary
   Daily Table Talk

Check/Reteach 5–10 min
Poster, Word Cards
   Leveled Support Reteach

DAY 2 — Language: Category Words

Preteach/Review 10–15 min
Poster
   Leveled Support Preteach
   Practice Stations Review

Teach 35–45 min
   Category Words
   Daily Table Talk

Check/Reteach 5–10 min
Poster, Word Cards
   Leveled Support Reteach

Fluency: Writing or Speaking

CALIFORNIA Standards

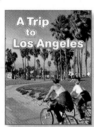

GK Sci 4.e Communicate observations orally and through drawings.

ELA LS 2.3 Relate an experience or creative story in a logical sequence.

ELA R 1.17 Identify and sort common words in basic categories (e.g., colors, shapes, foods).

Academic Language

Vocabulary: clock

Category Words: cereal, eggs, toast, waffle

Get Online! www.pearsonsuccessnet.com

Concept Talk Video

Background Building Audio Slideshow

This Week
Unit 4, Week 1

A Day's Adventures

Next Week
Unit 4, Week 2
A Lucky Day

DAY 3 FORM & FUNCTION Read and Comprehend	**DAY 4** FORM & FUNCTION Language Arts	**DAY 5** Language Arts
Language: High Frequency Words	**Phonics**	**Think, Talk, and Recognize**
Preteach/Review 10–15 min Poster **Leveled Support Preteach** **Practice Stations Review**	**Preteach/Review** 10–15 min Poster **Leveled Support Preteach** **Practice Stations Review**	**Preteach/Review** 10–15 min Poster **Leveled Support Preteach** **Practice Stations Review**
Teach 35–45 min **High Frequency Words** **Daily Table Talk**	**Teach** 35–45 min **Phonics** **Daily Table Talk**	**Teach** 15–20 min **Think, Talk, and Recognize** **Concept Wrap Up**
Check/Reteach 5–10 min Poster, Word Cards **Leveled Support Reteach**	**Check/Reteach** 5–10 min Poster, Word Cards **Leveled Support Reteach**	**Check/Reteach** 30–40 min Poster, Word Cards, Song Book **Leveled Support Reteach**
		Fluency: Writing or Speaking
ELA R 1.15 Read simple one-syllable and high frequency words (i.e., sight words).	**ELA R 1.14** Match all consonant and short-vowel sounds to appropriate letters.	**ELA LS 1.2** Share information and ideas, speaking audibly in complete, coherent sentences.
High Frequency Words: are, do, that		

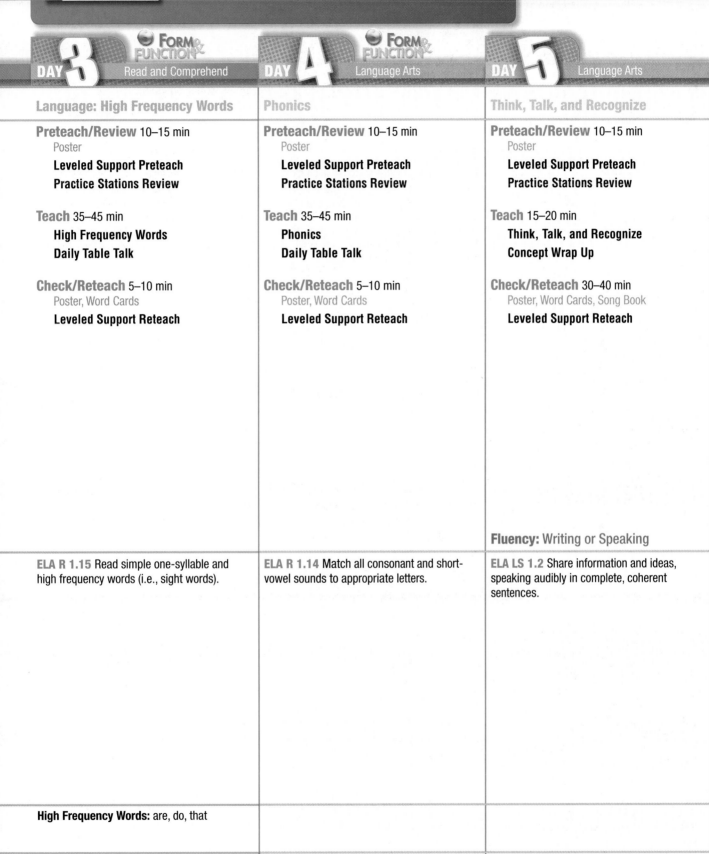

122b

Practice Stations

Materials and Activity

crayons, colored pencils, paper

My Day

Have children describe their day in pictures. Divide a sheet of paper into thirds and tell children to draw something they do in the morning, afternoon, and evening in each of the boxes. Share the activities with others. Now have children cut the page into those thirds. Have other children try to sequence their day.

index cards with the vocabulary words written on them, stacked face down

Use the Word

One child chooses a card and says a sentence with that vocabulary word. The next child chooses a card and says a sentence with that word. Children continue to choose cards and say sentences. When all of the words have been used, children can reshuffle the cards and start again.

play

I like to play with my dog.

Preteach/Reteach

Transfer and Common Misconceptions

Unstressed Syllables

Many unstressed syllables in American English are pronounced with a very short unclear vowel. The word rabbit is shown as /r ab ɪt/, but it may also be pronounced /r ab ət/.

Two Sounds of *C*

Children may want to say /k/ at the beginning of cereal. When *c* is found before *e* or *i*, it is pronounced /s/; otherwise it is pronounced /k/ as in *cook.*

Produce Language

Weekly Concept and Language Goal

CONCEPT GOALS

- understand the concept that adventures are fun activities that can happen any day
- describe adventures that can happen at school

By Day 5, children should be able to talk about their drawings and write a one-word label.

Daily Table Talk

❶ **Beginning**
> Children pantomime while you provide the language.

❷ ❸ **Early Intermediate/Intermediate**
> Children pantomime and say a word or phrase.

❹ ❺ **Early Advanced/Advanced**
> Children say a sentence while pantomiming.

Daily Table Talk

❶ **Beginning**
> Children talk about their drawings.

❷ ❸ **Early Intermediate/Intermediate**
> Children write one-word labels.

❹ ❺ **Early Advanced/Advanced**
> Children write a phrase or sentence.

DAY 3 — Read and Comprehend
FORM & FUNCTION

sheets of colored construction paper, crayons, colored pencils

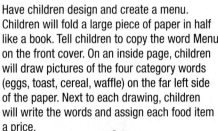

Make a Menu

Have children design and create a menu. Children will fold a large piece of paper in half like a book. Tell children to copy the word Menu on the front cover. On an inside page, children will draw pictures of the four category words (eggs, toast, cereal, waffle) on the far left side of the paper. Next to each drawing, children will write the words and assign each food item a price.

Oral Language

Very young children with little literacy in their home languages are likely to develop oral language skills before reading and writing skills.

Daily **Table Talk**

① Beginning
Name school activites or adventures and have children say yes or no.

② ③ Early Intermediate/Intermediate
Phrase: field trip, assembly

④ ⑤ Early Advanced/Advanced
Sentence: We took a field trip to the zoo.

DAY 4 — Language Arts
FORM & FUNCTION

Index cards with the high frequency words written on them, letter tiles, paper

Letter Tiles

Use Word Cards and Letter Tiles to spell high frequency words. Make placemats with two columns. Have them place the Word Card in the first column. Have them use the Letter Tiles to spell the word in the second column.

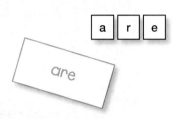

a r e

are

Producing /h/

/h/ is produced in the back of the throat with a completely open vocal tract. The air flows out of the tract in a similar fashion to a sigh. No sound is produced at the larynx.

Daily **Table Talk**

① Beginning
Name bedtime routine acivities; have chldren say yes or no

② ③ Early Intermediate/Intermediate
One or two word: brush teeth, put on pajamas

④ ⑤ Early Advanced/Advanced
Sentence: I listen to a story before bed.

DAY 5 — Language Arts

magazines, hangers, string, index cards, scissors, tape

Hang the /h/ Words

Give each child a hanger. Children will create an /h/ mobile. Tell children to find and cut out from magazines pictures of things that begin with /h/. Have children glue /h/ pictures to index cards and then tape a piece of string to the index card. Tie the other end of the string to the hanger to hang the /h/ pictures.

Classroom Structure

Because beginning English Learners may not initially understand verbal cues, predictable structures are even more important in order to reduce anxiety, promote feelings of comfort, and familiarize them to classroom expectons. Classroom patterns and predictable structures aid language development.

Daily **Table Talk**

① Beginning Child draws and speaks about the drawing.

② ③ Early Intermediate/Intermediate Child draws and speaks about the drawing using at least one concept vocabulary word.

④ ⑤ Early Advanced/Advanced Child draws and provides a label for the drawing that includes a vocabulary word.

OBJECTIVE

To introduce and discuss concepts and vocabulary related to the idea of daily adventures.

Build Background Get **Ready** to **Read!**

Question of the Week

What adventures can you have every day?

www.pearsonsuccessnet.com

Concept Talk

Use the Big Book Connect the Big Book to the unit theme, Adventures—Let's Go Exploring. Display and discuss the cover. Then read the book aloud.

Introduce the Weekly Concept Tell children that today, they will talk about things they do during the day and when they do them. Ask the weekly question: What adventures can you have every day?

Use the Poster Direct children's attention to the weekly poster. Use the Day 1 teaching notes at the bottom of the poster.

Sing the Song Use the song **We Like School** to reinforce children's understanding of the weekly concept. Have children sing or simply chant the words with you.

Use a Transparency Use the Sequence Map (Transparency 7) to help children organize the events that happen in one day.

Vocabulary

* Academic Vocabulary

bunnies another word for rabbits, used mostly by small children

* **clock** an instrument in a room or building that shows the time

nap short sleep during the day

play to do things that you enjoy, especially pretend or to use toys

rabbit a small animal with long ears and soft fur that lives in a hole in the ground

 ELA LS 2.3 Relate an experience or creative story in a logical sequence. (ELD LS.B3)

123

Introduce Concept Vocabulary

1. **Say the Word** Display the Word Card as you say *bunnies.* Have children repeat the word.

2. **Introduce Word Meaning** Ask questions about the bunnies. How do bunnies move around?

3. **Demonstrate** Show a stuffed animal or rabbit puppet and make it "hop" around the room. Have children role play being bunnies hopping around the room.

4. **Apply** Have children demonstrate their understanding.

Repeat with other vocabulary words.

Corrective Feedback If children have difficulty discriminating between bunnies and the rabbit, discuss similarities and differences between them and share pictures of other baby animals and their parents.

Concept Work

Discuss what is happening in each picture, having children point to it. Then talk about the time of day each event is taking place. Discuss if these events or similar events happen during their day. Have children color the pictures.

 **Leveled Support** **Vocabulary in Context**

❶ **Beginning** Point to the bunnies, rabbit, and clock on the Worktext page. Say the word for each picture as children point, and have them echo each word.

❷ ❸ **Early Intermediate/Intermediate** Do the Beginning activity, but have children say the words themselves. Give help if needed.

❹ ❺ **Early Advanced/Advanced** Ask children to draw three activities they do in a day: a morning, an afternoon, and an evening. Then ask them to use vocabulary words as they describe the activities.

Wrap Up **DAY** 1

 Daily **Table Talk** What adventures do you have throughout the day? Have children answer the question, using the vocabulary words.

Produce Language Play charades. Ask each child to act out something they do during the day. Say a sentence.

Today children should have:

☑ **Learned** and applied vocabulary related to daily events.

☑ **Spoken** complete sentences about daily events.

☑ **Recognized** concept vocabulary words.

 ELA LS 2.3 Relate an experience or creative story in a logical sequence. (ELD LS.B3)

123

To discuss adventures families have; to introduce category words for breakfast foods.

Concept Talk

Connect to Day 1 What adventures can you have every day?

Introduce the Daily Question What are some adventures your family has had? **Have children answer orally.**

Use the Poster Use the Day 2 teaching notes.

Introduce Category Words

1. **Say the Word** Have children point to the picture of eggs. Say the word and have children repeat.

2. **Introduce Word Meaning** Ask questions: Do you like eggs? Do you like them scrambled? With ketchup?

3. **Demonstrate** Have children role play cracking an egg on the side of their desk and then opening it.

4. **Apply** Repeat with other vocabulary words and elicit that they all belong to the category "breakfast food."

Have children draw other breakfast foods.

Corrective Feedback If children have difficulty identifying other breakfast foods, share pictures from magazines or menus, or discuss various breakfast items.

Breakfast Foods

Picture Dictionary

cereal

eggs

toast

waffle

 Draw Draw breakfast foods.

eggs   toast

124 ELA R1.17 Identify and sort common words in basic categories (e.g., colors, shapes, foods). (ELD R.B4)

 Leveled Support **Category Words**

① **Beginning** Have children point to each breakfast item on the Worktext page as you say it. Have children echo the word.

②③ **Early Intermediate/Intermediate** Say the name of a breakfast item. Have children point to it. Then reverse the activity.

④⑤ **Early Advanced/Advanced** Have children talk in pairs. Have them tell each other what they eat for breakfast. Encourage them to use the category words if possible.

Wrap Up   DAY 2

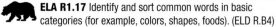

Table Talk Have children discuss family adventures such as trips.

Produce Language To build fluency, encourage children to label or write a sentence about their drawings. They can share their writing with partners.

Today children should have:

☑ **Learned** and applied vocabulary related to breakfast foods.

☑ **Spoken** complete sentences about a family adventure.

☑ **Recognized** words that belong in the same category.

What adventures can we find at school?

✏️ **Circle** Circle *are*.

We are happy to have a class pet.

✏️ **Circle** Circle *do*. Circle *that*.

We do projects that are fun.

🐻 ELA R1.15 Read simple one-syllable and high-frequency words (i.e., sight words). (ELD R.B2)

125

OBJECTIVE

To discuss adventures we can find at school; to introduce the high frequency words *are, that,* and *do*.

Concept Talk
 FORM & FUNCTION

Connect to Day 2 What are some adventures your family has had?

Introduce the Daily Question What adventures can we find at school? Discuss different things at school that could be called adventures, such as playing outside, having guests visit, taking a field trip, or celebrating special days.

Use the Poster Use the Day 3 teaching notes.

Review Concept Vocabulary Review the words introduced on Day 1.

Introduce High Frequency Words

Guide children to point to the word *are* in the direction line. Say: This is the word *are*. Let's say the word together. Now find and point to the word *are* in the sentence. Circle it. Continue wth the other high frequency words. Help children complete the Worktext page.

(LS) Leveled Support **High Frequency Words**

Preteach / Reteach

① **Beginning** Write the word *are*. Say This is the word *are*. Say the letters in *are* with me: *a, r, e, are*. Continue with *that* and *do*. Show the three words and distinguish between them.

② ③ **Early Intermediate/Intermediate** Write *are, that,* and *do*. Say a word and have children point to the correct word.

④ ⑤ **Early Advanced/Advanced** Have children find and circle the words *are, that,* and *do* in a newspaper article.

Wrap Up **DAY** 3

Daily **Table Talk** Have children discuss adventures they can find at school.

Produce Language Have each child say a sentence about an adventure they have had at school, such as a field trip, assembly, or special project.

Today children should have:

- ☑ **Learned** and applied the high frequency words *are, that,* and *do*.

- ☑ **Spoken** complete sentences about adventures children have at school.

- ☑ **Recognized** the high frequency words *are, that,* and *do*.

🐻 **ELA R1.15** Read simple one-syllable and high-frequency words (that is, sight words). (ELD R.B2)

To discuss what children do at night; to recognize initial /h/.

Concept Talk

FORM & FUNCTION

Connect to Day 3 What adventures can we find at school?

Introduce the Daily Question What do you do every night? Ask children what they do before they go to bed. They might hear a story, brush their teeth, say good night to their families, have a snack, and so on.

Use the Poster Use the Day 4 teaching notes.

Phonics

Identify Sound /h/ Have children point to each picture as you name it. When you point to the horse, say: Have you ever ridden a horse? That would be an adventure. Say: Now I'm going to read the pairs of words again. Listen for /h/ at the beginning. Which word begins with /h/, *hat* or *book?* Continue with remaining pairs of words: *cat, horse; hand, banana.*

Corrective Feedback If children have difficulty identifying the initial sound /h/, read each word again, separating the phonemes and emphasizing the initial phoneme in each word.

Identify Sound Hh

✏️ **Color** Color things with *h*.

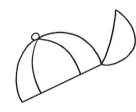

126 🐻 **ELA R1.14** Match all consonant and short-vowel sounds to appropriate letters. (ELD R.B10)

Preteach / Reteach **Leveled Support** Phonics

❶ **Beginning** Hold up a card on which you have written *H*. Say: The name of this letter is *h*. The sound for this letter is /h/. Have children echo you as you make the sound. Say a few words that begin with /h/.

❷ ❸ **Early Intermediate/Intermediate** Tell children you will read several words and they should listen for /h/. When you say a word that begins with /h/, children should hop and repeat the word. Say: Hannah likes to hop. She hops around her house. Hopping makes Hannah happy.

❹ ❺ **Early Advanced/Advanced** Have children identify the letter that makes /h/. Ask children to name other words that begin with /h/.

Wrap Up   DAY 4

Daily Table Talk What do you do every night? Have children discuss their bedtime routines.

Produce Language Have each child say a sentence about what they do every night.

Today children should have:

☑ **Learned** and applied vocabulary related to what they do at night.

☑ **Spoken** complete sentences about what they do at night.

☑ **Recognized** words that begin with /h/.

🐻 **ELA R1.14** Match all consonant and short-vowel sounds to appropriate letters. (ELD R.B10)

What adventures can you have every day?

 Draw

ELA LS. 1.2 Share information and ideas, speaking audibly in complete, coherent sentences. (ELD LS.B3)

127

To guide children to express their understanding of weekly concepts and vocabulary.

Think, Talk, and Recognize!

Concept Talk

Connect to Day 4 What do you do every night? Model how to answer yesterday's question with a sentence.

Review the Weekly Question Ask: What adventures can you have every day? Have children share an activity they do during the day. After children have answered, they can identify other children that do the same activity.

Use the Poster Use the Day 5 teaching notes.

Review Concept Vocabulary Review the vocabulary introduced on Day 1.

Concept Wrap Up

Have children draw to answer the question: What adventures can you have every day? Discuss the photo on the page with children. This family is playing a game. Playing a game can be an adventure.

Leveled Support — Concept Vocabulary

① Beginning Display the Word Cards for *bunnies, clock, nap, play,* and *rabbit.* Say each word. Ask children to repeat and point to the matching card. Provide an object or make a gesture for each word and have children point to the corresponding word.

② ③ Early Intermediate/Intermediate Display the Word Cards for *bunnies, clock, nap, play,* and *rabbit.* Ask children to say each word and point to the matching card. Then ask questions about the words, such as: Could you see a bunny in your yard? What games do you like to play? Continue with questions about the other words.

④ ⑤ Early Advanced/Advanced Display the Word Cards for *bunnies, clock, nap, play,* and *rabbit.* Pair children and have each pair choose one of the words. Have partners say a sentence or tell a story that includes the word.

Wrap Up DAY 5

Table Talk What adventures can you have every day? Have children discuss the question, using the vocabulary words they have learned this week.

Produce Language To build fluency, children can label, write about, or speak about their drawings. Ask children to respond to what they have heard or read.

Today children should have:

☑ **Reviewed** the weekly concept and concept vocabulary.

☑ **Spoken** about adventures they can have every day.

☑ **Drawn or written** to show adventures that they can have every day.

ELA LS. 1.2 Share information and ideas, speaking audibly in complete, coherent sentences. (ELD LS.B3)

127

Question of the Week
What adventures can you have on a lucky day?

	DAY **1** Get Ready to Read	DAY **2** Read and Comprehend
	Build Background	Language: Category Words

Instructional Plan and Materials

- **Word Cards**
  65–67

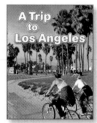

- **Poster**
  Poster 20 can be used at beginning or end of day.

- **Big Book**
  A Trip to Los Angeles

- **Song Book**, p. 20

Transparencies Explore content and vocabulary and model fluent reading.

For further information about using these components, see pages x–xv.

Preteach/Review 10–15 min
Poster, Song Book, Big Book
  Leveled Support Preteach
  Practice Stations Preteach

Teach 35–45 min
  Concept Talk
  Oral Vocabulary Routine
  Word Cards
  Build Concept Vocabulary
  Daily Table Talk

Check/Reteach 5–10 min
Poster, Word Cards
  Leveled Support Reteach

Preteach/Review 10–15 min
Poster
  Leveled Support Preteach
  Practice Stations Review

Teach 35–45 min
  Category Words
  Daily Table Talk

Check/Reteach 5–10 min
Poster, Word Cards
  Leveled Support Reteach

Fluency: Writing or Speaking

CALIFORNIA Standards

GK Sci 4.e Communicate observations orally and through drawings.

ELA LS 2.3 Relate an experience or creative story in a logical sequence.

ELA R 1.17 Identify and sort common words in basic categories (e.g., colors, shapes, foods).

Academic Language

Vocabulary: dinner

Category Words: pizza, salad, sandwich, soup, spaghetti, stew

---

Get Online! www.pearsonsuccessnet.com

Concept Talk Video

Background Building Audio Slideshow

This Week
Unit 4, Week 2

A Lucky Day

Next Week
Unit 4, Week 3
Animal Adventures

DAY 3 FORM & FUNCTION — Read and Comprehend

DAY 4 FORM & FUNCTION — Language Arts

DAY 5 — Language Arts

Language: High Frequency Words	**Phonics**	**Think, Talk, and Recognize**
Preteach/Review 10–15 min	**Preteach/Review** 10–15 min	**Preteach/Review** 10–15 min
Poster	Poster	Poster
Leveled Support Preteach	**Leveled Support Preteach**	**Leveled Support Preteach**
Practice Stations Review	**Practice Stations Review**	**Practice Stations Review**
Teach 35–45 min	**Teach** 35–45 min	**Teach** 15–20 min
High Frequency Words	**Phonics**	**Think, Talk, and Recognize**
Daily Table Talk	**Daily Table Talk**	**Concept Wrap Up**
Check/Reteach 5–10 min	**Check/Reteach** 5–10 min	**Check/Reteach** 30–40 min
Poster, Word Cards	Poster, Word Cards	Poster, Word Cards, Song Book
Leveled Support Reteach	**Leveled Support Reteach**	**Leveled Support Reteach**
		Fluency: Writing or Speaking
ELA R 1.15 Read simple one-syllable and high frequency words (i.e., sight words).	**ELA R 1.14** Match all consonant and short-vowel sounds to appropriate letters.	**ELA LS 1.2** Share information and ideas, speaking audibly in complete, coherent sentences.
High Frequency Words: are, do that		

Weekly Practice

Practice Stations

Materials and Activity

DAY 1 Get Ready to Read

colored construction paper, cooking or food magazines, scissors, glue

My Lucky Dinner 👫

Have children create a lucky dinner. Give them a large piece of construction paper for a placemat. Have children cut out pictures of food items and glue them on their placemats.

DAY 2 Read and Comprehend

index cards with the vocabulary words written on them, stacked face down

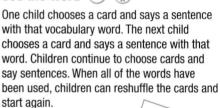

Use the Word 👫 👫

One child chooses a card and says a sentence with that vocabulary word. The next child chooses a card and says a sentence with that word. Children continue to choose cards and say sentences. When all of the words have been used, children can reshuffle the cards and start again.

bath

I gave my dog a bath on Saturday.

Preteach/Reteach

Transfer and Common Misconceptions

/th/ Sounds

Some of your students may find this sound difficult to pronounce because this phoneme is not found in Spanish.

S Words

Compare word features of the category words. Almost all of the words begin with the letter *s*. Which word is the longest word? Which word is the shortest word?

Produce Language

Weekly Concept and Language Goal

CONCEPT GOALS

- describe things that are done just for fun
- understand the concept of good luck and explain what might make a day a lucky one

By Day 5, children should be able to talk about their drawings and write a one-word label.

Daily Table Talk

❶ **Beginning**

Children pantomime while you provide the language.

❷ ❸ **Early Intermediate/Intermediate**

Children pantomime and say a word or phrase.

❹ ❺ **Early Advanced/Advanced**

Children say a sentence while pantomiming.

Daily Table Talk

❶ **Beginning**

Children talk about their drawings.

❷ ❸ **Early Intermediate/Intermediate**

Children write one-word labels.

❹ ❺ **Early Advanced/Advanced**

Children write a phrase or sentence.

DAY 3 FORM & FUNCTION Read and Comprehend

 DAY 4 FORM & FUNCTION Language Arts

DAY 5 Language Arts

colored construction paper, crayons, colored pencils

newspaper, highlighter, pens

picture cards

Make a Menu

Have children complete their menus from Week 1. Children will add dinner items to their menus. Have children use opposite inside or back pages of menus to draw pictures of the category words on the far left side of the page. Next to each drawing, children will write the words and assign each food item a price.

Word Search

A child chooses an article from a newspaper and looks for the high frequency words (*are, that,* and *do*). Have child locate and highlight these words in the article

Find the /l/ Words

Give each pair of children a pile of picture cards. Have children look through the cards and find words that begin with *l.*

The Word *are*

Children may often be confused by the word *are* as it only has one phoneme, yet three letters.

Producing /l/

/l/ is produced with the tongue tip against the alveolar ridge. Air flows over both edges of the tongue and sound is produced at the larynx. The lips are in a wide but relaxed position.

Visual Aids

Provide and use visual aids in the form of pictures or objects. Point to sections of text or materials as you mention them.

Daily Table Talk

❶ **Beginning**
> Name school activities or adventures and have children say lucky or not lucky.

❷ ❸ **Early Intermediate/Intermediate**
> Phrase: zoo, ballgame, water park

❹ ❺ **Early Advanced/Advanced**
> Sentence: On a lucky day, I get to go a waterpark.

Daily Table Talk

❶ **Beginning**
> Name activities that people might consider lucky and have children say yes or no.

❷ ❸ **Early Intermediate/Intermediate**
> One or two word: ball game, movies, friend's house

❹ ❺ **Early Advanced/Advanced**
> Sentence: I could go to a ball game on a lucky day.

Daily Table Talk

❶ **Beginning** Child draws and speaks about the drawing.

❷ ❸ **Early Intermediate/Intermediate** Child draws and speaks about the drawing using at least one concept vocabulary word.

❹ ❺ **Early Advanced/Advanced** Child draws and provides a label for the drawing that includes a vocabulary word.

OBJECTIVE

To discuss concepts and vocabulary related to the idea of lucky adventures.

Build Background Get Ready to Read!

Question of the Week

What adventures can you have on a lucky day?

www.pearsonsuccessnet.com

Concept Talk

Use the Big Book If you have not introduced the Big Book, consider reading it to children. Connect to the unit theme, Adventures—Let's Go Exploring.

Introduce the Weekly Concept Tell children that today, they will talk about times they felt lucky. Ask the weekly question: What adventures can you have on a lucky day?

Use the Poster Direct children's attention to the weekly poster. Use the Day 1 teaching notes at the bottom of the poster.

Sing the Song Use the song **A Lucky Day** to reinforce children's understanding of the weekly concept. Have children sing or simply chant the words with you.

Use a Transparency Use the Description Map (Transparency 4) to record children's ideas of what might happen on a lucky day.

A Lucky Day
Vocabulary

bath

dinner

rabbit

128

What adventures can you have on a lucky day?

Vocabulary

* **Academic Vocabulary**

bath an act of washing your body in the water that you put in a bathtub

* **dinner** the main meal of the day, usually eaten in the evening

rabbit a small animal with long ears and soft fur that lives in a hole in the ground

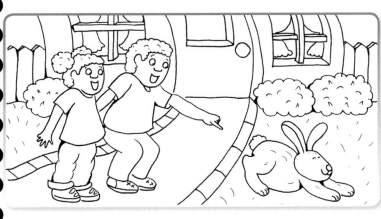

 ELA LS 2.3 Relate an experience or creative story in a logical sequence. (ELD LS.B3)   129

 Leveled Support Preteach LS Reteach **Vocabulary in Context**

❶ **Beginning** Point to the bath, rabbit, and dinner on the Worktext page. As children point to the picture, say the word. Have them echo each word.

❷ ❸ **Early Intermediate/Intermediate** Have children point to each picture and say the word. Offer help if needed. Ask questions about each word, using the illustrations on the Worktext page.

❹ ❺ **Early Advanced/Advanced** Ask children to work with partners to say a sentence using at least two of the vocabulary words.

Introduce Concept Vocabulary

1. **Say the Word** Display the Word Card as you say *dinner*. Have children repeat the word.

2. **Introduce Word Meaning** Tell children that dinner is the meal that we eat in the evening. Ask questions about dinner. What time do you eat dinner? What foods do you like to eat for dinner?

3. **Demonstrate** Have children role play eating dinner. They can discuss some of the foods they eat for dinner.

4. **Apply** Have children demonstrate their understanding. Repeat with other vocabulary words.

Corrective Feedback If children have difficulty understanding the word *dinner*, show pictures of dinner meals from magazines or menus. Provide visuals for the other words as well.

Concept Work

Discuss what is happening in each picture as children point to it. Talk about why someone may feel these events are lucky. The family feels lucky they are all together. The puppy getting a bath may not feel lucky, but the boy may feel lucky spending time with his dad. The children feel lucky to see the rabbit. Have children choose the picture that they think shows the luckiest day and color that picture. Children can share with partners why they chose to color what they did.

Wrap Up   **DAY 1**

Daily **Table Talk** What adventures can you have on a lucky day? Have children answer the question, using the vocabulary words.

Produce Language Role play going out to dinner. Have children say and complete this sentence: I feel lucky when we go to
_____ .

Today children should have:

☑ **Learned** and applied vocabulary related to lucky day adventures.

☑ **Spoken** complete sentences about lucky day adventures.

☑ **Recognized** concept vocabulary words.

 ELA LS 2.3 Relate an experience or creative story in a logical sequence. (ELD LS.B3)

129

OBJECTIVE

To discuss things that are fun to do; to introduce category words for dinner foods.

Concept Talk

Connect to Day 1 What adventures can you have on a lucky day?

Introduce the Daily Question What are some things you do that are fun? Give examples of fun activities. Tell children that things that are fun are enjoyable—we like them. Have children answer orally.

Use the Poster Use the Day 2 teaching notes.

Introduce Category Words

1. **Say the Word** Have children point to the picture of a sandwich. Say the word and have children repeat it.
2. **Introduce Word Meaning** Ask questions: What kind of sandwich do you like? What kind of bread do you like to use for a sandwich?
3. **Demonstrate** Have children role play making a peanut butter and jelly sandwich and then eating it.
4. **Apply** Repeat with other vocabulary words and elicit that they all belong to the category "dinner food."

Have children draw other dinner foods.

Corrective Feedback If children have difficulty identifying other dinner foods, share pictures from magazines or menus or discuss items. If the dinner foods pictured are unfamiliar to children, have them tell what foods they like to eat for dinner.

 **Wrap Up** DAY 2

Daily **Table Talk** Have children discuss things they do that are fun.

Produce Language To build fluency, encourage children to label or write a sentence about their drawings. They can share their writing with partners.

Today children should have:

☑ **Learned** and applied vocabulary related to dinner foods.

☑ **Spoken** complete sentences about something they do for fun.

☑ **Recognized** words that belong in the same category.

 ELA R1.17 Identify and sort common words in basic categories (colors, shapes, foods). (ELD R.B4)

130 A Lucky Day • Unit 4, Week 2

Dinner Foods

Picture Dictionary

pizza   salad   sandwich

soup   spaghetti   stew

 Draw Draw dinner foods.

130 **ELA R1.17** Identify and sort common words in basic categories (e.g., colors, shapes, foods). (ELD R.B4)

Preteach Reteach **LS Leveled Support** **Category Words**

❶ **Beginning** Have children point to each dinner item on the Worktext page as you say it. Have children echo the words.

❷ ❸ **Early Intermediate/Intermediate** Say the name of a dinner item. Have children point to it. Show pictures of foods and ask: Is this something you eat for dinner? Children can respond by nodding yes or no. Then reverse the activity.

❹ ❺ **Early Advanced/Advanced** Have children talk in pairs. Have them tell each other what they ate for dinner last night.

What things will you do on a lucky day?

✐ **Circle** Circle *are*. Circle *do*.
We do things that are special.

✐ **Circle** Circle *That*.
That is lucky!

 ELA R1.15 Read simple one-syllable and high-frequency words (i.e., sight words). (ELD R.B2)

131

To discuss things children would do on a lucky day; to review the high frequency words *are*, *that*, and *do*.

Concept Talk

 FORM & FUNCTION

Connect to Day 2 What are some things you do that are fun?

Introduce the Daily Question What things will you do on a lucky day? Discuss the meaning of *lucky* and ask children why they think those activities are lucky. How are activities on a lucky day different from what you do every day?

Use the Poster Use the Day 3 teaching notes.

Review Concept Vocabulary Review the words introduced on Day 1.

Introduce High Frequency Words

Guide children to point to the word *are* in the direction line. Say: This is the word *are*. Let's say the word together. Now find and point to the word *are* in the sentence. Circle it. Help children complete the Worktext page.

Corrective Feedback If children have difficulty circling the high frequency words, write the words on strips of paper and give them to children. Children can match the strips to the words on the page before they circle.

Preteach LS Reteach **Leveled Support** **High Frequency Words**

① **Beginning** Display the word *are*. Have children copy *are* in sand or shaving cream. Say the word and have children echo. Continue the tactile procedure with *that* and *do*.

② ③ **Early Intermediate/Intermediate** Have children write *are*, *that*, and *do* on index cards. Children work with partners reading aloud each word.

④ ⑤ **Early Advanced/Advanced** Have children find and use a paper marker to tab the words *are*, *that*, and *do* in a short story.

Wrap Up   DAY 3

Daily **Table Talk** Have children discuss things they will do on a lucky day.

Produce Language Have each child say a sentence about something they will do on a lucky day, such as going to a zoo, a ball game, or a water park.

Today children should have:

☑ **Learned** and applied the high frequency words *are*, *that*, and *do*.

☑ **Spoken** complete sentences about things they will do on a lucky day.

☑ **Recognized** the high frequency words *are*, *that*, and *do*.

 ELA R1.15 Read simple one syllable and high frequency words (sight words). (ELD R.B2)

131

OBJECTIVE

To discuss what could happen on a lucky day; to recognize initial /l/.

Concept Talk

FORM & FUNCTION

Connect to Day 3 What things will you do on a lucky day?

Introduce the Daily Question What could happen on your lucky day? Link the question to what children discussed yesterday.

Use the Poster Use the Day 4 teaching notes.

Phonics

Identify Sound /l/ Have children point to each picture as you name it. Say: Now I'm going to read the pairs of words again. Listen for /l/ at the beginning, like you hear in *lucky*. Which word begins with /l/, *ladybug* or *fish*? Continue with remaining pairs of words: *leaf, house; apple, lion.*

Corrective Feedback If children have difficulty identifying the initial sound /l/, read each word again, separating the phonemes and emphasizing the initial phoneme in each word.

Identify Sound Ll

 Color Color things with *l.*

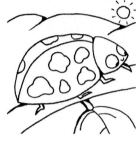

132 ELA R1.14 Match all consonant and short-vowel sounds to appropriate letters. (ELD R.B10)

Wrap Up

DAY 4

 Table Talk What could happen on your lucky day? Have children discuss things that might occur on a lucky day.

Produce Language Have each child say a sentence about what they want to happen if they had a lucky day.

Today children should have:

☑ **Learned** and applied vocabulary related to what could happen on a lucky day.

☑ **Spoken** complete sentences about what could happen on a lucky day.

☑ **Recognized** words that begin with /l/.

 ELA R1.14 Match all consonant and short-vowel sounds to appropriate letters. (ELD R.B10)

Leveled Support Phonics
Preteach / Reteach

① **Beginning** Hold up a card on which you have printed *L.* Say: The name of this letter is *l.* The sound for this letter is /l/. Have children echo the sound, exaggerating the movement of the tongue needed to make the sound /l/.

② ③ **Early Intermediate/Intermediate** Tell children you will read several words and they should listen for /l/. When you say a word that begins with /l/, children should make the letter *L* with their left thumb and index finger. Say: *lucky, salad, light, lamp, bath, dinner, like.*

④ ⑤ **Early Advanced/Advanced** Have children identify the letter that makes /l/. Now ask children to name words that end with /l/.

What adventures can you have on a lucky day?

 Draw

🐻 ELA LS. 1.2 Share information and ideas, speaking audibly in complete, coherent sentences. (ELD LS.B2)

133

OBJECTIVE

To guide children to express their understanding of weekly concepts and vocabulary.

Think, Talk, and Recognize!

Concept Talk

Connect to Day 4 What could happen on your lucky day? Model how to answer yesterday's question with a sentence.

Review the Weekly Question Ask: What adventures can you have on a lucky day? Have children share their ideas of a lucky day. After children have answered, they can identify other children that have similar ideas.

Use the Poster Use the Day 5 teaching notes.

Review Concept Vocabulary Review the vocabulary introduced on Day 1.

Concept Wrap Up

Have children draw to answer the question: What adventures can you have on a lucky day? Talk about the photograph on the page. This looks lucky! It looks like fun to run with so many balloons.

Leveled Support — Concept Vocabulary

Preteach / Reteach

① Beginning Display the Word Cards for *bath, dinner,* and *rabbit.* Say each word. Ask children to repeat and point to the matching card.

② ③ Early Intermediate/Intermediate Display the Word Cards for *rabbit, bath,* and *dinner.* Ask children to say each word and point to the matching card. Ask questions about the words. Which word is an animal? Which word is a meal? Children can point to cards and say the words.

④ ⑤ Early Advanced/Advanced Display the Word Card for *rabbit.* Ask children to identify two words about rabbits and explain how they are related. Continue for the words *bath* and *dinner.*

Wrap Up DAY 5

Table Talk (Daily) What adventures can you have on a lucky day? Have children discuss the question, using the vocabulary words they have learned this week.

Produce Language To build fluency, children can label, write about, or speak about their drawings. Ask children to respond to what they read or heard.

Today, children should have:

☑ **Reviewed** the weekly concept and concept vocabulary.

☑ **Spoken** about adventures they can have on a lucky day.

☑ **Drawn or written** to show adventures they could have on a lucky day.

 ELA LS 1.2 Share information and ideas, speaking audibly in complete, coherent sentences. (ELD LS.B3)

Question of the Week
What adventures can animals have?

DAY 1 — Get Ready to Read

Build Background

Preteach/Review 10–15 min
Poster, Song Book, Big Book
- **Leveled Support Preteach**
- **Practice Stations Preteach**

Teach 35–45 min
- **Concept Talk**
- **Oral Vocabulary Routine**
  Word Cards
- **Build Concept Vocabulary**
- **Daily Table Talk**

Check/Reteach 5–10 min
Poster, Word Cards
- **Leveled Support Reteach**

DAY 2 — Read and Comprehend

Language: Category Words

Preteach/Review 10–15 min
Poster
- **Leveled Support Preteach**
- **Practice Stations Review**

Teach 35–45 min
- **Category Words**
- **Daily Table Talk**

Check/Reteach 5–10 min
Poster, Word Cards
- **Leveled Support Reteach**

Instructional Plan and Materials

- **Word Cards**
  68–72

- **Big Book**
  A Trip to Los Angeles

- **Poster**
  Poster 21 can be used at beginning or end of day.

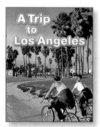

- **Song Book**, p. 21

Transparencies Explore content and vocabulary and model fluent reading.

For further information about using these components, see pages x–xv.

Fluency: Writing or Speaking

ELA LS 2.3 Relate an experience or creative story in a logical sequence.

ELA R 1.17 Identify and sort common words in basic categories (e.g., colors, shapes, foods).

CALIFORNIA Standards

GK Sci 1.a Students know objects can be described in terms of the materials they are made of and their physical properties (e.g., color, size, shape).

GK Sci 4.e Communicate observations orally and through drawings.

Academic Language

Category Words: small, large, short, tall

Get Online! www.pearsonsuccessnet.com

Concept Talk Video

Background Building Audio Slideshow

Animal Adventures

Next Week
Unit 4, Week 4
Goldilocks's
Adventures

DAY **3** Read and Comprehend	DAY **4** Language Arts	DAY **5** Language Arts
Language: High Frequency Words	**Phonics**	**Think, Talk, and Recognize**
Preteach/Review 10–15 min Poster **Leveled Support Preteach** **Practice Stations Review**	**Preteach/Review** 10–15 min Poster **Leveled Support Preteach** **Practice Stations Review**	**Preteach/Review** 10–15 min Poster **Leveled Support Preteach** **Practice Stations Review**
Teach 35–45 min **High Frequency Words** **Daily Table Talk**	**Teach** 35–45 min **Phonemic Awareness** **Daily Table Talk**	**Teach** 15–20 min **Think, Talk, and Recognize** **Concept Wrap Up**
Check/Reteach 5–10 min Poster, Word Cards **Leveled Support Reteach**	**Check/Reteach** 5–10 min Poster, Word Cards **Leveled Support Reteach**	**Check/Reteach** 30–40 min Poster, Word Cards, Song Book **Leveled Support Reteach**
		Fluency: Writing or Speaking
ELA R 1.15 Read simple one-syllable and high frequency words (i.e., sight words).	**ELA R 1.14** Match all consonant and short-vowel sounds to appropriate letters.	**ELA LS 1.2** Share information and ideas, speaking audibly in complete, coherent sentences.
High Frequency Words: one, two, three, four, five		

Practice Stations

Materials and Activity

yarn, green construction paper, party favor blowers, scissors, hole punch

Frog Mask 🧍

Have mask shapes outlined on green paper. Tell children to make frog masks. Have children cut out masks and then cut out eye holes. Attach yarn to the sides and have other children tie the mask at the back of their head. Use the party blower as the frog's tongue. Have children pretend they are frogs.

clay, colored construction paper, crayons, colored pencils, glue, tape, paint

Animal Art 🧍🧍

Have children design and create vocabulary animals. Provide children with various art supplies. Display animals in a table woodland habitat.

Preteach/Reteach

Transfer and Common Misconceptions

Plurals

Most nouns in English form the plural by adding *-s* or *-es*. You can help children understand singular and plural nouns by covering up the *s* at the end of the vocabulary words.

Large

Large is mostly used to express physical size. It is also commonly used with nouns connected with numbers or measurements. For example: a large number, a large quantity.

Produce Language

Weekly Concept and Language Goal

CONCEPT GOALS

- describe adventures that animals could have
- describe characteristics of a home in the woods
- name some exciting places in which animals live

By Day 5, children should be able to talk about their drawings and write a one-word label.

Daily Table Talk

❶ **Beginning**
> Children pantomime their favorite animals.

❷ ❸ **Early Intermediate/Intermediate**
> Children pantomime and name favorite their animals.

❹ ❺ **Early Advanced/Advanced**
> Children each say a sentence while pantomiming their favorite animals.

Daily Table Talk

❶ **Beginning**
> Children talk about their drawings.

❷ ❸ **Early Intermediate/Intermediate**
> Children write one-word labels.

❹ ❺ **Early Advanced/Advanced**
> Children write a phrase or sentence.

attribute pieces, yarn

What's My Sort?

Display several attribute pieces. Create a large circle of yarn. One at a time, begin placing small pieces in the circle and large pieces outside of circle. Ask children to guess how the groups are sorted. List children's suggestions to further develop oral language as well as the concept of categories.

Literacy Skills

The more children's literacy skills in their home languages have developed, the better foundation there is for English literacy skills; if the two languages are similar, the easier it is to transfer literacy from one to the other.

paper, colored dot stickers, stapler, pencil

Number Book

Each child or group gets two pieces of paper. Fold the papers like a book and staple them on the fold. Tell children to copy the word *Numbers* on the front cover. On the first page, place one dot sticker and have children write *one*. Have children put two dots on the next page and write the word *two*. Continue with stickers and numbers for the remainder of book.

Final Blends

Children may have trouble identifying *-nd* at the end of words. Children can trace their hand on a piece of paper. Write the letters *nd* in the open space of the traced hand. Have children say the word *hand* and listen for the blend at the end of the word.

paper with the following words written on it: *crab, clap, skip, band, mask, left, walk,* and *nest;* letter tiles

Segment and Blend

Tell children they are going to use letter tiles to create words. Have children find the letter tiles to spell the words on the sheet of paper. Have children try and sound out the words they spelled. Have partners check their tiles. Take turns creating words with letter tiles.

| s | k | i | p |

Build Background

Building background before reading a text helps readers understand it. Children do not all bring the same kinds of knowledge to a text. Some children may know a lot about squirrels, but nothing about frogs. Taking time to build background is essential.

Daily Table Talk

❶ Beginning

> Name different places. Have children say yes or no.

❷ ❸ Early Intermediate/Intermediate

> Phrase: tree, bush, hollow tree

❹ ❺ Early Advanced/Advanced

> Sentence: I might try and stay in a hollow tree.

Daily Table Talk

❶ Beginning

> Have children say yes or no as you name woodland and sea animal habitats.

❷ ❸ Early Intermediate/Intermediate

> One or two words: hollow log, under a bush

❹ ❺ Early Advanced/Advanced

> Sentence: An exciting place an animal might live is a cave.

Daily Table Talk

❶ Beginning Child draws and speaks about the drawing.

❷ ❸ Early Intermediate/Intermediate Child draws and speaks about the drawing using at least one concept vocabulary word.

❹ ❺ Early Advanced/Advanced Child draws and provides a label for the drawing that includes a vocabulary word.

OBJECTIVE

To introduce and discuss vocabulary and concepts related to animals' adventures.

Build Background Get Ready to Read!

Question of the Week What adventures can animals have?

www.pearsonsuccessnet.com

Concept Talk

Use the Big Book If you have't introduced the Big Book, consider reading it to children. Connect to the unit theme, Adventures—Let's Go Exploring.

Introduce the Weekly Concept Tell children that today, they will talk about adventures animals can have. Ask the weekly question: What adventures can animals have?

Use the Poster Direct children's attention to the weekly poster. Use the Day 1 teaching notes at the bottom of the poster.

Sing the Song Use the song **Animals Are Having Fun** to reinforce children's understanding of the weekly concept. Have children sing or simply chant the words with you.

Use a Transparency Use the Fantasy Transparency (Transparency 12) to share an animal fantasy and compare the adventures of fantasy animals to the adventures of real animals.

Animal Adventures

Vocabulary

cottontails

mouse

snakes

squirrels

frogs

134

What adventures can animals have?

Vocabulary

cottontails small rabbits with a white tail

mouse a small, furry animal with a long tail and a pointed nose that lives in buildings or in fields

snakes animals with a long, thin body and no legs

squirrels small animals with a long, furry tail that live in trees and eat nuts

frogs small animals with smooth skin that live in or near water, make a deep sound, and have long legs for jumping

ELA LS 2.3 Relate an experience or creative story in a logical sequence. (ELD LS.B3)

135

Introduce Concept Vocabulary

1. **Say the Word** Display the Word Card as you say *frogs.* Have children repeat the word.

2. **Introduce Word Meaning** Ask questions about frogs. How do frogs move? What do frogs eat? How do frogs sound?

3. **Demonstrate** Have children role play being a frog, hopping, croaking and eating flies.

4. **Apply** Have children demonstrate their understanding.

Repeat with other vocabulary words.

Corrective Feedback If children have difficulty understanding what a frog is, show pictures of frogs from books or the Internet. Continue with the other animals.

Concept Work

Discuss each animal as children point to it. Talk about adventures animals can have. Have children color the pictures. Children can choose a picture and describe the adventure in the picture.

 Leveled Support **Vocabulary in Context**

❶ **Beginning** Point to the each animal on the Worktext page. Name the animal and have children repeat.

❷ ❸ **Early Intermediate/Intermediate** Have children point to each picture and name the animal. Have them describe the animal in a word or two, make the animal's sound or movement, or demonstrate their understanding in another way.

❹ ❺ **Early Advanced/Advanced** Give each child a Word Card. Ask a child to describe the animal, imitate the animal, or use another way to tell which animal is on the card. Other children can guess what animal is being described.

Wrap Up   **DAY** 1

 What adventures can animals have? Have children answer the question, using the vocabulary words.

Produce Language Identify a favorite animal. Discuss adventures that animals can have. Children can each say a sentence.

Today children should have:

☑ **Learned** and applied vocabulary related to adventures animals can have.

☑ **Spoken** complete sentences about adventures animals can have.

☑ **Recognized** concept vocabulary words.

 ELA LS 2.3 Relate an experience or creative story in a logical sequence. (ELD LS.B3)

135

DAY 2

CALIFORNIA

OBJECTIVE

To discuss adventures animals can have; to introduce category words for sizes.

Concept Talk

Connect to Day 1 What adventures can animals have?

Introduce the Daily Question What kind of adventures do you think four or five animals could have? Have children answer orally.

Use the Poster Use the Day 2 teaching notes.

Introduce Category Words

1. **Say the Word** Have children point to the picture of the small mouse. Say *small* and have children repeat the word.

2. **Introduce Word Meaning** Ask questions: Is the mouse smaller than your shoe? What other animals are small?

3. **Demonstrate** Have children demonstrate *small* by making themselves as small as possible, or by using their hands or fingers to show how small something could be.

4. **Apply** Repeat with other vocabulary words and elicit that they all belong to the category "sizes."

Have children identify and circle something small and something tall.

Corrective Feedback If children have difficulty discriminating between short and tall, use cubes or blocks to demonstrate.

Wrap Up   DAY 2

Daily **Table Talk** Have children discuss adventures animals can have in a group.

Produce Language To build fluency, encourage children to label or write sentences about the things they circled. They can share their writing with partners.

Today children should have:

☑ **Learned** and applied vocabulary related to sizes.

☑ **Spoken** complete sentences about adventures animals can have together.

☑ **Recognized** words that belong in the same category.

 ELA R1.17 Identify and sort common words in basic categories (colors, shapes, foods). (ELD R.B4)

136 Animal Adventures • Unit 4, Week 3

Sizes

Picture Dictionary

small

large

short

tall

✏ **Circle** Circle a thing that is small.

✏ **Circle** Circle a thing that is tall.

136 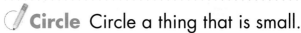 **EELA R1.17** Identify and sort common words in basic categories (e.g., colors, shapes, foods). (ELD R.B4)

Preteach **LS** Reteach **Leveled Support** **Category Words**

❶ **Beginning** Point to each picture on the Worktext page. Say the related size word and have children repeat it. Then hold up an object and ask: Is this object small? Is it tall? Is it short? Children can respond by nodding or gesturing.

❷ ❸ **Early Intermediate/Intermediate** Say a size word and have children point to the related picture. Then have children classify objects that are short, tall, small, and large.

❹ ❺ **Early Advanced/Advanced** Ask children to point to and name the size word for each picture. Have children identify the ending sound and corresponding letter for tall and small. (/l/, /l) Then have them describe an object in the classroom using a size word. Others can guess what object is being described.

Where would you stay in the woodland?

✏️ **Circle** Circle *One*. Circle *two*.
One squirrel will eat two acorns.

✏️ **Circle** Circle *Three*.
Three birds live in the tree.

✏️ **Circle** Circle *Four*. Circle *five*.
Four or five birds can live in the tree.

🐻 ELA R1.15 Read simple one-syllable and high-frequency words (i.e., sight words). (ELD R.B2)

137

OBJECTIVE

To discuss the woodland; to introduce high frequency words *one, two, three, four,* and *five.*

Concept Talk

🌀 **FORM & FUNCTION**

Connect to Day 2 What kind of adventures do you think four or five animals could have?

Introduce the Daily Question Where would you stay in the woodland? Show pictures or describe the woodland for children.

Use the Poster Use the Day 3 teaching notes.

Review Concept Vocabulary Review the words introduced on Day 1.

Introduce High Frequency Words

Write the word *one* on the board and hold up one finger. Say *one.* Draw one leaf on the board, next to the word *one.* Continue procedure with the words *two, three, four,* and *five.* Say: Point to the word *one* in the direction line. This is the word *one.* Let's say the word together. *One.* Now find and point to the word *one* in the sentence. Circle it. Help children complete the Worktext page.

Leveled Support High Frequency Words

Preteach / Reteach
LS

① **Beginning** Display the words *one, two, three, four,* and *five.* As you point to a word, show the number with your fingers and say the word. Have children show the number with their fingers and echo the word.

② ③ **Early Intermediate/Intermediate** Have children use connecting cubes to represent *one, two, three, four,* and *five.* Match the correct number word card to the cube representation.

④ ⑤ **Early Advanced/Advanced** Have children write *one, two, three, four,* and *five* on a piece of paper. Next to each word, they should draw the corresponding number of circles.

Wrap Up DAY 3

Daily **Table Talk** Have children discuss where they would try to stay in the woodland.

Produce Language Have each child say a sentence about where they would try to stay in the woodland.

Today children should have:

☑ **Learned** and applied the high frequency words *one, two, three, four,* and *five.*

☑ **Spoken** complete sentences about where they would try to stay in the woodland.

☑ **Recognized** the high frequency words *one, two, three, four,* and *five.*

🐻 **ELA R1.15** Read simple one syllable and high frequency words (sight words). (ELD R.B2)

OBJECTIVE

To discuss exciting places animals live; to identify initial and final blends.

Concept Talk

FORM & FUNCTION

Connect to Day 3 Where would you stay in the woodland?

Introduce the Daily Question What are some exciting places animals live? Discuss, drawing on children's knowledge, different habitats where animals live.

Use the Poster Use the Day 4 teaching notes.

Phonemic Awareness

Blends Draw a picture of a snake on the board. Say: Say this word with me. *Snake.* The word begins with two sounds blended together. Let's say the word slowly /s/ /n/ /ā/ /k/. What two sounds do you hear at the beginning of the word *snake*? The two sounds /s/ and /n/ are blended together. Repeat the procedure to model identifying a final blend using the word *nest*. Help children complete the Worktext page.

Corrective Feedback If children have difficulty completely the Worktext page, say each word slowly, separating the phonemes. Say the words in the photos, using both the initial and final blends shown. Children can hear which sounds make the words correct.

Match Blends

 Circle Circle the beginning sounds.

tr	cr

sp	sk

 Circle Circle the ending sounds.

nd	ft

st	sk

138   ELA R1.14 Match all consonant and short-vowel sounds to appropriate letters. (ELD R.B10)

Preteach LS Reteach Leveled Support Phonemic Awareness

① **Beginning** Hold up cards on which you have printed *s* and *n*. Say: The names of these letters are s and n. The sounds for these letters are /s/ and /n/. *Blended* together, the sound is /sn/. Have children echo you. Continue procedure with blends *st, cr, sl, nd, ft,* and *sk.*

② ③ **Early Intermediate/Intermediate** Tell children you will read several words and they should listen for blends. Children will identify if they hear a blend at the beginning or end of a word. Say: *skip, nest, desk, left, clap, band, mask, crab, rest.*

④ ⑤ **Early Advanced/Advanced** Write final blends *ft, nd, sk, st* on the board. Have children name the letters in each blend and name a word for each of the blends.

Wrap Up   DAY 4

Daily Table Talk What are some exciting places animals live? Have children name different places.

Produce Language Have each child say a sentence about exciting places animals might live.

Today children should have:

☑ **Learned** and applied vocabulary related to some exciting places animals live.

☑ **Spoken** complete sentences about some exciting places animals live.

☑ **Identified** initial and final blends.

ELA R1.14 Match all consonant and short-vowel sounds to appropriate letters.(ELA R.B10)

What adventures can animals have?

 Draw

OBJECTIVE

To guide children to express their understanding of weekly concepts and vocabulary.

Think, Talk, and Recognize!

Concept Talk

Connect to Day 4 What are some exciting places animals live? Model how to answer yesterday's question with a sentence.

Review the Weekly Question Ask: What adventures can animals have? Have children share adventures animals can have. After children have answered, use several adventures to tell a story.

Use the Poster Use the Day 5 teaching notes.

Review Concept Vocabulary Review the vocabulary introduced on Day 1.

Concept Wrap Up

Have children draw to answer the question: What adventures can animals have? Discuss the photo on the page. These animals seem to be talking to each other. What adventures do you think they might be planning?

Leveled Support Concept Vocabulary

① **Beginning** Display the Word Cards for *mouse, frogs, snake, cottontails,* and *squirrels.* Say each word. Ask children to repeat and point to the matching card.

② ③ **Early Intermediate/Intermediate** Display the Word Cards for *mouse, frogs, snake, cottontails,* and *squirrels.* Ask children to say each word and point to the matching card. Describe one of the animals in a few words and have children point to the corresponding card as they say the word.

④ ⑤ **Early Advanced/Advanced** Distribute the Word Cards to partners. Have each pair use the word in a sentence describing the animal and telling about an adventure it could have. Pairs can share their work with the class.

Wrap Up   **DAY 5**

Daily Table Talk What adventures can animals have? Have children discuss the question, using the vocabulary words they have learned this week.

Produce Language To build fluency, children can label, write about, or speak about their drawings. Ask children to respond to what they have read or heard.

Today, children should have:

☑ **Reviewed** the weekly concept and concept vocabulary.

☑ **Spoken** about adventures that animals can have.

☑ **Drawn or written** about animals' adventures.

ELA LS.12 Share information and ideas, speaking audibly in complete, coherent sentences. (ELD LS.B1)

139

Question of the Week
What kind of adventures can a child have?

Instructional Plan and Materials

- **Word Cards**
  73–76

- **Poster**
  Poster 22 can be used at beginning or end of day.

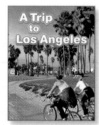

- **Big Book**
  A Trip to Los Angeles

- **Song Book**, p. 22

Transparencies Explore content and vocabulary and model fluent reading.

For further information about using these components, see pages x–xv.

CALIFORNIA Standards

GK Sci 2.b Students know stories sometimes give plants and animals attributes they do not really have.

Academic Language

DAY 1 — Get Ready to Read

Build Background

Preteach/Review 10–15 min
Poster, Song Book, Big Book
- **Leveled Support Preteach**
- **Practice Stations Preteach**

Teach 35–45 min
- **Concept Talk**
- **Oral Vocabulary Routine**
  Word Cards
- **Build Concept Vocabulary**
- **Daily Table Talk**

Check/Reteach 5–10 min
Poster, Word Cards
- **Leveled Support Reteach**

ELA R 2.4 Retell familiar stories.

Vocabulary: father, mother, baby

Concept Talk Video

DAY 2 — Read and Comprehend

Language: Category Words

Preteach/Review 10–15 min
Poster
- **Leveled Support Preteach**
- **Practice Stations Review**

Teach 35–45 min
- **Category Words**
- **Daily Table Talk**

Check/Reteach 5–10 min
Poster, Word Cards
- **Leveled Support Reteach**

Fluency: Writing or Speaking

ELA R 1.17 Identify and sort common words in basic categories (e.g., colors, shapes, foods).

Category Words: bed, chair, table, dresser

Background Building Audio Slideshow

Get Online! www.pearsonsuccessnet.com

This Week
Unit 4, Week 4

Goldilocks's Adventures

Next Week
Unit 4, Week 5
Cold Adventures

DAY 3 FORM & FUNCTION Read and Comprehend	**DAY 4** FORM & FUNCTION Language Arts	**DAY 5** Language Arts
Language: High Frequency Words	**Phonics**	**Think, Talk, and Recognize**
Preteach/Review 10–15 min Poster **Leveled Support Preteach** **Practice Stations Review**	**Preteach/Review** 10–15 min Poster **Leveled Support Preteach** **Practice Stations Review**	**Preteach/Review** 10–15 min Poster **Leveled Support Preteach** **Practice Stations Review**
Teach 35–45 min **High Frequency Words** **Daily Table Talk**	**Teach** 35–45 min **Phonics** **Daily Table Talk**	**Teach** 15–20 min **Think, Talk, and Recognize** **Concept Wrap Up**
Check/Reteach 5–10 min Poster, Word Cards **Leveled Support Reteach**	**Check/Reteach** 5–10 min Poster, Word Cards **Leveled Support Reteach**	**Check/Reteach** 30–40 min Poster, Word Cards, Song Book **Leveled Support Reteach**
		Fluency: Writing or Speaking
ELA R 1.15 Read simple one-syllable and high frequency words (i.e., sight words).	ELA R 1.14 Match all consonant and short-vowel sounds to appropriate letters.	ELA LS 1.2 Share information and ideas, speaking audibly in complete, coherent sentences.
High Frequency Words: one, two, three, four, five		

Practice Stations

Materials and Activity

---

several versions of "Goldilocks," tape recorder/CD player, headset

Goldilocks

Tell children to look at various versions of "Goldilocks." Compare pictures. Include a book on tape/CD if one is available.

---

index cards with vocabulary words written on them, paper

One of These Things Is Not Like the Others

Display index cards with vocabulary words written on them. Have partners work together to divide a piece of paper into four sections and illustrate each vocabulary word. Now have children play the game "One of These Things is Not Like the Others" to determine which word/picture doesn't belong with the others. Tell children to put an X through the word *woods.*

Preteach/Reteach

Transfer and Common Misconceptions

Deleted /r/

Some children have difficulty pronouncing the sound /r/, and it is often reduced or deleted in final positions: fathuh (father); mothuh (mother).

Pronoun or Ending?

In Spanish, *le* is often used as an objective pronoun and pronounced /lay/. This may lead to confusion as the child is introduced to English words that end in *le,* such as table.

Produce Language

Weekly Concept and Language Goal

CONCEPT GOALS

- describe the adventures of a fictional character
- explain characters and plot details in a story
- name real-life adventures that children can have

By Day 5, children should be able to talk about their drawings and write a one-word label.

Daily Table Talk

❶ Beginning
Children pantomime while you provide the language.

❷ ❸ Early Intermediate/Intermediate
Children pantomime and say a word or phrase.

❹ ❺ Early Advanced/Advanced
Children say a sentence while pantomiming.

Daily Table Talk

❶ Beginning
Children talk about their drawings.

❷ ❸ Early Intermediate/Intermediate
Children write one-word labels.

❹ ❺ Early Advanced/Advanced
Children write a phrase or sentence.

DAY 3 — **FORM& FUNCTION** — Read and Comprehend

pictures of furniture from magazines or decorator catalogs, scissors, wallpaper samples, glue, pencil

Decorating Den (★)

Tell children they are going to create a bedroom. Give children wall paper samples books and pictures of furniture. Have partners design the bedroom by using wallpaper as the wall of a room and then placing furniture in the room. Place furniture in the room and label the furniture with category words: *bed, table, chair, dresser.*

 DAY 4 — **FORM& FUNCTION** — Language Arts

crayons, paper, scissors

High Five! (★★)

Have children place their hands on colored sheets of paper with their fingers spread apart. Have their partners trace around their hands. Now have the second child trace the first partner's hand in each pair. Have each child cut out their hand and write a number word on each of their five fingers. Display these High Fives on a bulletin board.

 DAY 5 — Language Arts

picture cards that begin or end with *g,* index card that has *beginning* written on left side and *ending* written on right side, one clothespin

Beginning or End? (★★)

Have children take turns naming the picture, saying the word and identifying whether the /g/ sound is at the beginning or end of the word. Put the clothespin on the correct place on the card, beginning or end. Have partners check the card before they take their turns. Continue until all picture cards have been used.

Two Sounds of *g*

In English, when *g* is found before *e* or *i* it is pronounced like the Spanish *j*; otherwise it is hard, as in *get,* /g/.

Beginning Sound of *one*

Children are likely to be confused by the beginning of the word *one*. It sounds as if it begins with the letter *w.*

Welcome!

Seating children near the front of the room or near the teacher's desk can help make a child feel welcome. Frequent eye contact with children can communicate care and inclusiveness. Encourage children to participate in any way that makes them comfortable, but do not force participation.

 **Daily Table Talk**

❶ **Beginning** Name reasons Goldilocks might be visiting the three bears. Have children say yes or no.

❷ ❸ **Early Intermediate/Intermediate** Phrase: hungry, tired, friendly

❹ ❺ **Early Advanced/Advanced** Sentence: Goldilocks was tired.

 **Daily Table Talk**

❶ **Beginning** Have children act out an adventure they have had.

❷ ❸ **Early Intermediate/Intermediate** One or two word: swimming in lake, on an airplane

❹ ❺ **Early Advanced/Advanced** Sentence: I went rock climbing.

 **Daily Table Talk**

❶ **Beginning** Child draws and speaks about the drawing.

❷ ❸ **Early Intermediate/Intermediate** Child draws and speaks about the drawing using at least one concept vocabulary word.

❹ ❺ **Early Advanced/Advanced** Child draws and provides a label for the drawing that includes a vocabulary word

To introduce concepts and vocabulary related to adventures that children can have.

Build Background Get **Ready to Read!**

Question of the Week

What kind of adventures can a child have?

www.pearsonsuccessnet.com

Concept Talk

Use the Big Book If you haven't introduced the Big Book, consider reading it to children. Connect to the unit theme, Adventures—Let's Go Exploring.

Introduce the Weekly Concept Tell children that today, they will talk about adventures a child can have. They will be talking about the story "Goldilocks and the Three Bears." Ask the weekly question: What kind of adventures can a child have?

Use the Poster Direct children's attention to the weekly poster. Use the Day 1 teaching notes at the bottom of the poster.

Sing the Song Use the song **Playing With Family** to reinforce children's understanding of the weekly concept. Have children sing or simply chant the words with you.

Use a Transparency Use the Humorous Fiction Transparency (Transparency 15) to introduce children to the genre of humorous fiction. Ask if "Goldilocks and the Three Bears" belongs to that category.

Goldilocks's Adventure

Vocabulary

baby

father

mother

woods

140

What kind of adventures can a child have?

Vocabulary

* Academic Vocabulary

* **baby** a very young child

* **father** a male parent

* **mother** a female parent

woods a small forest

 ELA R 2.4 Retell familiar stories. (ELD R.B7)

141

Introduce Concept Vocabulary

1. **Say the Word** Display the Word Card as you say *baby*. Have children repeat the word.

2. **Introduce the meaning** Ask questions about babies. *How do babies talk? How do babies eat?*

3. **Demonstrate** Have children role play being a baby: crawling, crying, and sucking a thumb.

4. **Apply** Have children demonstrate their understanding.

Repeat with other vocabulary words.

Corrective Feedback If children have difficulty understanding what a baby is, show pictures of babies from magazines or books. Talk with children about how they used to be babies before they grew.

Concept Work

Discuss each picture and help children remember the story "Goldilocks and the Three Bears." Have children retell the story as they look at each picture. Then have children color the pictures.

Preteach / Reteach
LS Leveled Support Vocabulary in Context

❶ **Beginning** Point to the baby, father, mother, and woods on the Worktext page. Name the words and have children echo.

❷ ❸ **Early Intermediate/Intermediate** Ask children to find a mother, father, baby, and the woods in the illustrations in the Worktext. They can circle the pictures of these words.

❹ ❺ **Early Advanced/Advanced** Ask children to draw a picture a family having a picnic in the words and use vocabulary words to label their drawing.

Wrap Up DAY 1

Daily
Table Talk What kind of adventures can a child have? Have children answer the question, using the vocabulary words.

Produce Language Discuss adventures a child can have. Say a sentence using the sentence starter: *One day a child had so much fun when she _____ .*

Today children should have:

☑ **Learned** and applied vocabulary related to adventures little girls can have.

☑ **Spoken** complete sentences about adventures a little girl can have.

☑ **Recognized** concept vocabulary words.

 ELA R 2.4 Retell familiar stories. (ELD R.B7)

OBJECTIVE

To discuss adventures a child can have; to introduce category words for furniture.

Concept Talk

Connect to Day 1 What kind of adventures can a child have?

Introduce the Daily Question Are there one, two, three, four, or five bears in the story? Retell the story if necessary. Have children answer orally.

Use the Poster Use the Day 2 teaching notes.

Introduce Category Words

1. **Say the Word** Have children point to the picture of the bed. Say *bed,* and have children repeat the word.

2. **Introduce the Meaning** Ask questions: Do you sleep in a bed? Do you make your bed?

3. **Demonstrate** Have children demonstrate getting into bed by pulling down the covers, crawling in, and then pulling up the covers.

4. **Apply** Repeat with other vocabulary words and elicit that they all belong to the category "furniture."

Have children draw furniture.

Corrective Feedback If children have difficulty, have them choose a room to draw, such as a bedroom or kitchen. What kind of furniture would they find in the room?

Wrap Up   DAY 2

Daily

Table Talk Have children discuss the number of bears in the story.

Produce Language To build fluency, encourage children to label or write a sentence about their drawings. They can share their writing with partners.

Today children should have:

☑ **Learned** and applied vocabulary related to furniture.

☑ **Spoken** complete sentences about the number of bears in a story.

☑ **Recognized** words that belong in the same category.

ELA R1.17 Identify and sort common words in basic categories (for example colors, shapes, foods). (ELD R.B4)
ELA R 2.4 Retell familiar stories. (ELD R.B7)

Furniture

Picture Dictionary

bed

chair

table

dresser

Draw Draw furniture.

 ELA R1.17 Identify and sort common words in basic categories (e.g., colors, shapes, foods). (ELD R.B4)

Preteach / Reteach **LS Leveled Support** **Category Words**

❶ **Beginning** Point to each picture on the Worktext page. Say the related furniture word and have children repeat the word.

❷ ❸ **Early Intermediate/Intermediate** Say a furniture word and have children point to the corresponding picture. Say a simple description, such as: You sleep on this. You put your breakfast on this. Children can point to the word you are describing and say the corredsponding word.

❹ ❺ **Early Advanced/Advanced** Ask children to point to and name the furniture word for each picture. Have children say what each piece of furniture is used for. Then have partners compose sentences using one of the category words.

Why is Goldilocks visiting the bears?

✏️ **Circle** Circle *One.* Circle *three.*
One girl visited three bears.

✏️ **Circle** Circle *two.*
She saw two squirrels in the woods.

✏️ **Circle** Circle *four.* Circle *five.*
She saw four or five birds.

🐻 ELA R1.15 Read simple one-syllable and high-frequency words (i.e., sight words). (ELD R.B2)

OBJECTIVE

To discuss why Goldilocks is visiting the bears; to review high frequency words *one, two, three, four,* and *five.*

Concept Talk FORM & FUNCTION

Connect to Day 2 Are there one, two, three, four, or five bears in the story?

Introduce the Daily Question Why is Goldilocks visiting the bears? Have children retell that part of the story, using the illustrations on pages 140–141.

Use the Poster Use the Day 3 teaching notes.

Review Concept Vocabulary Review the words introduced on Day 1.

Review High Frequency Words

Write the word *one* on the board and hold up one finger. Say *one.* Continue the procedure with words *two, three, four,* and *five.* Say: Put your finger on the directions. It says circle *one,* circle *three.* Now find those number words in the sentence. Help children complete the Worktext page.

Corrective Feedback If children have difficulty finding the number words in the sentence, have them look at the first letter of the word *one* and then look for an *o* in the sentence. Then have them look for the *t* in *three.*

Preteach Reteach (LS) **Leveled Support** **High Frequency Words**

① **Beginning** Write the words *one, two, three, four,* and *five.* As you point to a word, say the word and show the number with your fingers. Have children echo the word and show the number with their fingers.

② ③ **Early Intermediate/Intermediate** Have children draw circles to represent *one, two, three, four,* and *five.* Children can match cards with the words printed on them to the pictures.

④ ⑤ **Early Advanced/Advanced** Have children write *one, two, three, four,* and *five* on a piece of paper. Next to each word, they can draw the corresponding number of squares. Have them use the words in sentences and share those sentences with partners.

Wrap Up DAY **3**

Daily **Table Talk** Have children discuss why Goldilocks is visiting the bears.

Produce Language Review the story. Have each child say a sentence about why Goldilocks is visiting the bears.

Today children should have:

☑ **Learned** and applied the high frequency words *one, two, three, four,* and *five.*

☑ **Spoken** complete sentences about why Goldilocks is visiting the bears.

☑ **Recognized** the high frequency words *one, two, three, four,* and *five.*

 ELA R1.15 Read simple one syllable and high frequency words (i.e., sight words). (ELD R.B2)

To discuss adventures; to identify initial and final /g/.

Concept Talk

FORM & FUNCTION

Connect to Day 3 Why is Goldilocks visiting the bears?

Introduce the Daily Question What adventures have you had? Discuss with children. You have probably not met three bears in the woods like Goldilocks did! What have you done that you would call an adventure?

Use the Poster Use the Day 4 teaching notes.

Phonics

Initial & Final /g/ Write the word *good* on the board. Say: Say this word with me. *Good.* What letter is at the beginning of the word? (*g*) What sound does the letter *g* make? (/g/) Good! Repeat procedure to model identifying final /g/ using the word *pig.* Tell children they are going to be listening for /g/ in words. Help children complete the Worktext page.

Corrective Feedback If children have difficulty completing the Worktext page, say the word for each picture very slowly, separating the phonemes and accentuating the /g/. Remind children that the sound will not always be at the beginnings of words. The sound can also appear at the ends of words.

Wrap Up   DAY 4

Daily
Table Talk What adventures have you had? Have children discuss adventures they have had.

Produce Language Have each child say a sentence about an adventure they have had.

Today children should have:

☑ **Learned** and applied vocabulary related to an adventure they have had.

☑ **Spoken** complete sentences about adventures they have had.

☑ **Recognized** initial and final /g/.

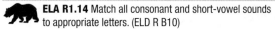
ELA R1.14 Match all consonant and short-vowel sounds to appropriate letters. (ELD R B10)

144 Goldilocks's Adventures • Unit 4, Week 4

Identify Sound Gg

✏️ **Circle** Circle things with *g*.

144 🐻 **ELA R1.14** Match all consonant and short-vowel sounds to appropriate letters. (ELD R.B10)

Preteach LS Reteach **Leveled Support** **Phonics**

① **Beginning** Hold up a card on which you have printed *g*. Say: This letter is *g*. G makes the sound /g/. Have children repeat after you. *g*/g/.

②③ **Early Intermediate/Intermediate** Hold up a card on which you have printed *g*. Say: What letter is this? What sound does the letter make? Offer help if needed. Have children say words beginning with /g/.

④⑤ **Early Advanced/Advanced** Give children pictures and name each picture with children. Ask children to put words in two categories: words that begin with /g/ and words that end with /g/. Ask children to draw pictures of some of the words and label them if they can.

What kind of adventures can a child have?

 Draw

OBJECTIVE

To guide children to express their understanding of weekly concepts and vocabulary.

Think, Talk, and Recognize!

Concept Talk

Connect to Day 4 What adventures have you had? Model how to answer yesterday's question with a sentence.

Review the Weekly Question Ask: What kind of adventures can a child have? Have children share adventures. After children have answered, they can identify other children that had similar ideas.

Use the Poster Use the Day 5 teaching notes.

Review Concept Vocabulary Review the vocabulary introduced on Day 1.

Concept Wrap-Up

Have children draw to answer the question: What kind of adventures can a child have? Discuss the photo. This family looks like it is exploring in the woods. This trip could be an adventure!

Leveled Support   Concept Vocabulary

① **Beginning** Display the Word Cards for *woods, father, mother,* and *baby.* Ask children: Is this a baby? Is this a mother? Children can nod to respond and then repeat the words.

② ③ **Early Intermediate/Intermediate** Display the Word Cards for *woods, father, mother,* and *baby.* Ask children to say each word as they point to it. Have children identify pictures that show these words on pages 140–141.

④ ⑤ **Early Advanced/Advanced** Give pairs of children the Word Cards, one word per pair. Ask children to work together to create a sentence using the word.

Wrap Up   DAY 5

Table Talk *Daily* What kind of adventures can a child have? Have children discuss the question, using the vocabulary words they have learned this week.

Produce Language To build fluency, children can label, write about, or speak about their drawings. Ask children to respond to what they read or heard.

Today, children should have:

☑ **Reviewed** the weekly concept and concept vocabulary.

☑ **Spoken** about Goldilocks's adventures and other adventures children can have.

☑ **Drawn or written** about adventures that children can have.

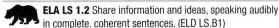 **ELA LS 1.2** Share information and ideas, speaking audibly in complete, coherent sentences. (ELD LS.B1)

145

WEEK 5
CALIFORNIA

Last Week
Unit 4, Week 4
Goldilocks's
Adventures

Weekly Lesson Plan

	DAY 1 Get Ready to Read	**DAY 2** Read and Comprehend
	Build Background	**Language: Category Words**

Question of the Week

What is it like in the Antarctic?

Instructional Plan and Materials

- **Word Cards** 77–80

- **Poster**
  Poster 23 can be used at beginning or end of day.

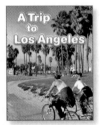

- **Big Book**
  A Trip to Los Angeles

- **Song Book**, p. 23

Transparencies Explore content and vocabulary and model fluent reading.

For further information about using these components, see pages x–xv.

DAY 1 — Build Background

Preteach/Review 10–15 min
Poster, Song Book, Big Book
- **Leveled Support Preteach**
- **Practice Stations Preteach**

Teach 35–45 min
- **Concept Talk**
- **Oral Vocabulary Routine**
  Word Cards
- **Build Concept Vocabulary**
- **Daily Table Talk**

Check/Reteach 5–10 min
Poster, Word Cards
- **Leveled Support Reteach**

DAY 2 — Language: Category Words

Preteach/Review 10–15 min
Poster
- **Leveled Support Preteach**
- **Practice Stations Review**

Teach 35–45 min
- **Category Words**
- **Daily Table Talk**

Check/Reteach 5–10 min
Poster, Word Cards
- **Leveled Support Reteach**

Fluency: Writing or Speaking

CALIFORNIA Standards

G1 Sci 2.a Students know different animals inhabit different kinds of environments and have external features that help them thrive in different kinds of places.

G1 His-Soc Sci 1.2.4. Describe how location, weather, and physical environment affect the way people live, including the effects on their food, clothing, shelter, transportation, and recreation.

ELA LS 1.2 Share information and ideas, speaking audibly in complete, coherent sentences.

ELA R 1.17 Identify and sort common words in basic categories (e.g., colors, shapes, foods).

Academic Language

Vocabulary: thunder

Category Words: hot, cold, warm, freezing

Concept Talk Video

Background Building Audio Slideshow

This Week
Unit 4, Week 5

Cold Adventures

Next Week
Unit 4, Week 6
City Adventures

DAY **3** Read and Comprehend	DAY **4** Language Arts	DAY **5** Language Arts
FORM & FUNCTION	FORM & FUNCTION	
Language: High Frequency Words	**Phonics**	**Think, Talk, and Recognize**
Preteach/Review 10–15 min Poster **Leveled Support Preteach** **Practice Stations Review**	**Preteach/Review** 10–15 min Poster **Leveled Support Preteach** **Practice Stations Review**	**Preteach/Review** 10–15 min Poster **Leveled Support Preteach** **Practice Stations Review**
Teach 35–45 min **High Frequency Words** **Daily Table Talk**	**Teach** 35–45 min **Phonics** **Daily Table Talk**	**Teach** 15–20 min **Think, Talk, and Recognize** **Concept Wrap Up**
Check/Reteach 5–10 min Poster, Word Cards **Leveled Support Reteach**	**Check/Reteach** 5–10 min Poster, Word Cards **Leveled Support Reteach**	**Check/Reteach** 30–40 min Poster, Word Cards, Song Book **Leveled Support Reteach**
		Fluency: Writing or Speaking
ELA R 1.15 Read simple one-syllable and high frequency words (i.e., sight words).	**ELA R 1.14** Match all consonant and short-vowel sounds to appropriate letters.	**ELA LS 1.2** Share information and ideas, speaking audibly in complete, coherent sentences.
High Frequency Words: from, here, go		

Practice Stations

Materials and Activity

DAY 1 — Get Ready to Read

books about Antarctica, batting or cotton balls

Antarctica

Provide Antarctica-related pictures and books from the library for children to look through. Have children begin to create an Antarctica bulletin board by stapling batting or stretched cotton balls to a bulletin board.

DAY 2 — Read and Comprehend

paper bags, construction paper, glue, newspaper, scissors, markers, stapler

Paper Bag Penguins

Create a paper-bag penguin for children to copy. Have them color a paper bag black. Draw an oval on white paper and cut it out. Glue it onto the bag to be the penguin's belly. The bottom of the bag is the bottom of the penguin. Stuff the bag with balled up newspaper. Fold down the top opening, corner to corner, meeting in the back. Staple the bag closed. Cut a black circle and glue it above the white tummy (over the stapled part) for the penguin's head. Cut and attach 2 orange webbed feet, 1 yellow triangle beak, and eyes. Talk about cold weather. Have children hold up their penguins when you say something related to cold or Antartica. Then have them add their penguins to the bulletin board.

Preteach/Reteach

Transfer and Common Misconceptions

/th/ sound

The English phoneme /th/ is not used in Spanish. Children may have difficulty producing the sound /th/ in the word *thunder*.

Deleting Final Sound

Some children may delete final consonants in word–final consonant clusters: col (cold). Remind children to pay attention to every phoneme.

Produce Language

Weekly Concept and Language Goal

CONCEPT GOALS

- describe what it might be like to have an adventure in the Antarctic
- explain the kind of transportation needed to get to and get around in the Antarctic
- name and describe different winter adventures

By Day 5, children should be able to talk about their drawings and write a one-word label.

Daily Table Talk (Day 1)

❶ **Beginning** — Name objects that might be found in the Antarctic and have children answer yes or no.

❷❸ **Early Intermediate/Intermediate** — One- or two-word response: penguin, iceberg

❹❺ **Early Advanced/Advanced** — Sentence: In the Antarctic I saw a penguin.

Daily Table Talk (Day 2)

❶ **Beginning** — Children talk about their drawings.

❷❸ **Early Intermediate/Intermediate** — Children write one-word labels

❹❺ **Early Advanced/Advanced** — Children write a phrase or sentence.

DAY 3 Read and Comprehend

 DAY 3 Read and Comprehend

six jars of water, six thermometers, paper, pencils

 DAY 4 Form & Function Language Arts

newspaper; highlighter pens

 DAY 5 Language Arts

egg carton, picture cards

Hot or Cold? 👫

Have six jars of water, numbered 1–6, of various temperatures. Tell children to place a thermometer in each jar of water. Wait several minutes and then check the temperature of each jar. Have children record the temperatures on a sheet of paper, according to the number on the jar. Have partners check thermometer readings and compare results.

Highlight! 👤

A child chooses an article from a newspaper and looks for the high frequency words (*go, from,* and *here*). Have child locate and highlight these words in the article.

Egg-citing! 👤 👫 👪

Provide picture cards and an egg carton. Have children identify words that begin with *e*. Have children place *e* picture cards in the carton. Children work together to get a dozen *e* words.

Do and Go

Children may be confused when they recognize that these two high frequency words have very similar structure and yet very different vowel sounds.

Producing /e/

The short vowel /e/ is produced with a wide lip shape and the tongue in a neutral position.

skipping Sounds

Children may often skip pronouncing the first *c* in Antarctica. Practice saying *Antarctica* instead of *Antartica*.

Daily Table Talk

❶ **Beginning** Name a word that might describe sledding and have children say yes or no.

❷ ❸ **Early Intermediate/Intermediate**
Phrase: snow, fast, cold

❹ ❺ **Early Advanced/Advanced**
Sentence: Sledding is cold and fun!

Daily Table Talk

❶ **Beginning** Name snowy activities and have children identify the ones they like to do by saying say yes or no.

❷ ❸ **Early Intermediate/Intermediate**
One- or two-word response: sledding, building a snowman

❹ ❺ **Early Advanced/Advanced**
Sentence: Building a snowman is a winter adventure.

Daily Table Talk

❶ **Beginning** Child draws and speaks about the drawing.

❷ ❸ **Early Intermediate/Intermediate** Child draws and speaks about the drawing using at least one concept vocabulary word.

❹ ❺ **Early Advanced/Advanced** Child draws and provides a label for the drawing that includes a vocabulary word.

OBJECTIVE

To introduce and discuss concepts and vocabulary related to adventures in the Antarctic.

Build Background Get Ready to Read!

Question of the Week What is it like in the Antarctic?

www.pearsonsuccessnet.com

Concept Talk

Use the Big Book If you haven't introduced the Big Book, consider reading it to children. Connect the Big Book to the unit theme, Adventures—Let's Go Exploring.

Introduce the Weekly Concept Tell children that today, they will talk about taking an adventure to the Antarctic. Ask the weekly question: What is it like in the Antarctic?

Use the Poster Direct children's attention to the weekly poster. Use the Day 1 teaching notes at the bottom of the poster.

Sing the Song Use the song **To Antarctica** to reinforce children's understanding of the weekly concept. Have children sing or simply chant the words with you.

Use a Transparency Use the Central Concept Map (Transparency 2) to capture children's thoughts. Write *Antarctica* in the middle circle. Record ideas about what it is like in Antarctica and what would be found there in the outer circles.

Cold Adventures

Vocabulary

penguin

ship

sled

thunder

What is it like in the Antarctic?

146

Vocabulary

* Academic Vocabulary

penguin a large, black and white Antarctic sea bird that cannot fly but uses its wings for swimming

ship a large boat that can carry people or goods over water

sled a vehicle that slides over snow, often used by children

* **thunder** the loud noise that you hear during a storm, usually after a flash of lightning

Introduce Concept Vocabulary

1. **Say the Word** Display the Word Card as you say *penguin.* Have children repeat the word.

2. **Introduce Word Meaning** Ask questions about penguins. Show pictures of penguins if necessary. How do penguins walk? What color are penguins?

3. **Demonstrate** Have children walk like a penguin, hands at side, shuffling feet.

4. **Apply** Have children demonstrate their understanding.

Repeat with other vocabulary words.

Corrective Feedback If children have difficulty understanding the word *penguin,* show pictures of penguins from magazines or books. Repeat with other vocabulary words.

Concept Work

Discuss each picture. Help children describe what is happening in each picture. Discuss the environment in the Antarctic, the animals that live there, and how people travel there. Have children color the pictures. Then have them describe one of the pictures to a partner.

Table Talk What is it like in the Antarctic? Have children answer the question, using the vocabulary words.

Produce Language Discuss adventures a person could have in the Antarctic. Have children say a sentence about what they might see in the Antarctic using the sentence starter: One day in the Antarctic I saw _____ .

Today children should have:

☑ **Learned** and applied vocabulary related to Antarctic adventures.

☑ **Spoken** complete sentences about Antarctic adventures.

☑ **Recognized** concept vocabulary words.

 ELA LS 1.2 Share information and ideas, speaking audibly in complete, coherent sentences. (ELD LS.B2)

147

 Leveled Support Vocabulary in Context

Preteach LS Reteach

❶ **Beginning** Point to the penguin, ship, and sled on the Worktext page. Name the words and have children echo.

❷ ❸ **Early Intermediate/Intermediate** Have children point to each vocabulary word picture and say the word. Then have them find and circle the items in the illustrations on the Worktext page.

❹ ❺ **Early Advanced/Advanced** Ask children to draw a picture of a ship in the Antarctic waters. Have children put a caption under their picture.

OBJECTIVE

To discuss travel to the Antarctic; to introduce category words for temperatures.

Concept Talk

Connect to Day 1 What is it like in the Antarctic?

Introduce the Daily Question How can you go from Antarctica to here? Have children answer orally. Refer to the illustrations on the Worktext page if children need ideas about travel in the Antarctic.

Use the Poster Use the Day 2 teaching notes.

Introduce Category Words

1. **Say the Word** Have children point to the picture of the flames. Say *hot* and have children repeat the word.

2. **Introduce Word Meaning** Ask questions: Is fire hot? Is a stove hot? What else is hot?

3. **Demonstrate** Have children demonstrate touching something hot by quickly pulling hand away.

4. **Apply** Repeat with other vocabulary words and elicit that they all belong to the category "temperature."

Have children draw lines to match temperature words to corresponding pictures.

Corrective Feedback If children have difficulty identifying what is hot and cold, let them feel ice cubes. Say *cold* as they touch the ice and have them echo. Guide them to the word *cold* by emphasizing the /k/ sound at the beginning of *cold*.

Temperatures

Picture Dictionary

hot

cold

warm

freezing

 Match Match temperatures.

cold

hot

148 ELA R1.17 Identify and sort common words in basic categories (e.g., colors, shapes, foods). (ELD R.B4)

Wrap Up   DAY 2

Daily Table Talk Have children discuss how you go from Antarctica to here.

Produce Language To build fluency, encourage children to label or write a sentence about the items they matched. They can share their writing with partners.

Today children should have:

☑ **Learned** and applied vocabulary related to temperatures.

☑ **Spoken** complete sentences about getting from Antarctica to here.

☑ **Recognized** words that belong in the same category.

ELA R1.17 Identify and sort common words in basic categories (for example colors, shapes, foods). (ELD R.B4)

Preteach/Reteach LS Leveled Support Category Words

❶ **Beginning** Point to each picture on the Worktext page. Say the related temperature word and have children repeat the word.

❷ ❸ **Early Intermediate/Intermediate** Say a temperature word and have children point to the corresponding picture. Ask questions to build understanding, such as: Is an ice cube hot? Is it cold in the desert? Children can nod to show their understanding and then say the temperature words.

❹ ❺ **Early Advanced/Advanced** Ask children to point to and name the temperature word for each picture. Have children say a sentence about whether they prefer hot or cold temperatures.

Do you want to sled in Antarctica?

✏️ **Circle** Circle *from.* Circle *here.*
Start sledding from here.

✏️ **Circle** Circle *go.*
Penguins go sledding too.

🐻 ELA R1.15 Read simple one-syllable and high-frequency words (i.e., sight words). (ELD R.B2)

149

To discuss sledding in Antarctica; to introduce high frequency words *from*, *here*, and *go*.

Concept Talk

 FORM & FUNCTION

Connect to Day 2 How can you go from Antarctica to here?

Introduce the Daily Question Do you want to sled in Antarctica? Discuss reasons.

Use the Poster Use the Day 3 teaching notes.

Review Concept Vocabulary Review the words introduced on Day 1.

Introduce High Frequency Words

Write the words *from here* on the board and draw a circle. On the other side of the board, draw an X. Say Let's start *from here* and go there. Have children echo *from here* and *go there.* Write the words *from here* and *go there.* Have children underline the words *from*, *here*, and *go.* Help children complete the Worktext page.

Leveled Support **High Frequency Words**
Preteach / Reteach

① **Beginning** Write the words *from, here,* and *go.* Have children identify and name the letters in each of the words.

② ③ **Early Intermediate/Intermediate** Write the words *from, here,* and *go.* Say a word and have children point to it and repeat after you. Then write the words on index cards. Say sentences and have children hold up the cards when they hear the words.

④ ⑤ **Early Advanced/Advanced** Display the words *from, here,* and *go.* Have children use each of the words in a sentence.

Wrap Up DAY 3

Table Talk Daily Have children discuss sledding in Antarctica.

Produce Language Have children look at the photos of people and penguins sledding. Have each child say a sentence about sledding in Antarctica.

Today children should have:

☑ **Learned** and applied the high frequency words *from, here,* and *go.*

☑ **Spoken** complete sentences about sledding in Antarctica.

☑ **Recognized** the high frequency words *from, here,* and *go.*

🐻 **ELA R1.15** Read simple one syllable and high frequency words (sight words). (ELD R.B2)

To discuss winter adventures; to identify initial and medial /e/.

Concept Talk

FORM & FUNCTION

Connect to Day 3 Do you want to sled in Antarctica?

Introduce the Daily Question What adventures can you have in the winter? Ask children if they have ever been sledding, skiing, built a snowman, or simply took a walk outside on a wintry day.

Use the Poster Use the Day 4 teaching notes.

Phonics

Identify Sound /e/ Write the word *pet* on the board. Say: Say this word with me *pet*. What letter is in the middle of the word? *e*. What sound does the letter e make? /e/. Repeat the procedure to model identifying initial /e/ using the word *egg*. Tell children they are going to be listening for /e/ in words. Help children complete the Worktext page.

Corrective Feedback If children have difficulty completely the Worktext page, say the word for each picture very slowly, separating the phonemes and accentuating the /e/. Remind children that the sound may be at the beginning or middle of a word.

Wrap Up   DAY 4

Daily Table Talk What adventures can you have in the winter? Have children discuss adventures they can have.

Produce Language Have each child say a sentence about a winter adventure they can have.

Today children should have:

- ☑ **Learned** and applied vocabulary related to a winter adventure they can have.

- ☑ **Spoken** complete sentences about a winter adventure they can have.

- ☑ **Identified** initial and medial /e/.

 ELA R1.14 Match all consonant and short-vowel sounds to appropriate letters. (ELD R.B10)

Identify Sound Ee

🖊 **Color** Color things with e.

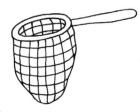 

150 🐻 **ELA R1.14** Match all consonant and short-vowel sounds to appropriate letters. (ELD R.B10)

Preteach LS Leveled Support Phonics Reteach

① **Beginning** Hold up a card on which you have printed *e*. Say: This letter is e. One sound e makes is /e/. Have children repeat after you. *e*/e/.

② ③ **Early Intermediate/Intermediate** Hold up a card on which you have printed *e*. Say: What letter is this? What is one sound *e* can make? Have children name a word that begins with the sound /e/.

④ ⑤ **Early Advanced/Advanced** Have children sort words into two categories: those with initial /e/ and those with medial /e/. Children can draw pictures and label them for each category.

...king audibly in complete, coherent sentences. (ELD LS.B1)

151

...rds
...ds).

Concept Vocabulary

...Word Cards for *penguin, ship, sled,* and *thunder.* Say each
...nd point to the matching card.

...**termediate** Display the Word Cards for *penguin,*
... children to say each word as they point to it. Ask
...ng: What kind of animal is a penguin? When would
... ask questions of partners or classmates.

...**ced** Display the Picture Card for *penguin.* Ask
...us this word. Continue for the other words.

To guide children to express their understanding of weekly
concepts and vocabulary.

Think, Talk, and Recognize!

Concept Talk

Connect to Day 4 What adventures can you have in the
winter? Model how to answer yesterday's question with a
sentence.

Review the Weekly Question Ask: What is it like in the
Antarctic? Have children share adventures. After children
have answered, they can identify other children that had
similar ideas.

Use the Poster Use the Day 5 teaching notes.

Review Concept Vocabulary Review the vocabulary
introduced on Day 1.

Concept Wrap-Up

Have children draw to answer the question: *What is it
like in the Antarctic?* Use the photo to prompt discussion.
The picture shows penguins. I can't see any trees in
the picture, just snow and water. It's icy and cold in the
Antarctic.

Wrap Up **DAY** 5

Table Talk What is it like in the Antarctic? Have
children discuss the question, using the vocabulary words
they have learned this week.

Produce Language To build fluency, children can label, write
about, or speak about their drawings. Ask children to respond to
what they read or heard.

Today, children should have:

- ☑ **Reviewed** the weekly concept and concept vocabulary.
- ☑ **Spoken** about what it is like in the Antarctic.
- ☑ **Drawn or written** to show what it is like in the Antarctic.

 ELA LS. 1.2 Share information and ideas, speaking
audibly in complete, coherent sentences. (ELD LS.B1)

151

Question of the Week What are some city adventures?

	DAY 1 Get Ready to Read	**DAY 2** Read and Co
	Build Background	**Language: Category Word**

Instructional Plan and Materials

- **Word Cards** 81–83

- **Big Book** A Trip to Los Angeles

- **Poster** Poster 24 can be used at beginning or end of day.

- **Song Book**, p. 24

Transparencies Explore content and vocabulary and model fluent reading.

For further information about using these components, see pages x–xv.

DAY 1 — Build Background

Preteach/Review 10–15 min
Poster, Song Book, Big Book
- **Leveled Support Preteach**
- **Practice Stations Preteach**

Teach 35–45 min
- **Concept Talk**
- **Oral Vocabulary Routine**
  Word Cards
- **Build Concept Vocabulary**
- **Daily Table Talk**

Check/Reteach 5–10 min
Poster, Word Cards
- **Leveled Support Reteach**

DAY 2 — Language: Category Word

Preteach/Review 10–15 min
Poster
- **Leveled Support Preteach**
- **Practice Stations Review**

Teach 35–45 min
- **Category Words**
- **Daily Table Talk**

Check/Reteach 5–10 min
Poster, Word Cards
- **Leveled Support Reteach**

Fluency: Writing or Speaking

CALIFORNIA Standards

ELA LS 1.2 Share information and ideas, speaking audibly in complete, coherent sentences.

ELA R 1.17 Identify and sort comm basic categories (e.g., colors, shape

GK Sci 4.e Communicate observations orally and through drawings.

Academic Language

Vocabulary: grandma

Category Words: clouds, moon, sta

Get Online! www.pearsonsuccessnet.com

Concept Talk Video

Background Building Audio Sli

This Week
Unit 4, Week 6

City Adventures

Next Week
Unit 5, Week 1
Getting Places

FORM & FUNCTION **DAY 3** Read and Comprehend	FORM & FUNCTION **DAY 4** Language Arts	**DAY 5** Language Arts
Language: High Frequency Words	**Phonics**	**Think, Talk, and Recognize**
Preteach/Review 10–15 min Poster **Leveled Support Preteach** **Practice Stations Review**	**Preteach/Review** 10–15 min Poster **Leveled Support Preteach** **Practice Stations Review**	**Preteach/Review** 10–15 min Poster **Leveled Support Preteach** **Practice Stations Review**
Teach 35–45 min **High Frequency Words** **Daily Table Talk**	**Teach** 35–45 min **Phonics** **Daily Table Talk**	**Teach** 15–20 min **Think, Talk, and Recognize** **Concept Wrap Up**
Check/Reteach 5–10 min Poster, Word Cards **Leveled Support Reteach**	**Check/Reteach** 5–10 min Poster, Word Cards **Leveled Support Reteach**	**Check/Reteach** 30–40 min Poster, Word Cards, Song Book **Leveled Support Reteach**
		Fluency: Writing or Speaking
ELA R 1.15 Read simple one-syllable and high frequency words (i.e., sight words).	**ELA R 1.14** Match all consonant and short-vowel sounds to appropriate letters.	**ELA LS 1.2** Share information and ideas, speaking audibly in complete, coherent sentences.
High Frequency Words: from, here, go		

Practice Stations

Materials and Activity

black construction paper, yellow tissue paper, tape, scissors

Cityscape

Have children design skyscrapers out of paper and other materials. Have children cut rectangle windows in tall black paper (buildings). Put yellow tissue paper on the back of the black paper to look as if lights are on in the building. Create a cityscape bulletin board or tape the buildings on the windows so the light will shine through the skyscraper windows.

grandma accessories/props: gray wig, spectacles, cane, handbag

A Day with Grandma

Give children props and accessories for one of them to transform into a grandma. Act out or pantomime grandma making bread with a grandchild and grandma taking her grandchild to the park. Now reverse roles so the other person gets a chance to be grandma.

Preteach/Reteach

Transfer and Common Misconceptions

Build Background

Books are not the only background source available. Videos, computer software, and websites are resources that can also be used to build background knowledge through their visual or interactive nature.

/ou/ and /oo/ Sounds

Learning to read English is not just a matter of learning to sound out phonemes and blending the sounds. To decode the *ou* in *cloud, touch,* and *soup,* children must look at other letters in the word as well.

Produce Language

Weekly Concept and Language Goal

CONCEPT GOALS

- describe some of the adventures people can have in the city
- compare and contrast the city to other places
- name and describe different ways to get to the city

By Day 5, children should be able to talk about their drawings and write a one-word label.

Daily Table Talk

❶ **Beginning**
> Children pantomime while you provide the language.

❷ ❸ **Early Intermediate/Intermediate**
> Children pantomime and say a word or phrase.

❹ ❺ **Early Advanced/Advanced**
> Children say a sentence while pantomiming.

Daily Table Talk

❶ **Beginning**
> Children talk about their drawings.

❷ ❸ **Early Intermediate/Intermediate**
> Children write one-word labels.

❹ ❺ **Early Advanced/Advanced**
> Children write a phrase or sentence.

DAY 3 — Read and Comprehend

FORM & FUNCTION

paper, markers, colored pencils, crayons

Things in the Sky ★ ★★

Tell children to draw a picture to show how the category words are related.

Have children share their pictures in a small group.

H is written as *j*

The word *here* may pose problems for some children. Spanish is written with the Roman alphabet like English, but there are a few orthographic differences of note. In Spanish the letter *h* is not pronounced, although the sound /h/ is written as *j* or *g*.

Daily Table Talk

❶ **Beginning** | Name things that can be found in the city and country and have children say city or country

❷ ❸ **Early Intermediate/Intermediate** | Phrase: skyscrapers, taxis, buses

❹ ❺ **Early Advanced/Advanced** | Sentence: We take a taxi.

DAY 4 — Language Arts

FORM & FUNCTION

markers, index cards, scissors

Puzzle Spelling ★★

Tell children to copy high frequency words onto large index cards with markers. Cut up the words into letters. Have children trade cards with a partner and put the letters together to spell the high frequency words.

Two sounds of *e*

Children may often see the letter and say it as its name, /ē/

Daily Table Talk

❶ **Beginning** | Have children act out forms of transportation.

❷ ❸ **Early Intermediate/Intermediate** | One or two word response: bus, train, plane

❹ ❺ **Early Advanced/Advanced** | Sentence: I take the train to the city.

DAY 5 — Language Arts

letter tiles; piece of paper with these endings written on it: *et, ed, en, ell;* paper, pencil

Rhyming words ★ ★★

Give children letter tiles and paper. Have children use the tiles to create word families. Tell children to add different beginning letters to create new words. Children work together to see how many words they can make in each of the families. Have partners take turns writing the words they create on paper.

| n | e | t |

Vowels

Most languages in the world have about 5 vowels. English has around 13 vowels, which means that many students of English must learn more vowel distinctions than there may be in their native languages.

Daily Table Talk

❶ **Beginning** Child draws and speaks about the drawing.

❷ ❸ **Early Intermediate/Intermediate** Child draws and speaks about the drawing using at least one concept vocabulary word.

❹ ❺ **Early Advanced/Advanced** Child draws and provides a label for the drawing that includes a vocabulary word.

To introduce concepts and vocabulary related to adventures people can have in the city.

Build Background Get **Ready** to **Read!**

Question of the Week

What are some city adventures?

www.pearsonsuccessnet.com

Concept Talk

Use the Big Book If you haven't introduced the Big Book, consider reading it to children. Connect to the unit theme, Adventures—Let's Go Exploring.

Introduce the Weekly Concept Tell children that today, they will talk about adventures you can have in the city. Ask the weekly question: What are some city adventures?

Use the Poster Direct children's attention to the weekly poster. Use the Day 1 teaching notes at the bottom of the poster.

Sing the Song Use the song **In the City** to reinforce children's understanding of the weekly concept. Have children sing or simply chant the words with you.

Use a Transparency Use the Fork Map (Transparency 5) with children. Children can name things they can do in the city and things they can see in the city as you record their ideas.

City Adventures

Vocabulary

bread

grandma

park

What are some city adventures?

152

Vocabulary

* **Academic Vocabulary**

bread a common food made from flour, water, and yeast

* **grandma** your grandmother

park a large, open area with grass and trees in a town, where people can walk or play games

Introduce Concept Vocabulary

1. **Say the Word** Display the Word Card as you say *bread.* Have children repeat the word.
2. **Introduce Word Meaning** Ask questions about bread. *What kind of bread do you like? Have you ever made bread?*
3. **Demonstrate** Have children role play making bread, pouring ingredients together in a bowl, kneading the dough, putting it in a pan and in an oven.
4. **Apply** Have children demonstrate their understanding.

Repeat with other vocabulary words.

Corrective Feedback If children have difficulty with the words, say the words again more slowly, separating the phonemes and then blending them as you say the word. Children can repeat after you.

Concept Work

Discuss the pictures with children. Talk about the adventures that are shown. Have children ever had these adventures in a city? Have children compare the city to adventures that they could have in the Antarctic or adventures that animals have. Have children circle details in the illustrations that show these adventures take place in the city.

Leveled Support Vocabulary in Context

❶ **Beginning** Point to the pictures and words on the Worktext page. Name the words and have children repeat them.

❷ ❸ **Early Intermediate/Intermediate** Have children point to each vocabulary picture and say the word. Then ask questions to build understanding: *Can a man be your grandma? Can you play baseball in a park?* Children respond to the yes/no questions by nodding. They can ask questions of their own.

❹ ❺ **Early Advanced/Advanced** Ask children to draw a picture of each vocabulary word and then label their pictures. Partners can make up sentences using the words.

Wrap Up DAY **1**

 Table Talk What kind of adventures can you have in the city? Have children answer the question, using the vocabulary words.

Produce Language Ask each child to act out an adventure they could have in the city and say a sentence about their adventure.

Today children should have:

☑ **Learned** and applied vocabulary related to city adventures.

☑ **Spoken** complete sentences about city adventures.

☑ **Recognized** concept vocabulary words.

ELA LS 1.2 Share information and ideas, speaking audibly in complete, coherent sentences. (ELD LS.B2)

153

To discuss the differences and similarities between the city and where children live; to introduce category words for things in the sky.

Concept Talk

Connect to Day 1 What are some city adventures?

Introduce the Daily Question How is the city the same or different from here? Have children answer orally.

Use the Poster Use the Day 2 teaching notes.

Introduce Category Words

1. **Say the Word** Have children point to the picture of the stars. Say *stars* and have children repeat the word.

2. **Introduce Word Meaning** Ask questions: Where do you see stars? When do you see stars?

3. **Demonstrate** Have children demonstrate looking at stars by pointing up at the sky or using hands to make binoculars.

4. **Apply** Repeat with other vocabulary words and elicit that they all belong to the category "things in the sky."

Have children draw things they can find in the sky.

Corrective Feedback If children have difficulty thinking of things to draw, invite them to look at sky pictures in books or magazines.

Wrap Up   DAY 2

Daily

Table Talk Have children discuss how the city is the same or different from here.

Produce Language To build fluency, encourage children to label or write a sentence about their drawings. They can share their writing with partners.

Today children should have:

☑ **Learned** and applied vocabulary related to things in the sky.

☑ **Spoken** complete sentences about how the city is the same or different from here.

☑ **Recognized** words that belong in the same category.

 ELA R1.17 Identify and sort common words in basic categories (for example, colors, shapes, foods). (ELD R.B4)

Things in the Sky

Picture Dictionary

clouds

moon

stars

sun

✏ **Draw** Draw things in the sky.

154   **ELA R1.17** Identify and sort common words in basic categories (e.g., colors, shapes, foods). (ELD R.B4)

Preteach Reteach LS Leveled Support **Category Words**

① **Beginning** Point to each picture on the Worktext page. Say the related word and have children echo it. You can also point to a picture and ask: Is this a star? Is this the moon? Children can nod to show their understanding.

② ③ **Early Intermediate/Intermediate** Say a category word and have children point to the corresponding picture. Have children describe the words in a sentence or two for partners to guess.

④ ⑤ **Early Advanced/Advanced** Pair children. Have each pair choose one word to use in a sentence. They can share their sentences with the group.

What can you do on a city adventure?

✏️ **Circle** Circle *Here*.

Here is the city market.

✏️ **Circle** Circle *Go*. Circle *from*.

Go from the museum to the park.

OBJECTIVE

To discuss what you do on a city adventure; to review high frequency words *here*, *go*, and *from*.

Concept Talk
FORM & FUNCTION

Connect to Day 2 How is the city the same or different from here?

Introduce the Daily Question What can you do on a city adventure? Discuss city adventures that children may have had.

Use the Poster Use the Day 3 teaching notes.

Review Concept Vocabulary Review the words introduced on Day 1.

Review High Frequency Words

Model the meanings of the high frequency words by saying simple sentences and using gestures, such as: *I am standing here. I will go from here to there.* Help children complete the Worktext page.

Corrective Feedback If children have difficulty circling the high frequency words, write the words on strips of paper. Children can match the words to the words in the Worktext.

Preteach / Reteach

LS **Leveled Support** **High Frequency Words**

① **Beginning** Write the words *from*, *here*, and *go* on index cards. Have pairs of children show cards to one another and say the word as it is shown.

② ③ **Early Intermediate/Intermediate** Give children index cards on which you have written the high frequency words, one word per card. Show cloze sentences and read them to children. Have them say and hold up the card that corresponds to the missing word in the sentence.

④ ⑤ **Early Advanced/Advanced** Have children design a postcard. Have children draw a city on one side and copy these words on the other side: *Wish you were here! From, _____ .*

Wrap Up **DAY**

Daily **Table Talk** Have children discuss what you can do on a city adventure.

Produce Language Have each child say a sentence about what you can do on a city adventure.

Today children should have:

☑ **Learned** and applied the high frequency words *here*, *go*, and *from*.

☑ **Spoken** complete sentences about what you can do on a city adventure.

☑ **Recognized** the high frequency words *here*, *go*, and *from*.

OBJECTIVE

To discuss how to travel to the city; to identify initial and final /e/.

Concept Talk

FORM & FUNCTION

Connect to Day 3 What can you do on a city adventure?

Introduce the Daily Question Ask: How can you get to the city? Discuss different forms of transportation, such as bus, train, car, or bicycle.

Use the Poster Use the Day 4 teaching notes.

Phonics

Identify Sound /e/ Write the word *red* on the board. Say: What sounds are in this word? /r/ /e/ /d/. Let's blend these sounds and say the word. *red.* What letter is in the middle of the word? e. What sound does the letter *e* make? /e/ Tell children they are going to be listening for /e/ in words. Help children complete the Worktext page.

Corrective Feedback If children have difficulty completing the Worktext page, say the word for each picture very slowly, emphasizing the /e/. Remind them that the sound may be at the beginning or in the middle of the word.

Identify Sound Ee

✏️ **Circle** Circle things with e.

156 🐻 **ELA R1.14** Match all consonant and short-vowel sounds to appropriate letters. (ELD R.B10)

Preteach / Reteach 🔵 **Leveled Support Phonics**

① **Beginning** Display a card on which you have written *Ee.* Say: This letter is *e*. One sound *e* makes is /e/. Have children repeat after you. *e* /e/. Say the words on the Worktext page with /e/, emphasizing the sound in each word.

② ③ **Early Intermediate/Intermediate** Say: I am going to say words. When you hear the sound /e/ in the word, raise your hand. Say words that do and do not have the sound /e/.

④ ⑤ **Early Advanced/Advanced** Give children pictures of items cut out from magazines. The items should have /e/ in both the initial and medial positions. Have children categorize them: words that start with /e/, and words with /e/ in the middle.

Wrap Up   DAY 4

Daily **Table Talk** How can you get to the city? Have children discuss ways to get to the city.

Produce Language Have each child say a sentence about ways to get to the city.

Today children should have:

☑ **Learned** and applied vocabulary related to ways to get to the city.

☑ **Spoken** complete sentences about ways to get to the city.

☑ **Recognized** initial and medial /e/.

🐻 **ELA R1.14** Match all consonant and short-vowel sounds to appropriate letters. (ELD R.B10)

What are some city adventures?

 Draw

OBJECTIVE

To guide children to express their understanding of weekly concepts and vocabulary.

Think, Talk, and Recognize!

Concept Talk

Connect to Day 4 How can you get to the city? Model how to answer yesterday's question with a sentence.

Review the Weekly Question Ask: What are some city adventures? Have children share adventures.

Use the Poster Use the Day 5 teaching notes.

Review Concept Vocabulary Review the vocabulary introduced on Day 1.

Concept Wrap-Up

Have children draw to answer the question: *What kind of adventures can you have in the city?* Discuss the photo: Where is this family? What adventure might they have?

Leveled Support　Concept Vocabulary

1 Beginning Display the Word Cards for *grandma, park,* and *bread.* Say each word. Ask children to repeat and point to the matching card.

2 3 Early Intermediate/Intermediate Display the Word Cards for *grandma, park,* and *bread.* Ask children to say each word as they point to it. Have children each choose a word and give a simple description of it. Others can guess what word is being described.

4 5 Early Advanced/Advanced Have children work with partners to tell a story using all three words. The story should tell about an adventure that someone could have in the city.

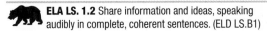
Wrap Up　　　　　　**DAY 5**

Table Talk What are some city adventures? Have children discuss the question, using the vocabulary words they have learned this week.

Produce Language To build fluency, children can label, write about, or speak about their drawings. Ask children to respond to what they read or heard.

Today, children should have

☑ **Reviewed** the weekly concept and concept vocabulary.

☑ **Spoken** about city adventures.

☑ **Drawn or written** about adventures they could have in the city.

ELA LS. 1.2 Share information and ideas, speaking audibly in complete, coherent sentences. (ELD LS.B1)

157

 How do people get from here to there?

Discuss the Big Question

Read and discuss the unit question. Introduce the word *transportation*. Transportation is the different ways that people get from one place to another. Cars, buses, and airplanes are some different kinds of transportation. What are some other kinds of transportation that people use?

Have children use the pictures along the side of the page to preview the weekly concepts for this unit. Read the weekly questions together. Discuss the weekly questions and how they relate to the big question.

Get Online! **www.pearsonsuccessnet.com**

• Unit 5 Big Question Video

CONCEPT/ LANGUAGE GOALS

Use the Concept and Language Goals throughout the unit to develop the big idea.

Children develop concepts and language as they talk about, use, and practice:

• Concept Vocabulary
• Academic Language
• Language Forms and Functions
• Category Words
• High Frequency Words

Get Online!
PearsonSuccessNet.com

Hear it!
See it!
Do it!

• Big Idea
• Concept Talk Video
• Background Building Audio Slideshow
• eBooks

Transportation— Going Places

How do people get from here to there?

158

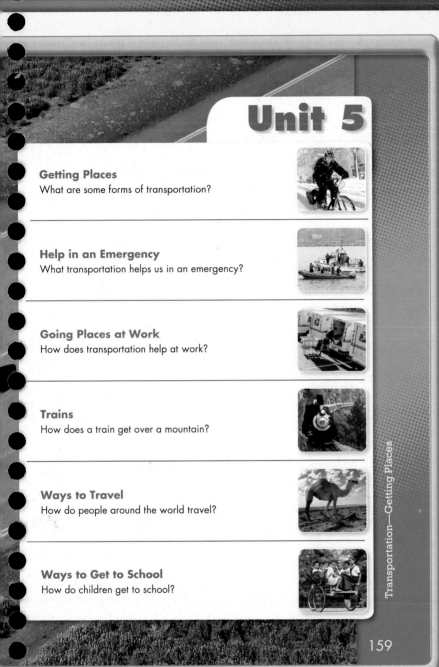

Unit 5

Getting Places
What are some forms of transportation?

Help in an Emergency
What transportation helps us in an emergency?

Going Places at Work
How does transportation help at work?

Trains
How does a train get over a mountain?

Ways to Travel
How do people around the world travel?

Ways to Get to School
How do children get to school?

Transportation—Getting Places

159

Read Aloud

Read the **Big Book** *One Morning in May.* Prompt discussion about the book.

• How do people get from place to place on the ground? In the air? On water?

• What is the best way to get to a place that is far away? Tell why you think so.

• What is the best kind of transportation people might use to travel back and forth to work or school?

For more read alouds related to the theme, see the Big Book Anthology.

Unit Project: Transportation

After discussing the unit question, provide children with newspapers and magazines. This week you will make a Big Book of Getting Places. Each day, you will work with partners to look through newspapers and magazines to find pictures that show different ways people get from place to place.

After children have gathered their pictures, have small groups of children paste the pictures in a large book made of sheets of poster paper stapled or tied together to make a book. You may have small groups create several books or create one large book as a class project. Pair children of mixed abilities to encourage participation. Encourage children to add labels or short sentences to accompany their pictures. Have children display and discuss the pictures in their books.

Question of the Week

What are some forms of transportation?

	DAY 1 Get Ready to Read	**DAY 2** Read and Comprehend
	Build Background	**Language: Category Words**

Instructional Plan and Materials

- **Word Cards**
  84–85

- **Big Book**
  One Morning in May

- **Poster**
  Poster 25 can be used at beginning or end of day.

- **Song Book**, p. 25

Transparencies Explore content and vocabulary and model fluent reading.

For further information about using these components, see pages x–xv.

Build Background

Preteach/Review 10–15 min
Poster, Song Book, Big Book
Leveled Support Preteach
Practice Stations Preteach

Teach 35–45 min
Concept Talk
Oral Vocabulary Routine
Word Cards
Build Concept Vocabulary
Daily Table Talk

Check/Reteach 5–10 min
Poster, Word Cards
Leveled Support Reteach

Language: Category Words

Preteach/Review 10–15 min
Poster
Leveled Support Preteach
Practice Stations Review

Teach 35–45 min
Category Words
Daily Table Talk

Check/Reteach 5–10 min
Poster, Word Cards
Leveled Support Reteach

Fluency: Writing or Speaking

CALIFORNIA Standards

GK Sci 4.e Communicate observations orally and through drawings.

ELA R 1.18 Describe common objects and events in both general and specific language.

ELA R 1.17 Identify and sort common words in basic categories (e.g., colors, shapes, foods).

Academic Language

Category Words: boat, car, train, truck

Get Online! www.pearsonsuccessnet.com

Concept Talk Video

Background Building Audio Slideshow

This Week

Unit 5, Week 1

Getting Places

Next Week

Unit 5, Week 2

Help in an Emergency

DAY 3 FORM & FUNCTION Read and Comprehend	**DAY 4** FORM & FUNCTION Language Arts	**DAY 5** Language Arts
Language: High Frequency Words	**Phonics**	**Think, Talk, and Recognize**

Preteach/Review 10–15 min
Poster
  Leveled Support Preteach
  Practice Stations Review
	Preteach/Review 10–15 min
	Poster
	  Leveled Support Preteach
	  Practice Stations Review
		Preteach/Review 10–15 min
		Poster
		  Leveled Support Preteach
		  Practice Stations Review

Teach 35–45 min
  High Frequency Words
  Daily Table Talk
	Teach 35–45 min
	  Phonics
	  Daily Table Talk
		Teach 15–20 min
		  Think, Talk, and Recognize
		  Concept Wrap Up

Check/Reteach 5–10 min
Poster, Word Cards
  Leveled Support Reteach
	Check/Reteach 5–10 min
	Poster, Word Cards
	  Leveled Support Reteach
		Check/Reteach 30–40 min
		Poster, Word Cards, Song Book
		  Leveled Support Reteach

		Fluency: Writing or Speaking
ELA R 1.15 Read simple one-syllable and high frequency words (i.e., sight words).	**ELA R 1.14** Match all consonant and short-vowel sounds to appropriate letters.	**ELA LS 1.2** Share information and ideas, speaking audibly in complete, coherent sentences.
High Frequency Words: yellow, blue, green		

Practice Stations

Materials and Activity

---

construction paper, scissors, markers, popsicle sticks

Kinds of Transportation 🏃

Have children trace different forms of transportation on construction paper, such as a train, bus, car, truck, or bicycle. Then have children cut out each vehicle and paste each one onto a popsicle stick. Children can pretend to race their vehicles.

---

plain paper, pencils, crayons, markers, vocabulary word list

Illustrate the Words 🏃

Have children create an illustration for each vocabulary word. Children should write a label for their drawings that include the vocabulary word.

Preteach/Reteach

Transfer and Common Misconceptions

Transportation Words

Reinforce similarities between English and Spanish by pointing out words that are similar, like *train* and *tren*.

---

oa Pronounced as Long *o*

Because vowels in Spanish are never silent, Spanish speakers may pronounce the *oa* in *boat* with two vowel sounds, as *bo-at*.

Produce Language

Weekly Concept and Language Goal

CONCEPT GOALS

- name and describe different forms of transportation
- explain what it means to walk through a jet way
- describe how a family can travel to the store

By Day 5, children should be able to write a one-word label or a sentence.

Daily Table Talk

❶ Beginning
> Children pantomime while you provide the language.

❷ ❸ Early Intermediate/Intermediate
> Children pantomime and say a word or phrase.

❹ ❺ Early Advanced/Advanced
> Children say a sentence while pantomiming.

Daily Table Talk

❶ Beginning
> Children talk about their drawings.

❷ ❸ Early Intermediate/Intermediate
> Children write one-word labels.

❹ ❺ Early Advanced/Advanced
> Children write a phrase or sentence.

DAY 3 — Read and Comprehend

index cards with category words written on them; pictures of the following vehicles pasted onto index cards: *car, boat, truck, train*

Transportation Match Game

Have word cards in one pile and picture cards in another. A child chooses a card from each pile. If the picture matches the word, the child keeps both cards. If they don't match, the cards go under each pile. Children take turns until all the cards have been matched.

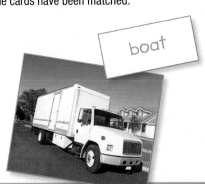

boat

The Word *yellow*

Some children may want to pronounce the *ll* in yellow as /y/, which is the way *ll* is pronounced in Spanish.

Daily Table Talk

❶ **Beginning**
Name different places and have children answer yes or no.

❷ ❸ **Early Intermediate/Intermediate**
Phrase: an airport

❹ ❺ **Early Advanced/Advanced**
Sentence: You can walk through an airport.

DAY 4 — Language Arts

index cards with the words *yellow, blue, green;* one set of cards for each team

What's Your Color?

Group children into teams of three. Each team member is given a color word. Then begin by asking, "If you have yellow, please stand up." The first yellow to stand up gets a point for the team. Repeat with various actions for each color so that every child has a chance to earn points for his or her team.

yellow

The Letter *j*

Spanish speakers may pronounce the letter *j* as /h/, which is how this letter is pronounced in Spanish.

Daily Table Talk

❶ **Beginning**
Name different ways people can travel to the store and have children answer yes or no.

❷ ❸ **Early Intermediate/Intermediate**
Phrase: by car

❹ ❺ **Early Advanced/Advanced**
Sentence: My family takes a car.

DAY 5 — Language Arts

index cards with these words: *jump, juice, jet, jam, wet, water, wing, wig*

Letter Sort

Have children sort the word cards into two groups. The first group of words begins with the letter *j* and the second group begins with the letter *w*.

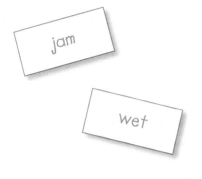

jam

wet

Plurals

Children may forget to add *s* when using the plural form of a noun. Some languages, including Cantonese, Hmong, and Korean, do not use a plural marker.

Daily Table Talk

❶ **Beginning** Child speaks about the drawing and may write a label.

❷ ❸ **Early Intermediate/Intermediate** Child writes a label that includes a concept vocabulary word.

❹ ❺ **Early Advanced/Advanced** Child writes a label or sentence that includes a vocabulary word.

OBJECTIVE

To introduce and discuss concepts and vocabulary related to different forms of transportation.

Build Background Get Ready to Read!

Question of the Week What are some forms of transportation?

www.pearsonsuccessnet.com

Concept Talk

Use the Big Book Connect the Big Book to the unit theme, Transportation—Going Places. Display and discuss the cover. Then read the book aloud.

Introduce the Weekly Concept Tell children that today they will talk about different ways people travel to get from place to place. Ask the weekly question: What are some forms of transportation?

Use the Poster Direct children's attention to the weekly poster. Use the Day 1 teaching notes at the bottom of the poster.

Sing the Song Use the song **All Around Town** to reinforce children's understanding of the concept. Have children sing or simply chant the words with you.

Use a Transparency Use the Shared Description Map (Transparency 8) to help children compare and contrast two forms of transportation.

Vocabulary

bus a large vehicle that people travel in

train a long vehicle that travels along a railroad carrying people or goods

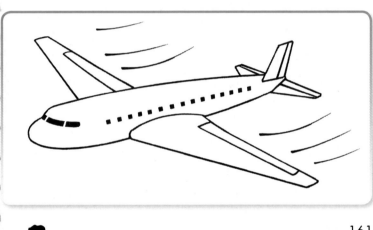

 ELA R 1.18 Describe common objects and events in both general and specific language. (ELD R.B2)

161

Introduce Concept Vocabulary

1. **Say the Word** Display the Word Card as you say *bus.* Have children repeat the word.

2. **Introduce Word Meaning** Ask questions about buses. *Do you ride a bus to school?*

3. **Demonstrate** Have children role play riding in a bus.

4. **Apply** Have children demonstrate their understanding.

Repeat with other vocabulary words.

Corrective Feedback If children have difficulty pronouncing the words, separate the phonemes. Then combine them to form the word. Have children repeat after you, blending the phonemes.

Concept Work

Name each form of transportation in the pictures and have children point to it. Then point to different forms of transportation as children name them. Have children color the pictures.

Preteach
LS **Leveled Support** **Vocabulary in Context**
Reteach

❶ **Beginning** Point to the bus and train on the Worktext page. Say the word for each picture as children point, and have them echo each word.

❷ ❸ **Early Intermediate/Intermediate** Do the Beginning activity, but have children say the words themselves, providing help if needed.

❹ ❺ **Early Advanced/Advanced** Ask children to draw a bus and a train and have them label their pictures. Then they can tell stories about places they might visit by bus and train. They should use the vocabulary words as they tell their stories.

Wrap Up DAY 1

Daily
Table Talk What are some forms of transportation? Have children answer the question, using the vocabulary words.

Produce Language Ask each child to act out riding in one form of transportation and say a sentence about it.

Today children should have:

☑ **Learned** and applied vocabulary related to different forms of transportation.

☑ **Spoken** complete sentences about different forms of transportation.

☑ **Recognized** concept vocabulary words.

 ELA R 1.18 Describe common objects and events in both general and specific language. (ELD R.B2)

161

DAY 2 — CALIFORNIA

OBJECTIVE

To discuss the different colors forms of transportation can be; to introduce category words for transportation.

Concept Talk

Connect to Day 1 What are some forms of transportation?

Introduce the Daily Question Ask: What forms of transportation can be yellow, blue, or green? Have children answer orally.

Use the Poster Use the Day 2 teaching notes.

Introduce Category Words

1. Say the Word Have children point to the car. Say the word and have children repeat.

2. Introduce Word Meaning Ask questions: Do you like to ride in a car? What do you like to do when you ride in a car?

3. Demonstrate Role play driving a car.

4. Apply Repeat with other vocabulary words and elicit that they all belong to the category "transportation."

Have children draw their favorite form of transportation.

Corrective Feedback If children have difficulty with the forms of transportation, say each word again and have children point to the corresponding picture.

Wrap Up — DAY 2

Table Talk Have children discuss the color of their family's method of transportation.

Produce Language To build fluency, encourage children to label or write a sentence about their drawings. They can share the writing with partners.

Today children should have:

- ☑ **Learned** and applied vocabulary related to transportation.
- ☑ **Spoken** complete sentences about forms of transportation that can be yellow, blue, or green.
- ☑ **Recognized** words that belong in the same category.

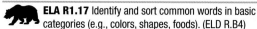 **ELA R1.17** Identify and sort common words in basic categories (e.g., colors, shapes, foods). (ELD R.B4)

Picture Dictionary

boat

car

train

truck

✏ **Draw** Draw a kind of transportation.

162 ELA R1.17 Identify and sort common words in basic categories (e.g., colors, shapes, foods). (ELD R.B4)

Leveled Support — Category Words

Beginning Have children point to each form of transportation on the Worktext page as you say it. Have children echo the word.

Early Intermediate/Intermediate Say the name of a form of transportation. Have children point to it. Then reverse the activity.

Early Advanced/Advanced Have children tell a partner which forms of transportation they have ridden in and which is their favorite.

Where can you walk through a jetway?

✏ **Circle** Circle *yellow*.
The plane was near a yellow line.

✏ **Circle** Circle *blue*. Circle *green*.
A green plane flew in the blue sky.

ELA R1.15 Read simple one-syllable and high-frequency words (i.e., sight words). (ELD R.B2)

163

OBJECTIVE

To discuss where you can walk through a jetway; to introduce the high frequency words *yellow, blue,* and *green*.

Concept Talk   🌐 FORM & FUNCTION

Connect to Day 2 What forms of transportation can be yellow, blue, or green?

Introduce the Daily Question Ask: Where can you walk through a jetway? Describe a jetway to children. A jetway is a place where people walk to get on a plane. Have children answer the question orally.

Use the Poster Use the Day 3 teaching notes.

Review Concept Vocabulary Review the words introduced on Day 1.

Introduce High Frequency Words

Guide children to point to the word *yellow* in the direction line. Say: This is the word *yellow*. Let's say the word together. Have them find the word in the text and circle it. Help children complete the activity on the Worktext page.

Corrective Feedback If children have difficulty with the high frequency words, write them on sticky notes. Give the notes to children and have them place the words on items in the classroom that are yellow, blue, and green.

Preteach LS Leveled Support Reteach   **High Frequency Words**

➊ **Beginning** Write the word *yellow*. Say: This is the word *yellow*. Say the word after me: *yellow*. Model using the word by holding up a yellow crayon. Say: This crayon is yellow. Repeat with blue and green.

➋ ➌ **Early Intermediate/Intermediate** Write *yellow, blue, green*. Say a word and have children point to the correct word.

➍ ➎ **Early Advanced/Advanced** Have children match the words *yellow, blue, green* with objects or pictures of objects that are yellow, green, and blue.

Wrap Up   **DAY** 3

Daily **Table Talk** Children can pretend to walk on a jetway and then talk about where you can walk through a jetway.

Produce Language Have each child say a sentence about walking through a jetway.

Today children should have:

☑ **Learned** and applied the high frequency words *yellow, blue,* and *green*.

☑ **Spoken** complete sentences about where you can walk through a jetway.

☑ **Recognized** high frequency words that name colors.

ELA R1.15 Read simple one-syllable and high frequency words (i.e., sight words). (ELD R.B2)

OBJECTIVE

To discuss where children's families travel when they go to the store; to identify sounds /j/ and /w/.

Concept Talk

FORM & FUNCTION

Connect to Day 3 Where can you walk through a jetway?

Introduce the Daily Question Ask: How does your family travel when they go to the store? Ask children if their family walks to the store or takes a car, bus, or train. Children can raise their hand for the appropriate answer.

Use the Poster Use the Day 4 teaching notes.

Phonics

Identify Sounds /j/ and /w/ Have children point to each picture as you name it. Say: Now I'm going to read the words again. Listen for /j/ at the beginning of the words. Which word starts with the /j/ sound? Have children identify the words that start with /j/. Then repeat for /w/ words.

Corrective Feedback If children have difficulty identifying the initial sounds, read each word again, separating the phonemes and emphasizing the initial phoneme in each word.

Wrap Up

DAY 4

 How does your family travel when they go to the store? Have children discuss the question.

Produce Language Have each child say a sentence about how their family gets to the store.

Today children should have:

☑ **Learned** and applied vocabulary related to how their family travels when they go to the store.

☑ **Spoken** complete sentences about how their family travels when they go to the store.

☑ **Recognized** words that begin with /j/ and /w/.

 ELA R1.14 Match all consonant and short-vowel sounds to appropriate letters. (ELD R.B10)

Identify Sounds Jj and Ww

✏ **Circle** Circle things with *j*.

✏ **Circle** Circle things with *w*.

164 ELA R1.14 Match all consonant and short-vowel sounds to appropriate letters. (ELD R.B1)

Preteach / Reteach **LS** **Leveled Support** **Phonics**

① **Beginning** Hold up a card on which you have printed *j*. Say: The name of this letter is *j*. The sound for this letter is /j/. Have children echo you. Then repeat for *w*.

② ③ **Early Intermediate/Intermediate** Tell children you will read several words and they should listen for /j/. Ask them to raise their hands when they hear a word beginning with a /j/. Say: juice, hat, joke, jam, wet, water. Then say the words again, asking children to raise their hands when they hear a word beginning with /w/.

④ ⑤ **Early Advanced/Advanced** Have children identify the letter that makes /j/. Ask children to name other words that being with /j/. Repeat with /w/. Have children work with you to create a chart, classifying words that have the two sounds. They can draw and label pictures to go on the chart.

What are some forms of transportation?

 Draw

OBJECTIVE

To guide children to express their understanding of weekly concepts and vocabulary.

Think, Talk, and Recognize!

Concept Talk

Connect to Day 4 How does your family travel when they go to the store? Model how to answer yesterday's question with a sentence.

Review the Weekly Question Ask: What are some forms of transportation? Ask the children to name all the forms of transportation they have learned about this week. Ask children what their favorite form of transportation is.

Use the Poster Use the Day 5 teaching notes.

Review Concept Vocabulary Review the vocabulary introduced on Day 1.

Concept Wrap Up

Have children draw to answer the question: *What are some forms of transportation?* Use the photograph on the page to prompt discussion. This form of transportation helps you travel on water. It's a boat. What would it be like to travel on a boat?

Preteach / Reteach **Leveled Support   Concept Vocabulary**

① **Beginning** Display the Word Cards for *bus* and *train.* Say each word. Ask children to repeat and point to the matching card.

② ③ **Early Intermediate/Intermediate** Display the Word Cards for *bus* and *train.* Have children choose a card and give a simple description of the word.

④ ⑤ **Early Advanced/Advanced** Pair children and have each pair take a Word Card. Have them describe the word on the card so that other children can guess the word. Children can tell a story about traveling by one of these forms of transportation.

Wrap Up   DAY 5

Daily Table Talk What are some forms of transportation? Have children discuss the question, using the vocabulary words they have learned this week.

Produce Language To build fluency, children can label, write about, or speak about their drawings. Ask children to respond to what they read or heard.

Today, children should have:

☑ **Recognized** the weekly concept and concept vocabulary.

☑ **Spoken** about forms of transportation.

☑ **Drawn or written** about forms of transportation.

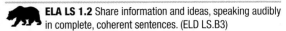 **ELA LS 1.2** Share information and ideas, speaking audibly in complete, coherent sentences. (ELD LS.B3)

Question of the Week What transportation helps us in an emergency?

DAY 1 — Get Ready to Read

Build Background

Preteach/Review 10–15 min
Poster, Song Book, Big Book
Leveled Support Preteach
Practice Stations Preteach

Teach 35–45 min
Concept Talk
Oral Vocabulary Routine
Word Cards
Build Concept Vocabulary
Daily Table Talk

Check/Reteach 5–10 min
Poster, Word Cards
Leveled Support Reteach

DAY 2 — Read and Comprehend

Language: Category Words

Preteach/Review 10–15 min
Poster
Leveled Support Preteach
Practice Stations Review

Teach 35–45 min
Category Words
Daily Table Talk

Check/Reteach 5–10 min
Poster, Word Cards
Leveled Support Reteach

Fluency: Writing or Speaking

Instructional Plan and Materials

- **Word Cards**
86–88

- **Big Book**
One Morning in May

- **Poster**
Poster 26 can be used at beginning or end of day.

- **Song Book**, p. 26

Transparencies Explore content and vocabulary and model fluent reading.

For further information about using these components, see pages x–xv.

CALIFORNIA Standards

GK Sci 4.e Communicate observations orally and through drawings.

ELA LS 2.1 Describe people, places, things (e.g., size, color, shape), locations, and actions.

ELA R 1.17 Identify and sort common words in basic categories (e.g., colors, shapes, foods).

Academic Language

Category Words: Coast Guard, firefighters, nurse, police

Concept Talk Video

Background Building Audio Slideshow

This Week

Unit 5, Week 2

Help in an Emergency

Next Week

Unit 5, Week 3

Going Places at Work

DAY 3 — FORM & FUNCTION — Read and Comprehend

DAY 4 — FORM & FUNCTION — Language Arts

DAY 5 — Language Arts

Language: High Frequency Words	Phonics	Think, Talk, and Recognize
Preteach/Review 10–15 min Poster **Leveled Support Preteach** **Practice Stations Review**	**Preteach/Review** 10–15 min Poster **Leveled Support Preteach** **Practice Stations Review**	**Preteach/Review** 10–15 min Poster **Leveled Support Preteach** **Practice Stations Review**
Teach 35–45 min **High Frequency Words** **Daily Table Talk**	**Teach** 35–45 min **Phonics** **Daily Table Talk**	**Teach** 15–20 min **Think, Talk, and Recognize** **Concept Wrap Up**
Check/Reteach 5–10 min Poster, Word Cards **Leveled Support Reteach**	**Check/Reteach** 5–10 min Poster, Word Cards **Leveled Support Reteach**	**Check/Reteach** 30–40 min Poster, Word Cards, Song Book **Leveled Support Reteach**
		Fluency: Writing or Speaking
ELA R 1.15 Read simple one-syllable and high frequency words (i.e., sight words).	**ELA R 1.14** Match all consonant and short-vowel sounds to appropriate letters.	**LS 1.2** Share information and ideas, speaking audibly in complete, coherent sentences.
High Frequency Words: yellow, blue, green		

Practice Stations

Materials and Activity

cut-out magazine photos of emergency vehicles (such as fire trucks, ambulances, police cars) pasted onto index cards

Emergency Transportation 🚸 🚸

Provide groups of children with cards. Then describe a simple emergency (such as, "There is a fire in a building"). Children hold up the card that corresponds to the emergency vehicle that could help in that emergency.

index cards with the vocabulary words written on them, stacked face down

Use the Word 🚸 🚸

One child chooses a card and says a sentence with that vocabulary word. The next child chooses a card and says a sentence with that word. Children continue to choose cards and say sentences. When all of the words have been used, children can reshuffle the cards and start again.

The boat is on the river

boat

Preteach/Reteach

Transfer and Common Misconceptions

The *sw* Blend

Some children may find this sound difficult to pronounce. Spanish does not have *s* blends, so pronouncing *sw*, as in *swimmer*, can be challenging.

Compound Words

Speakers of languages such as Cantonese, Hmong, and Vietnamese, in which words consist of one syllable, may need extra practice with compound words.

Produce Language

Weekly Concept and Language Goal

CONCEPT GOALS

- recognize the vehicles used in emergencies
- explain how people can help during an emergency
- describe specific emergency workers, such as the Coast Guard

By Day 5, children should be able to write a one-word label or a sentence.

Daily Table Talk

❶ Beginning

Children pantomime while you provide the language.

❷ ❸ Early Intermediate/Intermediate

Children pantomime and say a word or phrase.

❹ ❺ Early Advanced/Advanced

Children say a sentence while pantomiming.

Daily Table Talk

❶ Beginning

Children talk about their drawings.

❷ ❸ Early Intermediate/Intermediate

Children write one-word labels.

❹ ❺ Early Advanced/Advanced

Children write a phrase or sentence.

DAY 3 FORM & FUNCTION
Read and Comprehend

cut-out magazine or Internet pictures of firefighters, nurses, coast guard workers, police officers; the words *police, firefighters, nurse, coast guard* written on sticky notes

Label the Pictures

Provide children with pictures and sticky notes. Have children work together to place the correct label on each picture.

Color Words

Encourage children to tell the names of different colors in their home languages as they learn words for colors in English.

sentence strips, various objects in colors yellow, blue, and green (such as blocks, crayons, markers, beads, etc.)

What Color Is It?

Write these sentences on the strips: *The _____ is yellow. The _____ is blue. The _____ is green.* Have children choose one of the sentence strips. Then children choose an object that matches the color on the sentence strip. Children complete their sentence strip with the name of the object. Children take turns.

> The _____ is yellow

The Letter *x*

Speakers of Cantonese, Vietnamese, and Hmong may have trouble with the letter *x* as the sound /ks/ is not found in these languages.

DAY 5
Language Arts

stack of picture cards, including many words that end with *x* (such as *fox, ax, box, ox*), small box

X in a Box

A child chooses a picture card and says the word out loud. If the card has the same end sound as "box," the child places the card inside the box. Other cards go in a pile. Children choose cards until they have all been used.

Adjectives

When using color words, children may have trouble remembering that in English adjectives come before the nouns.

 Daily **Table Talk**

① **Beginning**
> Name different kinds of emergencies and have children answer yes or no.

② ③ **Early Intermediate/Intermediate**
> Phrase: on a boat

④ ⑤ **Early Advanced/Advanced**
> Sentence: They can help fix a boat fire.

Daily **Table Talk**

① **Beginning**
> Name different types of emergency transportation and have children answer yes or no.

② ③ **Early Intermediate/Intermediate**
> Phrase: an ambulance

④ ⑤ **Early Advanced/Advanced**
> Sentence: I saw an ambulance.

Daily **Table Talk**

① **Beginning** Child speaks about the drawing and may write a label.

② ③ **Early Intermediate/Intermediate** Child writes a label that includes a concept vocabulary word.

④ ⑤ **Early Advanced/Advanced** Child writes a label or sentence that includes a vocabulary word.

OBJECTIVE

To introduce and discuss concepts and vocabulary related to transportation in emergencies.

Build Background Get Ready to Read!

Question of the Week

What transportation helps us in an emergency?

www.pearsonsuccessnet.com

Concept Talk

Use the Big Book If you haven't introduced the Big Book, consider reading it to children. Connect to the unit theme, Transportation—Going Places.

Introduce the Weekly Concept Tell children that today they will talk about the kinds of transportation that are used in emergencies. Ask the weekly question: What transportation helps us in an emergency?

Use the Poster Direct children's attention to the weekly poster. Use the Day 1 teaching notes at the bottom of the poster.

Sing the Song Use the song **We Need Help** to reinforce children's understanding of the weekly concept. Have the children sing or simply chant the words with you.

Use a Transparency Use the Narrative Nonfiction Transparency (Transparency 16) to share a piece of text about a rescue dog. Children can tell a story about an emergency shown in the Worktext.

Help in an Emergency

Vocabulary

boat

swimmer

taxi

What transportation helps us in an emergency?

166

Vocabulary

boat a vehicle that travels over water

swimmer someone who swims, especially in competitions

taxi a car with a driver whom you pay to drive you somewhere

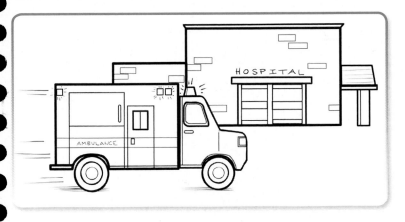

 ELA R 1.18 Describe common objects and events in both general and specific language. (ELD R.B2)   167

Introduce Concept Vocabulary

1. **Say the Word** Display the Word Card as you say *boat*. Have children repeat the word.

2. **Introduce Word Meaning** Ask questions about boats. Have you ever seen a boat? What did it look like? Where do boats travel?

3. **Demonstrate** Have children role play rowing a boat.

4. **Apply** Have children demonstrate their understanding. Repeat with other vocabulary words.

Corrective Feedback If children have difficulty identifying the words, show additional pictures from magazines or books that represent the words.

Concept Work

Discuss what is happening in each picture. What emergency situations are shown? Someone in a boat is rescuing a swimmer who needs help, a taxi is taking two parents to the hospital so the woman can have her baby, and an ambulance is going to the hospital. **Have children circle the forms of transportation. Then they can color the pictures.**

Leveled Support Vocabulary in Context

Preteach LS Reteach

❶ **Beginning** Point to the boat, taxi, and swimmer on the Worktext page. Say the word for each picture as children point, and have them echo each word.

❷ ❸ **Early Intermediate/Intermediate** Do the Beginning activity, but have children say the words themselves, providing help if needed. Ask children to describe one of the words for other children to guess.

❹ ❺ **Early Advanced/Advanced** Ask children to draw one kind of emergency transportation and have them label it with a vocabulary word.

Wrap Up   DAY 1

Daily
 Table Talk What kinds of transportation help us in an emergency? Have children answer the question, using the vocabulary words.

Produce Language Ask each child to say a sentence about one kind of transportation that people can use in an emergency.

Today children should have:

☑ **Learned** and applied vocabulary related to emergency transportation.

☑ **Spoken** complete sentences about emergency transportation.

☑ **Recognized** concept vocabulary words.

 ELA LS 2.1 Describe people, places, things (e.g., size, color, shape), locations, and actions. (ELD R.B2)

To discuss how people can help in an emergency; to introduce category words for people who help us.

Concept Talk

Connect to Day 1 What transportation helps us in an emergency?

Introduce the Daily Question Ask: What can we do to help in an emergency? Have children name at least one thing people can do to help in an emergency.

Use the Poster Use the Day 2 teaching notes.

Introduce Category Words

1. **Say the Word** Have children point to the firefighters. Say the word and have children repeat.

2. **Introduce Word Meaning** Ask questions: What do firefighters do? Have you ever seen firefighters? What do they wear?

3. **Demonstrate** Role play some actions that firefighters do, such as putting out a fire with a hose.

4. **Apply** Repeat with other category words and elicit that they all belong to the category "people who help us."

Have children draw a picture of someone helping another person in an emergency.

Corrective Feedback If children have difficulty comprehending who would help with what kind of an emergency, have them look at the Big Book or other sources of pictures of emergency helpers.

People Who Help Us

Picture Dictionary

Coast Guard

firefighters

nurse

police

 Draw Draw someone who helps us.

168 ELA R1.17 Identify and sort common words in basic categories (e.g., colors, shapes, foods). (ELD R.B4)

Wrap Up
DAY 2

Daily Table Talk Have children act out an emergency situation, such as a fire. Then have them discuss what people can do to help.

Produce Language To build fluency, encourage children to label or write a sentence about their drawings. They can share their writing with partners.

Today children should have:

☑ **Learned** and applied vocabulary related to people who help us.

☑ **Spoken** complete sentences about how people can help in an emergency.

☑ **Recognized** words that belong in the same category.

 ELA R1.17 Identify and sort common words in basic categories (e.g. colors, shapes, foods). (ELD R.B.4)

 Leveled Support **Category Words**

❶ **Beginning** Have children point to each person on the Worktext page as you say the name. Have children echo the word.

❷ ❸ **Early Intermediate/Intermediate** Say the name of a person who helps us, such as *nurse* or *firefighter.* Have children point to a picture of them. Then reverse the activity. Children can role play what people who have these various jobs do as they work.

❹ ❺ **Early Advanced/Advanced** Have children tell a partner what a nurse does (helps people who are sick or hurt) or what a firefighter does (helps put out fires).

What emergencies can the Coast Guard help fix?

✏️ **Circle** Circle *yellow*. Circle *blue*.
A yellow boat was in the blue water.

✏️ **Circle** Circle *green*.
They saved a green turtle.

🐻 **ELA R1.15** Read simple one-syllable and high-frequency words (i.e., sight words). (ELD R.B2)

169

OBJECTIVE

To discuss how the Coast Guard can help in emergencies; to review the high frequency words *yellow, blue,* and *green*.

Concept Talk

Connect to Day 2 What can we do to help in an emergency?

Introduce the Daily Question Ask: What emergencies can the Coast Guard help fix? Name types of emergencies and have children raise their hands if the Coast Guard can help fix it.

Use the Poster Use the Day 3 teaching notes.

Review Concept Vocabulary Review the words introduced on Day 1.

Introduce High Frequency Words

Introduce *yellow, blue,* and *green* by describing and holding up objects in the classroom, such as, This is a *yellow* crayon. This is a *blue* pen. Help children complete the Worktext page.

Corrective Feedback If children have difficulty with the high frequency words, write them on strips of paper so that children can match the words on paper to the words on the Worktext page.

Leveled Support **High Frequency Words**

Preteach
LS
Reteach

① **Beginning** Write the word *yellow*. Say: This is the word *yellow*. Say the word after me: *yellow*. Model using the word by holding up a yellow crayon. Say: This crayon is yellow. Repeat with blue and green.

② ③ **Early Intermediate/Intermediate** Write *yellow, blue, green*. Say a word and have children point to the correct word. Then hold up items and ask: Is this yellow? Is this green? Children can nod to respond.

④ ⑤ **Early Advanced/Advanced** Have children identify objects in the classroom that are yellow, blue, and green and say a sentence to describe the objects, using the color words.

Wrap Up **DAY** **3**

Daily
Table Talk Children can pretend to be driving a Coast Guard rescue boat and then talk about how the Coast Guard can help people in emergencies.

Produce Language Have each child say a sentence about how the Coast Guard can help people.

Today children should have:

☑ **Learned** and applied the high frequency words *yellow, blue, green*.

☑ **Spoken** complete sentences about emergencies the Coast Guard can help fix.

☑ **Recognized** high frequency words that name colors.

🐻 **ELA R1.15** Read simple one-syllable and high-frequency words (i.e., sight words). (ELD R.B2)

CALIFORNIA

To discuss emergency transportation children have seen; to identify sound /ks/.

Concept Talk

FORM & FUNCTION

Connect to Day 3 What emergencies can the Coast Guard help fix?

Introduce the Daily Question Ask: *What kinds of emergency transportation have you seen?* Name various kinds of emergency transportation and have children raise their hands if they have seen it.

Use the Poster Use the Day 4 teaching notes.

Phonics

Identify Sound /ks/ Have children point to each picture as you name it. Say: *Now I am going to read the words again. Listen for /ks/ in the word.* When you point to the taxi, say: *Have you ever ridden in a taxi? Where is the /ks/ sound in this word?* Continue with remaining words.

Corrective Feedback If children have difficulty identifying the sound /ks/, read each word again, emphasizing the medial or final /ks/ sound as appropriate.

Wrap Up   DAY 4

Daily

Table Talk *What kinds of emergency transportation have you seen?* Have children name as many as they can.

Produce Language Have each child say a sentence about one kind of emergency transportation they have seen.

Today children should have:

☑ **Learned** and applied vocabulary related to emergency transportation they have seen.

☑ **Spoken** complete sentences about emergency transportation they have seen.

☑ **Recognized** words with sound /ks/.

ELA R1.14 Match all consonant and short-vowel sounds to appropriate letters. (ELD R.B10)

Identify Sound Xx

✏️ **Circle** Circle things with x.

170 🐻 **ELA R1.14** Match all consonant and short-vowel sounds to appropriate letters. (ELD R.B10)

Preteach LS Reteach **Leveled Support** **Phonics**

① **Beginning** Hold up an index card on which you have printed the letter *x*. Say: *The name of this letter is x. The sound for this letter is /ks/.* Have children echo the sound, exaggerating the movements their mouths make to produce this sound.

② ③ **Early Intermediate/Intermediate** Tell children you will read several words and they should listen for /ks/. When you say a word that ends with /ks/, children should raise their hands and repeat the word. Say: *fox, box, hot, fax, fat.*

④ ⑤ **Early Advanced/Advanced** Have children identify the letter that makes the sound /ks/. Ask children to sort words into two categories: words with /ks/ and words with /k/. Provide words to sort and assist children in drawing pictures of the words and labeling them.

What transportation helps us in an emergency?

 Draw

 ELA LS. 1.2 Share information and ideas, speaking audibly in complete, coherent sentences. (ELD LS.B3)

171

To guide children to express their understanding of weekly concepts and vocabulary.

Think, Talk, and Recognize!

Concept Talk

Connect to Day 4 What kinds of emergency transportation have you seen? Model how to answer yesterday's question with a sentence.

Review the Weekly Question Ask: What transportation helps us in an emergency? Name various types of transportation, such as train, car, fire truck, ambulance, and bicycle. Ask children to raise their hands if that type of transportation can be used in an emergency.

Use the Poster Use the Day 5 teaching notes.

Review Concept Vocabulary Review the vocabulary introduced on Day 1.

Concept Wrap Up

Have children draw to answer the question: *What transportation helps us in an emergency?* Use the photograph to prompt discussion. What transportation is shown here? In what kind of emergency would this transportation help us?

Preteach / Reteach **Leveled Support** **Concept Vocabulary**

① **Beginning** Display the Word Cards for *boat, taxi, swimmer.* Say each word. Ask children to repeat and point to the matching card. Show photographs and ask: Is this a boat? Is this a swimmer? Children can nod to respond.

② ③ **Early Intermediate/Intermediate** Display the Picture Cards for *boat, taxi,* and *swimmer.* Ask children to say each word and point to the matching card.

④ ⑤ **Early Advanced/Advanced** Display the Picture Cards for *boat, taxi, swimmer.* Ask children to work with partners to tell a story using all three words. Print the words on index cards so that children can hold up the corresponding cards when they tell their stories to the group.

Wrap Up **DAY 5**

Daily Table Talk What transportation helps us in an emergency? Have children discuss the question, using the vocabulary words they have learned this week.

Produce Language To build fluency, children can label, write about, or speak about their drawings. Ask children to respond to what they read or heard.

Today, children should have:

☑ **Reviewed** the weekly concept and concept vocabulary.

☑ **Spoken** about forms of transportation used in emergencies.

☑ **Drawn or written** about emergency vehicles.

 ELA LS. 1.2 Share information and ideas, speaking audibly in complete, coherent sentences. (ELD LS.B3)

171

WEEK **3** CALIFORNIA

Last Week
Unit 5, Week 2
Helping in an
Emergency

Weekly Lesson Plan

 Question of the Week How does transportation help at work?

DAY **1** Get Ready to Read

Build Background

Preteach/Review 10–15 min
Poster, Song Book, Big Book
- **Leveled Support Preteach**
- **Practice Stations Preteach**

Teach 35–45 min
- **Concept Talk**
- **Oral Vocabulary Routine**
  Word Cards
- **Build Concept Vocabulary**
- **Daily Table Talk**

Check/Reteach 5–10 min
Poster, Word Cards
- **Leveled Support Reteach**

DAY **2** Read and Comprehend

Language: Category Words

Preteach/Review 10–15 min
Poster
- **Leveled Support Preteach**
- **Practice Stations Review**

Teach 35–45 min
- **Category Words**
- **Daily Table Talk**

Check/Reteach 5–10 min
Poster, Word Cards
- **Leveled Support Reteach**

Fluency: Writing or Speaking

Instructional Plan and Materials

- **Word Cards**
  89–95

- **Poster**
  Poster 27 can be used at beginning or end of day.

- **Big Book**
  One Morning in May

- **Song Book**, p. 27

Transparencies Explore content and vocabulary and model fluent reading.

For further information about using these components, see pages x–xv.

CALIFORNIA Standards

G1 His-Soc Sci 1.2.4. Describe how location, weather, and physical environment affect the way people live, including the effects on their food, clothing, shelter, transportation, and recreation.

ELA LS 2.1 Describe people, places, things (e.g., size, color, shape), locations, and actions.

ELA R 1.17 Identify and sort common words in basic categories (e.g., colors, shapes, foods).

Academic Language

Vocabulary: rain, snow, sun, wind

Category Words: astronaut, bike messenger, cashier, mechanic, teacher, writer

Get Online! www.pearsonsuccessnet.com

Concept Talk Video

Background Building Audio Slideshow

This Week
Unit 5, Week 3

Going Places at Work

Next Week
Unit 5, Week 4
Trains

DAY 3 — Read and Comprehend
FORM & FUNCTION

Language: High Frequency Words

Preteach/Review 10–15 min
Poster
- **Leveled Support Preteach**
- **Practice Stations Review**

Teach 35–45 min
- **High Frequency Words**
- **Daily Table Talk**

Check/Reteach 5–10 min
Poster, Word Cards
- **Leveled Support Reteach**

ELA R 1.15 Read simple one-syllable and high frequency words (i.e., sight words).

High Frequency Words: what, said, was

DAY 4 — Language Arts
FORM & FUNCTION

Phonics

Preteach/Review 10–15 min
Poster
- **Leveled Support Preteach**
- **Practice Stations Review**

Teach 35–45 min
- **Phonics**
- **Daily Table Talk**

Check/Reteach 5–10 min
Poster, Word Cards
- **Leveled Support Reteach**

ELA R 1.14 Match all consonant and short-vowel sounds to appropriate letters.

DAY 5 — Language Arts

Think, Talk, and Recognize

Preteach/Review 10–15 min
Poster
- **Leveled Support Preteach**
- **Practice Stations Review**

Teach 15–20 min
- **Think, Talk, and Recognize**
- **Concept Wrap Up**

Check/Reteach 30–40 min
Poster, Word Cards, Song Book
- **Leveled Support Reteach**

Fluency: Writing or Speaking

ELA LS 1.2 Share information and ideas, speaking audibly in complete, coherent sentences.

Practice Stations

Materials and Activity

paper, crayons, colored pencils

Transportation at Work

Have children draw pictures of a worker who uses some kind of transportation to do their job. Children can draw pictures of the worker at work or using the transportation in some way. Have children label the picture with one or two words.

paper, crayons, colored pencils

What's the Weather Like?

Help children divide a large sheet of construction paper into four parts. Have children create an illustration for the words *sun, wind, rain,* and *snow* in each box. Children can point to the picture that best describes the weather that day. Have them say a sentence about the weather.

Preteach/Reteach

Transfer and Common Misconceptions

Weather Words

Children will already be familiar with weather words in their own languages. They can compare them to the English words for *sun, wind, rain,* and *snow.*

Unstressed Syllables

Many syllables in English are pronounced with a short unstressed vowel sound. The words *astronaut, writer, teacher,* and *messenger* all contain unstressed syllables and may be difficult for some children to pronounce.

Produce Language

Weekly Concept and Language Goal

CONCEPT GOALS

- understand that some types of transportation are used on the job
- name and describe ways to send packages and messages

By Day 5, children should be able to write a one-word label or a sentence.

Daily Table Talk

❶ **Beginning**

| Children pantomime while you provide the language. |

❷ ❸ **Early Intermediate/Intermediate**

| Children pantomime and say a word or phrase. |

❹ ❺ **Early Advanced/Advanced**

| Children say a sentence while pantomiming. |

Daily Table Talk

❶ **Beginning**

| Children talk about their drawings. |

❷ ❸ **Early Intermediate/Intermediate**

| Children write one-word labels. |

❹ ❺ **Early Advanced/Advanced**

| Children write a phrase or sentence. |

DAY 3 FORM & FUNCTION — Read and Comprehend	**DAY 4** FORM & FUNCTION — Language Arts	**DAY 5** Language Arts
index cards with the category words: *astronaut, writer, teacher, bike messenger*	children's magazine, highlighter pens	index cards with the following words: *fun, cat, hot, duck, bug, pot, bun, run;* paper cups

What's My Job? ✵

Have a child choose a card and read the word silently. The child then must pantomime actions to indicate a particular job. Other children guess the job. Each child in the group should get a chance to act out a job.

Highlight the Words 🚶

Give children an article from a children's magazine and look for the high frequency words (*what, said, was*). Have child locate and highlight these words in the article.

In the Cup 🚶 🚶🚶

Say *cup* and emphasize the /u/ sound. Have the child put all the words with the same sound as *cup* in the cup. Then have children read the words either alone or with help.

fun

The Word *what*

Some children may have trouble with the letters *wh* pronounced /hw/.

The /u/ sound

Spanish speakers will probably find this sound easy to pronounce as an approximate /u/ sound also exists in Spanish.

Parts of Speech

Children may be confused by the way that English adds endings to verbs and then uses them as nouns and verbs. These constructions are part of natural speech and children will become familiar with them as they listen to fluent speakers.

Daily Table Talk

❶ **Beginning**
> Name different items of clothes and have children answer yes or no if it helps keep you warm in the winter.

❷ ❸ **Early Intermediate/Intermediate**
> Phrase: put on a scarf

❹ ❺ **Early Advanced/Advanced**
> Sentence: You can wear a scarf.

Daily Table Talk

❶ **Beginning**
> Name different types of transportation and have children answer yes or no.

❷ ❸ **Early Intermediate/Intermediate**
> Phrase: a truck

❹ ❺ **Early Advanced/Advanced**
> Sentence: They can drive a truck.

Daily Table Talk

❶ **Beginning** Child speaks about the drawing and may write a label.

❷ ❸ **Early Intermediate/Intermediate** Child writes a label that includes a concept vocabulary word.

❹ ❺ **Intermediate/Early Advanced** Child writes a label or sentence that includes a vocabulary word.

To introduce and discuss concepts and vocabulary related to transportation on the job.

Build Background Get Ready to Read!

How does transportation help at work?

www.pearsonsuccessnet.com

Concept Talk

Use the Big Book If you haven't introduced the Big Book, consider reading it to children. Connect to the unit theme, Transportation—Going Places.

Introduce the Weekly Concept Tell children that today they will be talking about different kinds of transportation that help people do their jobs. Ask the weekly question: How does transportation help at work?

Use the Poster Direct children's attention to the weekly poster. Use the Day 1 teaching notes at the bottom of the poster.

Sing the Song Use the song **People at Work** to build understanding of the concept. Have children sing or simply chant the words with you.

Use a Transparency Use the Relationship Map (Transparency 6) to help children connect forms of transportation to the jobs at which these forms of transportation are used.

Going Places at Work

Vocabulary

parking lots

rain

tunnels

bike

snow

sun

wind

How does transportation help at work?

172

Vocabulary
* Academic Vocabulary

parking lots open areas where cars can be parked

* **rain** water that falls in small drops from clouds in the sky

tunnels passages that have been dug under the ground or through a mountain, usually for cars or trains

bike a bicycle

* **snow** water frozen into soft, white pieces that fall like rain in cold weather

* **sun** the large, bright star in the sky that gives us light and heat

* **wind** the air outside when you can feel it moving around you

 ELA R 1.18 Describe common objects and events in both general and specific language. (ELD R.B2)

173

Introduce Concept Vocabulary

1. **Say the Word** Display the Word Card as you say *bike*. Have children repeat the word.

2. **Introduce Word Meaning** Ask questions about bikes. Can you ride a bike? What does your bike look like?

3. **Demonstrate** Have children role play getting on a bike, getting ready to ride, and riding.

4. **Apply** Have children demonstrate their understanding.

Repeat with other vocabulary words.

Corrective Feedback If children have difficulty pronouncing the vocabulary word, repeat the word again, separating it into phonemes. Have the children repeat the word after you, blending the phoneme.

Concept Work

Discuss each type of transportation, having children point to it. Discuss how these types of transportation help on the job. Ask children to circle the forms of transportation. Link them to specific jobs. Then children can color the pictures.

Preteach LS Reteach **Leveled Support** **Vocabulary in Context**

❶ **Beginning** Point to the pictures on the Worktext page. Say the word for each picture as children point and have them echo each word.

❷ ❸ **Early Intermediate/Intermediate** Provide clues for children, such as: This names something that falls from the sky in the winter. This is where you can put a car when you are not driving. Children can point to the word described by the clue.

❹ ❺ **Early Advanced/Advanced** Ask children to draw someone using transportation to do his or her job and then have them use vocabulary words to label their drawings.

Wrap Up **DAY** 1

 Daily **Table Talk** How does transportation help at work? Have children answer the question, using the vocabulary words.

Produce Language Have each child pretend to drive a truck or bike or another vehicle to work. Have children say a sentence about what they are doing.

Today children should have:

☑ **Learned** and applied vocabulary related to transportation that helps people do their jobs.

☑ **Spoken** complete sentences about kinds of transportation that help people do their jobs.

☑ **Recognized** concept vocabulary words.

 ELA LS 2.1 Describe people, places, things (e.g. size, color, shape), locations, and actions. (ELD R.B2)

173

OBJECTIVE

To discuss ways that people can send messages and packages; to introduce category words for jobs.

Concept Talk

Connect to Day 1 How does transportation help at work?

Introduce the Daily Question Ask: What are three ways people can send messages and packages? Gesture to show what it means to send a message or a package. Have children answer orally.

Use the Poster Use the Day 2 teaching notes.

Introduce Category Words

1. Say the Word Have children point to the astronaut. Say the word and have children repeat.

2. Introduce Word Meaning Ask questions: Would you like to fly in a spaceship like an astronaut? What would be exciting about being an astronaut?

3. Demonstrate Role play putting on a space helmet. As an astronaut, describe your job and what you do.

4. Apply Repeat with other vocabulary words and elicit that they all belong to the category "jobs."

Have children draw a picture of a job that they would like to do when they grow up.

Corrective Feedback If children have difficulty identifying how transportation helps at work, refer back to the picture examples from Day 1 to provide background (such as a bike messenger using a bike).

Wrap Up DAY 2

Table Talk Have children discuss ways people can send messages and packages.

Produce Language To build fluency, encourage children to label or write a sentence about their drawings. They can share the writing with partners.

Today children should have:

☑ **Learned** and applied vocabulary related to jobs.

☑ **Spoken** complete sentences about ways that people send messages and packages.

☑ **Recognized** words that belong in the same category.

 ELA R1.17 Identify and sort common words in basic categories (e.g. colors, shapes, foods). (ELD R.B.4)

174 Going Places at Work • Unit 5, Week 3

Jobs

Picture Dictionary

astronaut **bike messenger** **cashier**

mechanic **teacher** **writer**

✏ **Draw** Draw someone doing a job.

174 ELA R1.17 Identify and sort common words in basic categories (e.g., colors, shapes, foods). (ELD R.B4)

Leveled Support **Category Words**

① Beginning Have children point to each occupation picture on the Worktext page as you say it. Have children echo the word.

② ③ Early Intermediate/Intermediate Say the name of an occupation. Have children point to it. Describe what the pictured person does on the job. Then have children determine which worker you are describing based on the clues. Reverse the activity.

④ ⑤ Early Advanced/Advanced Have children tell a partner which of the jobs on the Worktext page they would like to do most and why.

How does a bike messenger bundle up in winter?

✏️ **Circle** Circle *what*.

The messenger knows what to wear.

✏️ **Circle** Circle *said*. Circle *was*.

He said the mask was warm.

ELA R1.15 Read simple one-syllable and high-frequency words (i.e., sight words). (ELD R.B2)   175

To discuss how a bike messenger bundles up in winter; to introduce the high frequency words *what*, *said*, and *was*.

Concept Talk

Connect to Day 2 What are three ways people can send messages and packages?

Introduce the Daily Question Ask: How does a bike messenger bundle up in winter? Name different items of clothing and have children raise their hands if it helps you keep warm in the winter.

Use the Poster Use the Day 3 teaching notes.

Review Concept Vocabulary Review the words introduced on Day 1.

Introduce High Frequency Words

Introduce *what*, *said*, and *was* by saying sentences, such as: *What* is this? Did you hear what I *said*? That *was* my book. Help children complete the Worktext page.

Corrective Feedback If children have difficulty finding the high frequency words in the sentences, highlight each word in the direction line and have children look for it in the sentence.

Wrap Up   DAY 3

Daily Table Talk Children can pretend to bundle up for winter and then discuss ways to keep warm in the winter.

Produce Language Have each child say a sentence about how a bike messenger stays warm by bundling up in winter.

Today children should have:

☑ **Learned** and applied the high frequency words *what*, *said*, and *was*.

☑ **Spoken** complete sentences about how a bike messenger bundles up in winter.

☑ **Recognized** high frequency words used in sentences.

ELA R 1.15 Read simple one-syllable and high-frequency words (that is, sight words). (ELD R B2)

175

Preteach Reteach LS Leveled Support **High Frequency Words**

❶ **Beginning** Write the word *what*. Say: This is the word *what*. Spell the word: *w,h,a,t*. Continue with *said* and *was*. Have children use letter tiles to spell the words that you have written on index cards.

❷ ❸ **Early Intermediate/Intermediate** Write *what*, *said*, and *was*. Say a word and have children point to the word. Then say sentences. Ask children to raise their hands when they hear the high frequency words.

❹ ❺ **Early Advanced/Advanced** Have children look for the high frequency words in classroom picture books. They can mark them with sticky notes.

To discuss the kind of transportation mail carriers use; to identify sound /u/.

Concept Talk

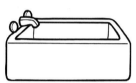 **FORM & FUNCTION**

Connect to Day 3 How does a bike messenger bundle up in winter?

Introduce the Daily Question Ask: What transportation can mail carriers use to do their jobs? Have children name one form of transportation mail carriers can use.

Use the Poster Use the Day 4 teaching notes.

Phonics

Identify Sound /u/ Have children point to each picture as you name it. Say: Now I'm going to read the pairs of words again. Listen for /u/. Which word has /u/? Help children complete the Worktext page.

Corrective Feedback If children have difficulty identifying the sound /u/, read each word again, separating the phonemes and emphasizing the medial phoneme of each word.

Wrap Up

DAY 4

 Table Talk Have children pretend to be mail carriers delivering mail in a truck and discuss what they are doing.

Produce Language Have each child say a sentence about how the mail carrier delivers the mail.

Today children should have:

- ☑ **Learned** and applied vocabulary related to what transportation mail carriers use to do their jobs.

- ☑ **Spoken** complete sentences about what transportation mail carriers use to do their jobs.

- ☑ **Recognized** words with /u/.

 ELA R1.1.4 Match all consonant and short-vowel sounds to appropriate letters. (ELD R.B1)

Identify Sound Uu

 **Color** Color things with *u*.

176 ELA R1.14 Match all consonant and short-vowel sounds to appropriate letters. (ELD R.B1)

Leveled Support Phonics

Preteach / Reteach

① **Beginning** Hold up an index card on which you have printed *u*. Say: The name of this letter is *u*. One sound this letter can make is /u/. Have children echo the sound and repeat after you as you say words with /u/ in the initial and medial positions.

② ③ **Early Intermediate/Intermediate** Tell children you will say several words and they should listen for /u/. When they hear a word with /u/, children should raise their hands. Say: nut, up, food, cat, bug, ant, fun.

④ ⑤ **Early Advanced/Advanced** Have children identify the letter that makes /u/. Ask children to name other words that have the sound /u/. Children can sort words based on their medial vowel sounds.

How does transportation help at work?

✏ Draw

ELA LS. 1.2 Share information and ideas, speaking audibly in complete, coherent sentences. (ELD LS.B3)

177

OBJECTIVE

To guide children to express their understanding of weekly concepts and vocabulary.

Think, Talk, and Recognize!

Concept Talk

Connect to Day 4 What transportation can mail carriers use to do their job? Model how to answer yesterday's question with a sentence.

Review the Weekly Question Ask: *How does transportation help at work?* Have each child pretend to be using a kind of transportation to do their job. Other children can try to guess what their job is based on the transportation they are using.

Use the Poster Use the Day 5 teaching notes.

Review Concept Vocabulary Review the vocabulary introduced on Day 1.

Concept Wrap Up

Have children draw to answer the question: *How does transportation help at work?* Use the photo to prompt discussion. What kind of trucks are these? Who uses these trucks to do their jobs?

Leveled Support Concept Vocabulary

① Beginning Display the Word Cards for *sun, wind, rain, snow, parking lots, bike, tunnels.* Say each word. Ask children to repeat and point to the matching card.

② ③ Early Intermediate/Intermediate Display the Word Cards for *sun, wind, rain, snow, parking lots, bike, tunnels.* Ask children to each choose one word and describe it in a word or sentence.

④ ⑤ Early Advanced/Advanced Display the Word Cards for *sun, wind, rain, snow, parking lots, bike, tunnels.* Have pairs each choose two words to use in a sentence.

Wrap Up   DAY 5

Daily Table Talk How does transportation help at work? Have children discuss the question, using the vocabulary words they have learned this week.

Produce Language To build fluency, children can label, write about, or speak about their drawings. Ask children to respond to what they read or heard.

Today, children should have:

☑ **Reviewed** the weekly concept and concept vocabulary.

☑ **Spoken** about forms of transportation used on the job.

☑ **Drawn or written** about vehicles that are used at work.

ELA LS. 1.2 Share information and ideas, speaking audibly in complete, coherent sentences. (ELD LS.B3)

Question of the Week How does a train get over a mountain?

DAY 1 — Get Ready to Read

Build Background

Preteach/Review 10–15 min
Poster, Song Book, Big Book
- **Leveled Support Preteach**
- **Practice Stations Preteach**

Teach 35–45 min
- **Concept Talk**
- **Oral Vocabulary Routine**
  Word Cards
- **Build Concept Vocabulary**
- **Daily Table Talk**

Check/Reteach 5–10 min
Poster, Word Cards
- **Leveled Support Reteach**

DAY 2 — Read and Comprehend

Language: Category Words

Preteach/Review 10–15 min
Poster
- **Leveled Support Preteach**
- **Practice Stations Review**

Teach 35–45 min
- **Category Words**
- **Daily Table Talk**

Check/Reteach 5–10 min
Poster, Word Cards
- **Leveled Support Reteach**

Fluency: Writing or Speaking

Instructional Plan and Materials

- **Word Cards**
  96–102

- **Big Book**
  One Morning in May

- **Poster**
  Poster 28 can be used at beginning or end of day.

- **Song Book**, p. 28

Transparencies Explore content and vocabulary and model fluent reading.

For further information about using these components, see pages x–xv.

CALIFORNIA Standards

GK Sci 4.e Communicate observations orally and through drawings.

ELA LS 2.1 Describe people, places, things (e.g., size, color, shape), locations, and actions.

ELA R 1.17 Identify and sort common words in basic categories (e.g., colors, shapes, foods).

Academic Language

Vocabulary: wheels

Category Words: ball, blocks, doll, puzzle, stuffed animal, top

Get Online! www.pearsonsuccessnet.com

Concept Talk Video

Background Building Audio Slideshow

This Week

Unit 5, Week 4

Trains

Next Week

Unit 5, Week 5

Ways to Travel

FORM & FUNCTION

DAY 3 Read and Comprehend

DAY 4 Language Arts

DAY 5 Language Arts

Language: High Frequency Words	Phonics	Think, Talk, and Recognize
Preteach/Review 10–15 min Poster **Leveled Support Preteach** **Practice Stations Review**	**Preteach/Review** 10–15 min Poster **Leveled Support Preteach** **Practice Stations Review**	**Preteach/Review** 10–15 min Poster **Leveled Support Preteach** **Practice Stations Review**
Teach 35–45 min **High Frequency Words** **Daily Table Talk**	**Teach** 35–45 min **Phonics** **Daily Table Talk**	**Teach** 15–20 min **Think, Talk, and Recognize** **Concept Wrap Up**
Check/Reteach 5–10 min Poster, Word Cards **Leveled Support Reteach**	**Check/Reteach** 5–10 min Poster, Word Cards **Leveled Support Reteach**	**Check/Reteach** 30–40 min Poster, Word Cards, Song Book **Leveled Support Reteach**
		Fluency: Writing or Speaking
ELA R 1.15 Read simple one-syllable and high frequency words (i.e., sight words).	**ELA R 1.14** Match all consonant and short-vowel sounds to appropriate letters.	**ELA LS 1.2** Share information and ideas, speaking audibly in complete, coherent sentences.
High Frequency Words: what, said, was		

Practice Stations

Materials and Activity

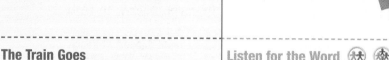
DAY 1

modeling clay, toy trains

The Train Goes Over the Mountain

Have children create a mountain out of modeling clay. Once the mountain is complete, children can take turns driving a toy train up and down the mountain.

DAY 2

index cards with the vocabulary words written on them

Listen for the Word

Distribute one vocabulary word to each child. Read sentences for each word. Have children listen for their vocabulary word. When they hear a sentence that includes the word on their card, they should hold up the card with that word.

dolls

Preteach/Reteach

Transfer and Common Misconceptions

/z/ Sound

Some children may want to pronounce the *s* at the end of *toys*, *cars*, and *wheels* as /s/. In English an *s* is often pronounced /z/ at the end of a word.

/ô/ Sound

Some children may have trouble with the word *ball*. Spanish has an approximate /ô/ sound, but children may pronounce the word as *boll*.

Produce Language

Weekly Concept and Language Goal

CONCEPT GOALS

- understand the concept that trains can travel over mountains
- describe ways that people can get around mountains
- name things that trains can carry on trips

By Day 5, children should be able to write a one-word label or a sentence.

Daily Table Talk

❶ **Beginning**
Children pantomime while you provide the language.

❷ ❸ **Early Intermediate/Intermediate**
Children pantomime and say a word or phrase.

❹ ❺ **Intermediate/Early Advanced**
Children say a sentence while pantomiming.

Daily Table Talk

❶ **Beginning**
Children talk about their drawings.

❷ ❸ **Early Intermediate/Intermediate**
Children write one-word labels.

❹ ❺ **Intermediate/Early Advanced**
Children write a phrase or sentence.

DAY 3 Read and Comprehend

DAY 4 Language Arts

DAY 5 Language Arts

cut-out magazine pictures of balls, dolls, stuffed animals, and tops; construction paper; glue; crayons or markers

index cards with the high frequency words written on them, letter tiles, paper

pairs of index cards with the following words: *rug, mug, sun, fun, luck, hug*

Toy Collage

Have children create a toy collage using the magazine cut-outs. Help children label each toy with the word *ball, doll, stuffed animal,* or *top.*

Letter Tiles

Use Word Cards and Letter Tiles to spell high frequency words. Make placemats with two columns. Have them place the Word Card in the first column. Have them use the Letter Tiles to spell the word in the second column.

Word Concentration

Place the cards facedown in three rows of four. Children take turns turning over two cards. If the cards match, they say the word and keep the cards. Play continues until all of the cards are matched.

The Word *said*

Spanish speakers may pronounce *said* as *side* because in Spanish the vowel pattern *ai* sounds like long *i.*

The /u/ Sound

Spanish speakers will probably find this sound easy to pronounce, as an approximate /u/ sound also exists in Spanish.

Pronouns

Speakers of Spanish may use inappropriate pronouns, particularly with neutral nouns, because all nouns in Spanish are either masculine or feminine.

Daily Table Talk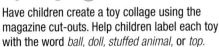

❶ Beginning Say *by* trying hard, *by* giving up, *by* walking, and have children answer yes or no.

❷ ❸ Early Intermediate/Intermediate
Phrase: *by* trying hard

❹ ❺ Intermediate/Early Advanced
Sentence: It can tug the train *by* trying hard.

Daily Table Talk

❶ Beginning Name different objects and have children answer yes or no if a train could carry it.

❷ ❸ Early Intermediate/Intermediate
One or two-word answer: people, some toys

❹ ❺ Intermediate/Early Advanced
Sentence: A train can carry people.

Daily Table Talk

❶ Beginning Child speaks about the drawing and may write a label.

❷ ❸ Early Intermediate/Intermediate Child writes a label that includes a concept vocabulary word.

❹ ❺ Intermediate/Early Advanced Child writes a label or sentence that includes a vocabulary word.

OBJECTIVE

To introduce and discuss concepts and vocabulary related to trains.

Build Background   Get Ready to Read!

Question of the Week

How does a train get over the mountain?

www.pearsonsuccessnet.com

Concept Talk

Use the Big Book If you haven't introduced the Big Book, consider reading it to children. Connect to the unit theme, Transportation—Going Places.

Introduce the Weekly Concept Tell children that today they will talk about trains, which are another kind of transportation, and how trains can get over mountains.

Use the Poster Direct children's attention to the weekly poster. Use the Day 1 teaching notes at the bottom of the poster.

Sing the Song Use the song **The Train** to build understanding of the concept. Have children sing or simply chant the words with you.

Use a Transparency Use the Cause and Effect Map (Transparency 1) to help organize causes and effects related to a train getting over a mountain.

Trains

Vocabulary

dining cars

dolls

sleeping cars

load
switching
toys
wheels

178

How does a train get over a mountain?

Vocabulary
* Academic Vocabulary

dining cars special cars on a train where meals are served

dolls toys that look like a small person or a baby

sleeping cars parts of a train with beds for passengers

load a large quantity of something that is carried by a person or a vehicle

switching changing from doing or using one thing to doing or using another

toys objects for children to play with

* **wheels** round things under a car, bicycle, etc. that turn and allow it to move

Introduce Concept Vocabulary

1. **Say the Word** Display the Word Card as you say *dolls*. Have children repeat the word.

2. **Introduce Word Meaning** Ask questions about dolls. What do dolls look like? Do you ever play with dolls?

3. **Demonstrate** Have children role play playing with a doll. Children can use dolls in the classroom to show how they play with dolls.

4. **Apply** Have children demonstrate their understanding.

Repeat with other vocabulary words.

Corrective Feedback If children have difficulty understanding the concept of mountain or train, have them look at photos from the Big Book or magazines.

Concept Work

Describe what is happening in each picture. In the top picture the train travels on tracks to get over a mountain. In the bottom picture, a family is ready to travel by train. Have children circle a wheel on the train. Children can color a train car in each picture.

 Leveled Support **Vocabulary in Context**

❶ **Beginning** Point to the pictures on the Worktext page. Say the word for each picture as children point and have them echo each word.

❷ ❸ **Early Intermediate/Intermediate** Do the Beginning activity, but have children say the words themselves, providing help if needed. Have children look for examples of the vocabulary words in the Worktext illustration. They can label what they find with sticky notes on which you have printed the words.

❹ ❺ **Early Advanced/Advanced** Have children talk about things you can do on a train, using vocabulary words, such as eating a meal in a dining car, playing with toys, and so on.

Wrap Up   DAY 1

 Table Talk How does a train get over the mountain? Have children answer the question, using the vocabulary words.

Produce Language Ask each child to pretend to be a train going over a mountain and to say a sentence about what they are doing.

Today children should have:

☑ **Learned** and applied vocabulary related to trains.

☑ **Spoken** complete sentences about a train going over a mountain.

☑ **Recognized** concept vocabulary words.

 ELA LS 2.1 Describe people, places, things (e.g. size, color, shape), locations, and actions. (ELD R.B2)

179

OBJECTIVE

To discuss other ways to get over a mountain; to introduce category words for toys.

Concept Talk

Connect to Day 1 How does a train get over a mountain?

Introduce the Daily Question Ask: What are other ways to get over a mountain? Name other ways and have children answer yes or no.

Use the Poster Use the Day 2 teaching notes.

Introduce Category Words

1. Say the Word Have children point to the picture of the ball. Say the word and have children repeat.

2. Introduce Word Meaning Ask questions: Do you ever play with a ball? What kinds of games can you play with a ball?

3. Demonstrate Role play throwing and catching a ball. You can play with a ball in the classroom or outdoors.

4. Apply Repeat with other vocabulary words and elicit that they all belong to the category "toys."

Have children point to items as you name them. Then have them draw their favorite toy.

Corrective Feedback If children have difficulty identifying toys, share pictures of other toys and compare them to non-toy items. Have them identify toys in the classroom.

Wrap Up   DAY 2

Daily Table Talk Have children discuss different ways to get over a mountain.

Produce Language To build fluency, encourage children to label or write a sentence about their drawings. They can share the writing with partners.

Today children should have:

☑ **Learned** and applied vocabulary related to toys.

☑ **Spoken** complete sentences about ways to get over a mountain.

☑ **Recognized** words that belong in the same category.

ELA R1.17 Identify and sort common words in basic categories (e.g. colors, shapes, foods).

Toys

Picture Dictionary

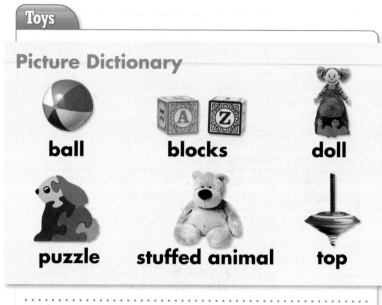

ball   blocks   doll

puzzle   stuffed animal   top

Draw Draw toys.

Leveled Support Category Words

Preteach / Reteach

① **Beginning** Have children point to each toy on the Worktext page as you say it. Have children echo the word.

②③ **Early Intermediate/Intermediate** Say the name of a toy. Have children point to it. Then reverse the activity.

④⑤ **Early Advanced/Advanced** Give directions using the vocabulary words:

1. Pretend to throw a **ball.**
2. Show how you might hold a **doll.**
3. Draw a **stuffed animal.**

Have children label each drawing.

How will the little engine tug the train?

✏️ **Circle** Circle *said*. Circle *what*.
The little engine said what it could do.

✏️ **Circle** Circle *was*.
The little engine was trying hard.

🐻 **ELA R1.15** Read simple one-syllable and high-frequency words (i.e., sight words). (ELD R.B2)

181

OBJECTIVE

To discuss how the little engine will tug the train up the hill; to introduce the high frequency words *what, said,* and *was.*

Concept Talk
FORM & FUNCTION

Connect to Day 2 What are other ways to get over a mountain?

Introduce the Daily Question Ask: How will the little engine tug the train up the hill? Read the sentences to children. Retell the story "The Little Engine That Could."

Use the Poster Use the Day 3 teaching notes.

Review Concept Vocabulary Review the words introduced on Day 1.

Introduce High Frequency Words

Guide children to point to the word *said* in the direction line. Say: Now find and point to the word *said* in the sentence. Circle it. Help children complete the Worktext page.

Corrective Feedback If children have difficulty finding the high frequency words in the sentences, write the words on sticky notes so that children can place them near the words on the Worktext page.

Preteach **LS** **Leveled Support** **High Frequency Words**
Reteach

① **Beginning** Read "The Little Engine That Could" aloud. Have children raise their hands when they hear *what, said, was.*

② ③ **Early Intermediate/Intermediate** Write *what, said, was* on index cards and give a set to each child. Say sentences with the words. When children hear the words, they should raise their cards.

④ ⑤ **Early Advanced/Advanced** Have children find and flag with a sticky note the high frequency words *what, said,* and *was* in a story book about trains or a newspaper article.

Wrap Up **DAY** 3

Table Talk Daily Have the children discuss why the little engine was able to tug the train up the hill.

Produce Language Have each child talk about the theme of "trying hard" in terms of the little engine. They can each say a sentence about something that they have tried hard to do.

Today children should have:

☑️ **Learned** and applied the high frequency words *what, said, was.*

☑️ **Spoken** complete sentences about how a little engine tugged a train up a hill.

☑️ **Recognized** high frequency words used in sentences.

🐻 **ELA R1.15** Read simple one-syllable and high-frequency words (i.e., sight words). (ELD R.B2)

To discuss what a train can carry on a trip; to identify initial and medial /u/.

Concept Talk

 FORM & FUNCTION

Connect to Day 3 How will the little engine tug the train up the hill?

Introduce the Daily Question Ask: What can a train carry on a trip? Name some items and ask children to raise their hands if they think a train could carry that item.

Use the Poster Use the Day 4 teaching notes.

Phonics

Identify Sound /u/ Have children point to each picture as you name it. Say: Now I'm going to read the pairs of words again. Listen for /u/. Which word has /u/? Is it in the beginning of the word or the middle of the word? Help children complete the Worktext page.

Corrective Feedback If children have difficulty identifying the sound /u/, read each word again, isolating the initial and medial sounds.

Wrap Up   DAY **4**

Table Talk What can a train carry on a trip? Have children discuss the question.

Produce Language Have each child say a sentence about items they have taken with them on a train trip or things that a train can carry on a trip.

Today children should have:

☑ **Learned** and applied vocabulary related to what a train can carry on a trip.

☑ **Spoken** complete sentences about what a train can carry on a trip.

☑ **Recognized** words with sound /u/.

 ELA R1.1.4 Match all consonant and short-vowel sounds to appropriate letters. (ELD R.B1)

✏ **Circle** Circle things with *u*.

Leveled Support **Phonics**
Preteach / Reteach

① **Beginning** Say words with the sound /u/. Then tell children to listen for the sound in other words you read. Children should raise their hands if they hear the sound in the word.

②③ **Early Intermediate/Intermediate** Ask children to stand up near their desks. Tell children you will read several words and they should listen for /u/. When you say a word that has /u/, children should step forward if it's initial /u/ and step back if it's medial /u/.

④⑤ **Early Advanced/Advanced** Have children identify the letter that makes /u/. Ask children to name other words with the /u/ sound. Then give words to children to sort: words with initial /u/ and words with medial /u/.

How does a train get over a mountain?

✏ Draw

ELA LS. 1.2 Share information and ideas, speaking audibly in complete, coherent sentences. (ELD LS.B1)

183

OBJECTIVE

To guide children to express their understanding of weekly concepts and vocabulary.

Think, Talk, and Recognize!

Concept Talk

Connect to Day 4 What can a train carry on a trip? Model how to answer yesterday's question with a sentence.

Review the Weekly Question Ask: How does a train get over a mountain? Have children use their hands to pretend to be a train going over a mountain and explain how they are doing it.

Use the Poster Use the Day 5 teaching notes.

Review Concept Vocabulary Review the vocabulary introduced on Day 1.

Concept Wrap-Up

Have children draw to answer the question: *How does a train get over the mountain?* Prompt discussion with the photo.

Leveled Support — Concept Vocabulary

① **Beginning** Display the Word Cards for *load, dolls, toys, sleeping cars, dining car, wheels,* and *switching.* Say each word. Ask children to repeat and point to the matching card.

② ③ **Early Intermediate/Intermediate** Display the Word Cards for *load, dolls, toys, sleeping cars, dining car, wheels,* and *switching.* Ask children to say each word and point to the matching card.

④ ⑤ **Early Advanced/Advanced** Display the Word Cards for *load, dolls, toys, sleeping cars, dining-car, wheels,* and *switching.* Ask children to tell a story about a train using the words.

Wrap Up DAY 5

Table Talk *Daily* How does a train get over a mountain? Have children discuss the question, using the vocabulary words they have learned this week.

Produce Language To build fluency, children can label, write about, or speak about their drawings. Ask children to respond to what they read or heard.

Today children should have:

☑ **Reviewed** the weekly concept and concept vocabulary.

☑ **Spoken** about how a train gets over a mountain.

☑ **Drawn or written** about a train getting over a mountain.

 ELA LS. 1.2 Share information and ideas, speaking audibly in complete, coherent sentences. (ELD LS.B3)

WEEK

CALIFORNIA

Weekly Lesson Plan

Last Week
Unit 5, Week 4
Trains

Question of the Week

How do people around the world travel?

DAY 1 — Get Ready to Read

Build Background

Preteach/Review 10–15 min
Poster, Song Book, Big Book
- **Leveled Support Preteach**
- **Practice Stations Preteach**

Teach 35–45 min
- **Concept Talk**
- **Oral Vocabulary Routine**
  Word Cards
- **Build Concept Vocabulary**
- **Daily Table Talk**

Check/Reteach 5–10 min
Poster, Word Cards
- **Leveled Support Reteach**

DAY 2 — Read and Comprehend

Language: Category Words

Preteach/Review 10–15 min
Poster
- **Leveled Support Preteach**
- **Practice Stations Review**

Teach 35–45 min
- **Category Words**
- **Daily Table Talk**

Check/Reteach 5–10 min
Poster, Word Cards
- **Leveled Support Reteach**

Fluency: Writing or Speaking

Instructional Plan and Materials

- **Word Cards**
  103–109

- **Big Book**
  One Morning in May

- **Poster**
  Poster 29 can be used at beginning or end of day.

- **Song Book**, p. 29

Transparencies Explore content and vocabulary and model fluent reading.

For further information about using these components, see pages x–xv.

CALIFORNIA Standards

G1 His-Soc Sci 1.2.4. Describe how location, weather, and physical environment affect the way people live, including the effects on their food, clothing, shelter, transportation, and recreation.

ELA LS 2.1 Describe people, places, things (e.g., size, color, shape), locations, and actions.

ELA R 1.17 Identify and sort common words in basic categories (e.g., colors, shapes, foods).

Academic Language

Vocabulary: air, land, ocean, water

Category Words: desert, lake, mountain, river, volcano, waterfall

Get Online! www.pearsonsuccessnet.com

Concept Talk Video

Background Building Audio Slideshow

This Week
Unit 5, Week 5

Ways to Travel

Next Week
Unit 5, Week 6
Ways to Get to School

DAY 3 — FORM & FUNCTION — Read and Comprehend

DAY 4 — FORM & FUNCTION — Language Arts

DAY 5 — Language Arts

Language: High Frequency Words	Phonics	Think, Talk, and Recognize
Preteach/Review 10–15 min Poster **Leveled Support Preteach** **Practice Stations Review**	**Preteach/Review** 10–15 min Poster **Leveled Support Preteach** **Practice Stations Review**	**Preteach/Review** 10–15 min Poster **Leveled Support Preteach** **Practice Stations Review**
Teach 35–45 min **High Frequency Words** **Daily Table Talk**	**Teach** 35–45 min **Phonics** **Daily Table Talk**	**Teach** 15–20 min **Think, Talk, and Recognize** **Concept Wrap Up**
Check/Reteach 5–10 min Poster, Word Cards **Leveled Support Reteach**	**Check/Reteach** 5–10 min Poster, Word Cards **Leveled Support Reteach**	**Check/Reteach** 30–40 min Poster, Word Cards, Song Book **Leveled Support Reteach**
		Fluency: Writing or Speaking
ELA R 1.15 Read simple one-syllable and high frequency words (i.e., sight words).	**ELA R 1.14** Match all consonant and short-vowel sounds to appropriate letters.	**ELA LS 1.2** Share information and ideas, speaking audibly in complete, coherent sentences.
High Frequency Words: where, come		

Weekly Practice

Practice Stations

Materials and Activity

mural paper, cut-out travel magazine pictures of various forms of travel around the world, crayons

Travel Around the World

Have children create murals of various forms of travel around the world. They can draw water on parts of the paper and paste pictures of boats in the water. They can draw roads and paste pictures of cars, trucks, and buses on them.

index cards with the vocabulary words written on them, stacked face down

Use the Word

One child chooses a card and says a sentence with that vocabulary word. The next child chooses a card and says a sentence with that word. Children continue to choose cards and say sentences. When all of the words have been used, children can reshuffle the cards and start again.

"airplane"

The airplane flew into the sky

Preteach/Reteach

Transfer and Common Misconceptions

The Word *ocean*

Spanish speakers may have trouble pronouncing this word. The letter *c* in Spanish is only pronounced as a hard or soft *c*, and the /sh/ sound is not found in Spanish.

/z/ Sound

Some children may want to pronounce the *s* in *desert* as /s/. In English an *s* can often be pronounced /z/ in the middle or end of a word.

Produce Language

Weekly Concept and Language Goal

CONCEPT GOALS

- describe ways in which people around the world travel
- name and describe favorite places
- explain how people travel in towns and on water

By Day 5, children should be able to write a one-word label or a sentence.

Daily Table Talk

❶ **Beginning**
> Children pantomime while you provide the language.

❷ ❸ **Early Intermediate/Intermediate**
> Children pantomime and say a word or phrase.

❹ ❺ **Intermediate/Early Advanced**
> Children say a sentence while pantomiming.

Daily Table Talk

❶ **Beginning**
> Children talk about their drawings.

❷ ❸ **Early Intermediate/Intermediate**
> Children write one-word labels.

❹ ❺ **Intermediate/Early Advanced**
> Children write a phrase or sentence.

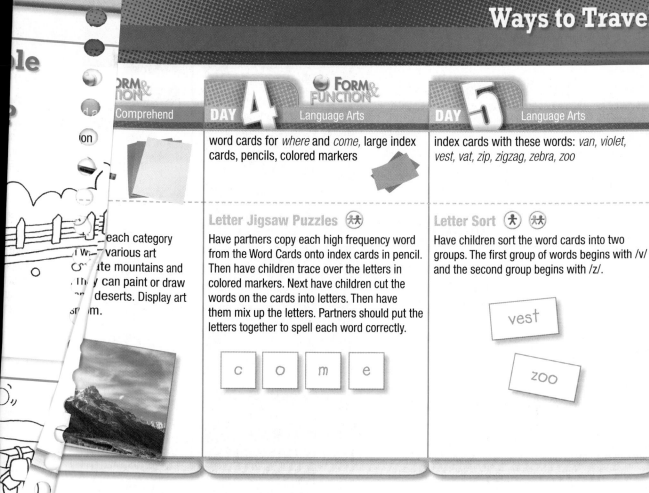

DAY 4 Language Arts

DAY 5 Language Arts

word cards for *where* and *come*, large index cards, pencils, colored markers

index cards with these words: *van, violet, vest, vat, zip, zigzag, zebra, zoo*

Letter Jigsaw Puzzles 👥

Have partners copy each high frequency word from the Word Cards onto index cards in pencil. Then have children trace over the letters in colored markers. Next have children cut the words on the cards into letters. Then have them mix up the letters. Partners should put the letters together to spell each word correctly.

| c | o | m | e |

Letter Sort 🧍 👥

Have children sort the word cards into two groups. The first group of words begins with /v/ and the second group begins with /z/.

vest

zoo

...me

...e confused by the word *come* ...one phoneme, yet four letters. ...t also pronounce it with a long *o* ...se it ends with an *e*.

The Letter z

Some children will have trouble pronouncing the letter *z* since this sound is not found in a number of languages, including Spanish, Cantonese, and Korean.

Subject Pronouns

Some children may drop subject pronouns because in Spanish the verb ending gives information about the number and/or gender of the pronoun.

Daily Table Talk

...nning
Name different places to go in your town and have children answer yes or no.

② Early Intermediate/Intermediate
Phrase: to the post office

④ ⑤ Intermediate/Early Advanced
Sentence: You can drive to the post office.

Daily Table Talk

① Beginning
Name different objects and have children answer yes or no if a train could carry them.

② ③ Early Intermediate/Intermediate
Phrase: by boat, by canoe

④ ⑤ Intermediate/Early Advanced
Sentence: You can travel by boat.

Daily Table Talk

① Beginning Child speaks about the drawing and may write a label.

② ③ Early Intermediate/Intermediate Child writes a label that includes a concept vocabulary word.

④ ⑤ Intermediate/Early Advanced Child writes a label or sentence that includes a vocabulary word.

Build Background Get **Ready** to **Read!**

Question of the Week

How do people around the world travel?

www.pearsonsuccessnet.com

Concept Talk

Use the Big Book If you haven't introduced the Big Book, consider reading it to children. Connect to the unit theme, Transportation—Going Places.

Introduce the Weekly Concept Tell children that today they will talk about how people use transportation in different parts of the world. Ask the weekly question: How do people around the world travel?

Use the Poster Direct children's attention to the weekly poster. Use the Day 1 teaching notes at the bottom of the poster.

Sing the Song Use the song **Ways to Travel** to build understanding of the concept. Have children sing or simply chant the words with you.

Use a Transparency Use the Description Map (Transparency 4) to help children describe different ways to travel.

Vocabulary
* **Academic Vocabulary**

camel a large animal with a long neck and one or two humps on its back that lives in the desert and carries goods or people

* **ocean** a particular area of salt water somewhere on Earth

trail a path across open country or through the forest

airplane a vehicle that flies by using wings on one or more engines

* **air** the gases around the Earth, which we breathe

* **land** the ground, especially when owned by someone and used for buildings or farming

* **water** the clear, colorless liquid that falls from the sky as rain; forms lakes, rivers, and oceans; and is used for drinking and washing

Introduce Concept Vocabulary

1. **Say the Word** Display the Word Card as you say *water.* Have children repeat the word.

2. **Introduce Word Meaning** Ask questions about water. Do you like to drink water? What kind of water can you swim in?

3. **Demonstrate** Have children role play swimming in water.

4. **Apply** Have children demonstrate their understanding.

Repeat with other vocabulary words.

Corrective Feedback If children have difficulty pronouncing the vocabulary words, repeat each word again, separating it into phonemes. Have children repeat the word after you, blending the phonemes.

Concept Work

Discuss the illustrations with children. Ask which pictures show ways that they have traveled. Have them circle the form of transportation in each picture. Then children can color the pictures.

Leveled Support   **Vocabulary in Context**

Preteach / Reteach

❶ **Beginning** Point to the pictures on the Worktext page. Say the word for each picture as children point and have them echo each word.

❷ ❸ **Early Intermediate/Intermediate** Do the Beginning activity, but have children say the words themselves. Give help if needed.

❹ ❺ **Early Advanced/Advanced** Ask children to draw a picture of an airplane flying over the ocean. Have them label the picture with as many vocabulary words as they can.

Wrap Up   **DAY** 1

Daily **Table Talk** How do people around the world travel? Have children answer the question, using the vocabulary words.

Produce Language Ask each child to act out traveling on some kind of transportation and say a sentence about it.

Today children should have:

☑ **Learned** and applied vocabulary related to how people travel in different parts of the world.

☑ **Spoken** complete sentences about how people travel in different parts of the world.

☑ **Recognized** concept vocabulary words.

 ELA LS 2.1 Describe people, places, things (e.g. size, color, shape), locations, and actions. (ELD R.B2)

185

OBJECTIVE

To discuss children's favorite places; to introduce category words for geography.

Concept Talk

Connect to Day 1 How do people around the world travel?

Introduce the Daily Question Ask: Where is your favorite place? Have children answer orally.

Use the Poster Use the Day 2 teaching notes.

Introduce Category Words

1. **Say the Word** Have children point to the picture of a mountain. Say the word and have children repeat.

2. **Introduce Word Meaning** Ask questions: Have you ever seen a mountain? What did it look like?

3. **Demonstrate** Role play climbing a mountain.

4. **Apply** Repeat with other vocabulary words and elicit that they all belong to the category "geography." *Geography* is a word that describes places on Earth and the special features there.

Have children point to items as you name them. Then have them draw one of the geographical features you have discussed.

Corrective Feedback If children have difficulty identifying the correct geographical term, point to the picture, say the word aloud, and have children repeat.

Geography

Picture Dictionary

desert   **lake**   **mountain**

river   **volcano**   **waterfall**

✎ **Draw** Draw a place in the world.

186 🐻 **ELA R1.17** Identify and sort common words in basic categories (e.g., colors, shapes, foods). (ELD R.B4)

Leveled Support Preteach/Reteach **Category Words**

❶ **Beginning** Have children point to each geography picture on the Worktext page as you say it. Have children echo the word.

❷❸ **Early Intermediate/Intermediate** Say a geographical term. Have children point to it. Then reverse the activity.

❹❺ **Early Advanced/Advanced** Have children tell a partner which of the geographical features they have seen in real life or would like to see. Have them describe it.

Wrap Up   DAY 2

Daily Table Talk Have children discuss their favorite places.

Produce Language To build fluency, encourage children to label or write a sentence about their drawings. They can share the writing with partners.

Today children should have:

☑ **Learned** and applied vocabulary related to geography.

☑ **Spoken** complete sentences about their favorite place.

☑ **Recognized** words that belong to the same category.

 ELA R1.17 Identify and sort common words in basic categories (e.g. colors, shapes, foods). (ELD R.B4)

 **Identify Sounds Vv and Zz**

 Circle Circle things with v.

 Circle Circle things with z.

188 ELA R1.14 Match all consonant and short-vowel sounds to appropriate letters. (ELD R.B1)

OBJECTIVE

To discuss ways to travel on the water; to identify sounds /v/ and /z/.

Concept Talk

FORM & FUNCTION

Connect to Day 3 Where can you zip through town in a [v]an?

Introduce the Daily Question Ask: What are some ways [p]eople travel on water? Name some ways to travel and [h]ave children raise their hands if it is a way to travel on [w]ater.

Use the Poster Use the Day 4 teaching notes.

Phonics

Identify sounds /v/ and /z/ Have children point to each [pi]cture as you name it. Say: Now I'm going to read the [w]ords again. Listen for the sound /v/ at the beginning of [th]e word. Which word begins with /v/, *bike* or *van*? Circle [th]e correct word. Then repeat for words with the sound /z/.

Corrective Feedback If children have difficulty [id]entifying the sounds /v/ and /z/, read each word again, [se]parating the phonemes and emphasizing the initial [ph]oneme in each word.

Wrap Up   DAY 4

Table Talk What are some ways people travel on [w]ater? Have children discuss the question.

Produce Language Have each child say a sentence about a [bo]at or other water transportation.

[To]day children should have:

☐ **Learned** and applied vocabulary related to ways to travel on water.

☐ **Spoken** complete sentences about how people travel on water.

☐ **Recognized** words that begin with /v/ and /z/.

ELA R1.14 Match all consonant and short-vowel sounds to appropriate letters. (ELD R.B10)

Preteach / Reteach

LS **Leveled Support** **Phonics**

① **Beginning** Hold up a card on which you have printed *Z*. Say: The name of this letter is *Z*. The sound for this letter is /z/. Have children echo you. Repeat for *V*.

② ③ **Early Intermediate/Intermediate** Read several words with /z/ and /v/ sounds. Ask children to clap when they hear a word that has the /z/ or /v/ sound.

④ ⑤ **Early Advanced/Advanced** Have children identify the letters that make the /z/ and /v/ sounds. Have children think of words that have the /v/ sound at the beginning and the /z/ sound at the beginning or end. They can sort the words, drawing pictures of them and labeling the pictures.

Where can you zip through town in a car?

✏️ **Circle** Circle *where.*

The driver knew where to go.

✏️ **Circle** Circle *Come.*

Come see the town.

To identify places in which you can drive a van throu[ ]
town; to introduce high frequency words *where* and [ ]

Concept Talk

Connect to Day 2 Where is your favorite place? [ ]

Introduce the Daily Question Ask: Where can [ ]
through town in a van? Have children name diffe[ ]
places in your town.

Use the Poster Use the Day 3 teaching notes.

Review Concept Vocabulary Review the word[ ]
introduced on Day 1.

Introduce High Frequency Word[ ]

Guide children to point to the word *where* in the [ ]
line. Say: This is the word *where.* Let's say the w[ ]
together: *where.* Now find and point to the word [ ]
in the sentence. Circle it. Help children complete [ ]
Worktext page.

Corrective Feedback If children have difficulty [ ]
the words, read the sentences slowly so that chi[ ]
pick out the high frequency words as they listen[ ]

Leveled Support · High Frequency Words

① **Beginning** Write the word *where.* Say This is the word *where.* Say the letters in *where* with me: w,h,e,r,e. Repeat with *come.*

② ③ **Early Intermediate/Intermediate** Write *where* and *come.* Say a word and have children point to the word. Then have children listen for the words in sentences, raising their hands when they hear the words.

④ ⑤ **Early Advanced/Advanced** Have children use the words *where* and *come* in a complete sentence.

Wrap Up **DA[ ]**

Table Talk Have children talk about what n[ ]
van different from a bus or train.

Produce Language Have each child say a sentence a[ ]
where you can drive a van through town.

Today children should have:

☑ **Learned** and applied the high frequency words w[ ]
come.

☑ **Spoken** complete sentences about driving a van t[ ]
town.

☑ **Recognized** high frequency words used in senten[ ]

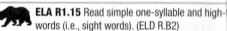 **ELA R1.15** Read simple one-syllable and high-[ ]
words (i.e., sight words). (ELD R.B2)

How do people around the world travel?

 Draw

ELA LS. 1.2 Share information and ideas, speaking audibly in complete, coherent sentences. (ELD LS.B3)

189

OBJECTIVE

To guide children to express their understanding of weekly concepts and vocabulary.

Think, Talk, and Recognize!

Concept Talk

Connect to Day 4 What are some ways people travel on water?

Review the Weekly Question Ask: How do people around the world travel? Ask the children if they always travel the same way.

Use the Poster Use the Day 5 teaching notes.

Review Concept Vocabulary Review the vocabulary introduced on Day 1.

Concept Wrap Up

Have children draw to answer the question: *How do people around the world travel?* Prompt discussion with the photo. This photo shows a city in Italy where people travel by boat rather than by car. How do people travel in other places in the world?

Leveled Support Concept Vocabulary

① **Beginning** Display the Word Cards for *water, land, air, airplane, trail, camel, ocean.* Say each word. Ask children to repeat and point to the matching card.

② ③ **Early Intermediate/Intermediate** Display the Word Cards for *water, land, air, airplane, trail, camel, ocean.* Ask children to say each word and point to the matching card.

④ ⑤ **Early Advanced/Advanced** Display the Word Cards for *water, land, air, airplane, trail, camel, ocean.* Ask children to tell a story using the words.

 Wrap Up   **DAY 5**

Table Talk How do people around the world travel? Have children discuss the question, using the vocabulary words they have learned this week.

Produce Language To build fluency, children can label, write about, or speak about their drawings. Ask children to respond to what they read or heard.

Today children should have:

☑ **Reviewed** the weekly concept and concept vocabulary.

☑ **Spoken** about forms of transportation people use around the world.

☑ **Drawn or written** about vehicles that are used all over the world for travel.

 ELA LS. 1.2 Share information and ideas, speaking audibly in complete, coherent sentences. (ELD LS.B3)

WEEK 6

CALIFORNIA

Weekly Lesson Plan

Last Week
Unit 5, Week 5
Ways to Travel

Question of the Week — How do children get to school?

	DAY 1 — Get Ready to Read	DAY 2 — Read and Comprehend
	Build Background	**Language: Category Words**

Instructional Plan and Materials

• **Word Cards**
110–115

• **Big Book**
One Morning in May

• **Song Book**, p. 30

• **Poster**
Poster 30 can be used at beginning or end of day.

Transparencies Explore content and vocabulary and model fluent reading.

For further information about using these components, see pages x–xv.

DAY 1 — Build Background

Preteach/Review 10–15 min
Poster, Song Book, Big Book
Leveled Support Preteach
Practice Stations Preteach

Teach 35–45 min
Concept Talk
Oral Vocabulary Routine
Word Cards
Build Concept Vocabulary
Daily Table Talk

Check/Reteach 5–10 min
Poster, Word Cards
Leveled Support Reteach

DAY 2 — Language: Category Words

Preteach/Review 10–15 min
Poster
Leveled Support Preteach
Practice Stations Review

Teach 35–45 min
Category Words
Daily Table Talk

Check/Reteach 5–10 min
Poster, Word Cards
Leveled Support Reteach

Fluency: Writing or Speaking

CALIFORNIA Standards

GK Sci 4.e Communicate observations orally and through drawings.

ELA LS 2.1 Describe people, places, things (e.g., size, color, shape), locations, and actions.

ELA R 1.17 Identify and sort common words in basic categories (e.g., colors, shapes, foods).

Academic Language

Category Words: countryside, farm, town, village

Get Online! www.pearsonsuccessnet.com

Concept Talk Video

Background Building Audio Slideshow

Ways to Get to School

DAY **3** FORM & FUNCTION Read and Comprehend	DAY **4** FORM & FUNCTION Language Arts	DAY **5** Language Arts
Language: High Frequency Words	**Phonics**	**Think, Talk, and Recognize**
Preteach/Review 10–15 min Poster **Leveled Support Preteach** **Practice Stations Review**	**Preteach/Review** 10–15 min Poster **Leveled Support Preteach** **Practice Stations Review**	**Preteach/Review** 10–15 min Poster **Leveled Support Preteach** **Practice Stations Review**
Teach 35–45 min **High Frequency Words** **Daily Table Talk**	**Teach** 35–45 min **Phonics** **Daily Table Talk**	**Teach** 15–20 min **Think, Talk, and Recognize** **Concept Wrap Up**
Check/Reteach 5–10 min Poster, Word Cards **Leveled Support Reteach**	**Check/Reteach** 5–10 min Poster, Word Cards **Leveled Support Reteach**	**Check/Reteach** 30–40 min Poster, Word Cards, Song Book **Leveled Support Reteach**
		Fluency: Writing or Speaking
ELA R 1.15 Read simple one-syllable and high frequency words (i.e., sight words).	**ELA R 1.14** Match all consonant and short-vowel sounds to appropriate letters.	**ELA LS 1.2** Share information and ideas, speaking audibly in complete, coherent sentences.
High Frequency Words: where, come		

Practice Stations

Materials and Activity

 DAY 1 Get Ready to Read

paper, crayons, colored pencils

Getting to School

Have children draw pictures of how they get to school. When the pictures are complete, children can label them with a word or two about the picture. Have children compare their pictures with classmates.

 DAY 2 Read and Comprehend

vocabulary words written on index cards

Match Game

Say the meaning of one of the vocabulary words aloud and the first letter in that word. Children work together to find the correct vocabulary word card to the definition. Continue until children have matched all words.

train

Preteach/Reteach

Transfer and Common Misconceptions

Extra Syllable

Some Spanish speakers may add the extra syllable "eh" before school, producing *eh school.*

The Letters ll

Some children may want to pronounce the *ll* in village as /y/, which is the way *ll* is pronounced in Spanish.

Produce Language

Weekly Concept and Language Goal

CONCEPT GOALS

- understand that children around the world travel to school in different ways
- name places where children can walk to school
- describe unusual ways to get to school, such as riding a yak

By Day 5, children should be able to write a one-word label or a sentence.

Daily Table Talk

❶ **Beginning**

Children pantomime while you provide the language.

❷ ❸ **Early Intermediate/Intermediate**

Children pantomime and say a word or phrase.

❹ ❺ **Intermediate/Early Advanced**

Children say a sentence while pantomiming.

 **Daily Table Talk**

❶ **Beginning**

Children talk about their drawings.

❷ ❸ **Early Intermediate/Intermediate**

Children write one-word labels.

❹ ❺ **Intermediate/Early Advanced**

Children write a phrase or sentence.

DAY 3 FORM & FUNCTION Read and Comprehend

 DAY 4 FORM & FUNCTION Language Arts

DAY 5 Language Arts

category words written on index cards, paper, crayons, colored pencils

cut-out paragraphs from children's magazines, word cards for *where, come*

index cards with these words: *yellow, yak, yard, yo-yo, queen, quilt, quiet, quack*

Places to Live

Have children choose one of the category words to illustrate. When the pictures are complete, have children who chose the same word discuss and compare their pictures. Put the illustrations together. Have children decorate a cover for the new "Places to Live" book.

Word Search

Give partners a set of word cards and have them read the words. Then have them look for the words in paragraphs and circle the words that they find.

Where do penguins live?

Letter Sort

Have children sort the word cards into two groups. The first group of words begins with /y/ and the second group begins with /qu/.

The Word *where*

Some children will have trouble with the sound /âr/ in *where*, which is an uncommon sound in many languages, including Spanish, Cantonese, Vietnamese, Hmong, and Korean.

The Letters *qu*

Spanish speakers may pronounce these letters as /k/, which is how they are pronounced together in Spanish.

Articles

Some children may omit articles, such as *a* and *the*, when speaking. Languages such as Cantonese, Hmong, Korean, Vietnamese, either have no articles or do not differentiate between *a* and *the*.

Daily Table Talk

❶ **Beginning**
Name different ways to get to school and have children answer yes or no.

❷ ❸ **Early Intermediate/Intermediate**
Phrase: by bus, by car

❹ ❺ **Intermediate/Early Advanced**
Sentence: I take a bus to school.

Daily Table Talk

❶ **Beginning**
Name different means of transportation for getting to school and have children answer yes or no.

❷ ❸ **Early Intermediate/Intermediate**
Phrase: by bike

❹ ❺ **Intermediate/Early Advanced**
Sentence: I would ride my bike to school.

Daily Table Talk

❶ **Beginning** Child speaks about the drawing and may write a label

❷ ❸ **Early Intermediate/Intermediate** Child writes a label that includes a concept vocabulary word.

❹ ❺ **Intermediate/Early Advanced** Child writes a label or sentence that includes a vocabulary word.

To introduce and discuss concepts and vocabulary related to how children around the world get to school.

Build Background Get **Ready** to **Read!**

Question of the Week

How do children get to school?

www.pearsonsuccessnet.com

Concept Talk

Use the Big Book If you haven't introduced the Big Book, consider reading it to children. Connect to the unit theme, Transportation—Going Places.

Introduce the Weekly Concept Tell children that today they will talk about how children around the world get to school. Ask the weekly question: How do children get to school?

Use the Poster Direct children's attention to the weekly poster. Use the Day 1 teaching notes at the bottom of the poster.

Sing the Song Use the song **Go To School** to build understanding of the weekly concept. Have children sing or simply chant the words with you.

Use a Transparency Use the Classification Map (Transparency 3) to help children classify different kinds of transportation.

Ways to Get to School

Vocabulary

bicycles

radio

train

bus
car
school

190

How do children get to school?

Vocabulary

bicycles vehicles with two wheels that you sit on and cause to move by pushing the pedals with your feet

radio a piece of electronic equipment that you use to listen to music or programs that are broadcast

train a long vehicle that travels along a railroad carrying people or goods

bus a large vehicle that people travel in

car a vehicle with four wheels and an engine, used by a small number of people traveling from one place to another

school a place where children are taught

 ELA R 1.18 Describe common objects and events in both general and specific language. (ELD R.B4)

191

Introduce Concept Vocabulary

1. **Say the Word** Display the Word Card as you say *school.* Have children repeat the word.

2. **Introduce Word Meaning** Ask questions about school: What do you do at school? What is your favorite thing about school?

3. **Demonstrate** Have children draw a picture of themselves doing something at school.

4. **Apply** Have children demonstrate their understanding.

Repeat with other vocabulary words.

Corrective Feedback If children have difficulty understanding the vocabulary words, use additional pictures or role play the meaning of each word.

Concept Work

Name each kind of transportation, having children point to it. Then point to transportation methods as children name them. Have children color the pictures.

Leveled Support   Vocabulary in Context

❶ Beginning Point to the pictures on the Worktext page. Say the word for each picture as children point, and have them echo each word.

❷ ❸ Early Intermediate/Intermediate Do the Beginning activity, but have children say the words themselves. Give help if needed.

❹ ❺ Early Advanced/Advanced Ask children to draw a picture showing how they get to school. Have them label the picture with vocabulary words.

Wrap Up   DAY 1

  How do children get to school? Have children answer the question, using the vocabulary words.

Produce Language Ask each child to act out something they do on their way to school and say a sentence about it.

Today children should have:

☑ **Learned** and applied vocabulary related to traveling to school.

☑ **Spoken** complete sentences about how children around the world get to school.

☑ **Recognized** concept vocabulary words.

 ELA LS 2.1 Describe people, places, things (e.g. size, color, shape), locations, and actions. (ELD R.B2)

191

To identify places where children can walk to school; to introduce category words for places to live.

Concept Talk

Connect to Day 1 How do children get to school?

Introduce the Daily Question Ask: Where can we walk to school? Have children answer the question orally.

Use the Poster Use the Day 2 teaching notes.

Introduce Category Words

1. **Say the Word** Have children point to the farm. Say the word and have children repeat after you.

2. **Introduce Word Meaning** Ask questions: Have you ever been to a farm? What animals live on a farm?

3. **Demonstrate** Role play some animals you might see on a farm.

4. **Apply** Repeat with other vocabulary words and elicit that they all belong to the category "places to live."

Have children point to items as you name them. Then have them draw a place where they would most like to live.

Corrective Feedback If children have difficulty identifying the correct place, point to the picture, say the word aloud, and have children repeat it. Ask questions that allow children to compare and contrast the places. Ask them, for example, how a farm is different from a town.

Wrap Up   DAY 2

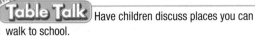
Daily **Table Talk** Have children discuss places you can walk to school.

Produce Language To build fluency, encourage children to label or write a sentence about their drawings. They can share the writing with partners.

Today children should have:

☑ **Learned** and applied vocabulary related to places to live.

☑ **Spoken** complete sentences about where children can walk to school.

☑ **Recognized** words that belong in the same category.

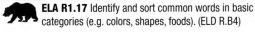
ELA R1.17 Identify and sort common words in basic categories (e.g. colors, shapes, foods). (ELD R.B4)

192 Ways to Get to School • Unit 5, Week 6

Places to Live

Picture Dictionary

countryside

farm

town

village

 Draw Draw a place to live.

192 **ELA R1.17** Identify and sort common words in basic categories (e.g., colors, shapes, foods). (ELD R.B4)

LS Leveled Support Category Words
Preteach / Reteach

① **Beginning** Have children point to each place on the Worktext page as you say it. Have children echo the word.

② ③ **Early Intermediate/Intermediate** Say the name of a place to live. Have children point to it. Then reverse the activity.

④ ⑤ **Early Advanced/Advanced** Have children tell a partner where they would like to live using the category words.

Did you ever ride a quiet yak to school?

🖊 **Circle** Circle *where*.

The yak goes where she goes.

🖊 **Circle** Circle *come*.

We come to school.

ELA R1.15 Read simple one-syllable and high-frequency words (i.e., sight words). (ELD R.B2)

193

To discuss the concept of riding a yak to school; to introduce high frequency words *where* and *come*.

Concept Talk FORM & FUNCTION

Connect to Day 2 Where can we walk to school?

Introduce the Daily Question Ask: Did you ever ride a quiet yak to school? Be sure that children understand what a yak is. Have children talk about where in the world children can ride a yak to school.

Use the Poster Use the Day 3 teaching notes.

Review Concept Vocabulary Review the words introduced on Day 1.

Introduce High Frequency Words

Guide children to point to the word *where* in the direction line. Say: This is the word *where*. Let's say the word together: *where*. Now find and point to the word *where* in the sentence. Circle it. Help children complete the Worktext page.

Corrective Feedback If children have difficulty with the high frequency words, write the sentences on the board or chart paper. Give children index cards with the high frequency words on them, and have them match the words on the cards to the words in the sentences.

Leveled Support — High Frequency Words

Preteach / Reteach

① **Beginning** Write the word *where*. Say: This is the word *where*. Say the letters in *where* with me: *w,h,e,r,e.* Repeat with *come*.

② ③ **Early Intermediate/Intermediate** Write *where* and *come* on index cards, one word on each side. Have children listen for the words as you say sentences. They can hold up the side of the card corresponding to the word they hear.

④ ⑤ **Early Advanced/Advanced** Write *where* and *come*. Have children say sentences using these words. Write their sentences. Have children circle the high frequency word in each sentence.

Wrap Up DAY **3**

Table Talk (Daily) Have children discuss what it would be like to ride a yak to school.

Produce Language Have each child talk about where a child would ride a quiet yak to school.

Today children should have:

☑ **Learned** and applied the high frequency words *where* and *come*.

☑ **Spoken** complete sentences about where a child would ride a yak to school.

☑ **Recognized** high frequency words in sentences.

ELA R1.15 Read simple one-syllable and high-frequency words (i.e., sight words). (ELD R.B2)

To discuss how children would like to get to school; to identify the sounds /y/ and /kw/.

Concept Talk

FORM & FUNCTION

Connect to Day 3 Did you ever ride a quiet yak to school?

Introduce the Daily Question Ask: If you could choose, how would you get to school? Name various ways to get to school and have children raise their hands when they hear their choice.

Use the Poster Use the Day 4 teaching notes.

Phonics

Identify /y/ and /kw/ Write the word *yak.* Say: Say this word with me: *yak.* What sound do you hear at the beginning of *yak*? What letter makes the /y/ sound in this word? Yes, *y* makes in the /y/ sound in many words. Now listen for /y/ in other words. Circle words with the sound. Repeat for *qu* and help children complete the Worktext page.

Corrective Feedback If children have difficulty identifying the initial sound, read each word again, separating the phonemes and emphasizing the initial phoneme in each word.

Identify Sounds Yy and Qu

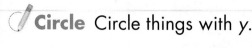

✎ Circle Circle things with *y.*

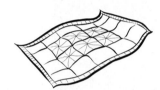

✎ Circle Circle things with *qu.*

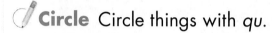

194 **ELA R1.14** Match all consonant and short-vowel sounds to appropriate letters. (ELD R.B10)

Preteach LS Reteach Leveled Support Phonics

① **Beginning** Say the words on the Worktext page. Ask children to raise their hands when they hear /y/ or /kw/.

②③ **Early Intermediate/Intermediate** Tell children you will read several words and they should listen for /y/. When you say a word that begins with /y/, children should take a step forward and repeat the word. Repeat the activity for *qu.*

④⑤ **Early Advanced/Advanced** Write the word *yak* and have children identify the first sound in the word. Ask children to name other words that begin with the /y/ sound spelled *y.* Repeat with *qu* and *queen.* Provide other words for children to sort.

Wrap Up   DAY 4

Daily **Table Talk** If you could choose, how would you get to school? Have children discuss the question.

Produce Language Have each child say a sentence about how they would choose to get to school.

Today children should have:

☑ **Learned** and applied vocabulary related to how they would like to get to school.

☑ **Spoken** complete sentences about how they would like to get to school.

☑ **Recognized** words with sounds /y/ and /kw/.

 ELA R1.14 Match sounds to appropriate letters. (ELD R.B10)

How do children get to school?

✏️ **Draw**

 ELA LS. 1.2 Share information and ideas, speaking audibly in complete, coherent sentences. (ELD LS.B3)

195

OBJECTIVE

To guide children to express their understanding of weekly concepts and vocabulary.

Think, Talk, and Recognize!

Concept Talk

Connect to Day 4 If you could choose, how would you get to school?

Review the Weekly Question Ask: How do children get to school? Ask the children if they always travel to school the same way.

Use the Poster Use the Day 5 teaching notes.

Review Concept Vocabulary Review the vocabulary introduced on Day 1.

Concept Wrap-Up

Have children draw to answer the question: *How do children get to school?* Discuss the photo with children before they draw. Ask children where in the world children might get to school this way.

Leveled Support Concept Vocabulary

Preteach / Reteach

➊ **Beginning** Display the Word Cards for *school, bus, car, train, bicycles, radio.* Say each word. Ask children to repeat and point to the matching card.

➋ ➌ **Early Intermediate/Intermediate** Display the Word Cards for *school, bus, car, train, bicycles, radio.* Describe a word in a phrase or sentence. Ask children to point to the word that you are describing.

➍ ➎ **Early Advanced/Advanced** Display the Word Cards for *school, bus, car, train, bicycles, radio.* Ask children to work in pairs to choose a word and then use the word in a sentence that tells about a way to get to school.

Wrap Up   DAY 5

Table Talk Daily How do children get to school? Have children discuss the question, using the vocabulary words they have learned this week.

Produce Language To build fluency, children can label, write about, or speak about their drawings. Ask children to respond to what they read or heard.

Today children should have:

☑ **Reviewed** the weekly concept and concept vocabulary.

☑ **Spoken** about forms of transportation children around the world use to get to school.

☑ **Drawn or written** about ways that children can get to school.

🐻 **ELA LS. 1.2** Share information and ideas, speaking audibly in complete, coherent sentences. (ELD LS.B3)

195

THE BIG ? What are different ways of building?

Discuss the Big Question

Read and discuss the unit question. Introduce the word *building.* When we build something, we put parts together to make something. Have you ever built anything? What was it? What parts did you use? What tools did you use?

Have children use the pictures along the side of the page to preview the weekly concepts for this unit. Read the weekly questions together. Discuss the weekly questions and how they relate to the big question.

Get Online! www.pearsonsuccessnet.com

• Unit 6 Big Question Video

CONCEPT/ LANGUAGE GOALS

Use the Concept and Language Goals throughout the unit to develop the big idea.

Children develop concepts and language as they talk about, use, and practice:

• Concept Vocabulary
• Academic Language
• Language Forms and Functions
• Category Words
• High Frequency Words

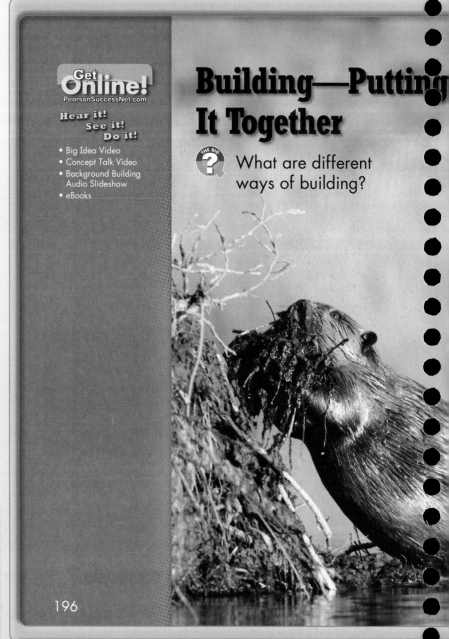

Get Online!
PearsonSuccessNet.com

Hear it!
See it!
Do it!

• Big Idea Video
• Concept Talk Video
• Background Building Audio Slideshow
• eBooks

Building—Putting It Together

THE BIG ? What are different ways of building?

196

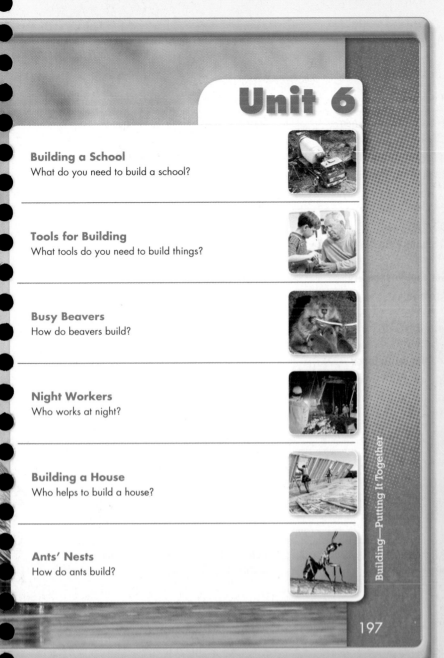

Unit 6

Building a School
What do you need to build a school?

Tools for Building
What tools do you need to build things?

Busy Beavers
How do beavers build?

Night Workers
Who works at night?

Building a House
Who helps to build a house?

Ants' Nests
How do ants build?

Building—Putting It Together

197

Read Aloud

Read the **Big Book** *Yoko Builds a Birdhouse.* Prompt discussion about the book.

- What materials does Yoko need to build the birdhouse? What tools does Yoko need?
- What is the last thing that Yoko does to build her birdhouse?
- What is something that you would like to build? What materials would you need? What tools would you use?

For more read alouds related to the theme, see the Big Book Anthology.

Unit Project: Building

After discussing the unit question, provide children with materials to make their own birdhouses following the steps in the **Big Book**. You may substitute black markers for shoe polish. This week you will make your own bird house. You will work with a group to make your birdhouse. You may also use the materials to build something you like, such as a house or place for another animal to live.

Group children of mixed abilities to encourage participation. Have children work together to build their birdhouses or other constructions. Display the finished buildings and have children talk about the steps they took from start to finish. Hang the birdhouses outside and observe them to see if birds make homes in them.

WEEK 1

CALIFORNIA

Weekly Lesson Plan

Last Week
Unit 5, Week 6
Ways to Get to School

Question of the Week
What do you need to build a school?

DAY 1 — Get Ready to Read

Build Background

Preteach/Review 10–15 min
Poster, Song Book, Big Book
- **Leveled Support Preteach**
- **Practice Stations Preteach**

Teach 35–45 min
- **Concept Talk**
- **Oral Vocabulary Routine**
  Word Cards
- **Build Concept Vocabulary**
- **Daily Table Talk**

Check/Reteach 5–10 min
Poster, Word Cards
- **Leveled Support Reteach**

DAY 2 — Read and Comprehend

Language: Category Words

Preteach/Review 10–15 min
Poster
- **Leveled Support Preteach**
- **Practice Stations Review**

Teach 35–45 min
- **Category Words**
- **Daily Table Talk**

Check/Reteach 5–10 min
Poster, Word Cards
- **Leveled Support Reteach**

Fluency: Writing or Speaking

Instructional Plan and Materials

pipes

Yoko Builds a Birdhouse

- **Word Cards**
  116–118

- **Big Book**
  Yoko Builds a Birdhouse

- **Poster**
  Poster 31 can be used at beginning or end of day.

- **Song Book**, p. 31

Transparencies Explore content and vocabulary and model fluent reading.

For further information about using these components, see pages x–xv.

CALIFORNIA Standards

GK Sci 4.e Communicate observations orally and through drawings.

ELA LS 2.3 Relate an experience or creative story in a logical sequence.

ELA R 1.17 Identify and sort common words in basic categories (e.g., colors, shapes, foods).

Academic Language

Category Words: bricks, cement, steel, wood

Get Online! www.pearsonsuccessnet.com

Concept Talk Video

Background Building Audio Slideshow

Building a School

DAY 3 · FORM & FUNCTION Read and Comprehend	DAY 4 · FORM & FUNCTION Language Arts	DAY 5 Language Arts
Language: High Frequency Words	**Phonics**	**Think, Talk, and Recognize**
Preteach/Review 10–15 min	**Preteach/Review** 10–15 min	**Preteach/Review** 10–15 min
Poster	Poster	Poster
Leveled Support Preteach	**Leveled Support Preteach**	**Leveled Support Preteach**
Practice Stations Review	**Practice Stations Review**	**Practice Stations Review**
Teach 35–45 min	**Teach** 35–45 min	**Teach** 15–20 min
High Frequency Words	**Phonics**	**Think, Talk, and Recognize**
Phonemic Awareness	**Daily Table Talk**	**Concept Wrap Up**
Daily Table Talk		
	Check/Reteach 5–10 min	**Check/Reteach** 30–40 min
Check/Reteach 5–10 min	Poster, Word Cards	Poster, Word Cards, Song Book
Poster, Word Cards	**Leveled Support Reteach**	**Leveled Support Reteach**
Leveled Support Reteach		
		Fluency: Writing or Speaking
ELA R 1.15 Read simple one-syllable and high frequency words (i.e., sight words).	**ELA R 1.14** Match all consonant and short-vowel sounds to appropriate letters.	**ELA LS 1.2** Share information and ideas, speaking audibly in complete, coherent sentences.
High Frequency Words: he, a, to, look, the, go		

Practice Stations

Materials and Activity

DAY 1   Get Ready to Read

classroom blocks, drawing paper, crayons

Building Together 👥

Have each pair work together to make a school building with building blocks. Have them talk about what their building looks like. Then discuss other features of a school building—windows, lights, pipes, and so on. Have children draw pictures of what they built.

DAY 2   Read and Comprehend

picture cards for *pipes, wires, spills;* drawing paper; drawing materials

School Building 👥

Have partners look at each picture, say the word, and describe what they see. Then have children talk about where they see pipes, wires, and spills at their school. Have each pair work together to draw a picture of where they see these things at their school.

Preteach/Reteach

Transfer and Common Misconceptions

Syntactic Order

For Korean speakers, the most common syntactic order is subject-object-verb. Provide many opportunities for Korean speakers to practice subject-verb-object order in short sentences.

Plurals

Children are likely to be familiar with plurals from their own languages. Have children think about how their own language changes a word from *one* to *more than one.* Help children connect this language rule to the way plurals are formed in English.

Produce Language

Weekly Concept and Language Goal

CONCEPT GOALS

- describe what it would be like to build a school
- name the people who might help build a school
- describe the machines and materials needed for building a school

By Day 5, children should be able to write a one-word label or a sentence.

Daily Table Talk

❶ **Beginning**
> Children point to items in the SE while you provide the language.

❷ ❸ **Early Intermediate/Intermediate**
> Words or Phrases: workers, machines

❹ ❺ **Early Advanced/Advanced**
> Sentence: Workers need machines.

Daily Table Talk

❶ **Beginning**
> Children talk about their drawings.

❷ ❸ **Early Intermediate/Intermediate**
> Children write one-word labels.

❹ ❺ **Early Advanced/Advanced**
> Children write a phrase or sentence.

FORM & FUNCTION

DAY 3   Read and Comprehend

FORM & FUNCTION

DAY 4   Language Arts

DAY 5   Language Arts

---

mural paper, markers, old magazines, glue, scissors

two sets of cards with these words for each player: *he, a, to, look, the,* and *go*

index cards with these words: *man, mat, bat, can, fan, tap, bit, lit, big, lip, fit,* and *tip*

More Materials

Label four sections of the mural paper: *wood, bricks, steel,* and *cement.* Read the words together. Have children find pictures in magazines of things made from these materials. Children glue the pictures in the matching section.

It's a Snap!

Each player places the cards in a stack, face down. Children play "Snap" by each turning over the top card. When someone turns over a card that matches a card already face up, the player says "snap!" The first player to say "snap" collects all of the cards and reads the word. Play resumes until someone collects all of the cards.

Sound Sort

Have children sort the word cards into two groups. The first group of words has the /a/ sound and the second group has the /i/ sound. After the cards are sorted, children read or repeat the words.

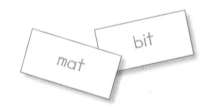

Modifiers

In Spanish, adjectives follow nouns. For example, Spanish speakers might say "bulldozer big" rather than "big bulldozer." Model correct placement of English modifiers.

Articles

Articles such as *a* and *an* are not used by Russian speakers. Using articles may be challenging for Russian-speaking children who are learning English.

Vowel Sounds

The Spanish language does not use the /a/ sound. The letter *a* can represent the /o/ sound. Children may say *top* instead of *tap.* Model the correct /a/ sound and emphasize how your jaw drops when you say /a/.

Daily Table Talk

① **Beginning** Point to pictures of machines in the Worktext. Say the name of each and have children repeat it.

② ③ **Early Intermediate/Intermediate** Words and phrases: cement truck, big bulldozer

④ ⑤ **Early Advanced/Advanced** Sentence: Cement is mixed in a big cement truck.

Daily Table Talk

① **Beginning** Children look at Vocabulary Cards for pipes and wires. They point and say each word.

② ③ **Early Intermediate/Intermediate** Words: wires, pipes, windows

④ ⑤ **Early Advanced/Advanced** Sentence: Workers use pipes to build a school.

Daily Table Talk

① **Beginning** Child speaks about the drawing and may write a label.

② ③ **Early Intermediate/Intermediate** Child writes a label that includes a concept vocabulary word.

④ ⑤ **Early Advanced/Advanced** Child writes a label or sentence that includes a vocabulary word.

To introduce and discuss concepts and vocabulary related to building a school.

Build Background

Get Ready to Read!

Question of the Week

What do you need to build a school?

www.pearsonsuccessnet.com

Concept Talk

Use the Big Book Connect the Big Book to the unit theme, Building—Putting It Together. Display the cover and discuss the picture. Then read the book aloud.

Introduce the Weekly Concept Ask children to describe the outside of the school building. Tell children that today they will talk about how a school is built. Ask the weekly question: What do you need to build a school?

Use the Poster Direct children's attention to the weekly poster. Use the Day 1 teaching notes at the bottom of the poster.

Sing the Song Use the song **What Do You Need?** to reinforce children's understanding of the weekly concept. Have the children sing or simply chant the words with you.

Use a Transparency Use the Realistic Fiction Transparency (Transparency 19) to share a story about a new school.

Building a School

Vocabulary

pipes

spills

wires

198

Vocabulary

pipes tubes through which a liquid or gas flows

spills flows from or falls out of a container, usually accidentally

wires metal that is long and thin like thread

ELA R 1.18 Describe common objects and events in both general and specific language. (ELD R.B4)

199

Introduce Concept Vocabulary

1. **Say the Word** Display the Word Card as you say *spills*. Have children repeat the word.

2. **Introduce Word Meaning** Ask questions about what happens when something spills. What happens when water spills? What do you do after something spills?

3. **Demonstrate** Fill a small cup with water and place it in a pan. Then tip the cup so that the water spills. Ask a volunteer to clean up the water with a paper towel.

4. **Apply** Have children demonstrate their understanding.

Repeat with other vocabulary words.

Corrective Feedback If children have difficulty pronouncing the vocabulary words, have them listen to separate phonemes, and then combine the phonemes to say the word. Have the children repeat the word after you.

Concept Work

Ask children to point to the pictures of the unfinished building, the worker laying the new floor, and the electrician installing the lights. Have children explain what is happening in each picture. Talk about the materials that the workers are using, such as cement, bricks, pipes, tiles, wires, and lights. Have children circle the materials that the workers are using.

 Leveled Support **Vocabulary in Context**

Preteach *Reteach*

① Beginning Have children point to the pictures of pipes, wires, and something that spills on the Worktext page. Say the word for each picture as children point. Then have them repeat the word.

② ③ Early Intermediate/Intermediate Say the word *pipes* and have children repeat it. Then have them point to a picture of pipes on the Worktext page. Continue with the other vocabulary words.

④ ⑤ Early Advanced/Advanced Draw a picture of *pipes, wires,* and something that *spills* on index cards. Turn the cards over and ask a child to choose a card. Have the child say a sentence describing what he or she sees.

Wrap Up   **DAY 1**

Table Talk *Daily* What do you need to build a school? Have children answer the question, using the vocabulary words.

Produce Language Have children point to things in your classroom that show what is needed to build a school, such as tiles, cement walls, lights, and so on. Have children say a sentence about what they see.

Today children should have:

☑ **Learned** and applied vocabulary related to building a school.

☑ **Spoken** complete sentences about what you need to build a school.

☑ **Recognized** concept vocabulary.

 ELA LS 2.3 Relate an experience or creative story in a logical sequence. (ELD LS.B3)

OBJECTIVE

To discuss who uses materials to build a school; to introduce category words for building materials.

Concept Talk

Connect to Day 1 Recall with children that yesterday they talked about materials that are used for building a school. What do you need to build a school?

Introduce the Daily Question Who helps to build a school? Have children answer orally.

Use the Poster Use the Day 2 teaching notes.

Introduce Category Words

1. **Say the Word** Have children point to the wood. Point to something in the room that is made out of wood as you say the word. Repeat so children can say it with you.

2. **Introduce Word Meaning** What does wood feel like? What things are made from wood?

3. **Demonstrate** Look for things in your classroom that are made from wood. Have children categorize items: things that are made from wood, things that are not made from wood.

4. **Apply** Repeat with other vocabulary words, and point out that they are all materials used for building.

Have children draw lines to match the materials and the buildings.

Corrective Feedback If children have difficulty matching the materials and the buildings, say the names of the materials. Point out the materials on the buildings.

Wrap Up

DAY **2**

Table Talk Who helps to build a school? What materials do we use for building? Have children discuss the questions.

Produce Language To build fluency, encourage children to label or write a sentence about a building they know and the material it is made of. They can share their writing with partners.

Today children should have:

☑ **Learned** and applied vocabulary related to building materials.

☑ **Spoken** complete sentences about people who help to build a school.

☑ **Recognized** words that belong in the same category.

 ELA R1.17 Identify and sort common words in basic categories (e.g., colors, shapes, foods). (EDL R.B4)

Building Materials

Picture Dictionary

bricks

cement

steel

wood

Match Match building materials.

200 ELA R1.17 Identify and sort common words in basic categories (e.g., colors, shapes, foods). (ELD R.B4)

Leveled Support Category Words

Preteach / Reteach

❶ **Beginning** Have children point to each building material on the Worktext page. Say the word for each picture. Then have children say the word with you.

❷ ❸ **Early Intermediate/Intermediate** Give a clue about each picture, such as: I see a sidewalk. Have children point to the picture and say the building material with you: cement.

❹ ❺ **Early Advanced/Advanced** Have partners look at a classroom picture book and find things made from wood, bricks, steel, or cement. Have them talk about what they see.

What machines can help build a school?

✎ **Circle** Circle *He*. Circle *a*. Circle *to*.
He uses a bulldozer to move dirt.

✎ **Circle** Circle *Look*. Circle *the*. Circle *go*.
Look at the truck go!

 **ELA R1.15** Read simple one-syllable and high-frequency words (i.e., sight words). (ELD R.B2)

201

Leveled Support High Frequency Words

1 Beginning Write the words *he, a, to, look, the,* and *go* and read the words together. Say a word and ask a volunteer to point to the words.

2 3 Early Intermediate/Intermediate Write the words *he, a, to, look, the,* and *go*. Read the words together. Then have children use each word in a sentence.

4 5 Early Advanced/Advanced Write the words *he, a, to, look, the,* and *go* on index cards. Give a card to each child and have him or her read the word. Then say one of the words in a sentence, emphasizing the high frequency word. Children stand if they are holding the matching card and repeat the word. Redistribute the cards and continue.

OBJECTIVE

To discuss machines used to build a school; to review the high frequency words *look, the, go;* to blend three or four phonemes in a word.

Concept Talk   FORM & FUNCTION

Connect to Day 2 Remind children that yesterday they talked about building materials. Who helps to build a school?

Introduce the Daily Question What machines are used to build a school? Discuss why machines are necessary to build a large building.

Use the Poster Use the Day 3 teaching notes.

Review Concept Vocabulary Review the words introduced on Day 1.

Introduce High Frequency Words

Review *he, look,* and *go* by saying a sentence and having children follow a direction, such as: *Look at the door.* Read the sentences on the Worktext page. Have children repeat the sentences and circle the words.

Phonemic Awareness

Sound Blending Have children listen to a sequence of separate phonemes and then have them combine the phonemes to say the word. Say /l/ /ù/ /k/. Children blend and say the word: *look.* Repeat with *wood* and *steel.*

Corrective Feedback For children who have difficulty blending longer words, review blending words with two phonemes, such as *go.*

Wrap Up DAY **3**

Table Talk What machines help to build a school? What jobs do the machines do? Have partners discuss the questions.

Produce Language Have children draw a picture of a machine that helps to build a school. Help children to label their pictures. Then have partners describe their pictures.

Today children should have:

☑ **Reviewed** and applied the high frequency words *he, a, to, look, the,* and *go.*

☑ **Spoken** complete sentences about machines that help to build a school.

☑ **Recognized** phonemes in words as they blended them.

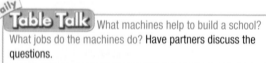 **ELA R.1.15** Read simple one-syllable and high-frequency words (i.e., sight words). (ELD R.B2)

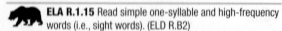

OBJECTIVE

To discuss what materials are needed to build a school; to reteach /a/, /i/.

Concept Talk

FORM & FUNCTION

Connect to Day 3 Elicit from children that yesterday they talked about what machines are needed to build a school.

Introduce the Daily Question What materials are needed to build a school? Ask children to think about their school as they name materials that were used to build it.

Use the Poster Use the Day 4 teaching notes.

Phonics

Sounds /a/ and /i/ Write *a* and have children identify the letter. Say *sat* and *hot.* Ask children which word has the /a/ sound. Then say each picture word and have children repeat the words. Have them complete the exercise on the Worktext page. Continue with the sound /i/.

Corrective Feedback For children having difficulty recognizing the /a/ and /i/ sounds, isolate the phonemes in each word in the Worktext. Remind children that the sounds may appear in the middle of the words rather than the beginnings.

Wrap Up DAY 4

Daily **Table Talk** What materials are needed to build a school? Have partners discuss the question.

Produce Language Have children draw a picture of their school. Help them to label some of the materials that were needed to build the school. Then have partners talk about their pictures, using complete sentences.

Today children should have:

☑ **Learned** and applied vocabulary related to building materials.

☑ **Spoken** complete sentences about building materials.

☑ **Recognized** the sounds /a/ and /i/.

ELA R.1.14 Match all consonant and short-vowel sounds to appropriate letters. (ELD R.B10)

Identify Sounds Aa and Ii

✏ **Circle** Circle things with *a.*

✏ **Circle** Circle things with *i.*

202 ELA R1.14 Match all consonant and short-vowel sounds to appropriate letters. (ELD R.B10)

Preteach / Reteach LS **Leveled Support Phonics**

① **Beginning** Say *hat* and *can,* emphasizing the /a/ sound. Write the letter *a* and have children repeat the words. Repeat with words for /i/.

② ③ **Early Intermediate/Intermediate** Write the letters *a* and *i* on each side of an index card. Say the following words and have children display the letter that matches the sound: *cat, hit, bin, Dan, tip, map, sick, nap.*

④ ⑤ **Early Advanced/Advanced** Write the letter *a* and have children make the /a/ sound with you. Ask children to think of words with that sound and make a list. Repeat with *i* and /i/. Then read the words and have children repeat them.

What do you need to build a school?

✏ Draw

 ELA LS. 1.2 *Share information and ideas, speaking audibly in complete, coherent sentences. (ELD LS.B3)*

203

To guide children to express their understanding of weekly concepts and vocabulary.

Think, Talk, and Recognize!

Concept Talk

Connect to Day 4 Remind children that yesterday they discussed what materials are needed to build a school.

Review the Weekly Question What do you need to build a school? Model how to use complete sentences to answer the question.

Use the Poster Use the Day 5 teaching notes.

Review Concept Vocabulary Review the vocabulary introduced on Day 1.

Concept Wrap Up

Have children draw in the Worktext to answer the question: *What do you need to build a school?* Discuss the picture of the construction site. What materials are needed? What do the workers do? How do the machines help?

Preteach LS Leveled Support Concept Vocabulary
Reteach

① **Beginning** Display the Word Cards for *pipes*, *wires*, and *spills*. Say each word. Ask children to repeat and point to the matching card.

② ③ **Early Intermediate/Intermediate** Write the word *pipes* and say it with the children. Ask them to describe where they have seen pipes at school. Continue with real-life examples of *wires* and *spills*.

④ ⑤ **Early Advanced/Advanced** Write the words *pipes*, *spills*, and *wires* on index cards. Have pairs each choose a card and use the card to speak or write a caption for an illustration on pp. 198–199.

Wrap Up   **DAY**

What do you need to build a school? Have children discuss the question, using the vocabulary words they have learned this week.

Produce Language To build fluency, children can label, write about, or speak about their drawings. Ask children to respond to what they read or heard.

Today children should have:

☑ **Reviewed** the weekly concept and concept vocabulary.

☑ **Spoken** about the materials needed to build a school.

☑ **Drawn or written** about materials that are needed to build a school.

 ELA LS. 1.2 *Share information and ideas, speaking audibly in complete, coherent sentences. (ELD LS.B1)*

203

WEEK 2
CALIFORNIA
Weekly Lesson Plan

Last Week
Unit 6, Week 1
Building a School

Question of the Week
What tools do you need to build things?

DAY 1 — Get Ready to Read

DAY 2 — Read and Comprehend

	DAY 1 Get Ready to Read	**DAY 2** Read and Comprehend
Instructional Plan and Materials    • **Word Cards** 119–125 • **Big Book** Yoko Builds a Birdhouse • **Poster** Poster 32 can be used at beginning or end of day. • **Song Book**, p. 32 **Transparencies** Explore content and vocabulary and model fluent reading. For further information about using these components, see pages x–xv.	**Build Background** **Preteach/Review** 10–15 min Poster, Song Book, Big Book **Leveled Support Preteach** **Practice Stations Preteach** **Teach** 35–45 min **Concept Talk** **Oral Vocabulary Routine** Word Cards **Build Concept Vocabulary** **Daily Table Talk** **Check/Reteach** 5–10 min Poster, Word Cards **Leveled Support Reteach**	**Language: Category Words** **Preteach/Review** 10–15 min Poster **Leveled Support Preteach** **Practice Stations Review** **Teach** 35–45 min **Category Words** **Daily Table Talk** **Check/Reteach** 5–10 min Poster, Word Cards **Leveled Support Reteach** **Fluency:** Writing or Speaking
CALIFORNIA Standards **GK Sci 4.e** Communicate observations orally and through drawings.	**ELA LS 2.3** Relate an experience or creative story in a logical sequence.	**ELA R 1.17** Identify and sort common words in basic categories (e.g., colors, shapes, foods).
Academic Language		**Category Words:** cow, goat, rooster, sheep
 **Get Online!** www.pearsonsuccessnet.com	**Concept Talk Video**	**Background Building Audio Slideshow**

This Week
Unit 6, Week 2

Tools for Building

Next Week
Unit 6, Week 3
Busy Beavers

FORM & FUNCTION

DAY 3 — Read and Comprehend

DAY 4 — Language Arts

DAY 5 — Language Arts

Language: High Frequency Words	Phonics	Think, Talk, and Recognize
Preteach/Review 10–15 min Poster **Leveled Support Preteach** **Practice Stations Review** **Teach** 35–45 min **High Frequency Words** **Phonemic Awareness** **Daily Table Talk** **Check/Reteach** 5–10 min Poster, Word Cards **Leveled Support Reteach**	**Preteach/Review** 10–15 min Poster **Leveled Support Preteach** **Practice Stations Review** **Teach** 35–45 min **Phonics** **Daily Table Talk** **Check/Reteach** 5–10 min Poster, Word Cards **Leveled Support Reteach**	**Preteach/Review** 10–15 min Poster **Leveled Support Preteach** **Practice Stations Review** **Teach** 15–20 min **Think, Talk, and Recognize** **Concept Wrap Up** **Check/Reteach** 30–40 min Poster, Word Cards, Song Book **Leveled Support Reteach**
		Fluency: Writing or Speaking
ELA R 1.15 Read simple one-syllable and high frequency words (i.e., sight words).	**ELA R 1.14** Match all consonant and short-vowel sounds to appropriate letters.	**ELA LS 1.2** Share information and ideas, speaking audibly in complete, coherent sentences.
High Frequency Words: we, are, here, is		

Weekly Practice

Practice Stations

Materials and Activity

shoe boxes or other small boxes, paint, paintbrushes, scrap art materials, pictures of farm animals

What's in the Barn? 👫

Look at the picture of the barn on the student page and have children discuss what a barn look like. Have partners work together to make a barn from a box. Demonstrate how to paint the box. Encourage them to use other materials to add details to the barn. Then have children use pictures of farm animals to complete the sentence: *A (pig) lives in my barn.*

large drawing paper, drawing materials

Down on the Farm ♻

Display the Vocabulary Cards for the animals and say the words together. Draw a simple barn in the middle of the paper. Then have children draw pictures of animals on the farm. Help them to label the animals. Display the pictures and have other children name the animals that they see.

Preteach/Reteach

Transfer and Common Misconceptions

Phonology

The English phoneme /sh/ is not used in Spanish. Spanish-speaking children may need extra practice saying words such as *sheep.*

Vowel Sounds

Help children to recognize the different sounds for *o* in the words *cow, rooster,* and *goat.*

Produce Language

Weekly Concept and Language Goal

CONCEPT GOALS

- understand the idea that tools are used to build things
- name things you can do with a saw
- describe things you can build with a hammer and with wood

By Day 5, children should be able to write a one-word label or a sentence.

Daily Table Talk

❶ **Beginning**

Children point to tools on the student page while you say the word.

❷ ❸ **Early Intermediate/Intermediate**

Words or phrase: saw, uses a hammer

❹ ❺ **Early Advanced/Advanced**

Phrase or sentence: A farmer uses a hammer to build.

Daily Table Talk

❶ **Beginning**

Children talk about their drawings.

❷ ❸ **Early Intermediate/Intermediate**

Children write one-word labels.

❹ ❺ **Early Advanced/Advanced**

Children write a phrase or sentence.

DAY 3 — Read and Comprehend

old magazines, scissors, yarn

Farm Animals 👥 👤

Have children cut out 10–12 pictures of different animals from old magazines. Make two large circles with yarn. Ask children to sort the animals into these categories: *Animals on a Farm* and *Animals Not on a Farm*.

DAY 4 — Language Arts

Letter tiles for *w, e, e, a, r, h, i, s,* paper

| w | e | e | a | r | h | i | s |

Spell and Read 👥

Write the high frequency words in a column: *we, are, here,* and *is.* Children take turns making the words with the tiles. After a child makes a word, the partner says the word.

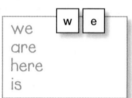

we
are
here
is

w e

DAY 5 — Language Arts

pot; index cards with the following words: *box, hop, hot, mop, not, on, top, bed, at, big, fun*

Put It in the Pot 👤

Say *pot* and emphasize the /o/ sound. Have the child put all the words with *o* in the pot. Then read the words together.

hot

Final Sounds

Many Vietnamese speakers do not pronounce final consonants. Continue to emphasize final consonants with Vietnamese speaking children.

Verbs

The Russian language does not have a present tense form of the verb *to be.* Children may need extra opportunities to practice these verb forms.

Vowel Sounds

In Spanish, the letter *a* can represent the /o/ sound. Point to the letter *o* in each word as you say it.

Daily Table Talk

1 Beginning

Have children look at the picture on the student page as they repeat the words *fence* and *barn.*

2 3 Early Intermediate/Intermediate

Words and phrases: *fence, barn*

4 5 Early Advanced/Advanced

Sentence: *Farmers build a fence with a hammer.*

Daily Table Talk

1 Beginning

Children repeat words after you to answer the question.

2 3 Early Intermediate/Intermediate

Words: *barn, fence,* and *doghouse*

4 5 Early Advanced/Advanced

Sentence: *A barn is built out of wood.*

Daily Table Talk

1 Beginning Child speaks about the drawing and may write a label.

2 3 Early Intermediate/Intermediate Child writes a label that includes a concept vocabulary word.

4 5 Early Advanced/Advanced Child writes a label or sentence that includes a vocabulary word.

Build Background Get Ready to Read!

Question of the Week

What tools do you need to build things?

www.pearsonsuccessnet.com

Concept Talk

Use the Big Book If you have not introduced the Big Book, consider reading it to children. Connect to the unit theme, Building—Putting It Together.

Introduce the Weekly Concept Tell children that today they will talk about tools and what they are used for. Ask the weekly question: What tools do you need to build things?

Use the Poster Direct children's attention to the weekly poster. Use the Day 1 teaching notes at the bottom of the poster.

Sing the Song Use the song **Farm Homes** to reinforce children's understanding of the weekly concept. Have the children sing or simply chant the words with you.

Use a Transparency Use the Sequence Map (Transparency 7) to help children organize the steps in building something.

Tools for Building

Vocabulary

cat

cow

goat

dog

mouse

rooster

sheep

204

What tools do you need to build things?

Vocabulary

cat a small animal that that is often kept as a pet or is used for catching mice

cow a large female animal that is kept on farms and used to produce milk or meat

goat a common farm animal with horns and with long hair under its chin

dog a very common animal with four legs that often kept as a pet or used for guarding buildings

mouse a small, furry animal with a long tail and a pointed nose that lives in buildings or in fields

rooster a male chicken

sheep a farm animal that is kept for its wool

 ELA R 1.18 Describe common objects and events in both general and specific language. (ELD R.B4)

205

Introduce Concept Vocabulary

1. **Say the Word** Display the Picture Card as you say *cow*. Have children repeat the word.

2. **Introduce Word Meaning** Ask questions about a cow. What kind of sound does a cow make? What does a cow look like? Where does a cow live?

3. **Demonstrate** Have children role play how a cow moves and the sounds it would make.

4. **Apply** Have children demonstrate their understanding.

Repeat with other vocabulary words.

Corrective Feedback If children have difficulty pronouncing the vocabulary word, demonstrate how to break the word into separate sounds. Tap as you say each sound. Have children do the same and then repeat the word.

Concept Work

Ask children to point to the pictures of the workers on the farm. Have children talk about what the people are doing and the tools that they are using. Have children circle the tools as you identify them: hammer, paintbrush, and saw. Then have children color the pictures.

Leveled Support   Vocabulary in Context

❶ **Beginning** Have children point to each pictured animal. Say the name of the animal and have children repeat it after you. Then ask them to make the animal sound.

❷ ❸ **Early Intermediate/Intermediate** Make lists of vocabulary words and read them together. Have partners look through classroom picture books and find pictures of each animal. Children make a check next to each animal that they find.

❹ ❺ **Early Advanced/Advanced** Display a list of vocabulary words and read them with the children. Then have children draw a picture of a farm and farm animals. Help them to label their pictures. Display the pictures and encourage others to read the vocabulary words.

Wrap Up   DAY 1

 Table Talk What tools do people use when they work on a farm? What animals live on the farm? Have children answer the question, using the vocabulary words.

Produce Language Have partners say a sentence about a tool and what it is used for.

Today children should have:

☑ **Learned** and applied vocabulary related to animals on a farm.

☑ **Spoken** complete sentences about tools and how they are used. Recognized concept vocabulary words.

ELA LS 2.3 Relate an experience or creative story in a logical sequence.(ELD LS.B3)

205

To discuss category words for farm animals; to discuss how a saw is used.

Concept Talk

Connect to Day 1 Recall with children that yesterday they talked about tools used on a farm. *What tools do you need to build things?*

Introduce the Daily Question *What kinds of things can you do with a saw?* Have children answer orally.

Use the Poster Use the Day 2 teaching notes.

Introduce Category Words

1. **Say the Word** Have children point to the sheep. Say the word and have children repeat it.

2. **Introduce Word Meaning** *What does a sheep look like? What sound does a sheep make?*

3. **Demonstrate** Have children make the sound of a sheep. Show several plastic or stuffed animals and have children identify which is a sheep.

4. **Apply** Repeat with other vocabulary words and point out that they all belong to the category of farm animals.

Have children draw pictures of animals that live on a farm.

Farm Animals

Picture Dictionary

cow

goat

rooster

sheep

 Draw Draw a farm animal.

206 ELA R1.17 Identify and sort common words in basic categories (e.g., colors, shapes, foods). (ELD R.B4)

Preteach **Reteach** **LS** **Leveled Support** **Category Words**

① **Beginning** Make a sound for each animal pictured in the Worktext. Have children point to the animal and say the word.

② ③ **Early Intermediate/ Intermediate** Sing "Old McDonald" with the children. Have children point to one of the animals pictured in the Worktext for each verse. Ask if they can name other farm animals for additional verses.

④ ⑤ **Early Advanced/Advanced** Ask children to think of other animals that live on a farm. Make a list. Encourage children to think of as many animals as they can. Then have them repeat each word on the list.

Wrap Up DAY 2

Daily **Table Talk** Suppose you wanted to build a barn for a cow. How could a saw help you? Have partners discuss the question.

Produce Language To build fluency, encourage children to label or write a sentence about their drawings. They can share their writing with partners.

Today children should have:

☑ **Learned** and applied vocabulary related to farm animals.

☑ **Spoken** complete sentences about using a saw.

☑ **Recognized** words that belong in the same category.

 ELA R1.17 Identify and sort common words in basic categories (e.g., colors, shapes, foods). (EDL R.B4)

What can you build with a hammer?

✏️ **Circle** Circle *We*. Circle *are*.
We are making a house.

✏️ **Circle** Circle *Here*. Circle *is*.
Here is the hammer.

ELA R1.15 Read simple one-syllable and high-frequency words (i.e., sight words). (ELD R.B2)

207

To discuss what you can build with a hammer; to review the high frequency words *we*, *are*, *here*, and *is*; review consonants and blends.

Concept Talk

 FORM & FUNCTION

Connect to Day 2 Remind children that yesterday they talked about what people do with a saw. What does a saw look like? What do you do with a saw?

Introduce the Daily Question What kinds of things can you build with a hammer? Discuss when people use a hammer.

Use the Poster Use the Day 3 teaching notes.

Review Concept Vocabulary Review the words introduced on Day 1.

Review High Frequency Words

Write *we*, *are*, *here*, and *is* on the board. Read the words together. Say one of the words and ask a child to point to the word and erase it. Continue with the rest of the words. Then read the sentences on the Worktext page. Children repeat the sentences and circle the words

Phonemic Awareness

Review Consonants and Blends Say the word *we* and have children repeat it Change /w/ to /h/. What's the new word? Continue with /f/, /k/, /m/, /n/, /s/, /b/, /sk/.

Corrective Feedback For children who have difficulty with phonemic substitution, model the new word. Then have children repeat it.

Leveled Support   High Frequency Words

Preteach / Reteach

① **Beginning** Write the words *we*, *are*, *here*, and *is*. Read the words together. Have the children repeat the words. Say one of the words in a sentence, emphasizing the word. Ask children to raise their hands when they hear one of the words.

② ③ **Early Intermediate/Intermediate** Make a list of the words *we*, *are*, *here*, and *is*. Read the words with the children. Then say a rhyming word for each and have children identify the high frequency word on the list: **we,** *knee*; **are,** *bar*; **here,** *clear*; **is,** *his*.

④ ⑤ **Early Advanced/Advanced** Make a list of the high frequency words for each child. Have them look for the words in classroom picture books.

Wrap Up **DAY** 3

Table Talk What can people build with a hammer? Have partners discuss the question.

Produce Language Have children draw a picture of someone working with a hammer. Help children label their pictures. Have partners talk about what they drew.

Today children should have:

☑ **Reviewed** and applied the high frequency words *we*, *are*, *here*, and *is*.

☑ **Spoken** complete sentences about building with a hammer.

☑ **Recognized** consonants and blends.

ELA R.1.15 Read simple one-syllable and high-frequency words (i.e., sight words). (ELD R.B2)

207

To discuss things that can be built out of wood; to review the sound /o/.

Concept Talk

FORM & FUNCTION

Connect to Day 3 Elicit from children that yesterday they talked about what people can build with a hammer. What kinds of things can you build with a hammer?

Introduce the Daily Question What kinds of things can you build out of wood? Have children discuss things on a farm that are made out of wood.

Use the Poster Use the Day 4 teaching notes.

Phonics

The Sound /o/ Write the letter *o* and say the /o/ sound. Write the word *hot,* blend the phonemes, and say the word with the children. Then have children say words that rhyme with *hot.* Identify the pictures on the Worktext page and have children complete the exercises.

Corrective Feedback For children having difficulty recognizing the /o/ sound in words, repeat the sound that the letter *o* makes. Then point to the pictures of *socks, fox, hop,* and *clock.* Have children repeat the words.

Identify Sound Oo

✏ **Circle** Circle things with *o*.

208 🐻 ELA R1.14 Match all consonant and short-vowel sounds to appropriate letters. (ELD R.B10)

 Leveled Support **Phonics**

① **Beginning** Say the words *hot* and *dot,* emphasizing the /o/. Write the letter *o* and associate it with the /o/ sound. Have children repeat the words.

② ③ **Early Intermediate/Intermediate** Slowly say these words: *hot, bat, lot, lit, bed, hop, bun, clock, sock, can.* Children raise their hands when they hear a word with /o/.

④ ⑤ **Early Advanced/Advanced** Write these words on chart paper: *h_t, h_p, cl_ck, n_t, s_ck, l_t, p_t, c_t.* Children write *o* to complete the word and say the word. Help them to use each word in a sentence.

Wrap Up **DAY 4**

Daily

Table Talk What kinds of things are made out of wood? Do we have things made out of wood in our classroom? Have partners discuss the questions.

Produce Language Have children draw a picture of something made out of wood. Have them say a sentence about their picture. Help them write the sentence.

Today children should have:

☑ **Learned** and applied vocabulary related to what one can make out of wood.

☑ **Spoken** complete sentences about things made out of wood.

☑ **Recognized** the sound of /o/ in words.

🐻 **ELA R.1.14** Match all consonant and short-vowel sounds to appropriate letters. (ELD R.B1)

What tools do you need to build things?

✏ Draw

OBJECTIVE

To guide children to express their understanding of weekly concepts and vocabulary.

Think, Talk, and Recognize!

Concept Talk

Connect to Day 4 Remind children that yesterday they talked about things that are made from wood. Model how to answer yesterday's question with a sentence.

Review the Weekly Question Ask: What tools do you need to build things? Have children talk about why people use a saw and hammer to build.

Use the Poster: Use the Day 5 teaching notes.

Review Concept Vocabulary Review the vocabulary introduced on Day 1

Concept Wrap Up

Have children draw a picture in the Worktext to answer the question: *What tools do you need to build things?* Discuss the picture of the person building a dollhouse. What tool do you see? What do you do with it?

(LS) Leveled Support   Concept Vocabulary

Preteach / Reteach

❶ **Beginning** Display the picture cards for *mouse* and *cow.* Say each word. Ask children to repeat and point to the matching card. Then ask questions such as: Which animal is bigger? Which animal lives in a pen? **Repeat with** *rooster* and *goat.*

❷ ❸ **Early Intermediate/Intermediate** Display picture cards for the vocabulary words. Say the words together. Then ask a child to give clues about one of the animals. Others guess the animal.

❹ ❺ **Early Advanced/Advanced** Choose one of the animals. Work together to make a word web with words and phrases that describe the animal.

 Wrap Up   DAY 5

Table Talk *Daily* What tools do you need to build things? Have children discuss the question, using the vocabulary words they have learned this week.

Produce Language To build fluency, children can label, write about, or speak about their drawings. Ask children to respond to what they read or heard.

Today children should have:

☑ **Reviewed** the weekly concept and concept vocabulary.

☑ **Spoken** about the tools people use to build things.

☑ **Drawn or written** to show how people use tools to build things.

 ELA LS. 1.2 Share information and ideas, speaking audibly in complete, coherent sentences. (ELD LS.B1)

209

Weekly Lesson Plan

Question of the Week How do beavers build?

	DAY 1 Get Ready to Read	**DAY 2** Read and Comprehend

Instructional Plan and Materials

- **Word Cards**
  126–130

- **Big Book**
  Yoko Builds a Birdhouse

- **Poster**
  Poster 33 can be used at beginning or end of day.

- **Song Book**, p. 33

Transparencies Explore content and vocabulary and model fluent reading.

For further information about using these components, see pages x–xv.

Build Background

Preteach/Review 10–15 min
Poster, Song Book, Big Book
- **Leveled Support Preteach**
- **Practice Stations Preteach**

Teach 35–45 min
- **Concept Talk**
- **Oral Vocabulary Routine**
  Word Cards
- **Build Concept Vocabulary**
- **Daily Table Talk**

Check/Reteach 5–10 min
Poster, Word Cards
- **Leveled Support Reteach**

Language: Category Words

Preteach/Review 10–15 min
Poster
- **Leveled Support Preteach**
- **Practice Stations Review**

Teach 35–45 min
- **Category Words**
- **Daily Table Talk**

Check/Reteach 5–10 min
Poster, Word Cards
- **Leveled Support Reteach**

Fluency: Writing or Speaking

CALIFORNIA Standards

G1 Sci 2.c Students know animals eat plants or other animals for food and may also use plants or even other animals for shelter and nesting.

ELA R 1.18 Describe common objects and events in both general and specific language.

ELA R 1.17 Identify and sort common words in basic categories (e.g., colors, shapes, foods).

Academic Language

Vocabulary: pond, teeth, trees

Category Words: grass, leaves, mud, sticks

Get Online! www.pearsonsuccessnet.com

Concept Talk Video

Background Building Audio Slideshow

Busy Beavers

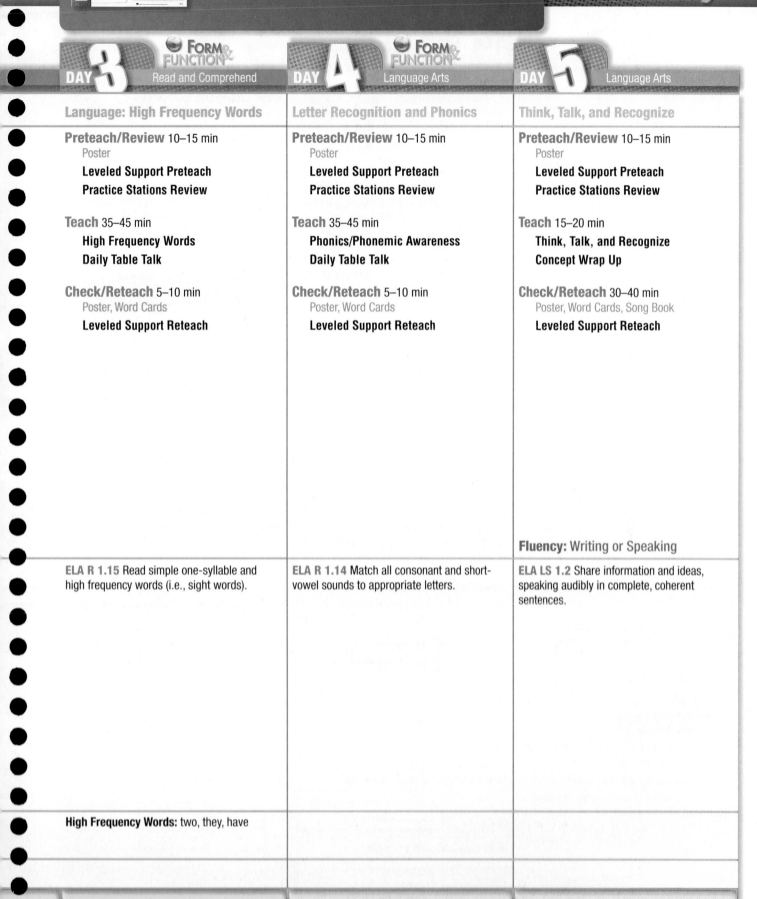

DAY 3 · Read and Comprehend
FORM & FUNCTION

Language: High Frequency Words

Preteach/Review 10–15 min
Poster
  Leveled Support Preteach
  Practice Stations Review

Teach 35–45 min
  High Frequency Words
  Daily Table Talk

Check/Reteach 5–10 min
Poster, Word Cards
  Leveled Support Reteach

ELA R 1.15 Read simple one-syllable and high frequency words (i.e., sight words).

High Frequency Words: two, they, have

DAY 4 · Language Arts
FORM & FUNCTION

Letter Recognition and Phonics

Preteach/Review 10–15 min
Poster
  Leveled Support Preteach
  Practice Stations Review

Teach 35–45 min
  Phonics/Phonemic Awareness
  Daily Table Talk

Check/Reteach 5–10 min
Poster, Word Cards
  Leveled Support Reteach

ELA R 1.14 Match all consonant and short-vowel sounds to appropriate letters.

DAY 5 · Language Arts

Think, Talk, and Recognize

Preteach/Review 10–15 min
Poster
  Leveled Support Preteach
  Practice Stations Review

Teach 15–20 min
  Think, Talk, and Recognize
  Concept Wrap Up

Check/Reteach 30–40 min
Poster, Word Cards, Song Book
  Leveled Support Reteach

Fluency: Writing or Speaking

ELA LS 1.2 Share information and ideas, speaking audibly in complete, coherent sentences.

Practice Stations

Materials and Activity

DAY **1**   Get Ready to Read

stuffed animal or picture of a beaver, drawing paper, crayons, small twig, tape

Busy As a Beaver

Draw a simple outline of a beaver on drawing paper for each child. Display a stuffed animal or picture of a beaver. Children talk about what it looks like. Then have them complete the picture by drawing eyes, ears, a mouth, and a tail. Have them color the picture. Then have them tape a small stick in the beaver's mouth to show what a beaver uses to build.

DAY **2**   Read and Comprehend

small bowls or containers partly filled with water, potting soil, toothpicks

Muddy Water

Have children work together to add soil to the water to make mud. Have them talk about how the mud feels. Then have them use the mud and toothpicks to make a model of a beaver lodge.

Preteach/Reteach

Transfer and Common Misconceptions

Phonology

The English phoneme /th/ is not used in Spanish. Provide ample opportunities for Spanish-speaking children to say words such as *teeth*.

Sounds

Some children may have difficulty with the initial sound in *trees*. Model similar words, such as *trap, trip, treat*.

Produce Language

Weekly Concept and Language Goal

CONCEPT GOALS

- describe beavers and how they build things
- tell what beavers look like
- explain how a beaver uses its tail

By Day 5, children should be able to write a one-word label or a sentence.

Daily Table Talk

❶ **Beginning**
> Children point to pictures on the student page while you say the words.

❷ ❸ **Early Intermediate/Intermediate**
> Words or phrases: carries sticks, cuts trees

❹ ❺ **Early Advanced/Advanced**
> Phrase or sentence: A beaver cuts trees down.

Daily Table Talk

❶ **Beginning**
> Children talk about their drawings.

❷ ❸ **Early Intermediate/Intermediate**
> Children write one-word labels.

❹ ❺ **Early Advanced/Advanced**
> Children write a phrase or sentence.

DAY 3 Read and Comprehend

vocabulary cards, mural paper, drawing materials

 DAY 4 Language Arts

cut-out headlines or paragraphs from children's magazines, word cards for *two, they, have*

DAY 5 Language Arts

Sticky notes with these words: *bed, bell, bet, get, led, let, red, pet, pen, wet, yes, mat, pat, it, sit, up,* and *lot;* paper

---

Beaver Lodge

Display the Vocabulary Cards and have children identify them. Draw a pond on the mural paper. Then have children draw things around the pond that beavers build with. Have children name the things that they drew and help them label their drawings.

Word Hunt

Give partners a set of word cards and have them read the words. Then have them look for the words in headlines or paragraphs and circle the words that they find.

Make 10

Write the number 10 on a sheet of paper and say the word, emphasizing /e/. Have the child find ten words with *e* and place them near the number. The partner reads the words. Children switch roles and repeat.

> 10
>
> bet

Plurals

Remind children that plurals are often formed in English by adding *s*. Have them find the concept words that are plurals.

Numbers

Point out that the word *two* is a number word. Have children say the word for *two* in other languages.

Consonant Clusters

Unlike English, the Khmer language uses many combinations of consonant clusters at the beginning of word. Children speaking Khmer may experience difficulty producing English phonemes.

Daily Table Talk

① Beginning Have children look at the picture on the student page. Point and say: Beavers swim. Children repeat the sentence.

②③ Early Intermediate/Intermediate Words and phrases: swim, build in the water

④⑤ Early Advanced/Advanced Sentences: Beavers swim. Beavers build in the water.

Daily Table Talk

① Beginning Children look at the picture of the beaver in the Student Edition and point to its tail. Have them say the word.

②③ Early Intermediate/Intermediate Words: swim, build

④⑤ Early Advanced/Advanced Sentence: A beaver uses its tail to swim.

Daily Table Talk

① Beginning Child speaks about the drawing and may write a label.

②③ Early Intermediate/Intermediate Child writes a label that includes a concept vocabulary word.

④⑤ Early Advanced/Advanced Child writes a label or sentence that includes a vocabulary word.

OBJECTIVE

To introduce and discuss how beavers build a home and related concept vocabulary.

Build Background Get **Ready** to **Read!**

Question of the Week   **How do beavers build?**

www.pearsonsuccessnet.com

Concept Talk

Use the Big Book If you haven't introduced the Big Book, consider reading it to children. Connect the Big Book to the unit theme, Building It—Putting It Together.

Introduce the Weekly Concept Tell children that today they will talk about beavers and where beavers live. Ask the weekly question: How do beavers build?

Use the Poster Direct children's attention to the weekly poster. Use the Day 1 teaching notes at the bottom of the poster.

Sing the Song Use the song **A Beaver Home** to reinforce children's understanding of the weekly concept. Have the children sing or simply chant the words with you.

Use a Transparency Use the Sequence Map (Transparency 7) to help children organize the sequence of steps a beaver takes to build a dam.

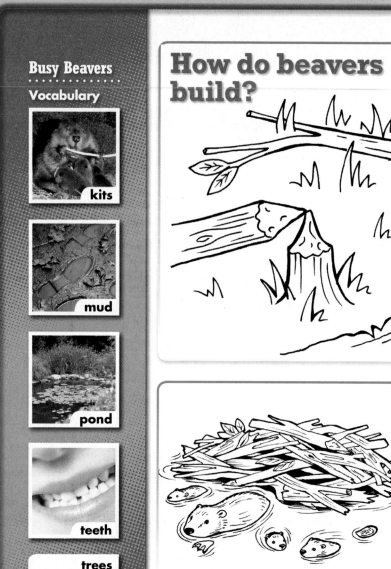

Busy Beavers

Vocabulary

kits

mud

pond

teeth

trees

How do beavers build?

210

Vocabulary

* **Academic Vocabulary**

  kits baby beavers

  mud wet earth that is soft and sticky

* **pond** a small area of fresh water that is smaller than a lake

* **teeth** more than one tooth

* **trees** very tall plants that have trunks

Introduce Concept Vocabulary

1. **Say the Word** Display the Word Card as you say *mud.* Have children repeat the word.

2. **Introduce Word Meaning** Ask questions about mud. What does mud look like? What does mud feel like?

3. **Demonstrate** Have children pretend to walk in mud.

4. **Apply** Have children demonstrate their understanding.

Repeat with other vocabulary words.

Corrective Feedback If children have difficulty pronouncing the words, separate the phonemes, and then say the word together.

Concept Work

Discuss with children what is happening in the pictures. Point out the beaver as you say the word. Tell children that beavers build their homes on water. They use their teeth to cut down trees. Discuss the sequence of events in the picture. Have children circle "tools" beavers use to build. Children can color the pictures.

 Leveled Support Vocabulary in Context

① ② Beginning/Early Intermediate Point to each picture and say the word. Have children repeat the word. Then say the word and have children point to the picture.

③ Intermediate Say a short definition for each word. Children point to the picture and say the word.

④ ⑤ Early Advanced/Advanced Give directions using the vocabulary words and have children draw a picture. Help children label their pictures.

1. Draw a *pond.*
2. Draw *trees* by the pond.
3. Draw *mud* by the pond.
4. Draw *kits* swimming in the pond.

Wrap Up   **DAY 1**

Table Talk How does a beaver build a place to live? Have children answer the question, using the vocabulary words.

Produce Language Have children draw a picture of a beaver's home. Help them to label the picture or write a sentence about it.

Today children should have:

☑ **Learned** and applied vocabulary related to beavers.

☑ **Spoken** complete sentences about how beavers build a place to live.

☑ **Recognized** concept vocabulary words.

 ELA R1.18 Describe common objects and events in both general and specific language. (ELD R.B6)

211

OBJECTIVE

To discuss what beavers look like; to introduce category words for things that animals use to build.

Concept Talk

Connect to Day 1 How do beavers build? Recall that beavers build by cutting things with their teeth.

Introduce the Daily Question What do beavers look like? Have children answer orally. Refer them back to pages 210–211 as they describe wah beavers look like.

Use the Poster Use the Day 2 teaching notes.

Introduce Category Words

1. **Say the Word** Have children point to *grass.* Say the word and have children repeat it.

2. **Introduce Word Meaning** Point to the floor. Is this grass? Where do you see grass? What color is grass? What does it feel like?

3. **Demonstrate** Ask children where they see grass. If possible, show some grass.

4. **Apply** Have children demonstrate their understanding.

Repeat with other category words.

Have children circle pictures that show things animals use.

Corrective Feedback If children have difficulty choosing the correct items, say the names of all the items. Model a sentence frame that you provide: This is a _____ . Who uses this to build? _____ use this to build.

Wrap Up   **DAY** 2

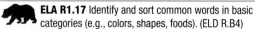 *Daily* **Table Talk** Have partners describe what a beaver looks like. Encourage them to use pictures in the Worktext to help.

Produce Language To build fluency, encourage children to label or write a sentence about a tool or building material on the Worktext page.

Today children should have:

☑ **Learned** and applied vocabulary related to things that animals use to build.

☑ **Spoken** complete sentences about what beavers look like.

☑ **Recognized** words that belong in the same category.

ELA R1.17 Identify and sort common words in basic categories (e.g., colors, shapes, foods). (ELD R.B4)

Things Animals Use To Build

Picture Dictionary

grass

leaves

mud

sticks

✏ **Circle** Circle what animals use.

212   **ELA R1.17** Identify and sort common words in basic categories (e.g., colors, shapes, foods). (ELD R.B4)

LS Leveled Support **Category Words**
Preteach / Reteach

① ② Beginning/Early Intermediate Have children point to each picture on the Worktext page. Say the word and have children repeat it.

③ ④ Intermediate/Early Advanced Write the vocabulary words on the board and read them together. Display a picture of a bird's nest. Talk about which materials on the list were used to make the nest.

⑤ Advanced Make a list of the vocabulary words and read them together. Then use word webs with these headings to find similarities: *Things that are green. Things that are wet.* Encourage children to use words from the list as well as other words. Record children's responses.

Why do beavers get wet?

🖊 **Circle** Circle *Two.*
Two beavers are swimming.

🖊 **Circle** Circle *They.* Circle *have.*
They have homes on the water.

🐻 ELA R1.15 Read simple one-syllable and high-frequency words (i.e., sight words). (ELD R.B2)

213

OBJECTIVE

To discuss why beavers get wet; to review the high frequency words *two, they,* and *have.*

Concept Talk

 FORM& FUNCTION

Connect to Day 2 What do beavers look like? Help children describe such features as fur, tail, and teeth.

Introduce the Daily Question Why do beavers get wet? Have children answer orally. Show illustrations of beavers swimming to help children answer the question.

Use the Poster Use the Day 3 teaching notes.

Review Concept Vocabulary Review the words introduced on Day 1.

Review High Frequency Words

Write *two* on the board and read it together. Ask children to hold up two fingers. Then write: *Here are two boys.* Ask a volunteer to circle *two.* Continue the activity with *they* and *have.* Then help children complete the Worktext page.

Corrective Feedback If children have difficulty recognizing the high frequency words, write each word on a sticky note and read it together. Make a list of the words on chart paper and have children match the words.

Preteach
LS Leveled Support **High Frequency Words**
Reteach

❶ **Beginning** Hold up two pencils. *I have two pencils.* Have children show pairs of items such as crayons, markers, and blocks and say the sentence.

❷ ❸ **Early Intermediate/Intermediate** Write this sentence on the board: *They have two _____ .* Give two children a crayon and model how to complete the sentence: *They have two crayons.* Use other objects and have children complete the sentence.

❹ ❺ **Early Advanced/Advanced** Write the words *two, they,* and *have* on sticky notes. Have partners work together to find the words in classroom picture books. Have them place the sticky note near the word. Then read the words together.

Wrap Up **DAY**

Table Talk Why do beavers get wet? Have partners discuss the question.

Produce Language Have each child say a sentence about why beavers get wet.

Today children should have:

☑ **Reviwed** and applied the high-frequency words *two, they,* and *have.*

☑ **Spoken** complete sentences about why beavers get wet.

☑ **Recognized** high frequency words.

🐻 **ELA R1.15** Read simple one-syllable and high-frequency words (i.e., sight words). (ELD R.B2)

OBJECTIVES

To discuss how a beaver uses its tail; to identify *e*, /e/; to blend words with three or four phonemes.

Concept Talk

FORM & FUNCTION

Connect to Day 3 Why do beavers get wet?

Introduce the Daily Question Ask: What does a beaver use its tail for? Have children look at the pictures of beavers in the Worktext and answer orally.

Use the Poster Use the Day 4 teaching notes.

Phonics/Phonemic Awareness

Review *e*/e/ Write *hen* and ask a child to circle the letter *e*. Say the word together. Then have children say rhyming words with you: *Ben, den, men, ten.* Have them complete the exercises on the Worktext page.

Blend Words What word is /b/ /e/ /d/? Have children say the word. Continue with *pan, dress, big, nest, pond, mud.*

Have children complete the activity in the Worktext.

Corrective Feedback If children have difficulty circling the correct pictures, say the words aloud emphasizing the vowel sounds. Have children raise their hands when they hear the word with /e/ in the pair.

Wrap Up
DAY 4

Daily Table Talk What does a beaver's tail look like? What does a beaver use its tail for? Have children discuss the questions.

Produce Language Have children draw a picture of a beaver and label its tail. Partners talk about what the tail looks like.

Today children should have:

- ☑ **Learned** and applied vocabulary related to a beaver's tail.
- ☑ **Spoken** complete sentences about beavers.
- ☑ **Recognized** the sound /e/.

 ELA R1.14 Match all consonant and short-vowel sounds to appropriate letters. (ELD B.10)

Identify Sound Ee

✏ **Circle** Circle things with e.

214  **ELA R1.14** Match all consonant and short-vowel sounds to appropriate letters. (ELD R.B10)

LS **Leveled Support** Phonics/Phonemic Awareness
Preteach / Reteach

① ② **Beginning/Early Intermediate** Hold up a card on which you have written *e*, identify the letter, and say the sound. Have children repeat these words, emphasizing the /e/ sound: *Ben, send, bed, ten, pen, let.*

③ **Intermediate** Slowly count from 1 to 10. Have children stand up when they hear a number with the /e/ sound. Write the numbers *seven* and *ten* and have volunteers circle the letter *e*.

④ ⑤ **Early Advanced/Advanced** Say groups of words. Ask children to identify the word that does *not* have the /e/ sound. ***pen, let,*** *cat; boat,* ***bed, men; dress,*** *run,* ***let; send,*** *man,* ***pen***

How do beavers build?

 Draw

OBJECTIVE

To guide children to express their understanding of weekly concepts and vocabulary.

Think, Talk, and Recognize!

Concept Talk

Connect to Day 4 What does a beaver use its tail for?

Review the Weekly Question How do beavers build? Have children look at the pictures on Day 1. Have them discuss where beavers live and what they use to build a place to live.

Use the Poster Use the Day 5 teaching notes.

Review Concept Vocabulary Review the vocabulary introduced on Day 1.

Concept Wrap Up

Have children draw to answer the question: *How do beavers build?* Use the photograph to prompt discussion: What tool do you see the beaver using? Beavers don't have saws—they have sharp teeth!

Leveled Support   Concept Vocabulary

Preteach / LS / Reteach

① **Beginning** Display the Word Cards for *kits, mud, pond, teeth,* and *trees.* Say each word. Ask children to repeat the word and point to the card.

② ③ **Early Intermediate/Intermediate** Place the Word Cards *kits, mud, pond, teeth,* and *trees* face down. Children take turns turning over a card and saying the word.

④ ⑤ **Early Advanced/Advanced** Do the intermediate activity. Then have children say a sentence using the vocabulary word.

Wrap Up   DAY 5

Daily **Table Talk** How do beavers build? Have children discuss the question, using the vocabulary words they learned this week.

Produce Language To build fluency, children can label, write about, or speak about their drawings. Ask children to respond to what they read or heard.

Today, children should have:

☑ **Reviewed** the weekly concept and concept vocabulary.

☑ **Spoken** about how beavers build.

☑ **Drawn or written** to show how beavers build.

 ELA LS1.2 Share information and ideas, speaking audibly in complete, coherent sentences. (ELD LS.B1)

215

WEEK 4

CALIFORNIA

Weekly Lesson Plan

Last Week
Unit 6, Week 3
Busy Beavers

Question of the Week — Who works at night?

	DAY 1 Get Ready to Read	**DAY 2** Read and Comprehend
	Build Background	**Language: Category Words**

Instructional Plan and Materials

policewoman

- **Word Cards**
  131–133

Yoko Builds a Birdhouse

- **Big Book**
  Yoko Builds a Birdhouse

Night Workers

- **Poster**
  Poster 34 can be used at beginning or end of day.

- **Song Book**, p. 34

Transparencies Explore content and vocabulary and model fluent reading.

For further information about using these components, see pages x–xv.

DAY 1 / Build Background

Preteach/Review 10–15 min
Poster, Song Book, Big Book
- **Leveled Support Preteach**
- **Practice Stations Preteach**

Teach 35–45 min
- **Concept Talk**
- **Oral Vocabulary Routine**
  Word Cards
- **Build Concept Vocabulary**
- **Daily Table Talk**

Check/Reteach 5–10 min
Poster, Word Cards
- **Leveled Support Reteach**

DAY 2 / Language: Category Words

Preteach/Review 10–15 min
Poster
- **Leveled Support Preteach**
- **Practice Stations Review**

Teach 35–45 min
- **Category Words**
- **Daily Table Talk**

Check/Reteach 5–10 min
Poster, Word Cards
- **Leveled Support Reteach**

Fluency: Writing or Speaking

CALIFORNIA Standards

GK His-Soc Sci K.3 Students match simple descriptions of work that people do and the names of related jobs at the school, in the local community, and from historical accounts.

ELA R 1.18 Describe common objects and events in both general and specific language.

ELA R 1.17 Identify and sort common words in basic categories (e.g., colors, shapes, foods).

Academic Language

Vocabulary: machinery

Category Words: bulldozer, cement mixer, concrete, crane, goggles, hard hat

---

Get Online! www.pearsonsuccessnet.com

Concept Talk Video

Background Building Audio Slideshow

This Week
Unit 6, Week 4

Night Workers

Next Week
Unit 6, Week 5
Building a House

DAY **3** FORM & FUNCTION Read and Comprehend	DAY **4** FORM & FUNCTION Language Arts	DAY **5** Language Arts
Language: High Frequency Words	**Phonics**	**Think, Talk, and Recognize**
Preteach/Review 10–15 min Poster **Leveled Support Preteach** **Practice Stations Review**	**Preteach/Review** 10–15 min Poster **Leveled Support Preteach** **Practice Stations Review**	**Preteach/Review** 10–15 min Poster **Leveled Support Preteach** **Practice Stations Review**
Teach 35–45 min **High Frequency Words** **Daily Table Talk**	**Teach** 35–45 min **Phonics** **Phonological Awareness** **Daily Table Talk**	**Teach** 15–20 min **Think, Talk, and Recognize** **Concept Wrap Up**
Check/Reteach 5–10 min Poster, Word Cards **Leveled Support Reteach**	**Check/Reteach** 5–10 min Poster, Word Cards **Leveled Support Reteach**	**Check/Reteach** 30–40 min Poster, Word Cards, Song Book **Leveled Support Reteach**
		Fluency: Writing or Speaking
ELA R 1.15 Read simple one-syllable and high frequency words (i.e., sight words).	**ELA R 1.14** Match all consonant and short-vowel sounds to appropriate letters.	**ELA LS 1.2** Share information and ideas, speaking audibly in complete, coherent sentences.
High Frequency Words: do, that, I like, see		

Practice Stations

Materials and Activity

drawing paper, crayons

Day and Night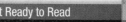

Have partners talk about what it looks like outside during the day and at night. Fold the drawing paper in half and label each side *Day* and *Night.* Children draw a picture to show something they do during each time of day. Then they discuss their pictures.

pictures of community workers; three sheets or drawing paper

When Do You Work?

Label the sheets of paper with a sun, a moon, and a sun and a moon. Children look at the pictures and decide if the job is done during the day, during the night, or if it could be done day or night. They place the pictures on the appropriate sheet of paper.

Preteach/Reteach

Transfer and Common Misconceptions

Word Meaning

Some children may have a difficult time understanding that only some jobs are done during the day or at night. Provide examples of familiar occupations, such as a doctor and a teacher. Ask questions such as: *When might a doctor work at night? Does a teacher teach children at night?*

Multi-syllable Words

Some children may have difficulty pronouncing four-syllable words. Say each word slowly and tap for each syllable. Have the child repeat the word with you several times, tapping for each syllable.

Produce Language

Weekly Concept and Language Goal

CONCEPT GOALS

- describe different workers who work at night
- explain what an engineer does at night
- describe jobs in which big machines are used

By Day 5, children should be able to write a one-word label or a sentence

Daily Table Talk

❶ **Beginning**

> Show pictures of familiar community workers and ask: Does (she) work at night? Children answer yes or no.

❷ ❸ **Early Intermediate/Intermediate**

> Phrase or sentence: delivery man; A delivery man works at night.

❹ ❺ **Early Advanced/Advanced**

> Sentence: A policewoman works at night.

Daily Table Talk

❶ **Beginning**

> Children talk about their drawings.

❷ ❸ **Early Intermediate/Intermediate**

> Children write one-word labels.

❹ ❺ **Early Advanced/Advanced**

> Children write a phrase or sentence.

DAY 3

Read and Comprehend

vocabulary cards, drawing paper, drawing materials

Construction Sites

Display the Vocabulary Cards and have partners take turns identifying each one. Then have them work together to draw a picture to show things that are used at a construction site. When the picture is completed, help them to label some of the items.

Plurals

Remind children that many plurals in English are formed by adding *s.* Help them to find the plural category words. Make sure they understand that the words mean *more than one.*

Daily Table Talk

① Beginning

> Children repeat names of big machines.

② ③ Early Intermediate/Intermediate

> Phrase or sentence: move dirt, mix cement

④ ⑤ Early Advanced/Advanced

> Sentence: A cement mixer mixes cement.

DAY 4

Language Arts

four sticky notes for each child, sentence strips

What Do You See?

Write these sentences on the strips:
I see _____. I like _____.

Have children draw pictures of two things that they see and two things that they like. Then children take turns putting a sticky note at the end of the matching sentence and reading the sentence. Children take turns.

> I see _____.

Pitch

In the Vietnamese language, words can have different meanings according to pitch. Help Vietnamese speakers understand that pitch is part of fluency in English.

Daily Table Talk

① Beginning

> Children repeat an answer to the question: It is dark.

② ③ Early Intermediate/Intermediate

> Phrase or sentence: dark outside, other people are sleeping

④ ⑤ Early Advanced/Advanced

> Sentence: It is dark outside.

DAY 5

Language Arts

pairs of index cards with the following words:
fun, but, sun, drum, bug, and *cut*

Concentration

Place the cards face down in a grid. Children take turns turning over two cards. If the cards match, they say the word and keep the cards. Play continues until all of the cards are matched.

The Sound /sh/

Some children may have difficulty pronouncing the /sh/ sound in *machinery,* as this sound is uncommon in some languages. Model one-syllable words with this sound until children become more proficient.

Daily Table Talk

① Beginning Child speaks about the drawing and may write a label.

② ⑤ Early Intermediate/Intermediate Child writes a label that includes a concept vocabulary word.

④ ⑤ Early Advanced/Advanced Child writes a label or sentence that includes a vocabulary word

OBJECTIVE

To introduce and discuss concepts and vocabulary related to the idea of jobs done at night.

Build Background Get **Ready** to **Read!**

Question of the Week Who works at night?

www.pearsonsuccessnet.com

Concept Talk

Use the Big Book If you haven't introduced the Big Book, consider reading it to children. Connect to the unit theme, Building—Putting It Together.

Introduce the Weekly Concept Tell children that today they will talk about the jobs that people do at night. Ask the weekly question: Who works at night?

Use the Poster Direct children's attention to the weekly poster. Use the Day 1 teaching notes at the bottom of the poster.

Sing the Song Use the song **Night Workers** to reinforce children's understanding of the weekly concept. Have the children sing or simply chant the words with you.

Use a Transparency Use the Classification Map (Transparency 3) to help children classify jobs into two categories: jobs done at night and jobs done during the day.

Night Workers
Vocabulary

delivery worker

machinery

policewoman

Who works at night?

216

Vocabulary

* **Academic Vocabulary**
  delivery worker a person who delivers goods to people
* **machinery** machines, especially large ones
  policewoman a female police officer

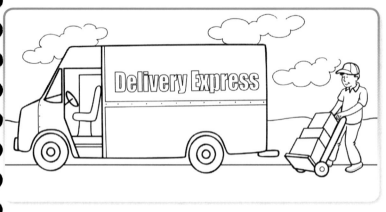

Delivery Express

 ELA R 1.18 Describe common objects and events in both general and specific language. (ELD R.B4)

217

Introduce Concept Vocabulary

1. **Say the Word** Display the Word Card as you say *delivery worker.* Have children repeat the words.

2. **Introduce Word Meaning** Give an example of a delivery worker. After cows give milk, the milk has to be brought to the store. People drive trucks to bring the milk. We say that the workers deliver the milk.

3. **Demonstrate** Have children role play loading a truck and delivering a package.

4. **Apply** Have children demonstrate their understanding.

Repeat with other vocabulary words.

Corrective Feedback If children have difficulty with the words, help them understand that two of these words are compound words. They are made of more than one word. Say both words: *delivery worker.* Tell children that separating the words helps you figure out the meaning of "someone who works to make deliveries."

Concept Work

Ask children questions about what the people in the pictures are doing. Point out that they are working at night, and talk about why people have to work at night. (We need to be safe at night. Some packages are important and have to arrive on time, so people deliver them at night. Road workers work at night so they won't interrupt people driving to work during the day.) Then have children circle each night worker.

Leveled Support Vocabulary in Context

❶ ❷ Beginning/Early Intermediate Have children point to the *delivery worker, machinery,* and *policewoman* on the Worktext page. Say the word for each picture as children point, and have them repeat each word.

❸ ❹ Intermediate/Early Advanced Label a large sheet of drawing paper with these headings: *Delivery Worker, Machinery, Policewoman.* Read the words together. Have children look through magazines to find pictures that belong in each category. Children paste the pictures in the correct section.

❺ Advanced Have partners work together to think of other jobs that people do at night. Then make a list of all of the responses.

Wrap Up   **DAY 1**

Daily Table Talk What jobs do people do at night? Have children answer the question, using the vocabulary words.

Produce Language Have children act out one of the night worker jobs. Ask them to say a sentence about what they are doing.

Today children should have:

☑ **Learned** and applied vocabulary related to jobs that people do at night.

☑ **Spoken** complete sentences about night workers.

☑ **Recognized** concept vocabulary words.

 ELA R1.18 Describe common objects and events in both general and specific language. (ELD R.B6)

217

OBJECTIVE

To discuss what an engineer does at night; to introduce category words for things at a construction site.

Concept Talk

Connect to Day 1 Who works at night?

Introduce the Daily Question What does an engineer do at night? Explain that an engineer designs and plans buildings and machines. Have children answer orally.

Use the Poster Use the Day 2 teaching notes.

Introduce Category Words

1. Say the Word Have children point to the picture of goggles as you say the word and children repeat.

2. Introduce Word Meaning Describe goggles. Goggles keep your eyes safe when you work. They are special kinds of glasses. Pat the top of your head. Would I wear goggles here? Show where you would wear goggles.

3. Demonstrate Hold up a pair of glasses. Talk about how goggles and glasses are similar and different.

4. Apply Have children demonstrate their knowledge.

Repeat with other vocabulary words and elicit that they all belong to the category "things at a construction site."

Have children draw something they would find at a construction site.

Corrective Feedback If children have difficulty understanding the meaning of the category words, show pictures in another book about building. Identify the things at a construction site.

Wrap Up
DAY 2

Daily
Table Talk Ask partners to name things that they would see at a construction site.

Produce Language To build fluency, encourage children to label or write a sentence about their drawings. They can share their writing with partners.

Today children should have:

☑ **Learned** and applied vocabulary related to things at a construction site.

☑ **Spoken** complete sentences about a construction site.

☑ **Recognized** words that belong in the same category.

 ELA R1.17 Identify and sort common words in basic categories (e.g., colors, shapes, foods). (ELD R.B4)

218 Night Workers • Unit 6, Week 4

Things at a Construction Site

Picture Dictionary

bull dozer **cement mixer** **concrete**

crane **goggles** **hard hats**

✏️ **Draw** Draw something at a site.

218 🐻 **ELA R1.17** Identify and sort common words in basic categories (e.g., colors, shapes, foods). (ELD R.B4)

Preteach / Reteach

LS **Leveled Support** **Category Words**

① ② **Beginning/Early Intermediate** Point to each picture on the Worktext page. Say the word and have children repeat.

③ **Intermediate** Play a guessing game. Give clues about each category word and have children say the word. I am thinking of something a worker wears on her head. It keeps the worker safe.

④ ⑤ **Early Advanced/Advanced** Have children look at the pictures in the Worktext for Day 1. Ask them to name other things that are found at a construction site. Make a list of their responses.

In which jobs can we run big machines?

✏ **Circle** Circle *do*. Circle *that*.
A crane can do that.

✏ **Circle** Circle *I*. Circle *like*. Circle *see*.
I like to see big trucks.

ELA R1.15 Read simple one-syllable and high-frequency words (i.e., sight words). (ELD R.B2)

219

Concept Talk

Connect to Day 2 What does an engineer do at night?

Introduce the Daily Question In which jobs can we run big machines? Talk about what some large machines are used for. Then have children answer orally.

Use the Poster Use the Day 3 teaching notes.

Review Concept Vocabulary Review the words introduced on Day 1.

Review High Frequency Words

Write *do* and read it together. Ask a volunteer to use the word in a sentence and write the sentence. Have another child circle the word *do*. Continue with *that, I, see,* and *like.* Then help children complete the Worktext page.

Corrective Feedback If children have difficulty recognizing the high frequency words, write two or three word sentences that use each word. Have children identify the words as you read the sentences.

Leveled Support   High Frequency Words

① ② **Beginning/Early Intermediate** Write the words *do, that, I, like,* and *see* on index cards. Make two cards for each word and place them facedown in a 5 x 2 grid. Children take turns turning over two cards and trying to make matches. When they make a match, they say the word.

③ **Intermediate** Write the letters *d, o, l, i, k, e, s, e, e, t, h, a,* and *t* on index cards. Mix up the letters for each word and have children put the letters in the correct order. Have them say the word and use it in a sentence.

④ ⑤ **Early Advanced/Advanced** Write the words *do, that, I, like,* and *see.* Read the words together. Then ask children to use two of the words in a sentence. Record the sentences.

Wrap Up   DAY 3

 Table Talk In which jobs can we run big machines? Have children refer to pictures in the Worktext and discuss the question.

Produce Language Have each child say a sentence about a big machine.

Today children should have:

☑ **Learned** and applied the high-frequency words *do, that, I, see,* and *like.*

☑ **Spoken** complete sentences about big machines.

☑ **Recognized** high frequency words.

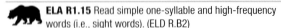 **ELA R1.15** Read simple one-syllable and high-frequency words (i.e., sight words). (ELD R.B2)

219

OBJECTIVES

To discuss what it is like to work at night; to reteach /u/; to review consonant sounds.

Concept Talk

FORM & FUNCTION

Connect to Day 3 In which jobs can we run big machines?

Introduce the Daily Question Ask: What is it like to work at night? Have children talk about factors such as sleeping on a different schedule and sometimes working in the dark.

Use the Poster Use the Day 4 teaching notes.

Phonics

Sound /u/ Write the letter *u* and have children identify it. Say the word *up* and have children repeat it, emphasizing the /u/ sound. Say the following words ask children if they hear /u/ at the beginning of the word or in the middle of the word: *tub, up, sun, umbrella, rub, us.* Help children complete the activity in the Worktext.

Phonological Awareness

Have children substitute phonemes to make new words. The word is *rub.* Change /b/ to /n/. What's the word? Continue with other examples.

Corrective Feedback If children have difficulty with phoneme substitution, say the new word and have them repeat it.

Wrap Up
DAY 4

Table Talk *Daily* What is it like to work at night? Have partners discuss the question.

Produce Language Have partners discuss what it might be like to work at night. Have partners ask each other: *Would you like to work at night?* Children answer in complete sentences.

Today children should have:

☑ **Learned** and applied vocabulary related to working at night.

☑ **Spoken** complete sentences about what it is like to work at night.

☑ **Recognized** the /u/ sound and substituted consonant sounds.

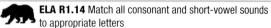
ELA R1.14 Match all consonant and short-vowel sounds to appropriate letters

220 Night Workers • Unit 6, Week 4

Identify Sound Uu

✏ **Circle** Circle things with *u.*

220  **ELA R1.14** Match all consonant and short-vowel sounds to appropriate letters. (ELD R.B10)

Leveled Support Phonics
Preteach / Reteach

❶ **Beginning** Hold up an alphabet card for *u.* Say the letter name and make the /u/ sound. Say the following words and have children repeat them: *duck, but, cup, cut, hug.*

❷ ❸ **Early Intermediate/Intermediate** Write the word *but* and have children read it with you. Ask them to think of rhyming words and make a list: *cut, hut, nut, rut.* Continue with *sun.*

❹ ❺ **Early Advanced/Advanced** Work together to make a list of words with the /u/ sound. Then give each child a sheet of drawing paper and label it with *u.* Children draw pictures to illustrate some words with the /u/ sound.

Who works at night?

 Draw

OBJECTIVE

To guide children to express their understanding of weekly concepts and vocabulary.

Think, Talk, and Recognize!

Concept Talk

Connect to Day 4 Recall that yesterday children talked about what it is like to work at night.

Review the Weekly Question Who works at night? Have children answer the question. Make a list of their responses.

Use the Poster Use the Day 5 teaching notes.

Review Concept Vocabulary Review the vocabulary introduced on Day 1.

Concept Wrap Up

Have children draw to answer the question: *Who works at night?* Discuss the photograph on the page. You can tell these people are working at night, because it is very dark. What machines are they using? Why do you think they are working at night?

Leveled Support   Concept Vocabulary

① ② **Beginning/Early Intermediate** Display the Word Cards for *delivery worker*, *machinery*, and *policewoman*. Say each word. Ask children to repeat and point to the matching card.

③ **Intermediate** Display the Word Cards for *delivery worker*, *machinery*, and *policewoman*. Ask children to choose a card and say a sentence about the picture.

④ ⑤ **Early Advanced/Advanced** Display the Word Cards for *delivery worker*, *machinery*, and *policewoman*. Point out that people and machines work during the day and at night. Give each child a sheet of drawing paper folded in half. Label each side *Day* and *Night*. Children choose a vocabulary word and draw an illustration for the word in each section. Have them include details to show day or night.

Wrap Up   DAY 5

Daily Table Talk Who works at night? Have partners discuss the question, using the vocabulary words they have learned this week.

Produce Language To build fluency, children can label, write about, or speak about their drawings. Ask children to respond to what they read or heard.

Today children should have:

☑ **Reviewed** the weekly concept and concept vocabulary.

☑ **Spoken** about people who work at night.

☑ **Drawn or written** about people and machines that work at night.

ELA LS1.2 Share information and ideas, speaking audibly in complete, coherent sentences. (ELD LS.B1)

221

WEEK 5

CALIFORNIA

Weekly Lesson Plan

Last Week
Unit 6, Week 4
Night Workers

Question of the Week

Who helps to build a house?

DAY 1 Get Ready to Read	DAY 2 Read and Comprehend
Build Background	**Language: Category Words**

Instructional Plan and Materials

- **Word Cards**
  134–136

- **Big Book**
  Yoko Builds a Birdhouse

- **Poster**
  Poster 35 can be used at beginning or end of day.

- **Song Book**, p. 35

Transparencies Explore content and vocabulary and model fluent reading.

For further information about using these components, see pages x–xv.

	DAY 1	DAY 2
	Preteach/Review 10–15 min Poster, Song Book, Big Book **Leveled Support Preteach** **Practice Stations Preteach** **Teach** 35–45 min **Concept Talk** **Oral Vocabulary Routine** Word Cards **Build Concept Vocabulary** **Daily Table Talk** **Check/Reteach** 5–10 min Poster, Word Cards **Leveled Support Reteach**	**Preteach/Review** 10–15 min Poster **Leveled Support Preteach** **Practice Stations Review** **Teach** 35–45 min **Category Words** **Daily Table Talk** **Check/Reteach** 5–10 min Poster, Word Cards **Leveled Support Reteach** **Fluency:** Writing or Speaking

CALIFORNIA Standards

GK His-Soc Sci K.3 Students match simple descriptions of work that people do and the names of related jobs at the school, in the local community, and from historical accounts.

	DAY 1	DAY 2
	ELA R 1.18 Describe common objects and events in both general and specific language.	**ELA R 1.17** Identify and sort common words in basic categories (e.g., colors, shapes, foods).

Academic Language

	DAY 1	DAY 2
	Vocabulary: neighbors	**Category Words:** apartment, house, hut, igloo, teepee, trailer

Get Online! www.pearsonsuccessnet.com

Concept Talk Video	**Background Building Audio Slideshow**

This Week
Unit 6, Week 5

Building a House

Next Week
Unit 6, Week 6
Ants' Nests

DAY 3 FORM & FUNCTION Read and Comprehend	DAY 4 FORM & FUNCTION Language Arts	DAY 5 Language Arts
Language: High Frequency Words	**Phonics**	**Think, Talk, and Recognize**
Preteach/Review 10–15 min Poster **Leveled Support Preteach** **Practice Stations Review**	**Preteach/Review** 10–15 min Poster **Leveled Support Preteach** **Practice Stations Review**	**Preteach/Review** 10–15 min Poster **Leveled Support Preteach** **Practice Stations Review**
Teach 35–45 min **High Frequency Words** **Daily Table Talk**	**Teach** 35–45 min **Phonics/Phonemic Awareness** **Daily Table Talk**	**Teach** 15–20 min **Think, Talk, and Recognize** **Concept Wrap Up**
Check/Reteach 5–10 min Poster, Word Cards **Leveled Support Reteach**	**Check/Reteach** 5–10 min Poster, Word Cards **Leveled Support Reteach**	**Check/Reteach** 30–40 min Poster, Word Cards, Song Book **Leveled Support Reteach**
		Fluency: Writing or Speaking
ELA R 1.15 Read simple one-syllable and high frequency words (i.e., sight words).	**ELA R 1.15** Read simple one-syllable and high frequency words (i.e., sight words).	**ELA LS 1.2** Share information and ideas, speaking audibly in complete, coherent sentences.
High Frequency Words: four, she, was		

Practice Stations

Materials and Activity

drawing paper, magazines, scissors, glue

Housing Project 👬

Have partners look at the pictures on the student page and talk about what they see. Then have children cut out pictures of houses in magazines and glue them on drawing paper. Have them talk about features that all houses have: walls, windows, doors, sinks and so on. Help them to label their pictures with common features.

Concept Vocabulary Cards, drawing paper, glue

People Puzzles 🚶 👬

Make copies of the Vocabulary Cards. Cut each picture into four puzzle pieces. Have children put the puzzles together and glue them on drawing paper. Children describe who is in the picture and what they are doing.

Preteach/Reteach

Transfer and Common Misconceptions

Vocabulary Development

Some children may need help developing vocabulary that relates to houses. Provide examples in your school that relate to features of houses, such as windows, doors, walls, and so on.

Phrases

Children may need help understanding that two words can describe one person. Show a picture of a truck and say the word. Then role-play driving a truck. Have children repeat the phrase *truck driver.*

Produce Language

Weekly Concept and Language Goal

CONCEPT GOALS

- understand that different people work together to build houses
- explain an architect's job in building a house
- describe how construction workers and plumbers help build houses

By Day 5, children should be able to write a one-word label or a sentence.

Daily Table Talk

❶ **Beginning**
> Children look at the photos on the student page and repeat names of workers in the pictures.

❷ ❸ **Early Intermediate/Intermediate**
> Phrases or sentences: construction workers, truck drivers

❹ ❺ **Early Advanced/Advanced**
> Sentence: A truck driver helps to build a house.

Daily Table Talk

❶ **Beginning**
> Children talk about their drawings.

❷ ❸ **Early Intermediate/Intermediate**
> Children write one-word labels.

❹ ❺ **Early Advanced/Advanced**
> Children write a phrase or sentence.

DAY 3 — FORM & FUNCTION — Read and Comprehend

drawing paper, drawing materials

Where Do You Live?

Have each child draw a picture of his or her home. Encourage them to add details. Then have children talk about homes that share similarities. Model examples, such as: *Jack and Suki live in apartments. The buildings are tall.*

Pronouncing /r/

Non-English speakers may have difficulty with the /r/ sound. Provide ample opportunities for children to repeat words with /r/ in initial, medial, and final positions.

Daily Table Talk

① Beginning Children point to pictures of workers on the student page and say or repeat the words.

② ③ Early Intermediate/Intermediate Phrases or sentences: construction workers, build walls

④ ⑤ Early Advanced/Advanced Sentence: Construction workers hammer nails.

DAY 4 — FORM & FUNCTION — Language Arts

Word Cards for *she* and *was*; small sticky notes with the letters *s, h, e, w, a, s*

Sticky Words

Display the Word Cards. Have children take turns putting the sticky notes in order to spell the words: *She was.* Then they complete the sentence.

Subject Pronouns

In Spanish, subject pronouns are not necessary. Help Spanish-speaking children to use pronouns such as *he* and *she* in sentences.

Daily Table Talk

① Beginning Children repeat the word plumber.

② ③ Early Intermediate/Intermediate Words or phrases: puts in pipes

④ ⑤ Early Advanced/Advanced Sentence: A plumber puts in pipes.

DAY 5 — Language Arts

Letter Tiles, index cards with the words *red, big, hug, cat, pot*

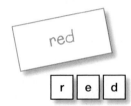

Say and Spell

Children choose a card and say the word. Then they use letter tiles to spell the word. Encourage children to use the words in sentences.

red

| r | e | d |

Phonemes

Children who speak Khmer may have difficulty pronouncing English phonemes. Provide many opportunities for segmenting words with three or four sounds.

Daily Table Talk

① Beginning Child speaks about the drawing and may write a label.

② ③ Early Intermediate/Intermediate Child writes a label that includes a concept vocabulary word.

④ ⑤ Early Advanced/Advanced Child writes a label or sentence that includes a vocabulary word.

OBJECTIVE

To introduce and discuss concepts and vocabulary related to building a house.

Build Background Get **Ready** to **Read!**

Question of the Week Who helps to build a house?
www.pearsonsuccessnet.com

Concept Talk

Use the Big Book If you haven't introduced the Big Book, consider reading it to children. Connect to the unit theme, Building—Putting It Together.

Introduce the Weekly Concept Tell children that today they will talk about people who work together to build a house. Ask the weekly question: Who helps to build a house?

Use the Poster Direct children's attention to the weekly poster. Use the Day 1 teaching notes at the bottom of the poster.

Sing the Song Use the song **Who Helps to Build a House?** to reinforce children's understanding of the weekly concept. Have the children sing or simply chant the words with you.

Use a Transparency Use the Sequence Map (Transparency 7) to help children organize the steps in building a house.

Vocabulary

* **Academic Vocabulary**
  construction workers someone who works in construction

* **neighbors** people who live very near you

  truck driver someone whose job is driving a truck

ELA R 1.18 Describe common objects and events in both general and specific language. (ELD R.B4)

223

Introduce Concept Vocabulary

1. Say the Word Display the Picture Card as you say *construction workers.* Have children repeat the words.

2. Introduce Word Meaning Ask questions about the construction workers. What do construction workers do?

3. Demonstrate Have children act out hammering, laying bricks, and other jobs that construction workers do.

4. Apply Have children demonstrate their understanding.

Repeat with other vocabulary words.

Corrective Feedback If children have difficulty pronouncing the words, point out that some vocabulary words are made up of two words. Place two blocks in front of children and tap each block as you say two words: *construction workers.* Repeat with *truck driver.*

Concept Work

Say each word and have children point to the matching picture. Discuss what construction workers do. Relate to children's experiences and knowledge of construction sites, equipment, and so on. Have children color the pictures.

Leveled Support   Vocabulary in Context

①② Beginning/Early Intermediate Say each vocabulary word. Children point to the matching picture and repeat the word.

③ Intermediate Write the following sentences on chart paper:

Construction workers _____ .

A truck driver _____ .

Read the incomplete sentences together, and have children complete each sentence with information about what the worker does.

④⑤ Early Advanced/Advanced Ask children to think of other workers who help to build houses. Make a list of their responses and talk about each job.

Wrap Up   DAY 1

Table Talk What do construction workers do? Have children answer the question, using the vocabulary words.

Produce Language Have a child role play one of the jobs that people do to build a house. The partner says a sentence about the worker.

Today children should have:

☑ **Learned** and applied vocabulary related to people who build houses.

☑ **Spoken** complete sentences about workers.

☑ **Recognized** concept vocabulary words.

 ELA R1.18 Describe common objects and events in both general and specific language. (ELD R.B6)

To discuss what an architect does; to introduce category words for different homes.

Concept Talk

Connect to Day 1 Who helps to build a house? Recall with children that yesterday they talked about who helps to build a house.

Introduce the Daily Question How does an architect help build a house? Explain that an architect designs and plans a building. Have children answer orally.

Use the Poster Use the Day 2 teaching notes.

Introduce Category Words

1. **Say the Word** Have children point to the *house*. Say the word and have children repeat it.

2. **Introduce Word Meaning** Gesture to show your classroom. Is this a house? What is a house?

3. **Demonstrate** Have children find pictures of houses in classroom picture books.

4. **Apply** Have children draw a house.

Repeat with other vocabulary words and elicit that they all belong to the category "types of homes."

Have children draw a type of home on the Worktext page.

Corrective Feedback If children have difficulty identifying different types of homes, explain that homes are different around the world. Say each word and have children repeat.

Wrap Up   DAY 2

 Table Talk Ask children to explain what an architect does. Discuss why the job is so important.

Produce Language To build fluency, encourage children to label or write a sentence about their drawings. They can share their writing with partners.

Today children should have:

☑ **Learned** and applied vocabulary related to different types of homes.

☑ **Spoken** complete sentences about homes.

☑ **Recognized** words that belong in the same category.

 ELA R1.17 Identify and sort common words in basic categories (e.g., colors, shapes, foods). (ELD R.B4)

Types of Homes

Picture Dictionary

apartment

house

hut

igloo

teepee

trailer

✏ **Draw** Draw a home.

224 🐻 **ELA R1.17** Identify and sort common words in basic categories (e.g., colors, shapes, foods). (ELD R.B4)

Preteach / Reteach LS Leveled Support **Category Words**

❶ ❷ **Beginning/Early Intermediate** Point to each picture in the Worktext. Have children say the word with you.

❸ **Intermediate** Point to one of the pictures in the Worktext. Ask children to say the word and then describe the house by using details.

❹ ❺ **Early Advanced/Advanced** Ask each child to draw a picture of a house that she or he would like to live in. Help them to label their pictures. Display the pictures.

How do construction workers build a house?

✏️ **Circle** Circle *Four*.
Four workers built a wall.

✏️ **Circle** Circle *She*. Circle *was*.
She was laying bricks.

 ELA R1.15 Read simple one-syllable and high-frequency words (i.e., sight words). (ELD R.B2)

225

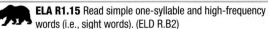

Leveled Support   **High Frequency Words**

Preteach / Reteach

① ② **Beginning/Early Intermediate** Write the sentence: *She was _____*. Have children read the sentence with you and complete it.

③ **Intermediate** Write the words *she, was,* and *four* on index cards. Turn the cards over. Children take turns choosing a card, reading the word, and using it in a sentence.

④ ⑤ **Early Advanced/Advanced** Help children write *four* on a sheet of drawing paper. Have them draw groups of four things.

OBJECTIVE

To discuss what construction workers do; to review the high frequency words *four, she,* and *was*.

Concept Talk   FORM & FUNCTION

Connect to Day 2 How does an architect help build a house? Recall with children that yesterday they talked about what an architect does.

Introduce the Daily Question Ask: How do construction workers help to build a house? Look at the picture in the Worktext for Day 1. Have children answer orally.

Use the Poster Use the Day 3 teaching notes.

Review Concept Vocabulary Review the words introduced on Day 1.

Review High Frequency Words

Ask children to hold up four fingers. Write the word *four* and read it together. Make a list of the words *four, she,* and *was.* Read each word and ask a volunteer to circle it. Help children complete the Worktext page.

Corrective Feedback If children have difficulty identifying the high frequency words, help them spell the words with magnetic letters. Read the words together.

Wrap Up   DAY **3**

Daily **Table Talk** How do construction workers help to build a house? What jobs do they do? Have children look at the pictures in the Worktext and discuss the question.

Produce Language Have partners each say a sentence about what construction workers do.

Today children should have:

☑ **Reviewed** and applied the high frequency words *four, she,* and *was*.

☑ **Spoken** complete sentences about construction workers.

☑ **Recognized** high frequency words in sentences about construction workers.

ELA R1.15 Read simple one-syllable and high-frequency words (i.e., sight words). (ELD R.B2)

225

To discuss what a plumber does; to identify initial, medial, and final sounds; to decode one syllable words.

Concept Talk

 FORM & FUNCTION

Connect to Day 3 How do construction workers help to build a house?

Introduce the Daily Question Ask: How does a plumber help build a house? Explain that a plumber puts in pipes and faucets for water. Have children answer orally.

Use the Poster Use the Day 4 teaching notes.

Phonics/Phonemic Awareness

Decode Words Write the word *bat*. Segment the sounds and blend them together. Write these words and help children decode: *man, bit, let, but, got*.

Identify Sounds Say the /b/ sound. Where do you hear /b/ in these words: *big? rabbit? rub?* Continue with similar examples. Children can raise their hands as they hear words with /b/ in the beginning, then in the middle, then at the end.

Match Words

 **Draw** Match words with pictures.

   **bed**

   **hat**

     log

     rug

     pig

Wrap Up   DAY 4

 Table Talk What does a plumber do? How does he or she help to build a house? **Have children discuss the question.**

Produce Language Have each say a sentence about what a plumber does.

Today children should have:

☑ **Learned** and applied vocabulary related to what plumbers do.

☑ **Spoken** complete sentences about plumbers.

☑ **Recognized** sounds in initial, medial, and final positions and decoded one-syllable words.

🐻 **ELA R1.15** Read simple one-syllable and high-frequency words. (i.e., sight words).

226   Building a House • Unit 6, Week 5

Preteach / Reteach — Leveled Support   Phonics/Phonemic Awareness

① ② **Beginning/Early Intermediate** Write *bed*. Segment the sounds. Then ask children to blend and say the word. Continue with *map, cat, dog, cup,* and *sit*.

③ **Intermediate** Write these words on chart paper: *pig, pot, cat, tap, bed*. Read the words together. Then say a sentence: *I cook with a _____ .* Children complete the sentence with a word from the list. Continue with similar sentences.

④ ⑤ **Early Advanced/Advanced** Write these words on the board: *lip, bib, top, mop, bug, bus, bag, can, red, hen*. Read the words together. Then give each child a sheet of drawing paper and ask him or her to draw a picture to illustrate one of the words. Children share their drawings and other children say the word that they chose.

Who helps to build a house?

 Draw

OBJECTIVE

To guide children to express their understanding of weekly concepts and vocabulary.

Think, Talk, and Recognize!

Concept Talk

Connect to Day 4 Remind children that yesterday they talked about what a plumber does.

Review the Weekly Question Ask: Who helps to build a house? Say the following: *nurse, plumber, teacher, construction worker, architect, fireman, waiter.* **Children stand when you name a worker who helps to build a house.**

Use the Poster Use the Day 5 teaching notes.

Review Concept Vocabulary Review the vocabulary introduced on Day 1.

Concept Wrap Up

Have children draw to answer the question: *Who helps to build a house?* Help children label their pictures. Discuss the photo on the page with children. These two people are building a house. What do you see in the picture?

 **Concept Vocabulary**

Preteach LS Reteach

① ② **Beginning/Early Intermediate** Display the Word Cards for the vocabulary words. Children point to each and say the words.

③ **Intermediate** Write the vocabulary words and read them together. Have children answer these questions using the words:

Who delivers wood for the house?

Who lives near the house?

Who lays bricks?

④ ⑤ **Early Advanced/Advanced** Display the Word Cards. Ask a child to choose a card and say a sentence that one of the people might say. Model by pointing to the picture of the truck driver and saying: *I like to drive.*

 Wrap Up DAY 5

Table Talk Daily Who helps to build a house? **Have children discuss the question, using the vocabulary words they learned this week.**

Produce Language To build fluency, children can label, write about, or speak about their drawings. Ask children to respond to what they read or heard.

Today children should have:

☑ **Reviewed** the weekly concept and concept vocabulary.

☑ **Spoken** about who helps to build a house.

☑ **Drawn or written** to show who helps to build a house.

 ELA LS1.2 Share information and ideas, speaking audibly in complete, coherent sentences. (ELD LS.B1)

227

Weekly Lesson Plan

 Question of the Week How do ants build?

	DAY **1** Get Ready to Read	DAY **2** Read and Comprehend

Instructional Plan and Materials

- **Word Cards** 137–141

- **Big Book** Yoko Builds a Birdhouse

- **Poster**
  Poster 36 can be used at beginning or end of day.

- **Song Book**, p. 36

Transparencies Explore content and vocabulary and model fluent reading.

For further information about using these components, see pages x–xv.

Build Background

Preteach/Review 10–15 min
Poster, Song Book, Big Book
  Leveled Support Preteach
  Practice Stations Preteach

Teach 35–45 min
  Concept Talk
  Oral Vocabulary Routine
    Word Cards
  Build Concept Vocabulary
  Daily Table Talk

Check/Reteach 5–10 min
Poster, Word Cards
  Leveled Support Reteach

Language: Category Words

Preteach/Review 10–15 min
Poster
  Leveled Support Preteach
  Practice Stations Review

Teach 35–45 min
  Category Words
  Daily Table Talk

Check/Reteach 5–10 min
Poster, Word Cards
  Leveled Support Reteach

Fluency: Writing or Speaking

CALIFORNIA Standards

GK Sci 2.a Students know how to observe and describe similarities and differences in the appearance and behavior of plants and animals (e.g., seed-bearing plants, birds, fish, insects).

ELA R 1.18 Describe common objects and events in both general and specific language.

ELA R 1.17 Identify and sort common words in basic categories (e.g., colors, shapes, foods).

Academic Language

Vocabulary: fall, hundreds, months, spring

Category Words: bee, beetle, cricket, wasp

Get Online! www.pearsonsuccessnet.com

Concept Talk Video

Background Building Audio Slideshow

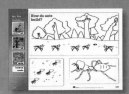

DAY 3 Read and Comprehend	**DAY 4** Language Arts	**DAY 5** Language Arts
Language: High Frequency Words	**Phonics**	**Think, Talk, and Recognize**
Preteach/Review 10–15 min Poster **Leveled Support Preteach** **Practice Stations Review**	**Preteach/Review** 10–15 min Poster **Leveled Support Preteach** **Practice Stations Review**	**Preteach/Review** 10–15 min Poster **Leveled Support Preteach** **Practice Stations Review**
Teach 35–45 min **High Frequency Words** **Daily Table Talk**	**Teach** 35–45 min **Phonemic Awareness** **Daily Table Talk**	**Teach** 15–20 min **Think, Talk, and Recognize** **Concept Wrap Up**
Check/Reteach 5–10 min Poster, Word Cards **Leveled Support Reteach**	**Check/Reteach** 5–10 min Poster, Word Cards **Leveled Support Reteach**	**Check/Reteach** 30–40 min Poster, Word Cards, Song Book **Leveled Support Reteach**
		Fluency: Writing or Speaking
ELA R 1.15 Read simple one-syllable and high frequency words (i.e., sight words).	**ELA R 1.15** Read simple one-syllable and high frequency words (i.e., sight words).	**ELA LS 1.2** Share information and ideas, speaking audibly in complete, coherent sentences.
High Frequency Words: come, one		

Practice Stations

Materials and Activity

clay, pipe cleaners

The Ants Go Marching ✿

Have children look at the drawing of an ant on the student page and describe what an ant looks like. Have children use clay and pieces of pipe cleaners to make model ants. After they make their model ants, have children complete the sentence: *My ant wants to go to _____.*

old magazines, scissors, glue, mural paper

Spring and Fall ✿

Divide the mural paper into two sections labeled Spring and Fall. Have children cut out pictures that represent each season. Discuss groups of items that may reflect the seasons, such as weather, clothing, and activities. After the mural is complete, help them label some items.

Preteach/Reteach

Transfer and Common Misconceptions

Vocabulary

Some children may be confused by the meaning of the word *nest* in this lesson. Point out that there are many different types of nests. The nest in the drawing looks like a pile of dirt, compared to the more familiar bird's nest.

Multiple Meaning Words

Be aware that some children may experience confusion with words that have multiple meanings. Say *fall* and role-play falling to the ground. Then show a picture that illustrates the season and explain that the word has two meanings.

Produce Language

Weekly Concept and Language Goal

CONCEPT GOALS

- understand that ants are animals that can build
- describe the parts of an ant nest
- explain how ants keep their nests safe

By Day 5, children should be able to write a one-word label or a sentence.

Daily Table Talk

| ❶ Beginning | Children repeat a sentence to answer the question. |

| ❷ ❸ Early Intermediate/Intermediate | Phrases or sentence: with leaves, dig in dirt |

| ❹ ❺ Early Advanced/Advanced | Sentence: Ants build with leaves. |

Daily Table Talk

| ❶ Beginning | Children talk about their drawings. |

| ❷ ❸ Early Intermediate/Intermediate | Children write one-word labels. |

| ❹ ❺ Early Advanced/Advanced | Children write a phrase or sentence. |

FORM & FUNCTION

DAY 3 Read and Comprehend

DAY 4 FORM & FUNCTION Language Arts

DAY 5 Language Arts

paper bowls, paint, drawing paper, drawing materials, scissors

white drawing paper cut into shapes of popcorn, bowl

index cards with a word on one side and a drawing to illustrate the word on the other side: *ant, cup, pig, mop, ten, Dad, bed, fan,* and *pan*

Busy Bees ✳ 👥

Have children make a bee by painting the bowl yellow. After the paint dries, children glue on a circular head, legs, and antennae. Have children tell what sound a bee makes and share information about bees.

Pass the Bowl, Please 👥

Write the following words on the paper popcorn shapes: *come, one, four, two, they, she, we, are, here,* and *is.* Place the papers in the bowl. Have children take turns choosing a "popcorn word" and reading it. Other children use the word in a sentence. Children take turns.

two

Picture This 👥

Place the cards in a stack with the words showing. One child takes a card and reads the word. The partner checks the picture on the back. Children take turns.

Word Families

Russian vocabulary has families of words. These words come from a root with prefixes and suffixes.

High Frequency Words

Since many high frequency words are not easily decodable, children need many opportunities to practice the words. Make word cards for children to use at school and at home.

Vowels

The Korean language has 10 vowels. Korean speakers may experience difficulty relating to the English alphabet system.

Daily Table Talk

❶ **Beginning** Children repeat words to answer the question.

❷ ❸ **Early Intermediate/Intermediate**
Words or phrases: tunnels, hills

❹ ❺ **Early Advanced/Advanced**
Sentence: Ants build tunnels.

Daily Table Talk

❶ **Beginning** Children repeat phrases to answer the question.

❷ ❸ **Early Intermediate/Intermediate**
Intermediate Phrases: watch for other ants

❹ ❺ **Early Advanced/Advanced**
Sentence: Ants keep other ants away.

Daily Table Talk

❶ **Beginning** Child speaks about the drawing and may write a label.

❷ ❸ **Early Intermediate/Intermediate** Child writes a label that includes a concept vocabulary word.

❹ ❺ **Early Advanced/Advanced** Child writes a label or sentence that includes a vocabulary word.

OBJECTIVE

To introduce and discuss concepts and vocabulary related to ants building their nests.

Build Background **Get Ready to Read!**

Question of the Week How do ants build?

www.pearsonsuccessnet.com

Concept Talk

Use the Big Book If you haven't introduced the Big Book, consider reading it to children. Connect to the unit theme, Building—Putting It Together.

Introduce the Weekly Concept Tell children that today they will talk about ants and how they build nests. Ask the weekly question: How do ants build?

Use the Poster Direct children's attention to the weekly poster. Use the Day 1 teaching notes at the bottom of the poster.

Sing the Song Use the song **Ants at Work** to reinforce children's understanding of the weekly concept. Have the children sing or simply chant the words with you.

Use a Transparency Use the Fable Transparency (Transparency 11) to share the fable of the ant and the grasshoppers. Children can compare the ants in the fable to real ants.

Ants' Nests

Vocabulary

ant

fall

spring

hundreds

months

228

How do ants build?

Vocabulary

* **Academic Vocabulary**
  ant a common, small, black or red insect that lives in groups

* **fall** the season between winter and summer, when leaves and flowers appear

* **spring** the season between winter and summer, when leaves and flowers appear

* **hundreds** a very large number of things or people

* **months** 12 periods of time that a year is divided into

ELA R 1.18 Describe common objects and events in both general and specific language. (ELD R.B4)

229

Introduce Concept Vocabulary

1. **Say the Word** Display the Word Card as you say *fall.* Have children repeat the word.

2. **Introduce Word Meaning** Ask questions about the fall. What season comes after summer? What happens to trees in the fall? What is it like outside in the fall?

3. **Demonstrate** Show a monthly calendar with pictures. Discuss the pictures for the fall season.

4. **Apply** Have children demonstrate their understanding.

Repeat with other vocabulary words.

Corrective Feedback If children have difficulty pronouncing the words, segment and blend the sounds. *Spring* and *fall* are both words that have more than one meaning. Help children understand that in this lesson, they should think of fall and spring as seasons of the year. Talk about other meanings of the words. Ask how children can know which meaning is being used.

Concept Work

Have children point to the picture of the ant and talk about what an ant looks like. Identify different parts of the ant, such as its legs and its antennae. Show children that ants can carry objects much larger than themselves to build nests. Have children talk about what the ants are doing and then color the pictures.

Leveled Support **Vocabulary in Context**

① ② **Beginning/Early Intermediate** Write the words *months, spring,* and *fall* and read them together. Display a monthly calendar and identify the months as you turn each page. Talk about the months during the spring and the fall seasons.

③ ④ **Intermediate/Early Advanced** Do the first activity. Then give each child a sheet of drawing paper divided in half. Help them to label each section with the words *spring* and *fall.* Have children draw a picture to illustrate each season.

⑤ **Advanced** Write the word *hundreds* and read it together. Have children work together to make ten groups of ten classroom objects, such as connecting cubes or pennies. Point out that they have made *one hundred.* Write the number.

Wrap Up **DAY 1**

Daily **Table Talk** How do ants build? Have children answer the question, using the vocabulary words.

Produce Language Have partners say a sentence that describes an ant nest.

Today children should have:

☑ **Learned** and applied vocabulary related to how ants build.

☑ **Spoken** complete sentences about ants and their nests.

☑ **Recognized** concept vocabulary words.

 ELA R1.18 Describe common objects and events in both general and specific language. (ELD R.B6)

 Insects

Picture Dictionary

bee

beetle

cricket

wasp

....

 Draw Draw an insect.

230   ELA R1.17 Identify and sort common words in basic categories (e.g., colors, shapes, foods). (ELD R.B4)

OBJECTIVE

To discuss where ants build nests; to introduce category words for insects.

Concept Talk

Connect to Day 1 Recall with children that yesterday they talked about how ants build.

Introduce the Daily Question Ask: Where do ants build nests? Refer to the pictures in the Worktext and talk about the setting. Have children answer orally.

Use the Poster Use the Day 2 teaching notes.

Introduce Category Words

1. Say the Word Have children point to *bee*. Say the word and children repeat.

2. Introduce Word Meaning Hold up a picture of an animal. Is this a bee? What does a bee look like? What sound does it make?

3. Demonstrate Have children act out how a bee flies and buzzes.

4. Apply Repeat with other vocabulary words, eliciting that they all belong to the category "insects."

Have children draw insects in the Worktext.

Corrective Feedback If children have difficulty identifying insects, point out some of the body parts: *antenna, legs, head, wings.* Say the name of each insect and have children repeat it.

Wrap Up   DAY 2

 Have partners describe where ants build nests.

Produce Language To build fluency, encourage children to label or write a sentence about their drawings. They can share their writing with partners.

Today children should have:

☑ **Learned** and applied vocabulary related to insects.

☑ **Spoken** complete sentences about where ants build nests.

☑ **Recognized** words that belong in the same category.

 ELA R1.17 Identify and sort common words in basic categories (e.g., colors, shapes, foods). (ELD R.B4)

230   Ants' Nests • Unit 6, Week 6

Preteach / Reteach LS **Leveled Support** Category Words

① ② **Beginning/Early Intermediate** Have children point to each insect on the Worktext page. Say the word and have children repeat.

③ **Intermediate** Say the name of each insect. Ask children to point to the picture.

④ ⑤ **Early Advanced/Advanced** Have children look closely at the pictures of insects and describe what they see. Make a list of the parts that insects have: *head, antenna, six legs, body, wings.* Read the words together.

What are the parts of an ant nest?

Circle Circle *come*.
Worker ants come to dig tunnels.

Circle Circle *One*.
One queen ant lays eggs.

ELA R1.15 Read simple one-syllable and high-frequency words (i.e., sight words). (ELD R.B2)

231

OBJECTIVE

To discuss the parts of an ant's nest; to review the high-frequency words *come* and *one*.

Concept Talk
FORM & FUNCTION

Connect to Day 2 Recall with children that yesterday they talked about where ants build nests.

Introduce the Daily Question Ask: What are the parts of an ant nest? Discuss the pictures in the Worktext. Explain that ants use soil, leaves, and other items to build their nest. Worker ants build tunnels. Have children answer the question orally.

Use the Poster Use the Day 3 teaching notes.

Review Concept Vocabulary Review the words introduced on Day 1.

Review High Frequency Words

Write the word *one* and read it together. Ask children to hold up one finger. Write the sentence: *I see one cat*. Ask a volunteer to circle *one*. Continue with *come*.

Corrective Feedback If children have difficulty reading the high frequency words, provide many opportunities for children to identify the words in short sentences. Write the words on sticky notes so children can place the notes near the words in the sentences.

Leveled Support — High Frequency Words
Preteach / Reteach

① ② Beginning/Early Intermediate Write the word *one* and read it together. Have each child use the word in a sentence. Repeat with *come*.

③ Intermediate Write the words *one* and *come* on sticky notes. Have children look for the words in classroom picture books. Have them place the notes on the pages where they find the words. Then have partners share their books.

④ ⑤ Early Advanced/Advanced Make Bingo cards with the high frequency words from Unit 6: *he, a, to, look, go, we, are, here, is, two, they, have, do, that, I, see, like, she, was four, one, come*. Write the words on index cards, say the words, and use counters to play Bingo.

Wrap Up   **DAY 3**

Table Talk *Daily* What are the parts of an ant nest? Have partners discuss the question.

Produce Language Have each child draw a picture of an ant nest. Help them label their pictures. Then have partners use a sentence to describe their pictures.

Today children should have:

☑ **Learned** and applied the high frequency words *one* and *come*.

☑ **Spoken** complete sentences about ant nests.

☑ **Recognized** the high frequency words *come* and *one*.

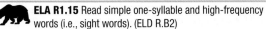 **ELA R1.15** Read simple one-syllable and high-frequency words (i.e., sight words). (ELD R.B2)

231

DAY 4

CALIFORNIA

OBJECTIVES

To discuss how ants keep their nests safe; to decode one-syllable words; to segment words with three or four phonemes.

Concept Talk

FORM & FUNCTION

Connect to Day 3 Recall with children that yesterday they talked about the parts of an ant nest.

Introduce the Daily Question How do ants keep their nests safe? Explain that some ants can tell if an ant is from another nest. Ants from the nest try to keep other ants away. Have children answer orally.

Use the Poster Use the Day 4 teaching notes.

Phonemic Awareness

Decode Words Write *ant.* Move your finger under each letter as you blend the sounds. Say *ant,* and have children repeat. Help children decode the words in the Worktext. Then have them complete the page.

Identify Sounds Give each child three blocks or index cards and make a row. Explain that the blocks show the beginning, middle, and end of a word. Say *bit.* Show me where you hear /t/. Point to the block. Continue with other words.

Wrap Up DAY 4

Daily Table Talk How do ants keep their nests safe? Have partners discuss the question.

Produce Language Have each child say a sentence about how ants protect their nests.

Today children should have:

☑ **Learned** and applied vocabulary related to how ants keep their nests safe.

☑ **Spoken** complete sentences about ants.

☑ **Recognized** and decoded one-syllable words.

ELA R1.15 Read simple one-syllable and high-frequency words (i.e., sight words).

Match Words

 Match Match words with pictures.

 **ant**

 **cup**

 **hen**

 pig

mop

Leveled Support Phonemic Awareness

Preteach Reteach

① ② **Beginning/Early Intermediate** Write *man.* Segment the sounds and say the word. Have children do the same and use the word in a sentence. Continue with *sit, can, pen, sun.*

③ ④ **Intermediate/Early Advanced** Write these words on index cards: *hen, sit, ant, cat, can, met, bat, cup, fun, pot.* Place the cards on the floor. Give a child a beanbag and have him or her toss it on a card. The child says the word and uses it in a sentence. Children take turns.

⑤ **Advanced** Give partners these letter tiles: *a, b, c, d, e, f, h, i, j, l, m, n, o, s, t, u, v, w.* Have them make and read three letter words.

How do ants build?

✏ Draw

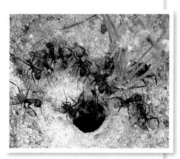

ELA LS. 1.2 Share information and ideas, speaking audibly in complete, coherent sentences. (ELD LS.B3)

233

OBJECTIVE

To guide children to express their understanding of weekly concepts and vocabulary.

Think, Talk, and Recognize!

Concept Talk

Connect to Day 4 Recall that yesterday they talked about how ants keep their nest safe.

Review the Weekly Question How do ants build? Have children explain what ants use to make nests.

Use the Poster Use the Day 5 teaching notes.

Review Concept Vocabulary Review the vocabulary introduced on Day 1.

Concept Wrap Up

Have children draw to answer the question: *How do ants build?* Prompt discussion with the photograph on the bottom of the page.

Leveled Support Concept Vocabulary

① ② **Beginning/Early Intermediate** Write *ant, fall, spring, hundreds, months.* Read the words together. Then say a short definition and ask children to say the vocabulary word: *This is a season when flowers start to grow.*

③ ④ **Intermediate/Early Advanced** Write *months* and read it together. Make a list of the months and make a tally to show when each child celebrates a birthday. Write *spring* and *fall* and read the words. Decide which birthdays occur during those seasons.

⑤ **Advanced** Write *spring, summer, fall, winter.* Have children discuss each season. Then have them label a sheet of drawing paper with their favorite season. Children draw a picture to show what they like to do during that season.

Wrap Up **DAY 5**

Table Talk How do ants build? Have children discuss the question, using the vocabulary words they learned this week.

Produce Language To build fluency, children can label, write about, or speak about their drawings. Ask children to respond to what they read or heard.

Today children should have:

- ☑ **Reviewed** concept vocabulary related to ants and nests.
- ☑ **Spoken** about how ants build.
- ☑ **Drawn or written** to show how ants build.

ELA LS12 Share information and ideas, speaking audibly in complete, coherent sentences. (ELD LS.B1)

233

Picture Glossary

Colors

blue	orange	red
green	purple	yellow

Numbers

1	one	
2	two	
3	three	
4	four	
5	five	
6	six	
7	seven	
8	eight	
9	nine	
10	ten	

234

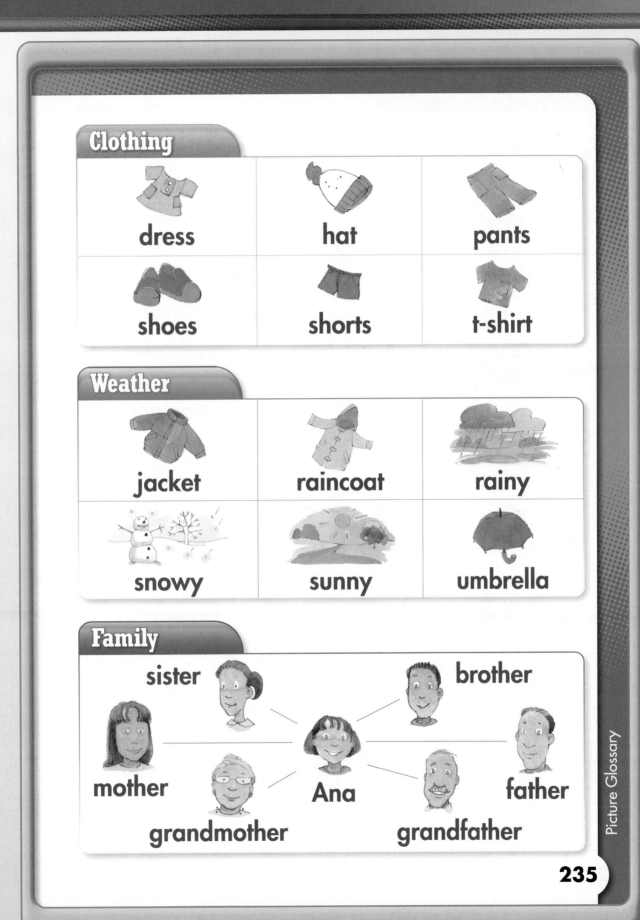

Clothing

dress	hat	pants
shoes	shorts	t-shirt

Weather

jacket	raincoat	rainy
snowy	sunny	umbrella

Family

sister   brother

mother   Ana   father

grandmother   grandfather

Picture Glossary

235

Picture Glossary

At Home

address

bathroom

bed

bedroom

couch

dining room

door

house

kitchen

living room

oven

phone

room

window

tub

236

At School

adding	book	chair
crayon	desk	globe
map	painting	pencil
reading	story	table
working on the computer		writing

Standards
CALIFORNIA

ENGLISH-LANGUAGE ARTS

Reading Standards

1.0 Word Analysis, Fluency, and Systematic Vocabulary Development
Students know about letters, words, and sounds. They apply this knowledge to read simple sentences.

Concepts About Print
1.1 Identify the front cover, back cover, and title page of a book.
1.2 Follow words from left to right and from top to bottom on the printed page.
1.3 Understand that printed materials provide information.
1.4 Recognize that sentences in print are made up of separate words.
1.5 Distinguish letters from words.
1.6 Recognize and name all uppercase and lowercase letters of the alphabet.

Phonemic Awareness
1.7 Track (move sequentially from sound to sound) and represent the number, sameness/difference, and order of two and three isolated phonemes (e.g., /f, s, th/, /j, d, j/).
1.8 Track (move sequentially from sound to sound) and represent changes in simple syllables and words with two and three sounds as one sound is added, substituted, omitted, shifted, or repeated (e.g., vowel-consonant, consonant-vowel, or consonant-vowel-consonant).
1.9 Blend vowel-consonant sounds orally to make words or syllables.
1.10 Identify and produce rhyming words in response to an oral prompt.
1.11 Distinguish orally stated one-syllable words and separate into beginning or ending sounds.
1.12 Track auditorily each word in a sentence and each syllable in a word.
1.13 Count the number of sounds in syllables and syllables in words.

Decoding and Word Recognition
11.14 Match all consonant and short-vowel sounds to appropriate letters.
1.15 Read simple one-syllable and high-frequency words (i.e., sight words).
1.16 Understand that as letters of words change, so do the sounds (i.e., the alphabetic principle).

Vocabulary and Concept Development
1.17 Identify and sort common words in basic categories (e.g., colors, shapes, foods).
1.18 Describe common objects and events in both general and specific language.

2.0 Reading Comprehension
Students identify the basic facts and ideas in what they have read, heard, or viewed. They use comprehension strategies (e.g., generating and responding to questions, comparing new information to what is already known). The selections in Recommended Literature, Kindergarten Through Grade Twelve (California Department of Education, 2002) illustrate the quality and complexity of the materials to be read by students.

Structural Features of Informational Materials
2.1 Locate the title, table of contents, name of author, and name of illustrator.

Comprehension and Analysis of Grade-Level-Appropriate Text
2.2 Use pictures and context to make predictions about story content.
2.3 Connect to life experiences the information and events in texts.
2.4 Retell familiar stories.
2.5 Ask and answer questions about essential elements of a text.

3.0 Literary Response and Analysis
Students listen and respond to stories based on well-known characters, themes, plots, and settings. The selections in *Recommended Literature, Kindergarten Through Grade Twelve* illustrate the quality and complexity of the materials to be read by students.

Narrative Analysis of Grade-Level-Appropriate Text
3.1 Distinguish fantasy from realistic text.
3.2 Identify types of everyday print materials (e.g., storybooks, poems, newspapers, signs, labels).
3.3 Identify characters, settings, and important events.

Writing Standards

1.0 Writing Strategies
Students write words and brief sentences that are legible.

Organization and Focus
1.1 Use letters and phonetically spelled words to write about experiences, stories, people, objects, or events.

238

1.2 Write consonant-vowel-consonant words (i.e., demonstrate the alphabetic principle).
1.3 Write by moving from left to right and from top to bottom.

Penmanship
1.4 Write uppercase and lowercase letters of the alphabet independently, attending to the form and proper spacing of the letters.

Written and Oral English Language Conventions Standards

The standards for written and oral English language conventions have been placed between those for writing and for listening and speaking because these conventions are essential to both sets of skills.

1.0 Written and Oral English Language Conventions

Students write and speak with a command of standard English conventions.

Sentence Structure
1.1 Recognize and use complete, coherent sentences when speaking.

Spelling
1.2 Spell independently by using pre-phonetic knowledge, sounds of the alphabet, and knowledge of letter names.

Listening and Speaking Standards

1.0 Listening and Speaking Strategies

Students listen and respond to oral communication. They speak in clear and coherent sentences.

Comprehension
1.1 Understand and follow one-and two-step oral directions.
1.2 Share information and ideas, speaking audibly in complete, coherent sentences.

2.0 Speaking Applications (Genres and Their Characteristics)

Students deliver brief recitations and oral presentations about familiar experiences or interests, demonstrating command of the organization and delivery strategies outlined in Listening and Speaking Standard 1.0.

Using the listening and speaking strategies of kindergarten outlined in Listening and Speaking Standard 1.0, students:
2.1 Describe people, places, things (e.g., size, color, shape), locations, and actions.

2.2 Recite short poems, rhymes, and songs.
2.3 Relate an experience or creative story in a logical sequence.

ENGLISH-LANGUAGE DEVELOPMENT

Reading Standards

Beginning

Word Analysis
B1. Recognize English phonemes that correspond to phonemes students already hear and produce in their primary language.

Fluency and Systematic Vocabulary Development
B2. Read aloud simple words (e.g., nouns and adjectives) in stories or games.
B3. Respond appropriately to some social and academic interactions (e.g., simple question/answer, negotiate play).
B4. Demonstrate comprehension of simple vocabulary with an appropriate action.
B5. Retell simple stories by using drawings, words, or phrases.
B6. Produce simple vocabulary (single words or short phrases) to communicate basic needs in social and academic settings (e.g., locations, greetings, classroom objects).

Reading Comprehension
B7. Respond orally to stories read aloud, using physical actions and other means of nonverbal communication (e.g., matching objects, pointing to an answer, drawing pictures).
B8. Respond orally to stories read aloud, giving one- or two- word responses (e.g., "brown bear") to factual comprehension questions.
B9. Draw pictures from one's own experience related to a story or topic (e.g., community in social studies).
B10. Understand and follow simple one-step directions for classroom activities.
B11. Identify, using key words or pictures, the basic sequence of events in stories read aloud.

Early Intermediate

Word Analysis
EI1. Produce English phonemes that correspond to phonemes students already hear and produce, including long and short vowels and initial and final consonants.

EI2. Recognize English phonemes that do not correspond to sounds students hear and produce, (e.g., *a* in *cat* and final consonants).

Phonemic Awareness

1.7 Track (move sequentially from sound to sound) and represent the number, sameness/difference, and order of two and three isolated phonemes (e.g., */f, s, th/,/j, d, j/*).

1.10 Identify and produce rhyming words in response to an oral prompt.

Fluency and Systematic Vocabulary Development

EI3. Produce vocabulary, phrases, and simple sentences to communicate basic needs in social and academic settings.

EI4. Read simple vocabulary, phrases, and sentences independently.

EI5. Read aloud an increasing number of English words.

EI6. Demonstrate internalization of English grammar, usage, and word choice by recognizing and correcting some errors when speaking or reading aloud.

Reading Comprehension

EI7. Respond orally to simple stories read aloud, using phrases or simple sentences to answer factual comprehension questions.

EI8. Draw and label pictures related to a story topic or one's own experience.

EI9. Understand and follow simple two-step directions for classroom activities.

EI10. Orally identify, using key words or phrases, the basic sequence of events in text read aloud.

EI11. Draw logical inferences from a story read aloud.

EI12. *Respond orally to factual comprehension questions about stories by answering in simple sentences.*

EI13. *Recite simple poems.*

EI14. *Identify orally the setting and characters by using simple sentences and vocabulary.*

Intermediate

Word Analysis

I1. Pronounce most English phonemes correctly while reading aloud.

I2. Recognize sound/symbol relationships and basic word-formation rules in phrases, simple sentences, or simple text.

I3. Recognize and name all uppercase and lowercase letters of the alphabet.

1.1 Identify the front cover, back cover, and title page of a book.

1.2 Follow words from left to right and from top to bottom on the printed page.

1.3 Understand that printed materials provide information.

1.4 Recognize that sentences in print are made up of separate words.

1.5 Distinguish letters from words.

Phonemic Awareness

1.7 Track (move sequentially from sound to sound) and represent the number, sameness/difference, and order of two and three isolated phonemes (e.g., */f, s, th/,/j, d, j/*).

Fluency and Systematic Vocabulary Development

I4. Demonstrate internalization of English grammar, usage, and word choice by recognizing and correcting errors when speaking or reading aloud.

I5. Use decoding skills to read more complex words independently.

I6. Use more complex vocabulary and sentences to communicate needs and express ideas in a wider variety of social and academic settings (e.g., classroom discussions, mediation of conflicts).

I7. Apply knowledge of content-related vocabulary to discussions and reading.

I8. Recognize simple prefixes and suffixes when they are attached to known vocabulary (e.g., *remove, jumping*).

Reading Comprehension

I9. Read stories and respond orally in simple sentences to factual comprehension questions about the stories.

I10. While reading aloud in a group, point out basic text features, such as the title, table of contents, and chapter headings.

I11. Draw inferences about stories read aloud and use simple phrases or sentences to communicate the inferences.

I12. Write captions or phrases for drawings related to a story.

I13. Understand and follow some multiple-step directions for classroom-related activities.

Early Advanced

Word Analysis

EA1. Use common English morphemes to derive meaning in oral and silent reading (e.g., basic syllabication rules, regular and irregular plurals, and basic phonics).

240

EA2. Recognize sound/symbol relationship and basic word-formation rules in phrases, simple sentences, or simple text.

Phonemic Awareness

1.8 Track (move sequentially from sound to sound) and represent changes in simple syllables and words with two and three sounds as one sound is added, substituted, omitted, shifted, or repeated (e.g., vowel-consonant, consonant-vowel, or consonant-vowel-consonant).

1.9 Blend vowel-consonant sounds orally to make words or syllables.

1.11 Distinguish orally stated one-syllable words and separate into beginning or ending sounds.

1.12 Track auditorily each word in a sentence and each syllable in a word.

1.13 Count the number of sounds in syllables and syllables in words.

Decoding and Word Recognition

1.14 Match all consonant and short-vowel sounds to appropriate letters.

1.15 Read simple one-syllable and high-frequency words (i.e., sight words).

1.16 Understand that as letters of words change, so do the sounds (i.e., the alphabetic principle).

Fluency and Systematic Vocabulary Development

EA3. Recognize simple antonyms and synonyms (e.g., good, bad; blend, mix) in stories or games.

EA4. Use simple prefixes and suffixes when they are attached to known vocabulary.

EA5. Use decoding skills and knowledge of academic and social vocabulary to begin independent reading.

Reading Comprehension

EA6. Read text and use detailed sentences to identify orally the main idea and use the idea to draw inferences about the text.

EA7. Read stories and orally respond to them by answering factual comprehension questions about cause-and-effect relationships.

EA8. Write a brief summary (three or four complete sentences) of a story.

EA9. Read and use basic text features, such as the title, table of contents, and chapter headings.

EA10. Read stories and texts from content areas and respond orally to them by restating facts and details to clarify ideas.

Writing Standards

Beginning

B1. Copy the English alphabet legibly.

Writing Strategies

EI1. Write simple sentences about events or characters from familiar stories read aloud by the teacher.

EI2. Write simple sentences by using key words posted and commonly used in the classroom (e.g., labels, number names, days of the week, and months (e.g., "Today is Tuesday").

EI3. Write one to two simple sentences (e.g., "I went to the park").

Intermediate

Writing Strategies

I1. Write short narrative stories that include the elements of setting and characters.

I2. Produce independent writing that is understood when read but may include inconsistent use of standard grammatical forms.

I3. Following a model, proceed through the writing process to independently write short paragraphs of at least three lines.

I4. Write simple sentences appropriate for language arts and other content areas (e.g., math, science, social studies).

I5. Write a friendly letter of a few lines.

Early Advanced

Writing Strategies

EA1. Write short narratives that include elements of setting, characters, and events.

EA2. Proceed through the writing process to write short paragraphs that maintain a consistent focus.

EA3. Use complex vocabulary and sentences appropriate for language arts and other content areas (e.g., math, science, social studies).

EA4. Write a formal letter.

EA5. Produce independent writing with consistent use of standard grammatical forms. (Some rules may not be followed).

Listening and Speaking Standards

Beginning

Strategies and Applications

B1. Begin to speak a few words or sentences by using some English phonemes and rudimentary English grammatical forms (e.g., single words or phrases).

California Standards

241

B2. Answer simple questions with one- to -two-word responses.

B3. Respond to simple directions and questions by using physical actions and other means of nonverbal communication (e.g., matching objects, pointing to an answer, drawing pictures).

B4. Independently use common social greetings and simple repetitive phrases (e.g., "Thank you," "You're welcome").

Early Intermediate

Strategies and Applications

EI1. Begin to be understood when speaking, but may have some inconsistent use of standard English grammatical forms and sounds (e.g., plurals, simple past tense, pronouns such as he or she).

EI2. Ask and answer questions by using phrases or simple sentences.

EI3. Retell familiar stories and short conversations by using appropriate gestures, expressions, and illustrative objects.

EI4. Orally communicate basic needs (e.g., "May I get a drink?").

EI5. Recite familiar rhymes, songs, and simple stories.

Intermediate

Strategies and Applications

I1. Ask and answer instructional questions by using simple sentences.

I2. Listen attentively to stories and information, and identify important details and concepts by using both verbal and nonverbal responses.

I3. Make oneself understood when speaking by using consistent standard English grammatical forms and sounds; however, some rules may not be followed (e.g., third-person singular, male and female pronouns).

I4. Participate in social conversations with peers and adults on familiar topics by asking and answering questions and soliciting information.

I5. Retell stories and talk about school-related activities by using expanded vocabulary, descriptive words, and paraphrasing.

Early Advanced

Strategies and Applications

EA1. Listen attentively to stories and information, and orally identify key details and concepts.

EA2. Retell stories in greater detail by including characters, setting and plot.

EA3. Make oneself understood when speaking by using consistent standard English grammatical forms, sounds, intonation, pitch, and modulation but may make random errors.

EA4. Participate in and initiate more extended social conversations with peers and adults on unfamiliar topics by asking and answering questions and restating and soliciting information.

EA5. Recognize appropriate ways of speaking that vary according to the purpose, audience, and subject matter.

EA6. Ask and answer instructional questions with more extensive supporting elements (e.g., "Which part of the story was the most important?").

English-Language Conventions

Beginning

English Language Conventions

B5. Use capitalization when writing one's own name.

Early Intermediate

English Language Conventions

EI5. Use a period or question mark at the end of a sentence.

EI6. Edit writing for basic conventions (e.g., capitalization and use of periods) and make some corrections.

Intermediate

English Language Conventions

I6. Produce independent writing that may include some inconsistent use of capitalization, periods, and correct spelling.

I7. Use standard word order but may have some inconsistent grammatical forms (e.g., subject/verb without inflections).

Early Advanced

English Language Conventions

EA6. Produce independent writing that may include some periods, correct spelling, and inconsistent capitalization.

EA7. Use standard word order with some inconsistent grammar forms (e.g., subject/ verb agreement).

EA8. Edit writing to check some of the mechanics of writing (e.g., capitalization and periods).

242

LETTERS!

Handbook

Aa Bb Cc Dd Ee Ff Gg Hh Ii Jj Kk Ll Mm
Nn Oo Pp Qq Rr Ss Tt Uu Vv Ww Xx Yy Zz
0 1 2 3 4 5 6 7 8 9

AC•1

The Alphabet cards can help you
with sounds in English.

a
a

b
b

c
c

d
d

AC•2

e

e

f

f

g

g

h

h

AC•3

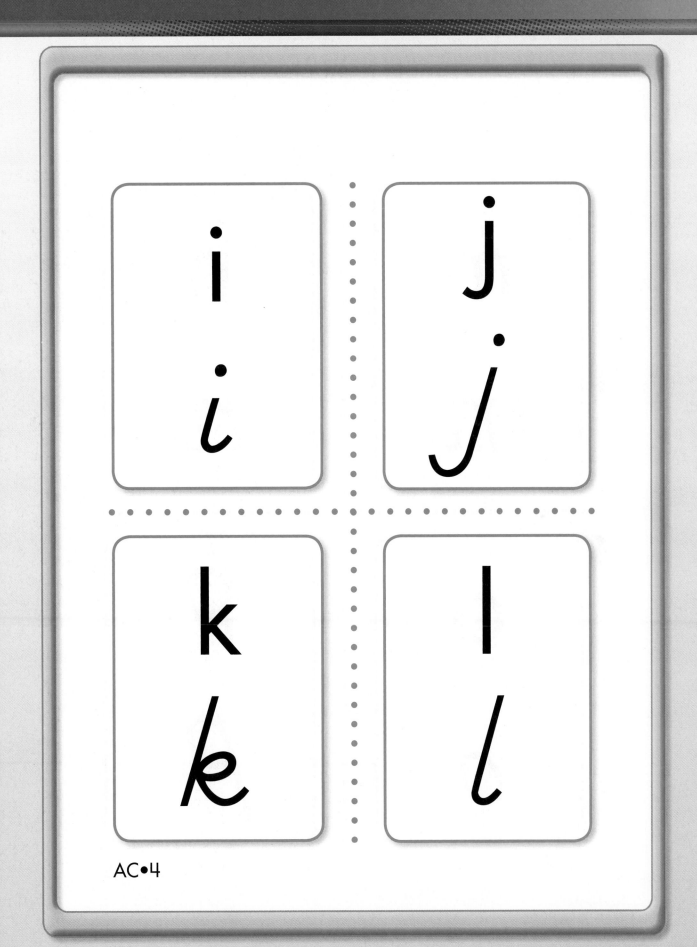

m

m

n

n

o

o

p

p

AC•5

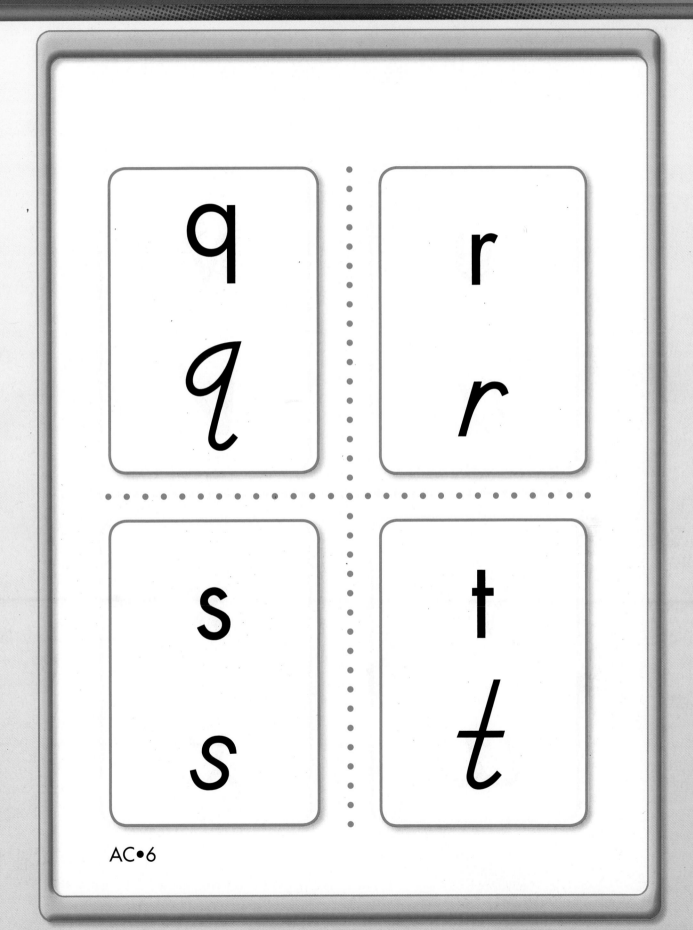

AC•6

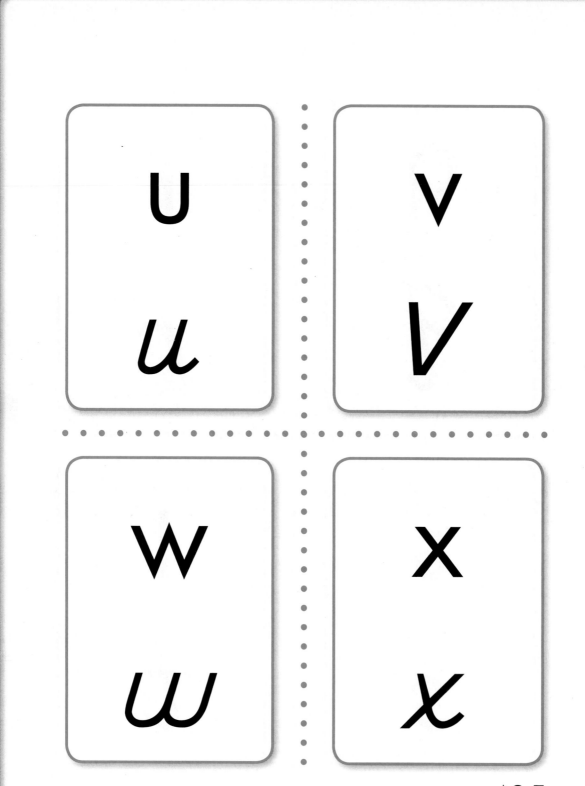

AC•7

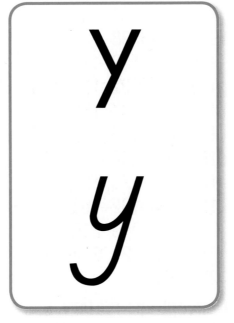

Y
y

z
z

AC•8

Illustrations

32C, 32D Liisa Guida; 58C David Preiss; 64C Ann W. Iosa; 64D, 70C, 70D, 102C, 102D, 146C, 146D, 184C Anette Heiberg; 76C, 96C Wednesday Kirwan 84C Jane Smith; 90C Sharon Vargo; 108C, 204D Donna Bizjak; 114C, 114D, 160C, 228C Marilyn Janovitz; 122C, 134C Sarah Beise; 128D Diane Greenseid; 140C, 140D Janet McDonnell; 166C, 190C Dani Jones; 172C, 216D Deborah C Johnson; 210C, 222C Liz Goulet Dubois

Photographs

Every effort has been made to secure permission and provide appropriate credit for photographic material. The publisher deeply regrets any omission and pledges to correct errors called to its attention in subsequent editions.

Unless otherwise acknowledged, all photographs are the property of Pearson Education, Inc.

Photo locators denoted as follows: Top (T), Center (C), Bottom (B), Left (L), Right (R), Background (Bkgd)

iii (TR) ©DK Images; iii (BL) Dave King/©DK Images; iii (C) Robert Llewellyn/Workbook Stock/Jupiter Images; iv (C) Robert Llewellyn/Workbook Stock/Jupiter Images; iv (L) ilian studio /Alamy Images; vi (C) Robert Llewellyn/Workbook Stock/Jupiter Images; vii (B) Dave King/©DK Images; 8C David Young-Wolff/Getty Images/Stone; 8D Howard Shooter/©DK Images; 20C ©MIXA Co., Ltd./Alamy; 20D Matt Carr/Photonica/Getty Images; 26C Martin Riedl/Getty Images; 38C George Hall/Corbis; 38D Richard Leeney/©DK Images; 46C William Manning/Corbis; 46D Clive Boursnell/©DK Images; 52B Cydney Conger/Corbis; 52C Getty Images; 58D Bill Ling/©DK Images; 76C (TR) DLILLC/Corbis; 76D ©Cultura/Alamy; 84D ©Jupiterimages/Brand X/Alamy; 90C (R) altrendo nature/Getty Images; 96C (R) Blend Images/Getty Images; 108D The Granger Collection, NY; 122D ©Jupiterimages/Brand X/ Alamy; 128C Jeffrey Coolidge/Iconica/Getty Images; 134D Ariel Skelley/Corbis; 140C (R) Juice Images/Punchstock; 152C david gregs /Alamy Images; 152D Kaz Chiba/Photographer's Choice/Getty Images; 160D ©Jupiterimages/Brand X/Alamy; 166D ©RubberBall/Alamy; 172D ©Blend Images/Alamy; 178C ©PhotoBliss/Alamy; 178D ©Jupiterimages/Polka Dot/ Alamy; 184D Jupiterimages/Brand X/Alamy; 190C (R) Steve Crise /TRANSTOCK/Transtock/ Corbis; 198C Jupiter Images; 198D Jupiter Images; 204C ©Jupiterimages/Brand X/Alamy; 210C (R) Allen Polansky/Stock Connection/Jupiter Images; 216D (L) David J. Green - work themes /Alamy Images; 222D Kevin Cooley/Stone+/Getty Images; 228D ©Jerry Young/ ©DK Images